LINCOLN THE PRESIDENT

SPRINGFIELD TO GETTYSBURG

VOLUME TWO

LINCOLN
THE PRESIDENT

SPRINGFIELD TO GETTYSBURG

VOLUME TWO

BY

J. G Randall

**PROFESSOR OF HISTORY
IN THE UNIVERSITY OF ILLINOIS**

GLOUCESTER, MASS.

PETER SMITH

1976

PRINTED IN THE UNITED STATES OF AMERICA

CONTENTS

CHAPTER XV

KENTUCKY TO THE RIGHT, FRÉMONT TO THE LEFT

I

STUNNING defeat and shake-up in army command had not fallen as isolated blows. With these troubles there came to Lincoln in the wretched summer and autumn of 1861 a concerted onslaught of opposite and incurably antagonistic forces. A fateful dualism it was to be, and as time went on it showed increasing power to pester and harass. It was the dualism of Kentucky on the one side and Frémont on the other, of border-state moderation against crusading zeal, of opportunist realism against impatient reform, of limited objectives, with emphasis on the Union, *versus* an all-out abolitionist program of virulent anti-Southernism. On the one hand were moderate men who wished the South to be satisfied when the Union was remade, meantime sparing Southern civilians the worst horrors of war; on the other hand were unctuous rebel-haters to whom suffering on the part of slaveholders and "traitors" seemed a kind of Divine vengeance.

This pervasive dualism was a veritable *leitmotif* in the drama of Lincoln's presidency; in its constant recurrence in varying forms Lincoln found a problem hardly less serious than the war itself. Whether it was a question of emancipation, of the definition of war aims, of legislation against Southerners, of choosing army commanders, of the tenure of cabinet advisers, or, later, of reconstructing a shattered Union, Lincoln's eye was continually to meet this spectre of internal discord looming before him. He was never to hear the last of it, nor in the outcome was his leadership to be successful.

One side of this struggle was embodied in Lincoln's native state.

It could be literally said that for Kentucky the Civil War had no meaning. In sympathy the state was Southern; in culture it was akin to Virginia. In the election of 1860 and the prewar crisis its supreme representative was Crittenden and its preoccupation had been with conciliation, union, and avoidance of war. Kentucky had, of course, its vigorous concept of state loyalty, but that loyalty was in terms of national integrity; it did not require an anti-Washington focus. To be loyal to both state and Union was, after all, not so strange a thing, no more strange than a person's loyalty to brother and father, or a nation's loyalty to itself and to the compelling cause of international order. This concept was, in fact, the essence of that federalism which was the American nation's essential characteristic if there was an American nation. In its recognition of a comprehensive instead of a merely local allegiance, it was to be as essential to the Confederate States as to the United States. In the discussion of this theme it is a misnomer to speak of "divided loyalty." That concept would imply that state and nation were incompatible opposites or enemies, instead of complementary elements fitting together. Unionism in Kentucky, as envisaged by its most distinguished leaders, implied no coexistence of inconsistent or conflicting loyalties.

Unwilling to interpret Southernism in anti-Union terms themselves, Kentuckians resented the precipitateness of South Carolina. They considered the "antics . . . of the Yanceyites . . . damaging" to the Southern cause on the border.[1] It irked and disgusted many of them to observe the easy nonchalance with which the cotton states stirred up trouble "at a safe distance"; it was felt that Virginia, Maryland, Kentucky, and Missouri had no desire to "sacrifice themselves" for a separatist cause they cared not for.[2] Moreover, Kentuckians kept emphasizing a plan of their own—a "border state convention" (to include the upper South with the Southern border) by which it was hoped that the whole unwelcome crisis could be resolved by joint consultation among eight of the fifteen slave states. Such consultation, of course, was to be friendly to the Union while safeguarding Southern interests. As the pioneer state of the great West while equally a part of the South, Kentucky held itself to have as much right as any state

---

[1] Letter of Thomas T. Grant, probably to Montgomery Blair, St. Louis, Oct. 29, 1860, Blair MSS.
[2] *Ibid.*

to develop and present a program; its initiative was as rightful as that of South Carolina, especially since the Kentucky plan involved co-operative effort among the states concerned.

After the formation of the Confederacy and the inauguration of Lincoln the Union element in Kentucky had been able (as in Maryland, Virginia, and the upper South) to stave off actual secession, which was vigorously sought by an active separatist faction. In sum, Kentucky, in general, had neither any motive to fight against the South nor any wish to break the Union, whose dissolution would sever commercial bonds and cut ties of blood kinship with thousands of fathers and brothers in nearby Northern commonwealths.

Policies become weaker when reduced to formulas; in this case the broad policy of the Union was whittled down to the formula of the Crittenden compromise. The failure of that compromise, marking the collapse and defeat of Kentucky's basic program, came as a heavy blow to border Southerners; this breakdown of constructive states-manship put ammunition into the hands of secessionists. Even so, there were enough good Kentuckians who felt that their contest was with Black Republicans rather than the United States to enable the legislature to scotch the secessionists' program and avoid calling the state convention which disunionists were promoting as the instrument of withdrawal.

This was the situation as of mid-April. Then came, with a cruel shock and a kind of dazed incredulity, the Sumter episode, unbe-lievable war, and the President's call for troops. Here began what E. M. Coulter calls a "maelstrom of events" in which "almost any re-action" might follow.[3] At this stage John M. Harlan, though Unionist in feeling, considered war inevitable unless Federal troops were with-drawn from the South; when war came he felt sure that the border states would join secessionist ranks.[4] Spirited agitation to promote Confederate influence was not lacking. By the familiar device of propaganda labels, Unionists were tagged as "Submissionists" and the Union policy was denounced as "suicidal madness" that would alienate Southern friends and isolate the state while "thirty millions of people . . . [were] engaged in bloody strife!"[5]

---

[3] E. M. Coulter, *Civil War and Readjustment in Kentucky*, 37.

[4] Harlan to Holt, March 11, 1861, Holt MSS. (cited in Coulter, 38).

[5] Louisville *Daily Courier*, April 18, 1861, in Dumond, *Southern Editorials on Seces-sion*, 494–495.

Governor Magoffin, who may be described as anti-Lincoln rather than fully pro-Confederate, answered the President's call for militia with the stinging comment that his state would "furnish no troops for the wicked purpose of subduing her sister Southern States." [6] Increasing secessionist activity in the state, however, caused him no less apprehension, and he acted to put a curb upon Confederate recruiting.[7] At this point Kentucky had not yet committed herself: ". . . there invoking peace, she stands" was for some months the post-Sumter as well as the pre-Sumter attitude of the state.[8]

II

With minds so conditioned, Kentuckians could not immediately adjust themselves to the violent reorientation forced by the outbreak of war. That outbreak left Kentucky with no place to go. It thickened the plot without offering a solution. Recruiting by both sides became active all over the state. Union and Confederate camps were quickly formed; families and communities were split; soldiers on opposite sides found themselves traveling on the same train. Unskillful Union agitation, particularly if couched in abolitionist terms, would hurt the Federal cause among its best friends. To offend the spirited pro-Confederate element would produce hot reaction. To force the issue prematurely might be the very factor that would precipitate secession.

Out of this confused situation there grew, as a natural if temporary *modus vivendi,* the famous Kentucky program of "neutrality." This soon became the state's declared policy, approved on May 16 by the lower house of the legislature, and on May 20 by Governor Magoffin's proclamation. "Thus was Kentucky . . . officially committed to a position which its people had been in the process of assuming since secession began." [1]

This neutral phase continued for some months, indeed through the summer of 1861, albeit individual Kentuckians were enlisting, and soldiers from the state fought on both sides at First Manassas. What this neutrality meant being interpreted, would require elaborate

---

[6] *Annual Cyclopaedia,* 1861, 396.   [7] Coulter, *Civil War . . . in Kentucky,* 49.
[8] "Kentucky," a poem by Forceythe Willson, in Moore, *Rebellion Record* (Poetry, etc.), II, 61.
[1] The quotation is from Coulter, 55; for references on Kentucky neutrality, see Randall, *Constitutional Problems Under Lincoln,* 407 n.

statement. Unable to conceive of war between the sections as other than a kind of nightmare, men of the border somehow hoped that a solution was yet possible in terms of peace and union. Meanwhile Kentucky would try not to enter the war, nor to let the war enter the state. The suspense and uneasiness of Kentucky were evidenced in an interview (June, 1861) between Simon Buckner of Kentucky, and George B. McClellan, Union general with headquarters at Cincinnati. Meeting informally and conversing without official guarantees, exchange of credentials, or agreements, these old friends talked over what would happen if Kentucky "should be invaded by the secession forces then collecting under Gen. Pillow . . . in Tennessee." The significance of this interview was seen in the ease of conference between the two military leaders (the one in the Union service, the other in Kentucky service as commandant of what were called "State Guards"), and in the earnest wish of Buckner to see that the neutrality of his state was respected; but the affair was formalized and magnified into a "Kentucky Concordat" or treaty, as represented to the public, the supposed terms being that Kentucky would respect Federal authority and keep Confederate troops out of the state, while no Union troops would be moved into the commonwealth.[2] The episode illustrates the extreme sensitiveness of Kentuckians at this time concerning "invasion" of their state by Federal troops. Such invasion might seriously have hurt the Union cause; yet Garret Davis noted another aspect of the situation when he wrote that a hundred Union companies were organizing over the state, that there was a great difference "between Union men armed and unarmed," and that thousands of Enfields or Sharps ought to be distributed where they would do the most good.[3]

Though there was constant fear that Kentucky could not be held for the Union, surprisingly few of the state's prominent leaders, in the spring and summer of '61, openly urged secession or adherence to the Confederacy. John C. Breckinridge, in this period, remained in the United States Senate and even after the Sumter crisis hoped for avoidance of general war. Just after Lincoln's call for troops Breckinridge urged that Kentucky call a Southern convention without delay, so

2 G. B. McClellan, *McClellan's Own Story*, 48–49; W. S. Myers, *General George Brinton McClellan*, 177–182; New York *Times*, June 24, 1861, p. 4, cc. 2–3; *Offic. Rec.*, 1 ser., II, 674–675.

3 *Offic. Rec.*, 1 ser., II, 678.

that Lincoln's special session of Congress would be confronted by fifteen opposing states. Thus alone, he thought, could general war be averted.[4] Vigorously assailing Lincoln's policy, Breckinridge nevertheless continued to profess lifetime attachment to the Union.[5] When, despite these protestations, he entered Confederate military service, his service was not yet terminated in the United States Senate; his equivocal membership in that body was ended by expulsion on December 4, 1861.[6]

Crittenden carried over his peacemaking attitude till it became a kind of wishful thinking after Sumter, advising that Kentucky take no part in the war but stand between the hostile sections as pacificator. Garret Davis and Guthrie worked untiringly for the Union. Magoffin wavered, being counted pro-Confederate, yet supporting neutrality and resenting Confederate interference. Young Henry Watterson, not then prominent, joined the Confederate army less from anti-Union conviction than from a wish to be associated with the Confederate set. Thomas E. Bramlette resisted the neutrality doctrine and took a commission with the Union army. Robert J. Breckinridge, staunch Unionist, opposed a secession convention, headed the "Unconditional Unionists," and became Lincoln's "chief counsellor" on Kentucky affairs. Other sturdy Kentuckians were strong Unionists, such as George D. Prentice, Benjamin H. Bristow, Joseph Holt, James F. Robinson, and the Speed brothers, James and Joshua F., these brothers being among the very few whose Unionism coexisted with genuine support of Lincoln. When Bell men joined with followers of Douglas to form the "Union State Central Committee,"[7] powerful support was offered by Prentice's paper, the influential Louisville *Journal.* Joseph Holt, recent secretary of war, addressed the citizens of Louisville in July, speaking unequivocally for the Union and denouncing secesion as a "great crime."[8]

---

4 New York *Times,* April 18, 1861, p. 8, c. 4.

5 Moore, *Rebellion Record* (Docs.), II, 305 ff.

6 *Cong. Globe,* 37 Cong., 2 sess., 9. On October 1, 1861, the legislature of Kentucky had instructed both its senators (John C. Breckinridge and L. W. Powell) to resign on the ground that they did not represent the will of people of the state.

7 Coulter, 28.

8 Moore, *Rebellion Record* (Diary), II, 29–30; *ibid.* (Docs.), II, 297–303. For the reference to the "great crime," see p. 298.

III

The Kentucky situation offered a grave challenge to Lincoln's leadership. Had the presidency been held by a man of less shrewdness and tact, or less understanding of border-state sentiment, this pivotal state might have been lost and the Ohio River might have become the boundary between the embattled sections. What this would have meant, no one knew better than Lincoln. "I think to lose Kentucky is nearly . . . to lose the whole game," he wrote. "Kentucky gone, we cannot hold Missouri, nor, as I think, Maryland. These all against us, and the job on our hands is too large for us. We would as well consent to separation at once, including the surrender of this capital." [1]

Knowing what was at stake and realizing the consequences of a false step, Lincoln did not rush things in Kentucky. He waited, observed, kept in touch, and conferred with Kentucky leaders of different shades and degrees. He encouraged ardent Union men in the state but kept them within bounds. Listening to hostile protests, he answered them in a conciliatory spirit without selling his cause down the river. On those matters that required secrecy he left "no written records to accuse," [2] conducting his Kentucky affairs largely by word of mouth. His few papers on the subject are masterpieces of noncommittal statement couched in phrases of utmost candor and frankness. On one occasion—a minor one—a suave and imperturbable answer from the White House went hand-in-hand with a touch of prairie humor when John Hay, writing for the President, replied to a Kentucky state senator who had protested against the stationing of troops at Cairo. Lincoln's secretary said that the matter would have "due consideration," and added: "He [the President] directs me to say that . . . he would never have ordered the movement of troops complained of had he known that Cairo was in your senatorial district." [3]

Lincoln showed respect for the neutral attitude of Kentucky without tying his hands by any stultifying agreement. He assured Garret Davis that he would not "force" the state, and had no military movements then in mind that would require sending troops through Ken-

---

[1] *Works*, VI, 360 (Sep. 22, 1861).

[2] Coulter, 90.

[3] *Works*, VI, 266 (May 6, 1861). This letter, not signed by the President, is here given as having been written by John Hay. See also Dennett, *John Hay*, 37–38.

tucky. He promised not to molest Kentucky so long as she made no forceful demonstration against the United States, nor resisted Federal laws. In a comment that looked both ways he told Senator Davis that until the meeting of Congress he would make no attempt to retake the forts belonging to the United States "unless he should be constrained to depart from that purpose by the continued military operations of the seceded States." Lest his words be misunderstood to imply weakness or indecision he added that events had reached a point to test whether "the Constitution formed a Government . . . with strength . . . sufficient to uphold its own authority, and to enforce . . . the laws . . . ." That authority he intended to uphold "to the extent that he should be sustained by the people of the United States." [4]

Lincoln continued this waiting policy till after the June elections in Kentucky. Indeed the expectation of such elections (to the Federal Congress) had much to do in shaping Lincoln's post-Sumter statesmanship. It has been stated, for example, that his postponement of the special session of Congress until July was because of the pivotal importance of Kentucky and the hazard of having an untoward thing happen at these elections.[5] The whole border situation was complicated by the intrigues and electioneering that preceded this Kentucky vote.[6] When the election occurred the Unionism of Kentucky was decisively demonstrated. Of the ten congressional districts all except one chose a "Union" candidate, the total Union vote in the state being 92,460 as compared to a "state rights" vote of 37,700.[7] It is true that many Southern-rights men did not vote at all, and that Unionism itself was a flexible and complex affair, capable of an interpretation that meant only neutrality.[8] Even so, it was important for Lincoln to have those Union congressmen from Kentucky, though no one knew better than the President how largely pro-Union votes came from men who detested the Republican party and were ready to rise in

---

[4] Garret Davis to George D. Prentice (concerning an interview between Davis and Lincoln), *Cong. Globe*, 37 Cong., 2 sess., appendix, 82–83. For another Lincoln conversation with Kentucky leaders, see J. W. Forney, *Anecdotes of Public Men*, I, 264–265.

[5] Blaine, *Twenty Years of Congress*, I, 309.

[6] As showing the apprehension of Unionists concerning this Kentucky election, J. F. Speed wrote to Joseph Holt on June 18, 1861, with anti-secession bitterness: ". . . we are contending with a foe that pays no respect to the will of a majority unless that majority shall be with them . . . ." Holt MSS.

[7] *Annual Cyclopaedia*, 1861, 397.   [8] Coulter, 95.

revolt against the abolitionist radicalism and anti-Southernism which gave evidence of becoming ever more powerful at Washington.

IV

In the summer of 1861 the Kentucky situation took shape and crystallized. The border-state convention, frustrated by the progress of secession and the outbreak of war, met at Frankfort on May 27 with only Kentucky and Missouri represented. It declared Kentucky's loyalty to the Union; yet it was an affair of distressingly small effect when compared to the ambitious hopes of those who had looked to it as the key to the sectional crisis. Military units were forming on both sides, "Home Guards" being organized to uphold the Union cause in opposition to Buckner's "State Guards" which were disunionist in intent. The legislature, suspecting the governor of secessionism, deprived him of his constitutional authority as commander-in-chief of the state militia, placing the military force of the state in the hands of a special group of five men known as a "Military Board." [1] Arms flowed into the state and were somehow distributed among safe Union men, while conflict was meanwhile averted as if by a miracle. In this phase the hand of the Union government was "deftly kept hidden," though indignation was soon directed against Lincoln's alleged "atrocity" in "arming one class . . . by . . . clandestine agents." [2]

Arguing that Kentucky had no need of a military force, Governor Magoffin urged the removal of "the military force now organized and in camp within the State." [3] To this Lincoln replied that such force was small, that it consisted of Kentuckians camped near their homes, that he was acting in accordance with the wishes of "the Union loving people of Kentucky," that of his numerous Kentucky advisers no others had asked that the force be removed, and that he "must respectfully decline to so remove it." [4]

It soon became evident that neutrality for Kentucky, in the sense of isolation from the war or non-participation in it, was impossible. If for no other reason, this impossibility would have been due to the intense concern of individual Kentucky citizens for one side or the

---

[1] Coulter, 87.
[3] *Annual Cyclopaedia*, 1861, 398.
[2] *Ibid.*, 90.
[4] *Works*, VI, 349–350 (Aug. 24, 1861).

other. Though the majority wanted avoidance of war, opposite sympathies were inevitable once the war was started; the very wish to
avoid war meant aversion to secession on the one hand or to what was
called Federal coercion on the other. The war could not be exorcized
nor wished away; geography in its relation to military strategy or
intersectional communication could not be ignored. It was the fate
of Americans of the time to be drawn into the war; Kentuckians were
among these Americans.

For obvious military reasons Union forces occupied Cairo, Illinois,
and Belmont, Missouri. This was but part of a chain of circumstances
in which Confederates under Leonidas Polk took Columbus and Hickman, Federals under Grant seized Paducah, and at the other end of the
state Zollicoffer, Confederate general, moved in from Tennessee in
the area of Cumberland Gap, heralding his action with a resounding
proclamation to the people of Kentucky to resist subjugation by
"Northern hordes." [5] As war clouds thickened all around them and
in their midst, the people of Kentucky saw the fabric of neutrality
collapse; when this was evident the policy was officially abandoned by
a resolution of the legislature (September 12, 1861) passed over the
governor's veto.[6] Declaring that Kentucky's neutrality had been "wan-
tonly violated" by the "so-called Southern Confederate forces," this
resolution demanded that the "invaders" be expelled and that Federal
aid and protection be sought. Magoffin reluctantly acquiesced in this
policy, then patriotically resigned the governorship, which passed to
James F. Robinson,[7] a Conservative who favored the United States.
From this point, though a pro-Confederate phantom government
was erected, Kentucky remained uncomfortably in the Union.

Because the project of neutrality proved temporary, it would be
easy to condemn it in sweeping terms. It was, in fact, condemned by
both sides, which is significant, as well as praised or appealed to by
both sides. In the matter of joining one side or the other Kentucky's
choice was harder than that of other states; a temporary neutrality
or quasi-truce was needful for the early months of difficult adjustment. To avert the war would have been a high accomplishment; Kentucky could not continue to work for this end if she took sides. Averting war was, however, more of a Kentucky motive than retreating into

5 *Annual Cyclopaedia*, 1861, 404.
6 Moore, *Rebellion Record* (Docs.), III, 129; Coulter, 114.   7 Coulter, 143.

a bomb-proof cellar of indifference after the conflict had started. In the weeks after mid-April 1861 the nation was psychologically inhibited from retracing its steps to the pre-secession status quo. Only if such a retracing had been possible could border neutrality have yielded any important result; there was in the policy an element that was essentially tentative, temporary, and provisional.

All told the policy contributed more good than otherwise to the Union cause; yet Lincoln condemned this "armed neutrality" as "disunion completed," and compared it to "the building of an impassable wall along the line of separation—and yet not quite an impassable one, for under the guise of neutrality it would tie the hands of Union men and freely pass supplies . . . to the insurrectionists, which it could not do as an open enemy. . . . It would do for the disunionists that which . . . they most desire . . . ." [8] Despite this rebuke, the attitude of impartiality and of marking time, besides being psychologically harmonious with the immediate postwar situation in the state, averted secession, kept the road open to conciliation, and averted civil war within the state in those heated days when fighting Kentuckians were rallying under opposing banners. It will not quite do to say that neutrality "broke down." It accomplished a number of definite results. Lincoln in general had no need to be disappointed in the ultimate course of his native state, which, as he reported to Congress in December 1861, was "decidedly, . . . unchangeably, ranged on the side of the Union." [9] His condemnation of border nonparticipation (in his July message) had occurred after Union benefits from that very policy had been reaped.[10]

V

Repercussions in northwestern Virginia did not follow the prevailing border pattern. Rather they fell, or were manipulated, into a unique formula not repeated elsewhere. Instead of statewide action stumbling through hesitation and indecision into a kind of reluctant

---

[8] *Works*, VI, 307 (July 4, 1861).   [9] *Ibid.*, VII, 53.

[10] In this specific historical account the intent is not to treat neutrality in general. The misguided isolationism of American neutrality from 1935 to 1939 is to be discussed in its own fearful setting. As to Kentucky, even if one regards its neutrality as understandable, it proved impossible. Kentucky's rightful contribution toward peace was frustrated. Denial of separatism and recognition of the imperative need of coöperation among states would have promoted such peaceful contribution.

Union allegiance, the program for the counties that became West Virginia was that of determined leaders in the Wheeling area who produced a fictitious adherence to the Union on the part of the whole state, and then, as if dissatisfied with their own fiction, created, perhaps unnecessarily, a detached commonwealth.[1] In Kentucky it was the pro-Confederate government that was a fabric of pretense; in Virginia the garb of fiction was worn by those who boldly asserted that the Old Dominion, none other than Virginia itself, adhered to the Union.

Since the story of Lincoln becomes too much clogged if one attempts to tell the complex history of the time, it will be possible only to glance at this development in the Kanawha region. Two diverse purposes were intertwined, the purpose of holding Virginia intact for the Union in defiance of the government at Richmond, and the further object of detaching the most Unionist part of the state by setting up a new political entity. The whole procedure is hardly intelligible unless one goes deep into historical backgrounds, intrastate sectionalism, geography, climate, topography, economic relations, and social diversities. When these are understood it will be seen that the mountain people of the Kanawha region had developed over the decades a marked diversity from the tidewater, middle, and piedmont areas. In contrast to dominant eastern forces, the westerners knew not the plantation economy, held few slaves or usually none at all, preferred evangelical sects to Episcopal forms, and dealt commercially with the area of the Ohio, having little converse with neighbors of the South. Wheeling was next door to Pittsburgh; the Panhandle was narrowly squeezed between Pennsylvania and Ohio; the Kanawha River was part of the Mississippi Valley.

Having no wish to secede from close neighbors and hotly resenting the action of the Richmond Convention, leaders in the western area, by a pattern that has been somewhat obscured in the older historical accounts,[2] moved with determination and vigor; once launched, the movement was about as easy to stop as an Appalachian torrent. Each

---

[1] On the theory that Virginia was adhering to the Union—in other words, that the Unionist efforts which erected a "restored state" were valid acts of the only legitimate Virginia government—the establishment of the new state, besides weakening the restored government, was logically unnecessary as a matter of federal relations.

[2] For a competent modern account see C. H. Ambler, *West Virginia, the Mountain State*.

step fitted into the whole comprehensive purpose. In mid-April, directly after the Sumter outbreak, preliminary organizational steps were taken; in May a mass convention of delegates at Wheeling prepared the road; in June a convention of doubtful authority, also at Wheeling, set up a reorganized government of Virginia on a Unionist pattern, at which point it could be asserted by the reorganizers that Virginia was a Union state; in August this same convention decreed that a new commonwealth by the name of "Kanawha" be formed, the name being later changed to West Virginia.

A few leaders arranged it so that forty-eight counties were included in the new state; ultimately, much against their will, two more, the counties of Jefferson and Berkeley in the Harpers Ferry area, were added. Half the area of the nascent commonwealth was unrepresented in the convention that gave it birth; in those parts that were "represented," some of the delegates bore the character of self-appointment or minority representation.

Other steps were taken as the months passed. A roster of state officials, with Francis Pierpoint [3] at the head as governor, was created for "restored [Unionist] Virginia"; Unionist senators for Virginia were chosen by the legislature at Wheeling; in due course a constitutional convention created an instrument of government for the new state of West Virginia. When completed, this constitution was ratified by a fragmentary vote of the people; then the "restored" legislature at Wheeling, in the alleged name of Virginia as a whole, gave the consent for the creation of the new state which the Constitution of the United States requires. Finally, by action of Congress, and reluctant consent on the part of President Lincoln,[4] West Virginia, in June of 1863, became one of the states in the American Union. Dispossessed by a government of its own creating, the restored government under Pierpoint stepped out of its true setting at Wheeling,

---

[3] This name is almost invariably given in historical accounts as "Pierpont," but contemporary usage, including the governor's own signature, was "Pierpoint."

[4] "Some conversation in Cabinet respecting the proposed new State of Western Virginia. The bill has not yet reached the President, who thinks the creation of this new State at this time of doubtful expediency." Welles, *Diary*, I, 191. Another indication of Lincoln's disapproval is found in a letter which Senator Willey wrote to Pierpoint, December 17, 1862, in which he said: "We have great fears that the President will veto the new State bill." Pierpoint Papers (MSS., Virginia State Archives). See also Browning, *Diary*, I, 596. Lincoln's recognition of the Pierpoint government, however, though never ostentatious, was generous and cordial.

moved to Alexandria where it abided under protection of Union arms, and, from that point until it was discarded by its friends in postwar years, maintained itself obscurely and precariously as the government of Virginia. From the wartime standpoint of Richmond, of course, both the new state and the Pierpoint government were pretending and illegal fabrications.

Efforts to promote the same type of separatist movement for the mountainous area of Eastern Tennessee, where Unionist sentiment was strong,[5] never proceeded beyond a preliminary and abortive stage. As noted above,[6] the people of all Tennessee, by referendum in February 1861 when the Confederacy was building, had emphatically rejected secession; in this rejection the eastern mountainous area had shown vigorous adherence to the Union. Since a mountainous region suggests a backwoodsy element, it must be added that some of the most cultured, conservative, and intellectually capable leaders of the state, such as Horace Maynard and Thomas A. R. Nelson, "regarded the secession movement with horror and disgust." [7] As in Virginia, though the points of the compass were reversed, intrastate sectionalism, compounded of many human and social factors, made the non-slaveholding area conscious of its distinctness from the rest of the state. Under the leadership of Nelson, who might have become the Pierpoint of East Tennessee, a convention was held at Knoxville in which pro-Union sentiments were vigorously expressed and the action of the governor and legislature in creating the military league with the Confederacy hotly denounced. This convention met on May 30, adjourned, and met again (at Greeneville, June 17), all without result so far as East-Tennessean independence was concerned. Realizing that a stroke for such independence would be revolutionary, the leaders of the movement allowed their efforts to dwindle to an indignant declaration of grievances and a "memorial" to the legislature, praying that counties in the eastern area be permitted to form a

[5] In saying that Unionism was strong or prevalent, one should not imply that the opposite sentiment was negligible. Though a matter of minority opinion, pro-Confederate sentiment was stoutly supported in eastern Tennessee by such a leader as Landon C. Haynes. Sentiment for the Confederacy, or at least for not promoting revolution against the Confederacy, was an appreciable factor also in the counties that became West Virginia, though it has never been adequately measured. In southwestern Virginia such sentiment was stronger than in either the West-Virginia area or eastern Tennessee.

[6] See vol. I, 357.

[7] J. W. Patton, *Unionism and Reconstruction in Tennessee*, 22.

separate state. This harmless memorial died in committee, and with it perished the feeble but sincere efforts to hold East Tennessee for the Union.[8]

VI

It was in Missouri that the complex of border issues produced the greatest turbulence and confusion. As in Kentucky, there was spirited opposition between unionists and secessionists, but with a difference; in Missouri, unionists themselves were sharply divided between pro-slavery (or anti-abolitionist) conservatives and uncompromising anti-slavery radicals, this latter being a class almost unknown in Kentucky.[1] The Missouri governor, Claiborne F. Jackson (later deposed), tried to promote secession, and internecine war impended as military units formed on opposing sides, with many a neighborhood shaken by guerrilla warfare and civilian sniping.

Efforts toward a truce between opposing armed camps, though starting out with promise, broke down because of the impatience of such unionists as Nathaniel Lyon and Frank Blair, Jr. As a result the state endured the torments of civil war in dead earnest, as at Wilson's Creek (August 10, 1861) where "this little, rough-visaged, red-bearded, weather-beaten Connecticut captain," [2] Nathaniel Lyon, was killed, after having promoted Union victory. Early in 1862 (March 7-8) another Union victory was achieved at Pea Ridge in the northeast corner of Arkansas near the Missouri line. By decision of battle and by other factors (especially a notable state convention) Missouri was held for the Union, though a rival state government, a minor affair, functioned obscurely and claimed Missouri's adherence to the Confederacy.

In the early months part of the difficulty as to Missouri was the problem of government itself, for with Confederate and Union rivalry, ill-defined military authority, non-observance of orders, martial law, and conflicts within Union ranks between military officers and civil leaders, the mere maintenance of order, to say nothing of going forward for the Union cause, was a matter of doubt and risk.

---

[8] *Ibid.*, 22-25.

[1] In that state Cassius Clay was a *rara avis;* he was a voice crying, not in the wilderness, but in cultured Lexington, whose citizens took measures to suppress him.

[2] Col. Thomas L. Snead (C. S. A.), in *Battles and Leaders of the Civil War*, I, 273.

Intrigues behind the lines, charges and counter charges, tattle-tale visits to Lincoln, presidential politics, and clashes of personal ambition, caused Missouri to be a kind of constant headache at the White House.

Among other things there was the serious problem, not fully appreciated by army heads at Washington, of developing the promising military possibilities of the West—not merely victories such as those at Forts Henry and Donelson, but far reaching movements that might have pushed the river campaigns deep into the Confederacy, and have notably shortened the war.[3] Large strategy was thus added to other factors to make the Mississippi Valley and its St. Louis focus a challenge to the best thought of the administration.

VII

Into the turbulent Missouri mêlée Lincoln had thrust the colorful "Pathfinder" and former Republican candidate, John C. Frémont. The measure of his provocative character may be seen in the violent reactions it produced. By some he was superlatively praised, these being often the most bitter opponents of Lincoln; by others he was relentlessly denounced. His Missouri assignment became for Lincoln an embarrassment, a hornet's nest, and a grave hazard. It could almost be said that the sum of Lincoln's intramural vexations was focused in the Frémont muddle. Before he was removed from his post this political general had alienated border sentiment, seized functions that belonged to civilian chiefs at Washington, laid his administration open to charges of fraud and extravagance, challenged the President's leadership, divided those elements which Lincoln was seeking to weld together, and had precipitated one of those military-and-civil clashes which are always troublesome in a democracy. Whether or not such was his purpose, he had rallied to his own combative person that unctuous and impetuous abolitionism which flowed increasingly in anti-Lincoln channels.

The Frémont explosion came in the form of a sensational and unauthorized "proclamation" which that general issued from his headquarters at St. Louis on August 30, 1861. Asserting that he found it

---

[3] These military problems, and the part taken in them by a spirited woman, are treated in Marjorie Barstow Greenbie, *My Dear Lady: The Story of Anna Ella Carroll, the "Great Unrecognized Member of Lincoln's Cabinet."* See below, pp. 66–67.

necessary to "assume the administrative powers of the State," he ordered that all persons taken with arms in their hands within his lines would be "tried by court-martial" and shot if guilty. In addition, property of all persons who supported the enemy was declared confiscated and their slaves "hereby declared freemen." Instead of proceeding within existing law, this proclamation supplied "such deficiencies as the conditions of war demand"; persons in correspondence with the enemy or fomenting tumult, were warned of "sudden and severe punishment." [1]

In the matter of suppressing disturbances among the civilian population, admittedly bad in Missouri, President Lincoln claimed the right to fix the pattern of executive conduct. As to confiscation, Congress had already acted in a sense far different from that of Frémont's order, by providing that seizures be handled by Federal courts and be confined to such property as was used in aid of the rebellion.[2] As to emancipation, that assuredly was a matter of high policy in which the government at Washington had not only to make the major decision, but to choose the moment, the form, and the circumstances of public action. To allow undelegated authority in these delicate and important matters to be seized by generals in the field, and to permit such weighty affairs to be handled by military departments in limited areas instead of as a whole, would have amounted almost to an abandonment of orderly government.

On hearing of the proclamation Joshua F. Speed wrote Lincoln of his serious apprehensions as to its effect in Kentucky. Union men from all parts of the state, he said, shared his fears. In a few days he wrote again to Lincoln and others. To Holt he said that "we could stand several defeats like that at Bulls run, better than we can this proclamation if endorsed by the Administration." Then he added: "Do not allow us by the foolish act of a mi[li]tary popinjay to be driven from our present active loyalty." With almost evangelistic fervor he exclaimed: "And Oh how I desire that my most intimate friend Mr Lincoln—whom I shall ever regard as one of the best & purest men I have ever known, should be the instrument in the hands of God for the reconstruction of this great republic—." [3]

---

[1] *Offic. Rec.*, 1 ser., III, 466–467.
[2] Law of Aug. 6, 1861, *U. S. Statutes at Large*, XII, 319.
[3] J. F. Speed to Joseph Holt, Louisville, Sep. 7, 1861, Holt MSS.

At this juncture, which was the critical phase in Kentucky's transition from neutrality to Union adherence, Lincoln was finding abundant reason to steer cautiously as to all the points of the Frémont episode, yet in seeking to coördinate the radical commander with national policy the President avoided rebuke. Writing to the general "in a spirit of caution, and not of censure," he made two points clear: (1) no man should be shot without the President's consent, lest there be indefinite retaliation, man for man, in the whole broad war; (2) the general was asked to modify his proclamation to make it conform to existing law. While dealing with Frémont Lincoln was thinking of the border situation; he feared that Frémont's act would "perhaps ruin our rather fair prospect for Kentucky." [4]

Though mildly worded, this note from Lincoln amounted to an instruction from the President on the two points specified; yet on both points Frémont refused compliance. On the matter of inflicting the military death penalty, though regularly such a penalty was subject to presidential approval even without Lincoln's special admonition, Frémont replied: "As promptitude is . . . an advantage in war, I have . . . to ask that you will permit me to carry out *upon the spot* [author's italics] the provisions of the proclamation . . . ." [5] Concerning the other point (modifying his proclamation according to law) he declined to make the alteration of his own accord, and, as if to put the President in the wrong before Frémont sympathizers, asked "that you will openly direct me to make the correction." [6] Lincoln wrote: "Your answer . . . expresses the preference . . . that I should make an open order for the modification, which I very cheerfully do. It is therefore ordered that . . . said proclamation be so modified . . . as to conform to . . . the act of Congress . . . [etc.]." [7] It is not revealed in the unsatisfactory interchange between Lincoln and Frémont that the general ever properly bowed to the President's authority. After Lincoln's clear admonition touching the shooting of civilians condemned on military trial, Frémont instructed one of his colonels that the shooting clause in his proclamation would be "strictly enforced." [8]

Despite his popularity and wide prestige, Frémont soon came under

---

[4] *Works*, VI, 350–351 (Sep. 2, 1861).   [5] *Offic. Rec.*, 1 ser., III, 477–478.   [6] *Ibid.*
[7] *Works*, VI, 353 (Sep. 11, 1861).   [8] *Offic. Rec.*, 1 ser., III, 492.

a cloud of accusations. Pomp, official swank, employment of "foreigners" (non-Missourians), graft in government contracts, extravagance, and favoritism were among the charges against him. To this was added the charge of military incompetence, especially failure to strengthen Lyon, leading to that general's defeat.[9] With headquarters at the Brant mansion in St. Louis, rented by the government at $6000 per year,[10] he was so importantly busy with trifles and so surrounded by guards and orderlies that men with serious business became disgusted in trying to interview him.[11] It was said that he occupied "more time in recruiting a 'body guard' than in attending to the affairs of the country." [12] A confidant of Governor Yates wrote that, while accomplishing nothing with Frémont, he "found the City filled with contractors and jobbers, [with] a great flurry in the Quartermaster's Department, but on every side . . . insufficiency of supplies." [13] At times he would be "seized with a spasmodic rashness and . . . [send] some small force into places greatly exposed and from which it . . . [could] not easily be extricated." [14]

But there were worse accusations. An observer wrote that the situation at St. Louis was "terrible and the frauds . . . shocking." [15] One of his associate officers, McKinstry, was denounced as a "robber and a traitor," the Frémont ménage being described as a "horde of pirates," [16] and again as a set of "California Vampires." [17] The general was accused of self importance and of a tendency to spread himself in the newspapers.[18] Lorenzo Thomas, adjutant general of the United States, reported questionable contracts, expensive barracks, inferior guns, ("20 out of 100 . . . would go off"), attention to Springfield when Price was marching toward Lexington, and, in general, unfitness for important command.[19]

In the sequel an elaborate official investigation was to reveal the

[9] Ibid., 545–546. [10] Ibid., 543.
[11] W. E. Smith, Blair Family, II, 69; F. P. Blair, Jr. to Montgomery Blair, Aug. 29, 1861, Blair MSS.
[12] Same to same, undated, Blair MSS.
[13] S. M. Wilson to Yates, Springfield, Ill., Sep. 30, 1861, Yates MSS.
[14] F. P. Blair, Jr. to Montgomery Blair, undated (about August 1861), Blair MSS.
[15] E. B. Washburne to S. P. Chase, Oct. 31, 1861 (typewritten copy filed among photostats of Trumbull MSS., Ill. Hist. Survey, Univ. of Ill.).
[16] Ibid. [17] S. S. to F. A. Dick, St. Louis, Sep. 3, 1861, Blair MSS.
[18] Ibid. [19] Offic. Rec., 1 ser., III, 540–549.

sordid details. A contract was granted without competitive bidding to a California friend to build thirty-eight mortar boats at $8250 each, though an experienced builder stated that the cost would not exceed $4927. Another Californian, a special friend of Frémont with no knowledge of military engineering, was paid $191,000 to build forts at St. Louis, this being "about three times what they should have cost." [20] It was found that the forts were useless and the secretary of war ordered their construction stopped; nevertheless the lucrative work was pushed to completion. In purchasing tents, horses, mules, and all kinds of supplies, huge commissions were taken by middlemen for inferior products. "The most stupendous contracts [so read the official report], involving an almost unprecedented waste of public money, were given out by him [Frémont] in person to favorites, over the heads of the competent and honest officers appointed by law." [21]

Of the personal results of this Missouri muddle the most distressing was the feud between the Frémonts and the Blairs, whose previous close friendship and intimacy turned into enmity and hostile intrigue. At one stage in the imbroglio Lincoln sent Postmaster General Montgomery Blair "as a friend" to St. Louis,[22] with the Quartermaster General, M. C. Meigs,[23] whereupon Mrs. Frémont, daughter of the illustrious Thomas Hart Benton, traveled to Washington, interviewed the President, and proceeded to set him right in the matter of emancipation. As the plot thickened Frank Blair, Jr. loomed as rival of Frémont for Unionist leadership and military glory in Missouri. When the rivalry was carried forward in the newspapers an anti-Frémont editor was arrested; finally Frémont clapped Blair himself in jail for insubordination. In hot retaliation Blair drew up a convincing list of charges and specifications against the Pathfinder, stressing lack of help at Lexington, failure to suppress guerrillas, employment of incompetents, defiance of the President, and "conduct un-

---

[20] *House Exec. Doc. No. 94,* 37 Cong., 2 sess., pp. 17–18, 25–26. Undue emphasis in Frémont's defense has sometimes been placed upon the so-called investigation and report on his case by the congressional committee on the conduct of the war, but the Jacobin slant, gross unfairness, and radical prejudice of that committee are too well known for its judgments to carry much weight. See Williams, *Lincoln and the Radicals,* 278–279. Williams writes: "The inquisitors applied liberal daubs of whitewash to the episodes in his [Frémont's] career which shrieked of inefficiency, and commended lavishly . . . his . . . grasping the need for an emancipation proclamation before the president did" (*ibid.,* 279).

[21] *House Exec. Doc. No. 94,* 37 Cong., 2 sess., p. 34.

[22] *Works,* VI, 354 (Sep. 12, 1861).   [23] Nicolay and Hay, *Lincoln,* IV, 413.

becoming an officer and a gentleman." [24] Blair was soon released, but the Blair-Frémont feud continued unabated.

VIII

Agitation for and against Frémont was more than a matter of intrigue and ambition. It was a thunderous tempest that shook the country and seriously endangered the administration. To William Lloyd Garrison it seemed that if Lincoln was 6 feet 4 inches high, he was "only a dwarf in mind." [1] A Connecticut friend wrote to Welles after talking with gentlemen from Ohio, Indiana, Illinois, and Michigan: "They unanimously condemn the President's letter [2] [overruling Frémont] & as unanimously approve of Frémont's Proclamation." [3] Another correspondent of Welles wrote: "It is very easy for Mr Lincoln to make a record against the Pathfinder but another Benton will arise and set the ball in motion—to end in another expunging process. It is said that we must consult the border states . . . . Now with all due respect . . . , permit me to say *damn* the border states. . . . A thousand Lincolns and Sewards cannot stop the people from fighting slavery. . . . Perhaps it is thought that there are no more John Browns." [4] Gustave Koerner, prominent German-American of Illinois, disapproved of Lincoln's challenge to a man so popular as Frémont. Warning that the Blair faction was "determined to break down General Frémont," he admonished that the removal of the general would be "disastrous" and would almost "produce a Revolution . . . in our ranks." "The Blairs," he added, "are . . . implacable, and . . . [are supported] . . . by the quasi-Union-Neutrality, secession factions of the Country. Unless we counteract them by strong efforts they may succeed. . . . Frémont is no politician. . . . He is impetuous . . . ." [5]

---

[24] MS. in Blair papers, Library of Congress, undated. The charges were to be laid before the President. This manuscript is in a clerk's hand; it bears the name, not the autograph, of Frank P. Blair, Jr. On the Frémont-Blair imbroglio see also New York *Times*, Oct. 7, 1861, p. 1, cc. 4–6.

[1] W. L. Garrison to Oliver Johnson, Oct. 7, 1861, Garrison MSS.

[2] See above, p. 18.

[3] E. H. Owen to Gideon Welles, Hartford, Sep. 20, 1861, MS., Ill. State Hist. Lib.

[4] Gen. J. R. Hawley to Gideon Welles, New Haven, Sep. 17, 1861, MS., Ill. State Hist. Lib.

[5] Gustave Koerner to Yates, Hq., Western Department, St. Louis, Sep. 18, 1861, Yates MSS.

It was one of those overwrought moments in American democracy when people take sides emotionally and when everyone is a partisan on one side or the other. Even the conservative Browning of Illinois wrote a severe letter criticizing the President for taking issue with Frémont.[6] Concerning this epistle Lincoln wrote: ". . . coming from you, I confess it astonishes me"; this was the equivalent of saying that Browning was rightly a conservative and that, by his background and connections, he ought to have understood the border. With care and at some length Lincoln answered Browning, showing that Frémont's proclamation as to confiscation and emancipation was "purely political and not within the range of military law or necessity." These matters, said the President, "must be settled . . . by law-makers, and not by military proclamations. The proclamation . . . is simply 'dictatorship.' . . . But I cannot assume this reckless position, ..." Lincoln pointed out that the "Kentucky legislature would not budge till that proclamation was modified; . . . on the news of General Frémont having actually issued deeds of manumission, a whole company of our volunteers threw down their arms and disbanded." The President also showed the highly dangerous possibilities of letting Frémont "shoot men under the proclamation." [7] That Frémont was exploiting abolitionist impatience for his own political purposes in the anti-Lincoln sense was hinted, though not stated, in the President's letter; yet the very restraint associated with the President's office put him at a disadvantage in such a partisan agitation. The wide extent of Frémont's command must also be remembered. Such a matter as the seizure of Paducah and Columbus, for example, came under his jurisdiction. Grant, Pope, Sherman, McClernand, and others in the West, were under his orders. What went on in St. Louis was of broad importance.

Lincoln had shown great patience toward Frémont and had assured Mrs. Frémont that he was not animated by hostility toward the general.[8] He did not remove him because of the proclamation alone. That was serious enough, but the President had also to consider border-state resentment, the growing list of complaints against Frémont's regime, and the apparent impossibility of getting the general to right the situation himself. Lincoln took his time, considered both sides,

---

[6] Browning, *Diary*, I, 502 n.   [7] *Works*, VI, 357–361 (Sep. 22, 1861).
[8] *Ibid.*, VI, 354 (Sep. 12, 1861).

or rather all sides, and finally removed the commander only when the Missouri situation had become virtually impossible. Before acting, Lincoln assembled and studied ample statements on the Frémont case, including a long report by General Thomas to the secretary of war.[9] Finally, on October 24, 1861, orders went out from Washington that David Hunter would "temporarily" relieve Frémont of the command of the Department of the West.[10] Even then, however, the delivery of this order was to be withheld if Frémont was engaged in battle, or "had fought and won a battle." On the same date Lincoln issued an order to Hunter as the new commander, with military instructions as to pursuing Price. Actual shift of command from Frémont to Hunter was effected on November 2, 1861. By that time Frémont had taken the field with his army; he was in southwestern Missouri advancing against Price. In a farewell to his men the deposed general expressed regret that he would not be there to lead them in the victory they were "about to win." [11]

IX

Various pleas in defense have been offered on Frémont's side. In his California career there had been the vindictive action of Stephen W. Kearny, leading to a severe court-martial decree, and there was the feeling that this episode exhibited an unfair attitude of West Point officers against army men who were not of the Academy. In the full and authoritative account by Allan Nevins it has been noted that "most historians have done less than justice to Frémont." [1] Nevins emphasizes the monumental difficulties of his command, when suddenly thrust into the newly created Western Department, "without organization, money, arms, or stores, without anything but raw recruits, . . . and compelled to deal with sedition at home as well as . . . enemies in the field." [2] "Beyond doubt," writes Nevins, "there was great waste and some corruption in St. Louis . . . ; but none of the corruption was Frémont's, and the waste was largely attributable to the War Department's own inefficiency." [3] Characteriz-

---

[9] See above, p. 19.   [10] *Offic. Rec.*, 1 ser., III, 553.   [11] *Ibid.*, 560.

[1] Allan Nevins, *Frémont, Pathmarker of the West*, 548. This one-volume work, published in 1939, supersedes the earlier two-volume work by Nevins. It is a most readable new study, with additional material, remodeled narrative, and fresh appraisal.
[2] *Ibid.*, 548.   [3] *Ibid.*, 627.

ing Frémont's personality, Nevins observes "a disproportion between his ardent imagination, and his mediocre grasp of practical means to achieve the goal he so vividly saw . . . ." [4] As to the President's action, Nevins concludes: "Unquestionably, Lincoln did wisely in removing Frémont," but he adds: "Nevertheless, . . . observers in Missouri believed then and always that he had acted, not merely with high patriotism, but with sagacity and efficiency." [5]

It had taken Lincoln much longer to come to the point of displacing Frémont than to reach an estimate concerning the man's qualities. As early as September 9, 1861, he had written: "General Frémont . . . is losing the confidence of men near him, whose support any man in his position must have to be successful. His cardinal mistake is that he isolates himself and allows nobody to see him, . . . by which he does not know what is going on in the very matter he is dealing with." [6]

There were many who agreed with Washburne that the government had ample reason to check Frémont and his "horde of pirates." To many also it would have been distasteful for Frémont to have become the Zachary Taylor, or perhaps one should say the General Grant, of the war. All along the border and the lower Middle West resentment against Frémont was burning fiercely. More vociferous and vocal, however, was the torrent of applause for Frémont and abuse of the President for removing him. According to the New York *Independent* the "great mass of earnest, thinking men" sided with the general, while the "tricksters, the old fogies, . . . and the Secessionists" opposed him. [7] A Missouri admirer of Sumner wrote that the modification of Frémont's proclamation was "one of the many great errors of the President." [8] The same writer considered that the episode had made the general "much more dear to the people" and had "shaken confidence in the Government." [9] Denouncing the President's disposition "to kill off Fremont," a Michigan citizen wrote that Lincoln and his cabinet "have already or intend betraying the trust placed in their hands." [10] Sympathy for Frémont was lengthily voiced by a writer to the New York *Times,* who considered the general a vic-

[4] *Ibid.,* 618.   [5] *Ibid.,* 543.
[6] Lincoln to General David Hunter, Sep. 9, 1861, *Works,* VI, 352.
[7] *The Independent,* Sep. 26, 1861, p. 1, c. 6.
[8] Thomas O'Reilly to Sumner, St. Louis, Oct. 27, 1861, Sumner MSS.
[9] Same to same, Nov. 22, 1861, *ibid.*
[10] T. P. Dunham to Sumner, Kalamazoo, Nov. 4, 1861, *ibid.*

tim of conspiracy, ramifying widely and extending to Washington, for the overthrow of "that energetic commander." He particularly stressed the fact that Frémont "possesses such a knowledge of the human character that he would not take into his confidence and give his plans to one who might betray them to the War Department, to go thence directly through the newspapers to the enemy." [11] When in late October, 1861, the Pennsylvania Anti-Slavery Society met at West Chester, Lincoln's treatment of Frémont was denounced and the President was compared to Pharaoh.[12] Such denunciation was an abolitionist *cliché*.

From this point the name of Frémont, along with that of Benjamin F. Butler, became a focus for radical attack upon the harassed President, while generals who were favored or kept in command by the President, McClellan especially, were by-words of radical denunciation. Though ill informed, such denunciation bore the fervid quality of righteous unction. It was the Anna E. Dickinsons, the Wendell Phillipses of the land who took up the pro-Frémont slogans. To them the whole war was viewed not only as a holy war against slavery but as a crusade against Southerners as wicked persons. For their inherent wickedness and for the centuries they had held the Negro in bondage these rebels of the South were to be punished. When Lincoln refused or omitted to do so, he was associated with "rebels," with the "traitorous" McClellan, with slave catchers. To such critics the President did nothing right. Even his handling of the *Trent* affair was denounced as weak bungling. Pulled at from right and left till he was nearly torn apart, the conservative Lincoln, President of the dis-United States, found among his own Republicans almost a greater vexation than among those of the opposite party, or even among enemies in arms.

X

Some concept of the difficulty of Lincoln's position can be had by noting the matters that pressed upon him at the turn of that year,

---

[11] Letter to Adjutant General Thomas from "An Impartial Reader," New York *Times*, Nov. 7, 1861, p. 2, c. 3–4.

[12] *National Anti-Slavery Standard*, Nov. 2, 1861, quoted in James Harvey Young, "Anna Elizabeth Dickinson and the Civil War" (ms. doctoral dissertation, Univ. of Ill., 1941), chap. 1. The same author has given a vivid account of this amazing girl orator and antislavery firebrand in *Miss. Vall. Hist. Rev.*, XXXI, 59–80 (June, 1944).

1861–62. Congress met and the Jacobins of Congress ominously whetted their blades. The affair of the *Trent,* with its appalling menace of war with Britain, was at the acute stage. English Tories and French aristocrats were persistently misunderstanding America and abusing its chief. An annual message to Congress, Lincoln's first, had to be prepared. Sinews of war had to be provided. A national military policy was yet to be devised. Troublesome aspects of the slavery question, including military emancipation, the use of Negro soldiers, and the treatment of fugitive slaves, could not much longer be evaded. Overdue appointments were awaiting the President's action, with three vacancies, for example, on the Supreme Court. Meanwhile, with a formidable enemy encamped near Washington, the secretary of war was about to be removed for good reason, while the head of the army (McClellan) was ill and could not be "disturbed with business." [1] "Since he had never delegated his powers," writes his biographer, "work at the headquarters of the army was paralyzed by his absence," while in the field a coördinating staff service was lacking. [2]

Not all these matters, nor the most serious of them, were treated in Lincoln's message of December 3, 1861. Comment on fundamentals was unsatisfactorily combined with miscellaneous departmental recommendations. What the President said about Haiti and Liberia, about the court of claims, patents, warfare against pirates, the land office, the international exhibition to be held at London, and the newly organized territories (Colorado, Dakota, and Nevada), can be passed over. On more critical matters he spoke confidently, though with no concealment of hard realities. Foreign nations, he thought, would not give the aid and comfort for which the enemies of the Union hoped. Even from the standpoint of commerce and self interest it seemed to him that governments abroad would prefer one strong nation on these shores rather than "the same nation broken in hostile fragments." Reviewing the war situation he found his chief encouragement on the border, where developments in Maryland, Kentucky, and Missouri were favorable to the Union side. Those three states, he said, while promising not a soldier at first, had sent no less than 40,000 men into the field for the Union, while in western Virginia the President was pleased to note that the winter found Union loving people masters of their own country. With footings ob-

---

[1] *Works,* VII, 70 (Jan. 1, 1862).   [2] Myers, *McClellan,* 228.

tained on the Southern coast the Union cause was advancing south-ward.

As to army command the President mentioned that McClellan was "in considerable degree" the choice of the country. This was faint praise, but even this much was hedged when the President added that one bad general was better than two good ones, and that if a ship is in a storm it may go down because "no single mind" is allowed to control. After ranging widely over many topics, Lincoln closed on the theme of popular government, the danger of despotism, and the superior claim of labor above capital. Predicting a nation of two hundred and fifty million souls within the lifetime of men then living, he reasoned that the "struggle of to-day is not altogether for to-day—it is for a vast future also." But this future was to be en-visaged in terms of "the popular principle, applied to government, through the machinery of the States and the Union . . . ."[3]

By the wonder of telegraphy the "7,578 words" of the message were received in New York in one hour and thirty-two minutes.[4] To the *Times* it seemed that the document showed "plain, clear common sense," being "written in the vigorous, compact and unostentatious style . . . characteristic of the President."[5] The *Herald* likewise considered it a "plain, concise, unpretending, business-like exposi-tion."[6] Not so William Lloyd Garrison. "What a wish-washy message from the President," he wrote. "It is . . . evident that he is a man of very small calibre, and had better be at his old business of splitting rails . . . . He has evidently not a drop of anti-slavery blood in his veins; . . . ."[7] "Not *one single manly, bold, dignified* position taken . . . but a . . . timid, timeserving, commonplace sort of an abor-tion of a message, cold enough . . . to *freeze* h-ll over," wrote a lesser abolitionist.[8] French journals read the message to imply that Lincoln considered war with Britain inevitable.[9] In Britain the na-tion's thought was so absorbed in the death of Prince Albert that the message received comparatively little attention, but the London *Herald* railed at Lincoln's "inexcusable" "*if not insulting, language*

---

[3] *Works*, VII, 28–60.   [4] New York *Times*, Dec. 4, 1861, p. 5, c. 1.
[5] *Ibid.*, Dec. 4, 1861, p. 4, cc. 2–3.   [6] New York *Herald*, Dec. 4, 1861, p. 6, c. 3.
[7] W. L. Garrison to Oliver Johnson, Boston, Dec. 6, 1861, Garrison MSS.
[8] S. York to Lyman Trumbull, Paris, Ill., Dec. 5, 1861, Trumbull MSS.
[9] Quotations from French newspapers as found in New York *Herald*, Jan. 3, 1862, p. 2, c. 5.

[which] *can only* . . . *apply to France and England,"* warning that Lincoln must back down, else a war would follow which would annihilate his country.[10] As if such pointless criticisms were not enough, the President had to deal with advisers at home, even in his cabinet, who doubted his ability to lead. On the last day of the year 1861 the Attorney General wrote in his diary: "The Prest. is an excellent man, . . . but he lacks *will* and *purpose,* and, I greatly fear he, has not *the power to command."* [11]

---

[10] Extracts from London *Herald* in New York *Herald,* Jan. 1, 1862, p. 2, c. 3. This London paper was characterized by the New York *Herald* as the Derby organ of aristocrats and oligarchists (*ibid.*).

[11] Bates, *Diary,* 220.

CHAPTER XVI

A SEA OF TROUBLES

I

IN THE international domain it appears that few presidents have done less—i. e., performed fewer obvious presidential acts—than Lincoln. In comparison with Woodrow Wilson, or Theodore Roosevelt, or Franklin Roosevelt, Lincoln's activity in the realm of diplomacy was slight. Yet if one subtracts from American international dealings those touches that were peculiarly Lincoln's own, the difference becomes so significant that his contribution must be regarded as a sizable factor. Lincoln did not have much time to take his international soundings before the sailing became stormy and hazardous. Diplomacy was Seward's province. Lincoln was content that it should be so, but in the first phase of his administration and the early months of the war Lincoln showed not only sounder judgment than Seward, but, which is essential in an executive, the will to use that judgment, albeit without destroying Seward's usefulness.[1]

While painfully occupied with the Sumter crisis, Lincoln received from his foreign secretary a confidential paper which might well have served as sufficient reason for dismissing that official. Bluntly indicating that the administration was "without a policy," Seward proceeded to supply one. At home he would evacuate Sumter, but keep and defend the Gulf ports. Then he would demand explanations from Spain and France (on matters that had in no way reached, or approached, a

---

[1] For Lincoln's foreign problems one should consult· Frank L. Owsley, *King Cotton Diplomacy* (closely devoted to the Confederate side); Ephraim Douglass Adams, *Great Britain and the American Civil War;* Jay Monaghan, *Diplomat in Carpet Slippers.* The work by Monaghan is a recent vivid treatment that emphasizes Lincoln. See also Martin P. Claussen, *The United States and Great Britain, 1861–1865: Peace Factors in International Relations* (abstract of thesis, Univ. of Ill., 1938); J. G. Randall, "Lincoln and John Bright," *Yale Rev.,* XXXIV, 292–304 (Dec., 1944).

crisis). He would demand these explanations categorically, at once! If the explanations were not satisfactory, he would convene Congress, and declare war! He would also seek an explanation from Great Britain and Russia, and would marshal on this side of the Atlantic a "vigorous . . . spirit of independence . . . against European intervention."

Whatever policy was adopted, it must be "somebody's business," said Seward, to direct it. Either the President must do it himself, "and be all the while active in it," or he must devolve it upon some cabinet member. Once a policy was determined, debate must end. Significantly the "premier" added: ". . . I neither seek to evade nor assume responsibility." [2]

Perhaps the kindest way to treat this amazing document, aside from noting its date (April 1), is to observe that its proposals never proceeded beyond the tentative stage, and that the history of Seward's diplomatic accomplishments could be written without even mentioning this fool's-day aberration. The secretary took no outward action in the terms of his "Thoughts for the President's Consideration." Foreign nations were not confronted with preposterous demands. Reason did not so rashly desert the state department. Next day and thereafter Seward was a reasonably normal person. If later he was to return (as on May 21) to his April illusion that European war had to result from the American situation and that such war would reunite the sections, the acute form of the illusion was definitely past.[3]

Before dismissing the subject, however, it is significant to note how Lincoln received this eccentric communication. In the first place, he protected his government, and his secretary too, by keeping the

---

[2] "Some Thoughts for the President's Consideration" [memorandum by Seward], April 1, 1861, Nicolay and Hay, *Lincoln*, III, 445–447. Evidently found among the President's papers after his death, this memorandum has been produced only by Nicolay and Hay. So far, their biography and their edition of Lincoln's works are the only traceable sources for the document. It is hardly to be supposed that they invented it or were misled by a forged document, and historians have accepted it as genuine. There is no corroboration, however, in the Seward papers.

[3] For a historical analysis of Seward's "Thoughts" see Frederic Bancroft, "Seward's Proposition of April 1, 1861 . . . ," 99 *Harper's Mo.*, 781–791 (1899). Bancroft shows how Seward, assuming in the winter of 1860–61 the function of saving the country, labored under strange illusions—e. g., that restoration of the Union would be promoted by a foreign war. The authenticity of the "Thoughts" is not questioned by Bancroft.

matter secret. His private secretaries, the sole agents in giving the document to the world, assert that "the affair never reached the knowledge of any other member of the Cabinet." ⁴ At the same time, without losing a day, the President sent a reply in which courteous patience was perfectly balanced by that firmness of which the pliable Lincoln was at times capable. He made it clear that the administration did have a foreign policy as displayed in circulars and instructions to ministers, and a domestic policy as announced in his own inaugural address. Then, with a dignity befitting the nation's elected chief who could not delegate final responsibility, Lincoln wrote: ". . . I remark that if this must be done [directing a policy], I must do it." ⁵ This carried no rebuke and had no apparent effect on the personal friendship of the two men; probably the matter was never "again alluded to by either Lincoln or Seward." ⁶ In a quiet episode of which the nation knew nothing the President had made it crystal clear that Seward was no "premier" and Lincoln no rubber stamp. What Lincoln may have thought about the matter was kept under his hat. Not a needless syllable was uttered. Nothing, probably, was said orally and face to face. Yet from that April day Lincoln was not only President but Chief; he was treated and recognized as such. Already, as in the Sumter affair, harm had been done by Seward's officious negotiation behind Lincoln's back. From this point there was less backstair diplomacy, while on vital matters there was on Lincoln's part at least a salutary minimum of attention to the wording of foreign despatches. Both in executive control and in international dealings the secret incident of the "Thoughts" had important consequences; to the biographer of Lincoln it has significance as a revelation of strength of personality combined with gentlemanly dealing.

II

As the foreign relations of Lincoln, Seward, and Company unfolded, they became enmeshed in a remarkable series of episodes, of which the most serious seemed to approach catastrophic proportions. At London Charles Francis Adams, Lincoln's chosen minister, represented the best of American statesmanship, while Lord John (later

---

⁴ Nicolay and Hay, *Lincoln*, III, 449.   ⁵ *Ibid.*, III, 448–449.   ⁶ *Ibid.*, III, 449.

Earl) Russell, British foreign secretary, with whom Adams had to deal, was a reasonable man whose readiness to understand the United States was a factor of importance. Yet the upper class in England tended toward sympathy with the Southern cause, and Her Majesty's prime minister Palmerston had a veritable penchant for intervention in the affairs of distant nations. From what he saw and heard, Adams was led to feel that among aristocratic Englishmen there was a strong desire "to see the United States go to pieces." [1] Though British statesmen would seek to conceal the fact, Adams thought they distrusted the American Union as "an overbearing and powerful democracy." [2] As for the Tories, there is little doubt that they wanted the American national experiment to fail. This, in general, was the attitude of the London Clubs; much of the conversation that floated around in excusive circles would be in this vein. Such also was the tone of that influential but arrogant paper, the *Times* of London.

Lord Lyons, British minister at Washington, did not adequately take Lincoln's measure, nor Seward's either. During the campaign of 1860 he had referred to Lincoln as "a rough Farmer—who began life as a Farm Labourer—and got on by a talent for stump speaking." [3] He distrusted Lincoln and his party; yet he felt that loud Republican protests against England may have been partly to counteract the suspicions aroused by Anglo-American sympathy on the slavery question.[4] Cobden, later a conspicuous friend of the Union, prayed in March 1861 for a peaceful dissolution of the Union without bloodshed, though seeing no political leader who could have the "courage" to advocate it. Of the new President he wrote: "Lincoln whom I saw at Springfield, is a backwoodsman of good sturdy common sense, but . . . unequal to the occasion." [5] Of Seward he said: "He is a sort of Brummagen Palmerston always talking in a low cunning way to *Bunkum*." [6] Even Bright regarded Seward as "capricious." [7] Earl Rus-

---

[1] W. C. Ford, ed., *A Cycle of Adams Letters*, I, 220.

[2] C. F. Adams to Edward Everett, London, July 12, 1861, Everett MSS.

[3] Lyons to Russell (private), July 23, 1860, Russell Papers, G. D. 22/34, MSS., Public Record Office (London).

[4] *Ibid.*

[5] Cobden to Bright, Mar. 25, 1861, Cobden MSS. (Add. MSS. 43649), British Museum.

[6] Cobden to William Slagg, Dec. 19, 1861, typescript copy, Cobden MSS. (Add. MSS. 43677, pt. 2), British Museum.

[7] Bright to Cobden, Oct. 3, 1861, Bright MSS. (Add. MSS. 43383, pt. 8), British Museum.

sell so far misjudged Lincoln that he could think him capable of "getting up war cries to help his declining popularity." [8] Early in 1861 Russell could write: "President Lincoln looming in the distance is a still greater peril than President Buchanan." [9] At the time of the Sumter crisis he feared that Lincoln would use force, by which he would "clinch the separation, but injure trade . . . this year." [10]

Francis Lieber's observation was that all the foreign ministers in Washington with the exception of the Russian, inclined to the South. Coining the phrase "Le Pouvoir Dinatoire," he thought Southern members of Congress had "used the Dinatory Power much better than the Northern Congressmen." [11] Americans in England did little to help their cause. Adams wrote: "Even intelligent Americans are quoted here as talking about the right to dissolve the partnership just as if we were a mere trading firm." [12] From quite a different quarter Americans were causing British apprehension by advocating the acquisition of Mexican territory. Edward Bates feared that such schemes would alienate the sympathy of the British middle class, represented by Mr. Bright, whose attitude was friendly and who were able "to check even the ministers of the crown." [13]

The very existence of war and the necessity of carrying it on by war measures, involved international complications. Such a policy as the blockade of Southern ports, proclaimed by Lincoln on April 19 and April 27,[14] produced a crop of legalistic objections. President Jefferson Davis denounced it as a "mere paper blockade" which "could only have been published under the sudden influence of passion," [15] while abroad it raised at once the question of international legality. Under the recent Declaration of Paris of 1856, a blockade, to be binding, had to be effective, and there was doubt at the time whether such effectiveness existed. Though the United States was not a signatory of the Declaration of Paris, this matter of effectiveness was always

---

[8] Russell to Lyons (private), Mar. 28, 1863 (copy), Russell Papers, G. D. 22/97, MSS., Public Record Office (London).

[9] Russell to Lyons (private), Feb. 16, 1861 (copy), Russell Papers, G. D. 22/96, MSS., *ibid.*

[10] Russell to Lyons, April 20, 1861, *ibid.*

[11] Francis Lieber to S. B. Ruggles, May 24, 1861, Lieber MSS.

[12] C. F. Adams to Edward Everett, London, July 26, 1861, Everett MSS.

[13] Bates, *Diary,* 193 (Aug. 27, 1861).   [14] *Works,* VI, 248–250, 256–257.

[15] Message of President Davis to the Confederate Congress, April 29, 1861, *Journal,* Confed. Cong. (Sen. Doc. No. 234, 58 [U. S.] Cong., 2 sess.), I, 166.

considered in the international discussion of the subject. The double nature of the war as a conflict between belligerents (each government having recognition of belligerency) and at the same time an internal problem of putting down insurrectionists conspiring (so it was said) to overthrow their own government, was the cause of constant difficulty, and led to a situation where foreign statesmen, in referring to the conflict, might use a different language than that of the Lincoln administration.[16]

This difference of language came into view when the United States government protested against the very idea of "neutrality" abroad. In the Queen's proclamation (issued on May 13, 1861, "the day Adams reached London, and before he had time to call at the Foreign Office") [17] the British government cast the official mold in which its main policy toward the American question was to be shaped. Throughout the war it deemed itself a neutral between the United States and the Confederate States. This ultimately was to disappoint the latter much more than the former, besides setting the pattern for substantial reparation to the Washington government in the course of time; but when it was issued the British neutrality announcement, quite natural considering the size and importance of the Southern *de facto* government, was the theme of frequent complaint on the part of Seward, to whom the proclamation seemed "designed to raise the insurgents to the level of a belligerent state," [18] while according to the state department at Washington, the Confederate government was a "pretended new State . . . existing in pronunciamento only." [19] It is true that Lincoln himself, in his blockade order, had virtually recognized the belligerent character of the Confederate government, as did the courts of the United States.[20] It is also true that in conducting semi-official communication with Southern agents the British government was careful to explain that such communication did "not imply any acknowledgment of the confederates as an independent state." [21] Remembering the non-application by the United States of the piracy or traitor theory of Southern status (in

---

[16] Randall, *Constitutional Problems Under Lincoln*, ch. iii.
[17] Bancroft, *Seward*, II, 176.
[18] Seward to Adams, June 8, 1861, *Sen. Doc. No. 1*, 37 Cong., 2 sess., p. 101.
[19] *Works*, VI, 282 (May 21, 1861). Seward's statement.
[20] Randall, *Constitutional Problems Under Lincoln*, 72.
[21] Russell to C. F. Adams, Nov. 26, 1861, *House Exec. Doc. No. 1*, 37 Cong., 3 sess., p. 9.

other words, the non-prosecution of Southern individuals as insurgents), it is now realized that the attitude of the British government on this point did not differ vitally from that of Washington. The variance was intangible; it was a matter of status. Serious difference, on the other hand, did exist between London and Richmond; the Confederacy urged intervention as well as full international recognition, which neither Britain nor any other foreign country gave.

As a kind of initial keynote for Anglo-American wartime relations, the secretary of state, on May 21, 1861, directed to Adams a paper designated as "Despatch no. 10" which has also been called Seward's "bold remonstrance." This paper has special interest as one of the few examples of Lincoln's editing of his government's international correspondence. All that Lincoln did was to go over Seward's words, changing a phrase here and deleting one there, but by these touches he transformed a bellicose and threatening despatch that might well have caused serious offense into a restrained instruction intended for Minister Adams's confidential guidance. In Seward's draft there was the comment that British intercourse with Confederate commissioners, even though unofficial, was injurious to the United States; then came the drastic admonition that Adams "desist from all intercourse whatever, unofficial as well as official, with the British government, so long as it shall continue intercourse of either kind with the domestic enemies of this country."

The President examined the despatch. Seward had written: "The President is surprised and grieved that Mr. Dallas [minister to Great Britain preceding Mr. Adams] did not protest against the proposed unofficial intercourse between the British Government and the missionaries of the insurgents as well as against the demand for explanations made by the British government." Instead of the words "is surprised and grieved" Lincoln substituted "regrets." Then he deleted the whole reference to the British demand with the comment: "Leave out, because it does not appear that such explanations were demanded." Where Seward remarked that British intercourse with the Confederate commissioners "would be none the less wrongful to us for being called unofficial," Lincoln struck out the accusing word "wrongful" and substituted "hurtful." Identifying the possibility of British recognition with intervention, Seward had written: ". . . we from that hour shall cease to be friends and become once more, as we have twice before been forced to be, enemies of Great Britain." Drawing a line around this truculent passage, Lincoln wrote simply: "Leave out." "If Great Britain . . . shall . . . recognize them," wrote Seward, "and give them shelter . . . , the laws of nations afford an adequate . . . remedy and we shall avail ourselves of it." Lincoln closed the sentence with the word "remedy"; the threatening conclusion was omitted.[22]

But Lincoln's chief suggestion was at the end of the despatch which in the Seward draft contained two wordy paragraphs of admonition dwelling upon the danger of war, putting the blame upon the British, accusing Britain of provoking the revolution, and warning "that nation" not to "repeat the . . . error." At the beginning of this warlike passage Lincoln wrote: "Drop all from this line to the end, and . . . write, 'This paper is for your own guidance only, and not [to] be read or shown to any one.'"

Instead of issuing the despatch in every particular as emended by Lincoln, Seward, with a good deal less than the clear brevity of Lincoln's words, added an introductory statement that the paper was not to be read or shown to Russell, though its spirit was to be Adams's guide; then he retained the final passage which Lincoln had wisely directed him to delete.[23] In Seward's eyes the confidential nature of the paper made this deletion unnecessary. Yet all this bellicose and rhetorical language was out of place when addressed confidentially to Adams; it was meaningless unless intended for the British government. Seward's retention of the passage which Lincoln had asked him to drop seemed to indicate a fondness for the products of his own brain and a partial unwillingness to be governed by the President's leadership. This, fortunately, did not dissipate the importance of Lincoln's

---

[22] This study of Seward's despatch with Lincoln's handwritten emendations is based on a photostat copy among the manuscripts in the Library of Congress. J. C. Bancroft Davis, assistant secretary of state, found the document in the files of the state department in 1869, whereupon Secretary of State Hamilton Fish showed it to President Grant, who authorized the making of twenty photographic copies which were distributed to high officials. The negative was then destroyed. (The original is no longer in the archives of the state department.) In 1886, over the disapproval of Mr. Fish, the *North American Review* (CXLII, 410–411) published a reduced facsimile, taken from the photographic copy belonging to Benjamin H. Bristow of the Grant cabinet. For a printed reproduction of Seward's draft with Lincoln's changes, see *Works*, VI, 277–286.

[23] For Seward's emended despatch as sent to C. F. Adams, May 21, 1861, see *Sen. Exec. Doc. No. 1*, 37 Cong., 2 sess., pp. 87–90.

revision. That revision had its immediate and continuing effect. Lincoln's influence in this bit of diplomacy had been more than that of advice or suggestion; it had carried through to the actual shaping of international intercourse.

III

As the year 1861 drew to a close the stormy Atlantic resounded to the thunders of a fearful Anglo-American crisis when two diplomats of the Confederacy, en route to foreign posts, were seized by a naval officer of the United States. This exploit was performed by Captain Charles Wilkes of the warship *San Jacinto* who had stopped the British steamer *Trent* and had arrested James M. Mason on his way to Britain, and John Slidell accredited to France. The diplomats, with their secretaries, were triumphantly brought to the United States and held as state prisoners in Fort Warren, Boston Harbor. Though the Blairs at once denounced the act of Wilkes,[1] Welles expressed approval of his conduct,[2] and in the House of Representatives opposing factions joined in voting a "high sense" of the captain's "good conduct." [3] Edward Everett, formerly secretary of state and minister to Britain, joined with Caleb Cushing, former attorney general, in praising Wilkes,[4] whose action was loudly applauded in the Northern press. Though the seizure occurred on November 8, it was not until nearly three weeks later (November 27), that word of it reached England. The news found Charles Francis Adams absent in Yorkshire on a social visit. Notified of the event by telegram he returned to London, full of "anxiety for the fate" of his "unhappy country." [5]

There is no denying that a miserable war threat resulted from this sensational affair. It was, perhaps, a small incident; yet, as viewed abroad, it seemed an affront to the British flag, a violation of the law of nations, and a deliberate American effort to provoke war. This

[1] Smith, *Blair Family*, II, 194.

[2] ". . . I congratulate you on the great public service you have rendered in the capture of the rebel commissioners . . . . Your conduct . . . has the emphatic approval of this Department." Secretary Welles to Captain Wilkes, Nov. 30, 1861, Moore, *Rebellion Record* (Docs.), III, 330.

[3] *Cong. Globe*, 37 Cong., 2 sess., 5.

[4] S. F. Bemis, ed., *American Secretaries of State*, VII, 63; Caleb Cushing to Fernando Wood, New York *Times*, Dec. 18, 1861, p. 6, cc. 3–5.

[5] Despatches nos. 80 and 81, C. F. Adams to Seward, London, Nov. 29, 1861, Dipl. Despatches (England, vol. 78), MSS., Dep. of State, Nat. Archives.

latter aspect was the serious factor. The incident was associated in British governmental minds with the conviction that Seward had been "acting with the desire of occasioning a war between the two countries . . . ." [6] From England it was privately reported that a foreign office employee had said at a dinner party that "it was the purpose of the Brittish [sic] government to have a war with us & that Lord Palmerston wanted to bring it on at once while we . . . [were] unprepared." [7] It "makes me sad," wrote one of Sumner's friends from Cardiff, "to see how many English presses are hot for war." [8] "This [the British] government expects—and I fear, welcomes war . . . [and] chooses its own time to strike . . . ," wrote Thurlow Weed from London. [9] "England is rampant," he wrote, "and France excited by the capture of Mason and Slidell. Everybody here expects war. An artificial . . . sentiment . . . has been . . . worked up against us. . . . London and Paris are full of noisy, adroit secessionists." [10]

The incident had brought into focus the main grievance against England—i. e., the reputed intention to interfere in the Civil War. The "first step toward interference in our domestic affairs," wrote John Jay, "will inaugurate war beyond all question." [11] Correspondence from London revealed such "bitterness and hostility" as to make it felt that Britain "must go to war." [12] Manchester was "intensely excited," with posters and "extra" papers dramatizing the crisis. [13] Journalists on both sides sensationally fanned the flames. The *Herald* of New York and the *Times* of London "seemed to be competing for a new high mark in jingo journalism." [14]

Speculation ranged widely as to probable developments in the expected war. Weed observed to Cameron that the Confederates wanted "us in war with England, that their ports may be opened and

6 E. Twistleton to William Dwight (of Boston), London, Dec. 7, 1861, Sumner MSS.

7 J. P. Usher to R. W. Thompson, Washington, Jan. 1, 1862, MS., Lincoln Nat. Life Foundation, Fort Wayne.

8 Charles D. Cleveland to Sumner, Cardiff, Dec. 17, 1861, Sumner MSS.

9 Thurlow Weed to Simon Cameron, London, Dec. 7, 1861, Cameron MSS.

10 Weed to Cameron, Paris, Dec. 3, 1861, *ibid.*

11 John Jay to Sumner, Nov. 8, 1861, Sumner MSS.

12 Joseph Cooper to Sumner, London, Dec. 28, 1861, *ibid.*

13 Henry W. Lord to Seward, Manchester, Nov. 27, 1861, Consular Letters (Manchester, vol. I), MSS., Dept. of State, Nat. Archives.

14 Martin Paul Claussen, *The United States and Great Britain, 1861–1865: Peace Factors in International Relations* (abstract of doctoral dissertation, University of Illinois, 1938), 1.

ours closed." [15] Another of Cameron's informants wrote glibly from Paris that the United States had no escape from a war with England and that the British fleet was all set for an attack in three grand divisions: (1) to open Southern ports; (2) to attack ports of New Hampshire and Maine (these to be held as "indemnity"); (3) to enter the Chesapeake, seize Baltimore and Annapolis, combine with Southern military forces, capture Washington, and destroy the Federal army.[16]

That so many people placed so low a value upon international good will while every element of misunderstanding was absurdly inflated, seems at this distance almost incredible. Tenseness of feeling destroyed the pleasure of social intercourse. Soon after the *Trent* affair an Englishman friendly to the United States found himself at a large dinner party "disagreeably prominent as the only advocate of the North against numberless taunts." [17] When, during this crisis, a distinguished English geologist, Sir Charles Lyell, pleaded the cause of the American union among his countrymen, the more effectively because he and Lady Lyell had enjoyed warm friendship with certain planters of the South, "the contumely became so fierce, that for a while they [Sir Charles and his lady] kept aloof from society, as it was too much for a lady's strength to bear it." [18]

IV

When it came to formulating Britain's policy in the *Trent* case, Palmerston at first took a threatening attitude, and governmental steps were taken that bore the appearance of preparations for possible war. Eight thousand troops were sent to Canada; [1] in Confederate correspondence this force was represented as "10,000 picked troops" together with "immense war material." [2] Warships were fitted out, officers were ordered to be in readiness for embarkation, and orders were issued forbidding the export of saltpetre, gunpowder, and munitions.[3] Seward was informed by the American consul in Manchester

---

[15] Thurlow Weed to Simon Cameron, London, Dec. 7, 1861, Cameron MSS.

[16] M. Balch to Simon Cameron, Paris, Dec. 11, 1861, *ibid.*

[17] Francis W. Newman to Epes Sargent, London, Feb. 22, 1865, MS., Boston Public Lib.

[18] Same to same, London, April 26, 1865, *ibid.*

[1] Theodore Martin, *Life of . . . the Prince Consort*, V, 419 n.

[2] W. L. Yancey to R. M. T. Hunter, London, Dec. 31, 1861, *Offic. Rec.* (Nav.), 2 ser., III, 313.

[3] C. F. Adams to W. H. Seward, London, Dec. 6, 1861, Despatch No. 84, Dipl. Despatches (England, vol. 78), MSS., Dept. of State, Nat. Archives.

that military and naval preparations were "going on with the greatest energy" and that the "whole nation" seemed to be "completely aroused." [4] War feeling was high in Quebec and a military board in that city was active in preparing the provinces for an expected contest with the United States.[5] In these circumstances, while diplomacy moved slowly, rumor spread like an epidemic, and it was reported in London that at the time of the American tour of the Prince of Wales "Mr. Seward . . . [had told] the Duke of Newcastle he was likely to occupy a high office; that when he did so it would become his duty to insult England, and he should insult her accordingly." [6]

Yet on the other side there were factors of a conciliatory nature; these indeed deserve more study than threats and alarms. The Queen, remembering American kindness to her son, made appeals to her ministers for peace as she signed proclamations.[7] The feeling of high excitement, the intensity of which has not been exaggerated, belonged to the period of two or three weeks following the reception of the news in England. As days passed British sentiment improved and arbitration came to be spoken of favorably. Leading British liberals, notably Bright and Cobden, spoke courageously of peace— for it took courage—even while military preparations were in progress and war feeling was up. When Americans began to think it over, it was realized that Slidell and Mason would be "a million times less mischievous" in London than in Fort Warren,[8] and that a policy of caution was indicated by all the rules of prudence. The strength of the Confederate wish for war between the United States and England was in itself sufficient evidence that this was a thing for Lincoln to avoid. Above all, thoughtful people began to realize the supreme folly of a needless war with so formidable a naval power as Britain when the government was desperately engaged with the domestic enemy, and when the occasion of such a war would have put the United States in the equivocal position of opposing its own traditional policy of supporting neutral rights at sea. It was reported from Boston, for example, that the "almost universal opinion . . . among intelligent men" was that this country must not have war with England, that

---

[4] Henry W. Lord to W. H. Seward, Manchester, Dec. 5, 1861, Consular Letters (Manchester, vol. I), MSS., Dep. of State, Nat. Archives.

[5] New York *Times*, Jan. 1, 1862, p. 5, c. 1.

[6] Benson J. Lossing, *Pictorial History of the Civil War*, II, 162.

[7] Weed to Cameron. Dec. 7, 1861, Cameron MSS.   [8] *Ibid.*

the envoys should be given up even though it be in response to peremptory demand, and that mortified pride was nothing compared to "a divided empire and a devastating war." [9]

This feeling became stronger when the legal aspects of the controversy were studied. While Wilkes had the belligerent right to search the *Trent* and take it into port for adjudication (on such a matter as carrying contraband), his summary procedure in the arrest of the envoys at sea and their forcible removal from the deck of the British steamer amounted to arbitrary disregard of legal usage and essential rights. On the other hand, a graceful yielding by the United States, while accomplishing everything in the avoidance of war, would involve no loss of "face" or sacrifice of prestige, since Wilkes's act was entirely unauthorized by his government. American concession could even be reasonably construed as gaining a point on England, because the Washington government would be disavowing such an act as it had traditionally complained of in "impressment" days. This would be putting England in the wrong, yet magnanimously yielding for the sake of peace—[10] something like eating one's cake and having it too! As a writer in a Washington newspaper expressed it, the United States was "as much estopped from defending the act of Capt[ain] Wilkes as Great Britain from complaining of it." [11]

V

In steering his country through this imbroglio, Lincoln gave his chief thought to avoiding the folly of having, as he said, "two wars on his hands at a time." [1] Benson J. Lossing, the historian, who participated in an interview with the President on the subject, quoted him as saying: "I fear the traitors will prove to be white elephants. . . . If Great Britain . . . demands their release, we must give them up . . . and thus forever bind her over to keep the peace in relation to neutrals, and so acknowledge that she has been wrong for sixty years." [2] Opinion in the cabinet was conflicting and not particularly

[9] Horatio Woodman to Charles Sumner, Boston, Dec. 20, 1861, Sumner MSS.
[10] Charles D. Cleveland to Charles Sumner, Cardiff, Dec. 17, 1861, *ibid.*
[11] Washington *National Intelligencer*, Dec. 9, 1861.
[1] Lincoln was so quoted in a letter from R. M. Mason to Amos Lawrence, Jan. 14, 1861 [1862], Amos Lawrence MSS.
[2] Lossing, *Pictorial Hist. of the Civ. War*, II, 156–157.

helpful. Seward, as reported by Welles, "at first approved" Wilkes's act,[3] while, as already noted, Welles commended the captain in a letter of congratulation. (Later both Seward and Welles came around to the position that Wilkes's method of procedure was incorrect.) The attorney general misread the situation, thinking Wilkes's seizure of the men lawful and apprehending no danger from Britain.[4] More than a month after the incident Lincoln passed a remark to Browning that indicated he was not worried; [5] this, however, was before information had been received of the official British attitude. The rash view of Browning himself was that the seizure was fully justified and that this country intended "at all hazards, to hold on to the prisoners" even though the result might be "a general upheaving of the nations." [6]

It should be remembered that it was not until about six weeks after the *Trent* incident that the official statement of the British government's position reached Washington; following that, it would be another three weeks before the American reply would be known in England. Cyrus Field's patient attempts to lay the Atlantic cable had failed prior to the Civil War and were not to achieve success until 1866. It is mere speculation to say what would have been the result in the crisis of the *Trent* affair if the cable had been in operation in 1861. The reasonable guess would seem to be that man's inventiveness would have been a menace in this case and that instantaneous communication between England and the United States would have been unfortunate. As it was, public feeling had time to cool down, sober opinion had a chance to mature, and the uses of diplomacy were allowed their opportunity. In this case diplomacy, in the sense of a sincere communication between governments for the purpose of arriving at a settlement, was genuine; it was not a mere façade or screen behind which, as in recent times, warmaking forces were ruthlessly operating. What Russell said to Lyons, or Seward to Russell, really counted; governments were speaking to governments through officially constituted spokesmen. A consultation as to the wording of an Anglo-American despatch was a matter of vital importance. What-

---

3 Welles, *Diary*, I, 299.

4 "While the fact gives . . . general satisfaction, . . . timid persons are alarmed, lest Great Britain should take offense . . . . There is no danger on that score. . . . Not only was it lawful to seise the men, but, I think, the ship itself was subject to confiscation," Bates, *Diary*, 202 (Nov. 16, 1861).

5 Browning, *Diary*, I, 513–514.   6 *Ibid.*, 514 n.

ever influence went into the shaping of such a despatch was pregnant with historic consequences. Under these circumstances, at a time when Palmerston and his cabinet seemed to be heading toward a breach with Washington, it was a matter of no small importance that the Queen and the Prince Consort took a hand at diplomacy.

Royal personages are supposed in Britain to be glorified figureheads, but this episode offered an important exception. On November 30 it had been decided at a meeting of the British cabinet that immediate reparation be demanded and a virtual ultimatum delivered.[7] A despatch to that effect (Russell to Lyons) was prepared and laid before the Prince Consort in his capacity as confidential adviser and private secretary to the Queen. It was the last official document submitted to the Prince, who was ill, "very wretched," and could eat no breakfast.[8] It was his last illness; he died on December 14. In this matter Albert's thoughts were those of Victoria; their combined deliberations appear in a memorandum of December 1, dated at Windsor Castle, written by Albert and only slightly modified by the Queen, in which it was suggested that Her Majesty would have liked to see the expression of a hope that the American captain had not acted under instructions, and that Her Majesty's government were unwilling to believe that the United States would do otherwise than spontaneously offer redress.

Whereas the tone of the contemplated British note had been that of peremptory demand, of putting the United States in the wrong, and of forcing a breach of relations if reparation and apology were not forthcoming, the modified note which Russell sent to Lyons, while firm enough in safeguarding the British position, was cast in far more conciliatory language. As sent, the despatch was "remodelled upon the lines indicated by the Prince, its language being little more than his own cast into official form." [9] It is the belief of the Prince's biographer that the peaceful decision of the United States government would hardly have occurred "but for the temperate and conciliatory tone in which, thanks to the Prince, the views of the [British] Government had been conveyed." [10] Her Majesty's government in the modified despatch took the attitude of believing the best of the United States, of recalling the friendly relations that had long subsisted between the countries, and of assuming that Wilkes's "aggression" had

---

[7] Spencer Walpole, *Life of Lord John Russell*, II, 346.
[8] Martin, *Prince Consort*, V, 421.   [9] *Ibid.*, V, 423.   [10] *Ibid.*, V, 425.

not been committed in compliance with his government's orders. The captain's affront, of course, could not be passed over without being set right, but it was believed that the United States government was fully aware of this and would not unnecessarily force a discussion on "a question of so grave a character, and with regard to which the whole British Nation would be sure to entertain such unanimity of feeling." Accordingly, the British expectation was that Washington, of its own accord, would give satisfaction by releasing the four gentlemen (the envoys with their secretaries) and would offer a suitable apology.[11]

VI

It was not alone on the British side that governmental restraint was apparent. When Lincoln submitted his first regular annual message to Congress on December 3, 1861, he made no mention of the *Trent* case, though the imbroglio was on everyone's tongue. The management of foreign affairs and the framing of diplomatic intercourse being so peculiarly executive in character, there is little evidence that the participation of Congress in this task of international adjustment would have been helpful. Heroically to take a stand, or to deliver a resounding stump speech in the form of a legislative resolution, was hardly calculated to improve the situation. On innocuous and collateral aspects, however, Lincoln did submit to Congress some of the correspondence. The Austrian authorities, for example, had expressed deep concern in the matter, and Seward had assured the imperial-royal government that the United States was incapable of disturbing the peace of the world and would in no sense fail as an advocate of the broadest liberality in matters of international law.[1] When the Prussian government complained, the secretary of state, mentioning in a typical bit of diplomatic patter that that government was eminently distinguished by a generous ambition to ameliorate the condition of mankind, produced evidence to show that, if the peace was to be broken, the fault would not lie in anything the United States had done.[2] On the same subject there were communications with France, whose government took the incident very seriously, with Russia, whose emperor expressed sentiments of warm friendship,

---

[11] *Ibid.*, V, 423.   [1] *Sen. Exec. Doc. No. 14*, 37 Cong., 2 sess.   [2] *Ibid.*, no. 18.

and with the King of Italy. The President formally submitted all these communications to the nation's legislature. What it amounted to was that if Congress wished to debate the Russian, Austrian, or Siamese aspects of the *Trent* affair, this was agreeable to Lincoln! [3]

In his anxiety to preserve American dignity while promoting reasonable adjustment, the President turned his thoughts to arbitration. Employing a characteristic technique which appeared on various other occasions, he carefully sketched a despatch on the subject; then the despatch was never sent. In this document, a kind of experimental draft of a possible letter from Seward to Lyons,[4] Lincoln showed considerable wariness as to yielding any American point, but stated that Wilkes had acted "without orders from or expectation of the government." Specifying matters regarding the existing conflict which he wished to "bring into view," Lincoln then proceeded to suggest that the United States would "go to such friendly arbitration as is usual among nations," and would abide by the award; or, in lieu of this, he proposed "reparation" by the United States, provided such reparation should become the law for future analogous cases.[5] This was about the time that matters were coming to a head, the British position having been communicated to Lord Lyons, and Lincoln now "feared trouble." He showed Browning his proposed letter. The matter was talked over fully and "both agreed that the question was easily susceptible of a peaceful solution . . . and . . . that it was a proper case for arbitration." [6]

Pacific influences now came into play. Seward, as early as November 27, had sent word to Adams that Wilkes had acted without instructions.[7] This cost Washington nothing and proved a very considerable factor. Charles Sumner, chairman of the Senate committee on foreign relations, even before the *Trent* affair, was in correspondence with two outstanding British liberals, Bright and Cobden. As the correspondence continued these British leaders stressed not only the need of peaceful adjustment, but also the necessity of America's release of the envoys, since no other solution would be adequate. At one point Bright wrote: "I need not tell you . . . that Nations *drift*

[3] *Ibid.*, nos. 8, 22, 30; *Works,* VII, 75, 86, 107–108, 111.

[4] Browning, *Diary,* I, 517.

[5] "Draft of a Despatch proposing Arbitration in the 'Trent' Affair—not used or sent," *Works,* VII, 63–65. Tentatively dated December 10 (?), 1861.

[6] Browning, *Diary,* I, 516 (Dec. 21, 1861).   [7] Bancroft, *Seward,* II, 233.

into wars . . . often thro' the want of a resolute hand at some moment early in the quarrel. So now, a courageous stroke, not of arms, but of moral action, may save you and us." [8] Sumner showed these letters to Lincoln; then he wrote Bright that the President was "pacific in disposition, with a natural slowness," adding, "Yesterday he said to me, 'There will be no war unless England is bent upon having one.' " [9] Sumner also quoted Lincoln as saying: "I never see Lord Lyons. If it were proper I should like to talk with him, that he might hear from my lips how much I desire peace. If we could talk together he would believe me." [10]

In Paris, three leading Americans—Thurlow Weed, John Bigelow, and Winfield Scott—made their contribution toward pacification. (Weed was an informal emissary of Seward; Bigelow was consul at Paris; Scott was simply a distinguished American abroad.) Weed wrote letters to his right bower Seward advising that Wilkes's act be not approved. Bigelow drafted a public letter to be signed by Scott; then Weed induced Scott to sign it as his own. This letter, to which the high prestige of Scott's name was attached, emphasized American friendship toward Britain and gave the assurance that, with understandings that "could emancipate the commerce of the world," the United States would willingly give up the envoys.[11] Weed also played his part by conferring in person with Earl Russell and by contributing a letter which appeared prominently in the *Times* of London, and was republished in Paris, Liverpool, Manchester, Dublin, and St. Petersburg. The main point of the letter was the emphatic assurance that Seward's "badinage" had no significance and that both the secretary and the American people had the earnest wish to maintain friendly relations with Britain.[12] While speaking thus to the British nation Weed did not fail in his letters to Seward to report the seriousness of the Wilkes incident as viewed from London; the same report was given to Seward by Adams and Bigelow.

British leaders had contemplated an ultimatum to the United

[8] Bright to Sumner, Rochdale, Dec. 5, 1861, *Proceedings*, Mass. Hist. Soc., XLV, 151.
[9] E. L. Pierce, *Memoir and Letters of Charles Sumner*, IV, 57.
[10] *Ibid.*, IV, 61.
[11] John Bigelow, *Retrospections of An Active Life*, I, 387–390.
[12] Thurlow Weed Barnes, *Memoir of Thurlow Weed* (Harriet A. Weed, ed., *Life of Thurlow Weed* . . . . vol. II), 354 ff.

States—i. e., a demand, with a time limit, that the men be released. This was to have been followed, in case of non-compliance, by withdrawal of the British legation from Washington. The next step would probably have been war. Since in some historical accounts it is erroneously stated that an "ultimatum" was *actually delivered* to the American government, it is necessary carefully to review the situation to see precisely what happened. On November 29, two days after England received news of the incident, the cabinet having held a meeting, Palmerston sent the Queen a note proposing that a release of the envoys be demanded, and that, on refusal, Lyons should leave Washington; along with this was a proposed despatch to Lyons to the same effect. This is the document which, as noted above, was modified and softened by the Prince and Queen. Russell's despatch to Lyons as actually sent (November 30) expressed the hope that the United States would of its own accord offer the needed redress—i. e., release of the men, with a suitable apology. All this was in a note which Lyons might show to Seward, and it contained no suggestion of an ultimatum, merely the statement that, if Seward did not offer the release, it should be proposed to him. The whole despatch was carefully worded to avoid any injury to American sensibilities. The factor that has caused some writers to think in terms of a British ultimatum came not in the despatch intended for Seward's perusal, but in a private note of Russell to Lyons, in which the Earl indicated that Lyons should consent to a delay of no more than seven days after the release demand was submitted; if at the end of that time such release had not been agreed to, Lyons was *confidentially* instructed to leave Washington with his whole legation. Having written the despatch and the private note, Russell thought the matter over yet again. Then he sent a second private note to Lyons on the same day, suggesting that in his first interview with Seward Lyons should not take the despatch with him but should prepare his mind for it, and allow him to arrange a settlement with the President and cabinet. Next time he was to bring the despatch and read it to Seward fully, but with not a word as to *delivering* any "ultimatum." If at this second interview Seward should ask what would be the consequence of noncompliance, Lyons was instructed to say that he wished to leave Seward and the President free to take their own course, and to add that he desired to abstain from anything like menace. It was also stated that the British cabinet would be "rather easy about the apology." [13]

This diplomatic maneuver can hardly be regarded as an ultimatum in the accepted sense of that word. An ultimatum involves a situation in which all the elements—demand, time limit, and threat as to what would happen on non-compliance—are communicated to the threatened government; such a process of governmental communication did not take place in the *Trent* case. Russell's first private note did suggest a rather menacing possibility; the saving features lay in the second private note and in the mildness and unthreatening character of the open despatch. In spite of all this the seven-day limit (even though not paraded publicly), and the suggestion to Lyons to leave Washington, were serious matters; to remember them is to point up the gravity of Lincoln's problem.[14]

Informed of the British position by Lyons, Seward sparred for a few days' time, realizing the while that settlement was rather urgent but giving no thought to a fact that must have constantly bothered Lyons—namely, that by December 30 the seven days would have expired. In preparation for the final decision, papers had been tentatively drafted for alternative courses. Lincoln, as above noted, had drawn up his paper suggesting arbitration or conditional release, while Seward had drafted a letter to Lyons [15] announcing simple release. Under these circumstances Lincoln's cabinet met on Christmas Day "impressed with the magnitude of the subject" and aware that upon their decision "depended . . . probably the existance [sic], of the nation." [16] Despite the reference to the "white elephant" already quoted, it appears that at the time of the assembling of the cabinet not even Lincoln was fully convinced of the necessity of release; "no one except [Montgomery] Blair and Seward seems to have favored a full compliance with the British demand." [17] Yet the Blair patriarch was blaming Seward for international troubles; at the time of this cabinet

---

[13] Walpole, *Lord John Russell*, II, 346–347.

[14] The purpose of British diplomacy has thus been described: ". . . publicly to browbeat and menace the United States by a . . . threat of war, . . . privately to pave the way for getting out of the difficulty without a resort to arms." Thomas L. Harris, *The Trent Affair*, 172. (A more friendly view would be that while diplomacy worked toward peace, a certain boldness in asserting national rights would, in the days of acute difficulty, give harmless outlet to the more belligerent sentiment at home. This dualism existed on both sides of the Atlantic.)

[15] Bates, *Diary*, 216.   [16] *Ibid*   [17] Bancroft, *Seward*, II, 235.

meeting Francis P. Blair, Sr., wrote to ex-President Van Buren that he did not care if "Billy Bowlegs" (Seward) were delivered up along with the envoys to appease British pride, Seward being held in lieu of an apology! [18]

This Christmas cabinet meeting may be regarded as one of those occasions when genuine deliberation on matters of high policy brought results. Though not a member of the cabinet, Sumner was invited in; the ponderous senator's reading of friendly letters "just rec'd" from Bright and Cobden was a unique feature of this consultation. It was realized that internal politics in Britain was a factor of importance, that if Palmerston's government did not obtain satisfaction from the United States the opposition might "force a ministerial crisis." The cabinet also realized that the United States could not hope for success "in a super added war with England." The hard facts in the case were realistically canvassed, and though all, "even the President," were reluctant to acknowledge "obvious truths," "all yielded to the necessity," and unanimously accepted Seward's letter to Lyons, "after some verbal . . . amendments." [19]

Thus was the important decision reached. The solution—yielding to the British wish—seems in retrospect so simple that one can easily miss the fatefulness of this moment in history, for this solution came exceedingly hard. Chase, who in cabinet meeting advised "surrender of the rebels," qualified the advice with anti-British remarks, and noted in his diary that his consent to Seward's solution was "gall and wormwood" to him.[20] That it was also wormwood to Bates is shown by his hope that three months later the case might be different "if we do half our duty." [21]

Lincoln's paper proposing arbitration, being less conciliatory than immediate release, seems not to have been presented at this cabinet meeting. That night the President told Browning at a White House dinner that the cabinet "had agreed not to divulge what had occurred, but that there would be no war with England." [22] Seward's letter went to Lyons; the envoys were released; the incident was closed. From that point one heard little of Mason and Slidell.

Speaking to full galleries with most of the foreign envoys present,

[18] Smith, *Blair Family*, II, 194.　　　[19] Bates, *Diary*, 214–216.
[20] Diary and Letter Book of S. P. Chase (MS., Lib. of Cong.), Dec. 25, 1861.
[21] Bates, *Diary*, 215.　　　[22] Browning, *Diary*, I, 518.

Sumner reviewed the whole question in the Senate,[23] and his conciliatory speech brought a flood of congratulatory comment. Chase thought it "admirable," [24] and Lincoln's secretary asked for a copy so the President could read it.[25] The Sumner manuscripts for this period contain numerous compliments on the senator's effort.[26] In Paris it produced an "excellent effect," wrote Bigelow, and "still better in England." [27] Even the adverse comment of the *Times* in London seemed to Henry Adams a measure of the excellence of the senator's effort.[28] To the unemotional Adamses in London the relief amounted to a complete change of atmosphere. Early in 1862 Charles Francis Adams wrote of a "complete lull" in London, noting that the *Trent* affair had done much good by dispelling the notion that "we were intending to pick a quarrel." [29]

Though Lincoln's part in the episode was not publicized, it was of decisive importance. It is now possible to see the President's contribution in his restraint, his avoidance of any outward expression of truculence, his early softening of the state department's attitude toward Britian, his deference toward Seward and Sumner, his withholding of his own paper prepared for the occasion, his readiness to arbitrate, his golden silence in addressing Congress, his shrewdness in recognizing that war must be averted, and his clear perception that a point could be clinched for America's true position at the same time that full satisfaction was given to a friendly country. This is not to say that Lincoln was entirely conversant with international dealings, nor that he was finding the solution through his own efforts. His deference to others who were finding the solution and his acceptance of other men's contributions were deliberate. Where he deemed it necessary he would sometimes overrule his own cabinet; his part in

---

[23] *Cong. Globe,* 37 Cong., 2 sess., 241–245 (Jan. 9, 1862).

[24] "Went to the Capitol and heard Mr. Sumner's speech. . . . [It was] admirable. . . . Most of the foreign Ministers were present, and full galleries." Diary and Letter Book of S. P. Chase (MS., Lib. of Cong.), Jan. 9, 1862.

[25] "The President would like to read your speech on the Trent question." J. G. Nicolay to Charles Sumner (undated but headed "Sunday Morning"), Sumner MSS., 56:19.

[26] Among those who wrote with glowing praise of Sumner's speech on the *Trent* affair were C. P. Huntington, Jan. 20, 1862; H. W. Torrey, Jan. 21; J. W. Hanson, Jan. 22; Orestes A. Brownson, Jan. 30. Sumner MSS.

[27] John Bigelow to Charles Sumner, Paris, Jan. 30, 1862, *ibid.*

[28] ". . . I was . . . pleased to see that the *Times* lost its temper in criticising you. It is a significant fact . . . ." Henry Adams to Charles Sumner, London, Jan. 30, 1862, *ibid.*

[29] C. F. Adams to Edward Everett, London, Feb. 21, 1862, Everett MSS.

the making of executive decisions was not often usurped. In this light, the peaceful outcome of the cabinet meeting of December 25, 1861, over which he presided, must be regarded as a matter of executive purpose and of presidential method.

It is beyond the scope of this book to exhibit the factors that worked effectively for peace between Britain and America: essential harmony of related peoples; antislavery sentiment in Britain; sympathy between laborers in the two lands; liberal opinion in England, exemplified by Bright, rising in response to enlightened sentiment on American shores; reasonableness on the part of men in official position; and finally, the realization that peace and economic interest go hand in hand. The economic factor has sometimes been misinterpreted and the importance of cotton overstated. Essentially it was realized in Britain that war with the United States, besides being otherwise unthinkable, would be economically disastrous by breaking down trade, overthrowing the countless advantages that go with world stability, closing profitable markets, inducing reprisals in shipping, and inflicting industrial and material injuries vastly greater than the supposed issues leading to war.[30]

VII

The tone of moderation and restraint which appeared in the *Trent* affair was carried over into later phases of Anglo-American relations during the Lincoln presidency.[1] The subject of these relations is not to be adequately understood by mentioning only a part of them or by overemphasizing those elements on both sides of the ocean that were pushing their governments toward a more truculent course. In America there were those who served their own short-sighted ends by

[30] Claussen, *United States and Britain, 1861–1865*. The shutting off of American wheat has been given more emphasis by other writers than by Claussen, who shows that little attention was given to the matter in the diplomatic correspondence of the time and that the American West supplied no controlling share of the whole British wheat consumption. See also Randall, *Civil War and Reconstruction*, 653 n.

[1] Further international phases—e. g., the blockade, the fitting out of warships, the peaceable adjustment in the matter of the Laird rams, the severe resentment of the Confederacy toward Britain from late 1863 to the end of the war, the preponderant influence of Union sympathizers in Britain, the distinguished service of John Bright, the notable friendliness of Russia toward the United States, and the difficulty with France concerning Napoleon III's intervention in Mexico—are reserved for treatment in a later companion work.

misrepresenting and denouncing Britain. Within England there were groups who looked with disdain upon the United States. The point to be remembered, however, is that in neither country did these trouble-making groups set the pattern of official action or determine the direction of international dealing. It is true that class-conscious aristocrats of British society wanted the United States adventure to fail and for that reason favored the Confederacy. On the other hand liberals in England, and with them the masses of the people, favored the American union even if, with Bright, they might regret the "folly" of the tariff in contrast to the Confederacy's gesture toward free trade, and in spite of the economic dislocation and real human distress produced by the Union blockade.

Whatever may have been these varying attitudes, it was the great English nation, rather than the few, who had their way. Britain's connection with Washington was not only unbroken; it grew notably more friendly in the latter half of the war. It is very important that this fact be understood, the more so since misconceptions in this field of history are all too common. It has even been mistakenly said that Britain "intervened" for the Confederacy. Such ignorant statements have appeared in American newspapers. This is the exact opposite of the truth. It is true that there were tensions; there were disputes; on two or three occasions there came what were called crises. It is precisely in such situations that the friendship of nations is tested. Peace does not depend upon the lack of dispute or difference. It depends upon the basic common sense of statesmen and the fundamental harmony of peoples when faced with disputes and confronted with international problems.

Summarizing the British attitude throughout the war in briefest terms, the Confederacy failed in its hope of a warlike outcome over the *Trent* affair; it failed in its strenuous drive for recognition as a nation of full standing; its hopes were dashed in the matter of mediation and intervention; its objectives were unrealized as to the breaking of the blockade. Even in the matter of furnishing warships to the Confederacy the British gave no help after the year 1862. The pattern of Britain's controlling policy in this field was set not by the case of the *Alabama* and a few sister ships in which help was extended (and reparation given after the war), but in the significant cases of the *Alexandra* and the Laird rams in 1863, in which the ardent efforts of the Richmond government to obtain the further delivery of British-built ships were entirely frustrated.

The British government refused to receive Confederate diplomats, and in other respects the Confederacy was so disappointed with the action of the English authorities that there occurred in the latter part of 1863 a complete breach between Richmond and London, if one can speak of a breach between governments that never had regular relations, nor anything approaching it. In September of 1863 the Southern diplomat, Mason, withdrew from London on the instruction of his own government, and in the same year British consuls, whose status was irregular, were expelled from cities within the Confederacy by the government of Jefferson Davis. This was but the natural result of repeated negative decisions by the British ministry on those fundamental matters—mediation, recognition, and actual support in the war—on which Confederate hopes were based and on which the diplomacy of Confederate agents was pivoted. Thus it was not Washington, but Richmond, that broke with England, and that in 1863, the middle year of the war.

There is another point on which a word should be said. The people of the South, with their leaders and warriors, commanded the admiration of many English minds. That admiration has become a long-standing tradition, but it needs to be rightly viewed. Where friendliness to the South was motivated by willingness to see the United States fail as a nation and as a democratic experiment, it became only a vexatious and complicating, but not a controlling, wartime factor. This, however, leaves much to be said; for in the long run, and in its healthier aspects, British interest in the South has somehow managed to transcend or by-pass the political implications of the American controversy. If Britons admired Lee and Jackson, that did not mean that they turned against Lincoln. Governmentally, their regular relations and their unbroken amity was with the United States. In the sense of ultimate American reunion that amity has embraced both North and South. One is by no means overlooking Southerners as Americans when he emphasizes British friendship for that government which preceded and survived the American struggle.

CHAPTER XVII

EXIT CAMERON

I

SIMON CAMERON, who had maneuvered his way into the cabinet against Lincoln's clearly expressed wish, was the first to leave it. While military effort was yet in its early stages the secretary of war was under a fire of criticism. Inefficiency in war administration, failure to provide for the new volunteers (many of whom were without tents), and unreadiness to accept recruits offered by the states, might have been passed over as curable faults traceable to the unpreparedness of the nation and the habit of putting politicians into cabinet posts without training for their duties. More serious than this, however, was the saturnalia of fraud and extravagance which characterized the business dealings of the war department. The report of the investigating committee on this subject is a stinging comment on the greed of profiteers and the shocking laxness of government officials. In 1109 pages of testimony one may read the disgusting details. Rejected and worthless Austrian muskets, twenty-five thouand of them, were purchased at $6.50 each only to be stored in an arsenal. But while buying arms discarded by European nations, the government condemned a lot of Hall carbines, sold them at a nominal price, bought them back at fifteen dollars each, sold them to a private firm at $3.50, and bought them again at $22 each! In a factual statement the committee referred to a "corrupt system of brokerage," "prostitution of public confidence to purposes of individual aggrandizement," "remarkable combinations . . . to rob the treasury," treatment of an act of Congress as "almost a dead letter," "contracts . . . universally injurious to the government," articles purchased as army supplies which bore no relation to regulations—in a word favoritism, corruption, waste, colossal graft, and baneful inefficiency.[1]

Having endured Cameron till endurance was no longer possible, Lincoln let it be known to close friends that a change was contemplated, suggesting indirectly that the secretaryship of war be given back to Holt.[2] "Cameron ought to be turned out forthwith for incompetency, to say nothing of the rumors of jobbing . . . ," wrote Lyman Trumbull in the summer of '61.[3]

But how could Cameron be eased down—i. e., induced to resign without loss of face? This was not simple in the case of a man who had boldly pushed his way into the President's official family when plainly told to stay out. Lincoln did not wish actually to dismiss Cameron. Removal of the politician-secretary would have seemed too drastic. Yet Cameron was so great a liability to the administration and so serious a drawback to the public service that a new secretary was necessary. Finding that Cassius M. Clay was tired of court routine at St. Petersburg and ambitious to serve his country in a military capacity commensurate with his importance,[4] Lincoln satisfied Clay by a generalship and thus eased the jolt for Cameron, who took the diplomatic post in Russia as a graceful way of withdrawing.

There was, however, more to the story, which illustrates the difficulty of constructing historical accounts on the basis of statesmen's letters. On January 11, 1862, Lincoln wrote a curt letter to Cameron indicating that he could gratify the latter's "desire for a change of position" and informing him that he was about to nominate him as minister to Russia. The situation was not so simple as this, however, for at this point Cameron had not actually resigned; his vague verbal comment that his resignation was at Lincoln's disposal did not mean that under the circumstances of January 1862 he was actually sub-

---

[1] *House Report No. 2*, 37 Cong., 2 sess., passim. (For specific statements quoted above, see pp. 34, 40, 53, 54.)

[2] R. W. Bush to Holt, Nov. 23, 1861, cited in A. Howard Meneely, *The War Department, 1861*, 365.

[3] Trumbull to Doolittle, Aug. 31, 1861, MS., Ill. St. Hist. Lib.

[4] "I asked him [Lincoln] if it was true that Cash M Clay was to be made a Major General—he said it was—I protested very earnestly against it— . . . asking . . . that we should not be troubled with him, remarking . . . that he was now in great hopes that the rebellion [sic] would be pretty much ended before he would get here." J. F. Speed to Joseph Holt, Feb. 4, 1862, Holt MSS. For Lincoln's mention of Clay's desire for military appointment, see *Works*, VII, 80 (Jan. 11, 1862). For Clay's brief acceptance of high command, his insistence on abolition of slavery as a condition of his service, his return to Russia in 1863 to remain till 1869, and his later dissatisfaction with the Republican party, see *Dic. of Amer. Biog.*, IV, 170.

mitting an unsolicited resignation. A. K. McClure relates that Lincoln's short letter was handed to Cameron by Chase and that he (McClure), in company with T. A. Scott, assistant secretary of war, conferred that night with Cameron, who, far from accepting this solution without question, "exhibited an extraordinary degree of emotion." According to McClure, Cameron "was affected even to tears, and wept bitterly over . . . [the] personal affront from Lincoln," [5] saying that it "meant personal as well as political destruction, and was an irretrievable wrong committed . . . by the President." [6]

Because of Cameron's agitation it was arranged as an afterthought that the secretary should write a letter of resignation predated to January 11, whereupon Lincoln wrote a similarly predated letter to Cameron expressing, as he had not done originally, "affectionate esteem" and confidence in the secretary's "ability, patriotism, and fidelity to public trust," and referring to the "not less important" services the Pennsylvanian could render in his new St. Petersburg location.[7] Considering that it took a bit of forcing to get Cameron out of the cabinet, one reads the public correspondence with a realization that it tactfully concealed the true situation. When this true situation is recalled, some of the newspaper comments of the time have an odd sound. The *Herald*, for instance, informed its readers that "General Cameron" [8] had accepted the secretaryship "with great reluctance" (!), had preferred the Senate, had always been ready to retire, and now, "having accomplished so much," could "well afford to lay aside his exhausting labors." [9]

For a striking example of Cameron's manner of coöperating with his chief one may go back to the previous month. Seizing advantage of radical displeasure with Lincoln, he had taken a step which seriously embarrassed the President while it gave Cameron some weeks of publicity and ill-won glory in antislavery circles. Without consulting the President, Cameron had included in his annual report of December 1861 a long passage advocating the employment of slaves as soldiers. In language sweet to vindictive ears the secretary gave less emphasis to the merits of the Negroes than to the punishment of "rebellious traitors" who had forfeited their rights.[10] Secretarial re-

[5] A. K. McClure, *Abraham Lincoln and Men of War-Times*, 165.
[6] *Ibid.*, 164. [7] *Works*, VII, 79–82.
[8] The misleading military title was a matter of informal courtesy.
[9] New York *Herald*, Jan. 14, 1862, p. 5, c. 1. [10] McPherson, *Rebellion*, 249.

ports were customarily assembled in the President's office and transmitted through him to Congress by assimilation with his own annual
message. What to do as to slaves and Negro troops was the President's
problem. It was an important and central matter of policy, yet of his
own initiative Cameron had his report "printed, and, without being
submitted to his [Lincoln's] inspection, mailed to the postmasters of
the chief cities to be handed to the press as soon as the telegraph should
announce . . . the reading of the message . . . in Congress." [11]

When Lincoln found what had been done behind his back he
caused advance copies of the Cameron report to be recalled by telegraph, a new edition being issued which omitted the questionable
passage. Lincoln was shocked, was "greatly grieved," and considered
the episode a "severe strain" upon his trust in his colleague's
"fidelity"; [12] yet the incident did not break their friendly relations. He
continued to extend kind treatment to a secretary who did not re-
ciprocate; yet in the "suppression" of the original report there was a
touch of presidential censorship which worked to Lincoln's detriment
because the passage was not in fact withheld from the public, but
appeared simultaneously with the expurgated version, so that the
attempted suppression was pointed up and emphasized. Persons who
did not ordinarily read a secretary's report began to make compari-
sons, and a Connecticut friend of Cameron wrote that he preferred the
"Simon pure" article printed in the *Tribune* to the "bogus report"
in the *World*.[13] Bishop Simpson, a power among Methodists, wrote:
"We are tired of the dilatory policy of the President," and added: "I
approve fully of your Report before it was *amended* by the Pres^t." [14]
Publishing the report in its original form, E. L. Baker of the *Illinois
State Journal*, wrote that Cameron was "*very strong in Illinois*," [15]
while from Pottsville, Pennsylvania, came the comment that the
President's message was "tame," and that the "overwhelming majority" favored Cameron's "great document." [16] "You have touched
the national heart," wrote a Pittsburgh friend. "Your Report . . .
is universally approved and you now occupy a position a head & shoul-

[11] Nicolay and Hay, *Lincoln*, V, 125.   [12] McClure, *Men of War-Times*, 162–163.
[13] D. Wellman, Jr., to Cameron, Watertown, Conn., Dec. 10, 1861, Cameron MSS.
[14] M. Simpson to Cameron, Evanston, Ill., Dec. 9, 1861, *ibid*.
[15] E. L. Baker to Cameron, Office of the *Illinois State Journal*, Springfield, Dec. 10,
1861, *ibid*.
[16] Wm. L. Helfenstein to Cameron, Pottsville, Pa., Dec. 9, 1861, *ibid*.

ders above the President & all the Cabinet beside." [17]

Despite Lincoln's avoidance of any sharp dealing, when the secretary's resignation became known in January there were many who put Cameron in the persecuted role of a man who was sacrificed for loyally serving the antislavery cause. Adulation of Cameron and denunciation of the President became once more the theme of abolitionist critics. One man wrote: "I am astonished to learn that you have been removed from the cabinet because you advocated the use of all the means within our reach to put down this outrageous rebellion. . . . I am . . . sad . . . to see the course Lincoln is pursuing." [18] Another supposed "that the policy of the border states . . . [had] triumphed in the councils of the President, and that the emancipationists . . . [had] to go under." [19] And another: "Yr resignation, when understood is not only approved by yr friends, but excites their admiration. . . . But I must confess yr resignation gives me some fears for the future of the country." [20] Even Cameron's supporters, however, if only between the lines, betrayed their realization that charges of corruption had something to do with his departure from the cabinet. In a letter of friendly sympathy Governor Morton of Indiana remarked: "It is a leading feature in the policy of the opponents of the war to charge corruption against every man engaged in its prosecution . . . ." [21]

Two branches of the United States government, the Supreme Court and the House of Representatives, put on record a denunciation of the practices that prevailed under Cameron. In a case at law involving the activity of a lobby "agent" (to the tune of $75,000 for no other "service" than the use of influence to place a contract) Justice Field on behalf of the Court wrote:

"All contracts for supplies should be made with those, and with those only, who will execute them most faithfully, and at the least expense to the Government. Considerations as to the most efficient and economical mode of meeting the public wants should alone control . . . the action of every department of the Government. No other consideration can lawfully enter into the transaction, so far as the Government is concerned.

---

17 Sam'l A. Purviance to Cameron, "Confidential," Pittsburgh, Dec. 6, 1861, *ibid.*
18 N. P. Sawyer to Cameron, Pittsburgh, Jan. 14, 1862, *ibid.*
19 Wm. S. Garvin to Cameron, Jan. 16, 1862, *ibid.*
20 Wm. L. Helfenstein to Cameron, Willards [Hotel], Jan. 13, 1862, *ibid.*
21 O. P. Morton to Cameron, Indianapolis, Jan. 13, 1862, *ibid.*

Such is the rule of public policy; and whatever tends to introduce any other elements into the transaction, is against public policy. That agreements, like the one under consideration, have this tendency, is manifest. They tend to introduce personal solicitation, and personal influence, as elements in the procurement of contracts; and thus directly lead to inefficiency in the public service, and to unnecessary expenditures of the public funds." [22]

In the same sense the House of Representatives, after an elaborate investigation, passed the following resolution:

"*Resolved,* That Simon Cameron, late Secretary of War, by investing Alexander Cummings with the control of large sums of the public money, and authority to purchase military supplies, without restriction, without requiring . . . any guarantee for the faithful performance of his duties . . . , and by involving the Government in a vast number of contracts with persons not legitimately engaged in the business pertaining to . . . such contracts, . . . has adopted a policy highly injurious to the public service, and deserves the censure of the House.[23]

With characteristic willingness to shield a colleague and bear the blame for subordinates, President Lincoln replied at length to this resolution. He was unwilling to "leave the censure . . . to rest . . . chiefly upon Mr. Cameron." He added: "It is due to Mr. Cameron to say that, although he fully approved the proceedings, they were not moved nor suggested by himself, and that not only the President but all the other heads of departments were at least equally responsible . . . for whatever error, wrong, or fault was committed in the premises." [24]

In this communication Lincoln reviewed the war crisis and the earlier methods of dealing with it. Stressing the sharpness of the emergency and the "condition of a siege" at the capital, he showed that, with Congress not in session, it was for the President to choose whether to let the government fall into ruin or avail himself of broad powers. After summoning advisers he had decided to take a number of quick steps to promote the public defense.[25] Intrusting distinguished citizens with important duties in the forwarding of supplies and troops, he

---

[22] The Court continued "Agreements for compensation contingent upon success, suggest the use of sinister and corrupt means for the accomplishment of the end desired. The law meets the suggestion of evil, and strikes down the contract from its inception." Tool Company *vs.* Norris, 69 U. S. 45, 54-55.

[23] *Cong. Globe,* 37 Cong., 2 sess., 1888, April 30, 1862.

[24] *Works,* VII, 193-194 (May 26, 1862).   [25] See vol. I, 374-375.

had directed that Governor Morgan of New York and Alexander
Cummings be authorized by Secretary Cameron "to make all necessary arrangements for the transportation of troops and munitions
. . . in aid . . . of the army . . . until communication should
be completely reëstablished between . . . Washington and New
York." Finding government departments shot through with disloyal
personnel, he had directed that public money be used "without
security" by selected non-official individuals. Confessing that these
measures were "without authority of law," Lincoln defended them
as his own and as necessary to save the government from overthrow.

Implicit in this relationship was the honorable obligation to avoid
abuse of so unusual a trust imposed by so high an official. Nevertheless an admission that things went wrong was suggested in the last
sentence of this message, in which Lincoln took for himself equal
responsibility for "such error" or "wrong" as might have been committed. Lincoln did not say that censure by the House was unjustified,
but that it should not be aimed exclusively at Mr. Cameron. The
financial transactions themselves, as they worked out, were not defended, nor did the President attempt to give the detailed history of
these transactions. That Cummings obtained his profitable opportunity only because he was a crony of Cameron was part of this history.

The Senate also was deeply moved by the charges against Cameron,
and there was formidable opposition to his confirmation as minister
to Russia. Protracted debate on this subject in executive session ended
inconclusively in adjournment. According to the *Herald* the "objections . . . were chiefly on the ground of alleged mismanagement of
the War Department, and favoritism in the appointment of military
officers and the award of contracts . . . ." It was not expected that
confirmation would be withheld, "but the array against the nomination . . . deprive[d] the confirmation of any complimentary complexion, and amount[ed] to a censure of the conduct of the War Department." [26] In this connection it must be remembered that Cameron
had been recently a member of the Senate, that readiness to confirm
a fellow senator was traditional, and that in spite of this several leading senators of Cameron's own party voted against the appointment
(Trumbull, Grimes, Harlan, Hale, Wilkinson, and Foster). John
Sherman was reported as speaking against the confirmation, then

---

[26] New York *Herald*, Jan. 17, 1862, p. 1, c. 1.

voting for it.[27] Trumbull's opposition to the appointment was expressed in "a very bitter speech." [28]

II

For the vital post of successor to Cameron, Lincoln chose Edwin M. Stanton of Pennsylvania, thus making his first cabinet appointment of an 1860 Democrat.[1] Originating in Ohio and shifting to Pittsburgh, Stanton had developed as a prominent lawyer, while in politics he was known as an antislavery Democrat. Coming at a late hour into the Buchanan cabinet when its stiffening was signalized by cabinet reorganization, his presence in that body was interpreted as giving solidity to a wavering administration. His fright on the eve of civil war and his ill words concerning Lincoln were not generally known, nor could one foresee that he would ultimately prove a worse headache than Cameron. Emphasis at the moment was upon his intellect, competence, and efficiency; J. F. Speed wrote of order and precision instead of "that loose shackeling way of doing business in the war office." [2]

The appointment of Stanton seemed to many a strange proceeding. Welles noted that no member of the cabinet "was aware of his selection until after it was determined upon, except Mr. Seward," [3] while Bates stated that the act took him by surprise, since no hint of it had been given in cabinet meeting, nor had the President or any cabinet member mentioned it to him.[4] Lincoln's act was indeed so unexpected as to appear sudden; Stanton himself, according to his own statement, had not spoken to Lincoln "from the 4th of March, 1861, until the day he handed me my commission." [5] Though at the time the emphasis was upon the expectation that Stanton would prove an efficient contrast to Cameron, the sequel was to show that the new secretary "loved antagonism, and there was hardly a period during

---

[27] *Ibid.*, Jan. 18, 1862, p. 1, c. 4.   [28] Browning, *Diary*, I, 524.

[1] See vol. I, 270–271.

[2] J. F. Speed to Joseph Holt, Washington, Feb. 4, 1862, Holt MSS.

[3] Welles adds that after the matter had been decided it was made to appear that Cameron had had a hand in choosing his successor. Since Chase was "sensitive in matters where Seward was operating," the treasury head, according to Welles, "was called in and consulted on a predetermined question." Welles, *Diary*, I, 58–59.

[4] Bates, *Diary*, 226.

[5] Stanton to Buchanan, May 18, 1862, quoted in McClure, *Men of War-Times*, 174.

his . . . service as War Minister in which he was not . . . in positive antagonism with the President." A. K. McClure, who made this comment, added: "In his antagonisms he was, as a rule, offensively despotic, and often pressed them upon Lincoln to the very utmost point of Lincoln's forbearance . . . ." [6]

Soon after the Cameron-Stanton shift there were rumors of other cabinet changes. It was whispered that Chase would withdraw and resume his place in the Senate,[7] and there were more persistent reports that Welles would step out and be replaced by his able assistant, Gustavus Fox, or, as some of the gossip would have it, by General Banks.[8] Part of the rumor as to Welles was that he would become minister to Spain.[9] Editorializing on this subject, the *Herald* remarked that Welles's successor, "if picked up in the streets at a venture, . . . [could not] possibly be worse." [10] Commenting in general on the President's cabinet early in 1862, Ebenezer Peck of Illinois made the displaced Cameron out to be a "nether millstone," Welles "worse than a granny," Smith "busy about his salary only," and Seward "eagerly looking for the succession." [11]

III

Immediately upon assuming his unexpected office Stanton had an interview at his own request (January 20, 1862) with a new fangled congressional organization known as the committee on the conduct of the war.[1] Whatever else this visit did, it made pro-Stanton copy in the newspapers, which did not omit to report the "magnetic influence" of the new secretary, his "honesty," his "regard to public economy," and his purpose to reduce the rebellion "with all possible despatch." [2] The story of this committee, and the grief it gave to Lincoln and to competent army leaders, is one of the most vexing phases of Civil War history. The movement for such a committee began with

6 McClure, 171.   7 New York *Herald*, Jan. 15, 1862, p. 1, c. 4.

8 *Ibid.*, Feb. 2, 1862, p. 5, c. 1; April 25, 1862, p. 4, c. 5; April 26, 1862, p. 10, c. 4.

9 *Ibid.*, April 25, 1862, p. 1, c. 3.   10 April 25, 1862, p. 4, c. 5.

11 Peck to Trumbull, Chicago, Feb. 15, 1862, Trumbull MSS.

1 ". . . all the members present, and [the committee] had a conference of several hours' duration with honorable Edwin M. Stanton, Secretary of War, at his request." Journal of the Committee, Jan. 20, 1862, Report, Committee on the Conduct of the War, *Sen. Rep. No. 108*, 37 Cong., 3 sess., I, 75.

2 New York *Herald*, Jan. 23, 1862, p. 8, c. 2.

Roscoe Conkling's resolution of December 2, 1861, calling for the investigation of the disasters at Bull Run and Ball's Bluff. The latter affair was a small engagement (October 21, 1861) on the Potomac not far above Washington, in which Union forces had been sharply defeated and cut to pieces. Bad though it was, the affair was exaggerated, the more so because of the death of Colonel (Senator) Edward D. Baker, a man of the radical type, whose error on the battlefield was largely responsible for the unfortunate outcome, but whose sacrifice called for a living scapegoat.

This Baker was Lincoln's close friend, indeed the namesake of one of his sons. Born in London, he had won political and legal success in Illinois, fought against Mexico, shifted to the Far West, and risen to the position of senator from Oregon. On the outbreak of the war he had defended the Union cause with fiery oratory in New York, and had then spectacularly entered the military service, in command of the "California regiment" which he had raised. Performing the "anomalous duty of commanding his regiment and representing Oregon in the Senate," [3] Baker had appeared in uniform on the floor of the Senate on August first and had theatrically denounced a pro-Confederate speech by Breckinridge of Kentucky. According to Blaine, in the history of the Senate "no more thrilling speech was ever delivered." [4]

Stirred by the death of a popular hero (who had rashly exposed himself and his brigade), and maddened by the inactivity of McClellan's main army, the "Jacobins" (or radicals) of Congress in December 1861 were in a mood to get action and punish those guilty of mistakes. Debate and proposals arising from Conkling's resolution led to the creation of a standing "joint committee on the conduct of the war," which consisted of three senators (B. F. Wade of Ohio, Zachariah Chandler of Michigan, and Andrew Johnson of Tennessee) and four representatives (D. W. Gooch of Massachusetts, George W. Julian of Indiana, John Covode of Pennsylvania, and Moses F. Odell of New York). Wade and Chandler, Republicans who vindictively hated the South and viewed the war as an opportunity for party gain, were its leading spirits. By the bold ruthlessness of its leaders, by the partisan vote which created it, and by the star-chamber quality of its proceedings, the character of the committee can be gauged. In the name of

---

[3] Blaine, *Twenty Years of Congress*, I, 344.　　　　[4] *Ibid.*, 345.

promoting military efficiency, injecting energy into the service, exposing mistakes, and "obtaining information" for the President, this impressively busy organization conducted elaborate inquisitions, took generals and war officials away from their proper duties, stirred the country with misplaced publicity, ruined the reputations of able generals while building up their own military pets, worried Lincoln, bandied unproved charges of treason, and created dissension and distrust within the lines. Not a member had had military experience,[5] yet the committee assumed a finality of military judgment commensurate with their marked intolerance toward men of West Point.

The chief targets of the committee were McClellan (he above all), Charles P. Stone, and Fitz-John Porter; their pets were Frémont, Burnside, Pope, and McDowell. By a preposterous inquisition which never got round to substantiation of specific charges, Charles P. Stone was blamed for Ball's Bluff, pilloried before popular opinion, arrested, imprisoned without trial (for 189 days in flagrant violation of law as to the discipline of officers), and subjected to such out-of-court persecution and defamation that he resigned the army in whose service his usefulness had been broken, and took a commission under the Khedive of Egypt.

When army officers spoke a language which the committee did not like, Wade and Chandler would hold back senate confirmation of an advanced commission.[6] With political motives constantly in view, they not only persecuted Democratic generals, but "became the spearhead of the radical drive against the [Lincoln] administration."[7] Though the full activity of this aggressive group is hard to visualize, the persistent energy of their "investigations" must be constantly remembered in any study of the military campaigns of the Army of the Potomac.[8]

---

[5] This was true of the committee as originally constituted. W. W. Pierson, in *Amer. Hist. Rev.*, XXIII, 558.

[6] T. Harry Williams, *Lincoln and the Radicals*, 74, citing: New York *Tribune*, Dec. 24, 1862; *ibid.*, Jan. 26, 1863; Col. W. B. Hazen to John Sherman, Dec. 10, 1862 (John Sherman MSS.); Detroit *Free Press*, April 7, 1863.

[7] T. Harry Williams, *Lincoln and the Radicals*, 64.

[8] Though not ignoring other sectors, they concentrated chiefly upon the Army of the Potomac, finding in that army "all that is necessary" for their investigation. Report, Com. on Conduct of the War, *Sen. Rep. No. 108*, 37 Cong., 3 sess., I, 4. The committee is treated by W. W. Pierson in *Amer. Hist. Rev.*, XXIII, 550–576; its work is more elaborately told by T. Harry Williams in the account above cited; for a brief summary, see J. G. Randall, *Civil War and Reconstruction*, 367–370.

CHAPTER XVIII

BEHIND McCLELLAN'S LINES

I

AFTER slight activity in 1861, the year 1862 was to witness for the Union army "stupendous . . . operations . . . on a theatre . . . almost the size of a continent." [1] Democracy's makeshift, the army was an aggregation of units indifferently commanded, inadequately equipped, and shot through with unmilitary procedures, distrust, disrespect for officers, and desertion. It was a slowly evolving volunteer army to which the drafts of 1862 (minor affairs) made slight contribution. Titles in the volunteer service were much higher for comparable training and experience than in the regular army, against which there seemed to be a kind of prejudice among men in authority. Those who had left the regular army, gone into civilian pursuits, and entered the volunteer service for the emergency, fared much better as to promotion and rank than those who continued their regular-army status. In the absence of a general staff the central control of the army was amorphous, changeable, and difficult to define.

Before large operations opened, or even the armies began to move, in the East, shining advances had been made in the West. General command in this area centered at St. Louis under Frémont till his removal in November 1861, then under Halleck. It was not the headquarters men, however, but commanders in the field, who achieved results. These results, in which gunboat flotillas coöperated with land forces, included the early occupation of river positions on the Ohio and upper Mississippi, the signal victory of Grant and Foote in the

---

[1] *Annual Cyclopaedia*, 1862, 25. Bull Run, of course, offers an outstanding exception to the statement as to slight activity in 1861.

capture of Forts Henry and Donelson on the Tennessee and Cumberland Rivers, Confederate retreat following the heaviest battle of the whole war in the West at Pittsburg Landing (Shiloh), the capture of Island Number Ten and New Madrid, and seizure of New Orleans in May 1862. These were major events, giving great prominence to such generals as Halleck (though this was hardly deserved), Pope, "Unconditional Surrender" Grant, and Sherman, and to such naval leaders as Foote, Farragut, and Porter. After Donelson had capitulated (February 16, 1862), soon after the surrender of Fort Henry (February 6), the *Times* remarked that the "monster" was in the "death struggle," [2] while Edward Bates considered that "the heart of the rebellion" had been broken.[3]

To give the story of these western military matters, assigning credit in exactly the right degree to leaders and participants—e. g., to say just how much was the contribution of Halleck, Frémont, Grant, Foote, Charles F. Smith, et cetera—is as impossible here as to discuss Confederate blame for the surrender of Donelson. Smith himself, with his "superb physique" [4] and perfect soldierly bearing whether on review or in battle, would deserve considerable attention. Nor can space be given to the obscure claims presented for Anna E. Carroll of Maryland. This able and energetic woman, overlooked and almost completely forgotten, has been credited in a remarkable recent biography with service of great significance. It is claimed (with an impressive show of documents) that she knew in advance of secession plots, worked on Governor Hicks and other leaders to save Maryland, and helped to prevent the secession of that crucially important state. Finding fatal flaws in the military plans of Halleck and Frémont, and envisaging the importance of the western rivers, she is said to have done much to invent and develop that land-and-water strategy which yielded such shining results in Union success, and which might well have yielded much larger results if her full program had been followed. For advising Lincoln, and preparing a paper on the war powers which helped the President's case when he was threatened with congressional assault upon his authority, she has even been called (perhaps with exaggeration) "the great unrecognized member of Lincoln's cabinet." It has been argued that she saw through the incompetence

---

2 New York *Times*, Feb. 17, 1862, p. 4, c. 4.   3 Bates, *Diary*, 248.
4 *Battles and Leaders of the Civil War*, I, 405 (portrait, 411).

of some of the highest generals, and that that may be the reason why the facts concerning her record seem for years to have been suppressed.[5]

To these Union advances in the West the navy was able, in eastern coastal operations, to add the famous ironclad duel in Hampton Roads [6] and the capture of such Atlantic positions as Norfolk, Virginia, Port Royal (approach to Beaufort, S. C.), and Fort Pulaski (approach to Savannah, Georgia). The city of Savannah, however, as well as Mobile, Charleston, and Wilmington, remained in possession of their Southern defenders. Coincident with the inland river campaigns was the amphibious operation at Roanoke Island on the North Carolina coast (February-March, 1862). Under the joint command of General Burnside and Admiral Goldsborough this campaign resulted in the capture of Confederate positions on the Island and at Newbern, a bitter setback as viewed from Richmond. These naval developments had the sharper effect in the South because until the *Monitor* swung into action Southerners had been led to expect great things of their naval forces, especially when the *Virginia,* in sending Union warships to the bottom, had produced a first class scare in Washington. Even the calmness of Lincoln was broken at this time. "The President . . . was so excited," noted Gideon Welles, "that he could not deliberate or be satisfied with the opinions of nonprofessional men, but ordered his carriage and drove to the navy yard to . . . consult with Admiral Dahlgren and other naval officers, who might be there." [7] The "most frightened" of all on that "gloomy day," [8] however, according to Welles, was Stanton. "He was . . . almost frantic, and . . . I saw well the estimation in which he held me with my unmoved and unexcited manner and conversation." [9] With sage prophecy Welles pointed out that the *Merrimack* "could not come to Washington and go to New York at the same time," and he had "no apprehension of her visiting either." [10] Despite Stanton's "sneering inquiry" concern-

[5] Marjorie Barstow Greenbie, *My Dear Lady: The Story of Anna Ella Carroll, the "Great Unrecognized Member of Lincoln's Cabinet."* Appended to Mrs. Greenbie's biography are reprints of slightly known documents of the United States government in which after the war her services were belatedly revealed.

[6] In which the *Monitor* met the Confederate ironclad *Virginia* (formerly the *Merrimack*), checking the destructive career of that much feared vessel, and giving infinite relief to Washington. The date was March 9, 1862.

[7] Welles, *Diary,* I, 62.

[8] March 9, 1862, before news had been received of the retirement of the *Virginia* after its duel with the *Monitor*.

[9] Welles, *Diary,* I, 62.   [10] *Ibid.,* I, 63.

ing the *Monitor*,[11] authorities at Washington and the people generally were mightily relieved when the ironclad argument was settled in Lincoln's favor.

II

For certain writers the military career of George B. McClellan has become a fixed stereotype. It is assumed that if one is pro-Lincoln, he must be anti-McClellan, though the most bitter of McClellan's foes were also opponents of Lincoln. According to his detractors McClellan remained for many months uselessly inactive with a magnificent army, suffered delusions and infatuation as to enemy superiority, snubbed the President, treated the congressional war committee with contempt, evaded questions as to his intentions, exhausted Lincoln's patience, made erroneous plans, missed golden opportunities, demanded needless reënforcements, was a victim (or accomplice) of his secret service, clamored loud and long when troops were denied him, blamed the government with the intention to destroy his army, allowed himself to be surprised by enemy maneuvers, permitted subordinates to endure heavy fighting without sending them reënforcements, instructed the President concerning political duties, and in the Seven Days failed to take Richmond when all he had to do was to brush aside Confederate defense under Johnston, then under Lee and Jackson! It was even charged that he was a colossal traitor, that he did not mean to whip the enemy, and that he planned (some say he "considered") a military *coup d'état* by which Congress would be ousted, Lincoln removed, and himself made dictator. Perhaps the best indication that this traitor charge is fantastically false is the admission by Nicolay and Hay that it is "totally unjust." [1] One must remember that Hay's purpose to tear down McClellan was self-confessed. In a letter to Nicolay he said: ". . . we ought to write . . . like two everlasting angels—who . . . tell the truth about everything and don't care a twang of their harps about one side or the other"; then he showed how he meant this only as a kind of pose when he added in the same letter, speaking of McClellan: "It is of the utmost moment that we should *seem* fair to him, while we are destroying him." [2]

---

[11] *Ibid.*   [1] Nicolay and Hay, *Lincoln*, V, 169.
[2] Hay's italics. Quoted in Tyler Dennett, *John Hay: From Poetry to Politics*, 139.

In attempting a fair appraisal of McClellan the following points should be noted: (1) Competent military writers speak favorably of his leadership. He is most bitterly assailed, not by those who have gone afresh into the elaborate sources to restudy his campaigns, but by those who repeat or perpetuate a party bias. (2) Even critics of McClellan give him credit for whipping an inefficient army into military shape. (3) McClellan's hold on the esteem and affection of his men was unmistakable; perhaps no tradition has been stronger among surviving veterans than approval of McClellan. (4) No one can measure the effect of non-coöperation in Washington in such matters as withholding McDowell's corps and Blenker's division, but the fact of such non-coöperation is a matter of record. (5) McClellan operated against the Confederacy at its military peak. (6) Only an amateur could suppose that the head of a reorganized and untried army was unwise in demanding full preparation and a heavy force when taking the offensive against Richmond. (7) The worst that Lee accomplished against him was to administer a momentary setback at Gaines's Mill; never did the Union army under McClellan suffer a major defeat.

(8) McClellan was going strong when recalled from the Peninsula; his campaign was in mid-progress; it had not spent itself. To picture McClellan as defeated in July 1862 was a misrepresentation due less to conditions at the front than to unmilitary factors behind his lines. (9) At an hour of agonizing peril McClellan saved Washington and the Union cause in the checking of Lee's invasion at Antietam; in its effect on both international and domestic policy this achievement was of untold importance. (10) It was when the Army of the Potomac was turned over to McClellan's successors that the Union cause suffered its worst military disasters. (11) Nothing worth while in the East was done on the Northern side in 1862 except under McClellan; yet 1862 was the turning point favorably for the Union in the matter of foreign intervention, a factor always closely linked with military events. Had McClellan collapsed at Antietam as Pope had done at Second Bull Run, it is hard to see how the Lincoln government and the Union cause could possibly have survived, to say nothing of launching an ambitious emancipation policy, which occurred directly after Antietam.

(12) Comparison of McClellan and Grant to the former's discredit is misleading. Had Grant been the target of furious partisan intrigue

that McClellan was, it is doubtful how far he could have gone. If one must compare generals it should be noted that, despite terrific butchery as at Cold Harbor, Grant's progress in 1864 was no more successful in a comparable period than McClellan's in 1862. If McClellan failed to "take Richmond" in '62, so did Grant in '64. Even with vastly better support and a better army, Grant's slowness and the seemingly fruitless butchery of his troops in 1864 was a bitter thing, so that August of that presidential year was an exceedingly dark period for the Lincoln administration. Had the main army of the East been *withdrawn from its position against the earnest protest of its commander* in midsummer of 1864 as McClellan's was for no better cause in midsummer of 1862, Grant would have gone down in history as a failure. McClellan in '62 had no Sherman or Sheridan in the East, but Lee did have Jackson. Finally, when at long last Grant succeeded in 1865, the Confederacy was a much weaker affair than in 1862. These things are by no means said as a disparagement of Grant, but any comparison of Grant and McClellan requires that one consider the inequality in conditions behind their lines and in the enemy strength that faced them. It requires one to remember that McClellan's slowness in getting results was certainly no greater than Grant's. Had McClellan at Antietam been merely another Pope, Grant might never have had his opportunity.

It was McClellan's destiny to take command of a demoralized and formless army, work it into shape, direct the Union effort as general-in-chief for a period, lead a difficult operation against the South's finest commanders, see his plan wrecked not by enemy action but by interference at home, suffer displacement at the height of a great campaign, step down not because of defeat but because of hostile intrigue, step back when disaster befell his first successor, direct a desperate yet successful defense when Lee struck north via Maryland, prepare another advance (his second offensive and third major campaign in a year), and, at the moment of forward movement, fall a victim to a relentless political pressure which Lincoln could not resist. A restudy of the manner in which the harassed general comported himself under these intolerable circumstances will give little evidence of self-promoting acumen nor ability to play "the game," but will assuredly reopen the case as to the condemnation of McClellan.

Assuming command at Washington (July 27, 1861) after the disaster of Bull Run, McClellan found what Stanton called a condition of "irretrievable misfortune . . . national disgrace . . . ruin . . . and national bankruptcy as the result of Lincoln's 'running the machine' for five months." [3] Approaches to Washington were virtually undefended, and, to quote the contemptuous Stanton again, it seemed "inevitable" that Washington would be captured and that Jeff Davis would turn out "the whole [Lincoln] concern." [4] What McClellan found "could not properly be called an army," [5] but a defeated, undisciplined, largely unarmed, ill supplied, demoralized, and even mutinous [6] mass. In succeeding months he instituted strict discipline (despite the "deficiency of instructed officers" and the utter lack of officers familiar with even the sight of a large army), reorganized and rearranged the troops, built fortifications, guarded the fordable Potomac, organized a staff,[7] constructed military telegraph lines, and, in sum, transformed the Army of the Potomac into a trained fighting machine ready to face a powerful foe. Passing "long days in the saddle and . . . nights in the office," [8] he by no means wasted his time, as critics have asserted. He knew thoroughly the Washington area [9] and visited every camp; [10] in another general such a knowledge of his army would have been counted a virtue. Having started with what was "not worthy to be called an army," he considered that it "would have been madness to renew the attempt until a complete change was made." [11]

In personality and the power to command respect McClellan was not wanting. After a three-hours conference with him H. W. Bellows wrote of a "well-knit, perfectly balanced form" that bent and swayed "as a panther," of an "eye, small but calm, direct and powerful," of "complexion deepened by exposure," of a man whose talk was "to the point," who was "not afraid of responsibility," and about whom there was "an indescribable *air of success*" and "something of the 'man of destiny.' " " '*How to do it*' [wrote Bellows] is stamped on his whole

---

[3] Stanton to Buchanan, Washington, July 26, 1861, quoted in *McClellan's Own Story*, 67 n.

[4] *Ibid*. Stanton added: ". . . what can he [McClellan] accomplish? Will not Scott's jealousy, cabinet intrigues, and Republican interference thwart him at every step?"

[5] *Ibid*., 68. [6] For mutiny, see *ibid*., 86.

[7] Col. R. B. Marcy was at its head (*ibid*., 112). In his life of Lee (II, 237) Douglas Freeman pays high tribute to the "excellence" of McClellan's staff.

[8] *McClellan's Own Story*, 69. [9] *Ibid*., 141. [10] *Ibid*. [11] *Ibid*., 71–72.

person." [12] To some, however, he seemed an egotist, and the diary of John Hay contains an amazing statement by which it appears that he went so far as to snub the President and secretary of state. According to this account Lincoln called at McClellan's house with Seward and Hay; finding the general not at home they all waited; McClellan came in and went upstairs without greeting his guests; when a servant "once more" reported their presence there came the cool answer that the general had gone to bed! The President, wrote Hay, seemed not to have noticed "this unparalleled insolence of epaulettes" and remarked that "it was better at this time not to be making points of etiquette & personal dignity." [13] To explain such incredible behavior in a manner favorable to McClellan seems impossible if the incident was fully and correctly reported by Hay. Though McClellan's home letters reveal an overwhelming strain of work in this period,[14] one balks at attempting an explanation and ends by wondering what refreshments were served "at the wedding of Col. Wheaton at General Buell's" which McClellan attended that night.[15] It would be helpful if one had a fuller record, or at least a confirmation, of the incident, which Hay himself referred to as the "first indication" he had "yet seen" [16] of this sort of thing. Only two nights before, Hay recorded a presidential visit to McClellan's house in which the "Tycoon [Lincoln] and the General were both very jolly." [17]

In general, McClellan's bearing toward Lincoln, while not comparable in deference to that of Lee toward Davis, was proper and respectful; nevertheless he did not relish conferences with the President, nor put a high value upon his ability. On one occasion he wrote to his wife of being "interrupted" by Lincoln and Seward; [18] at another time he mentioned a call by this pair before breakfast; [19] apropos of the *Trent* affair he deplored the weakness and unfitness of those who controlled the destinies of the nation; [20] a few days later he thought that the President was honest and meant well; [21] yet again, when "thoroughly tired out" and under heavy pressure and blame

12 H. W. Bellows to his wife, Willard's Hotel, Sep. 12, 1861, Bellows MSS.

13 Diary of John Hay, Nov. 13, 1861, in Tyler Dennett, *Lincoln . . . in the Diaries . . . of John Hay*, 34–35.

14 At 1:30 a. m., November 2, McClellan wrote: "I have been at work . . . since I arose yesterday morning—nearly eighteen hours." *McClellan's Own Story*, 173.

15 Dennett, *Lincoln . . . in the Diaries . . . of John Hay*, 34.

16 *Ibid.*, 35.   17 *Ibid.*, 34.   18 *McClellan's Own Story*, 170.

19 *Ibid.*, 174.   20 *Ibid.*, 175.   21 *Ibid.*, 176.

at a time when he was preparing a "very important" letter to Cameron, he confessed avoiding his home and concealing himself "at Stanton's to dodge all enemies in shape of 'browsing' Presidents, etc." [22] (It should be noted that McClellan was consulting Stanton at a time of the latter's scornful hostility to the Lincoln administration.)

Back in July 1861 McClellan had written:

I find myself in a new and strange position here—Presdt., Cabinet, Genl. Scott and all deferring to me—by some strange . . . magic I seem to have become *the* power of the land. I almost think that were I to win some small success now I could become Dictator or anything else that might please me—but nothing of that kind would please me,—*therefore* I *wont* be dictator. Admirable self denial! . . .

. . . .

. . . All tell me that I am held responsible for the fate of the nation, and that all its resources shall be placed at my disposal. It is an immense task that I have on my hands, but I believe I can accomplish it. . . . Oh! how sincerely I pray to God that I may be endowed with the wisdom and courage necessary to accomplish the work. Who would have thought, when we were married, that I should so soon be called upon to save my country? [23]

Such statements as these have been used by anti-McClellan writers to confirm the impression of arrogance and egotism. McClellan wrote these words, however, in confidential letters to his wife. They were a kind of unstudied release, not to be taken too seriously. They were written just after the new commander had assumed his duties at Washington in the wake of Bull Run. What the general wrote to Mrs. McClellan did no harm at the time. The letters are racy and quotable and have been used against him, but this resulted from their being printed after the war in *McClellan's Own Story*. At the age of thirty-six McClellan was at the head of the Union armies; it was not unnatural for a young man so placed to write to his wife of the immense task resting upon him. To be confident of his own ability was a lesser fault, if it was a fault, than to be uncertain and insecure in a time of crisis. McClellan had a monumental task to perform. Unlike certain other generals, his was not the confidence of rashness.

[22] *Ibid.*   [23] Myers, *McClellan*, 212–214.

III

Lincoln's comment that one bad general was better than two good ones was a canny aphorism rather than an effective guiding principle. Certainly in 1862 it could be said that neither in the field nor at the capital was there any coördinating and directing mind. In the period while McClellan was still general in chief the attorney general advised Lincoln to "act out the powers of his place, to command the commanders," and become "in fact, what he is in law, the *Chief Commander*." Bates thought this idea entirely feasible, since the President's "aids" could keep "his military . . . books and papers" and do his bidding. If he (Bates) were President he would know what to do with officers who were restive under a superior. As for Lincoln, he thought that a change for the better would occur "if he will only trust his own good judgment more, and defer less, to . . . subordinates." [1]

Whether the advice of "General Bates" was to be taken or not, the turn of the year found the North impatient for action. Summer, autumn, and early winter had passed and McClellan had not moved. End the war in a hurry, or else! This seemed to be the thought of loyal citizens generally as they tired of military parades, noted the mounting expense, watched the enemy grow, heard rumors of a revolution in the Northwest, and witnessed a constant slipping in the administration's hold upon popular confidence. As one of Trumbull's correspondents expressed it: "The people say if we can whip them let it be done at once if we cannot we want to know it now and save ourselves from bankruptcy if we cannot the nation from disunion." [2]

This unrest was evident in the applause given to Greeley on January 3, 1862, when in Washington he declared that national misfortune had been due to reluctance to meet the antagonist.[3] As the elected leader in a democracy the President naturally did not escape the effect of this widespread impatience and disapproval.

A kind of crisis in military affairs (one of many) came in December and January, 1861–62, when McClellan lay ill of typhoid fever for about three weeks. O. H. Browning records that at this time he had a

---

[1] Bates, *Diary*, 223–224.   [2] P. P. Enos to Trumbull, Jan. 7, 1862, Trumbull MSS.
[3] New York *Herald*, Jan. 4, 1862, p. 3, c. 3.

long talk with the President about the war. "He told me [wrote Browning] he was thinking of taking the field himself, and suggested several plans of operation." [4] McClellan's enemies took advantage of the situation, represented that army matters were at a standstill, and intrigued for his downfall. McClellan himself maintained that his intellect was not dulled, that his strong constitution enabled him to continue to transact business daily, and that each of "the chiefs of the staff departments" knew the condition of affairs and could deal, through him, with the President and secretary of war, so that no change in the machinery of army control was needed.[5] Nevertheless there began at this point a series of steps that tended progressively to create those elements of political interference which led at length to McClellan's ruin. Thinking that the sick general ought not to be "disturbed with business," [6] the President, with none of McClellan's confidence, took up the military part of his task with grim intensity. He gave close attention to western operations, advised Halleck to attack Columbus from up-river, concerned himself with affairs in eastern Tennessee where he noted that "our friends" were "being hanged and driven to despair," admonished Buell that "Delay is ruining us," and instructed that general to "name as early a day as you safely can" for a southward thrust.[7] It was at about this time that he took Halleck's *Science of War* out of the Library of Congress, and his secretaries relate that he "read a large number of strategical works," held long military conferences, and "pored over the reports from . . . the field of war." [8] On the tenth of January the President conferred with General Montgomery C. Meigs in the general's office. In "great distress," according to Meigs's account, the President said: "General, what shall I do? The people are impatient; Chase has no money . . . ; the General of the Army has typhoid fever. The bottom is out of the tub. What shall I do?" Meigs suggested a council of military chiefs. Accounts differ at this point. Meigs stated that a council of several generals and cabinet officials met on January 12, and that the President adjourned it till next day so that McClellan could attend.[9] McClellan stated that the conclave was called without his knowledge, that he mustered enough strength to be driven to the

---

4 Browning, *Diary*, I, 523 (Jan. 12, 1862).   5 *McClellan's Own Story*, 155–156.
6 *Works*, VII, 70 (Jan. 1, 1862).   7 *Ibid.*, VII, 71–74.
8 Nicolay and Hay, *Lincoln*, V, 155.
9 Montgomery C. Meigs, in *Amer. Hist. Rev.*, XXVI, 292.

White House, and that his unexpected appearance had "the effect of a shell in a powder-magazine." [10] Next day another conference was held, with McClellan present.[11] It was a strained and difficult meeting, at which Chase, according to McClellan's account, showed great anger because the "original and real purpose" was " 'to dispose of the military goods and chattels' of the sick man," and Chase could not bear the "sudden frustration of his schemes." [12] The meeting proceeded with a good deal of desultory whispering; then Chase, with "uncalled-for irritation" of manner, challenged McClellan to present his military program in detail. McClellan declined to reveal his plans in answer to Chase; when the same request came from the President, the general declined to submit his plans to that assembly, some of whom were "incapable of keeping a secret," unless the President would give the order in writing and assume the responsibility. On this note the council was declared adjourned by the President.[13] In the sullenness of McClellan's behavior one can see not only the caution of a field marshal who did not wish his intentions to become the property of everybody including the enemy, but also the resentment of a man who felt that the whole meeting was intended as a plot to destroy him.

In his impatience to get action Lincoln now took a step which almost suggested that he considered himself a general in chief or head of staff. On January 27, 1862, he issued "President's General War Order No. 1," which suggested that there were more to follow, in which he ordered a general forward movement of the land and naval forces to be launched on February 22, with details as to particular armies that were to move on that day. Secretaries, subordinates, the general in chief, and all other commanders were to be held severally to "strict and full responsibilities" for the "prompt execution of this order." [14]

---

10 *McClellan's Own Story*, 156.

11 Those present were the President, Generals McClellan, McDowell, Franklin, and Meigs, and Secretaries Seward, Chase, and Blair. Cameron, secretary of war, seems not to have been present.

12 *McClellan's Own Story*, 157. McClellan thought that Chase wished to put his friend McDowell into the chief military command.

13 It was not that McClellan refused to reveal his plans to the President, nor other chosen officials; he strongly distrusted the existing meeting, suspected insincere motives, and did not want his coming movements "spread over Washington." *Ibid.*, 158.

14 *Works*, VII, 89–90. The order was peculiarly the President's own; it was not prepared in the war department and merely signed by the President. It is stated by Nicolay and Hay (*Lincoln*, V, 160) that the President wrote the order "without con-

Two things may be said of this presidential paper: (1) It was no mere advice or admonition; it was a peremptory order from the constitutional commander in chief of the army and navy. If it was not an order to be obeyed by all, high and low, its title was a misnomer and its wording a misfit. (2) In terms of actual fact the order got nowhere; nothing happened that bore any resemblance to fulfillment of the President's command.

As a sort of expansion of his "President's General War Order No. 1" Lincoln issued four days later his "President's Special War Order No. 1" directing that on or before February 22 an expedition should move out for the seizure of a railroad point "southwestward of . . . Manassas Junction." [15] The nation's chief was getting down to particulars. One cannot say that military commands in the American army have never been debated; at any rate McClellan was given "permission" [16] to debate this one, and it was never carried out. The President's order got no farther than a proposal. Execution was not required, yet the order was never formally revoked.[17]

In the giving of these orders it was as if Lincoln, though ineffectively, were performing as "Chief Commander" in the manner of Bates's suggestion. The more significant fact was that he was under pressure from all sides, and particularly under political and popular pressure, to send the troops forward. In the sense of military commands his orders were not taken seriously, nor has American army practice proceeded on the theory that the President functions as supreme field marshal. The fundamental meaning of the constitutional provision making the President "Commander in Chief of the Army and Navy" is to be found in the Anglo-Saxon concept that the military power shall be subject to the civil. It is for this reason that the highest civil official is given the power to determine, broadly, the national purpose and occasion for which the troops are used. That he should actually command an army or direct a fleet is not contemplated. Lincoln's giving of these war orders must be considered exceptional,

---

sultation with any one, and read it to the Cabinet, not for their sanction, but for their information."

15 *Works*, VII, 91.

16 "I asked his excellency whether . . . I could be permitted to submit . . . my objections to his plan and my reasons for preferring my own. Permission was accorded . . . ." *McClellan's Own Story*, 228–229.

17 *Ibid.* 237.

rather than in line with established procedure. Nicolay and Hay state that they were issued when the President was "at the end of his patience." [18]

It is in this sense—i. e., in terms of troubled emergency, perplexing anxiety, and exceptional proposals—that one must read the above-noted remark of Lincoln to Browning as to the possibility of taking the field himself. To do that was not his function, nor is there reason to suppose, as some have superficially done, that such taking of the field would have promoted a better central war direction or strategic success, though it would have thrown the President more fully into the very midst of military controversy than he already was. To those who realize what the presidency involves, with all its civil responsibilities and its challenge of national leadership, the plan of the President becoming a great political general in actual command of the main army will be dismissed as beyond serious consideration. As for Lincoln, he was at his military best when he deferred to and supported able commanders, whom it was his duty to appoint, not when he overruled or displaced them.

Mention should be made of one other occasion on which Lincoln seemingly assumed the function of actual military-naval command. Early in May of 1862, though business was pressing in Washington, Lincoln made a somewhat curious visit to Fort Monroe, taking Secretary of the Treasury Chase and Secretary of War Stanton with him, and there is evidence that on this occasion he not only conferred with naval and military commanders but also took a hand in the actual direction of operations. Chase referred to "a brilliant week's campaign of the Prest." as if the President had been in command, and attributed the Union capture of Norfolk to Lincoln's direction of the movements involved.[19] A Massachusetts gentleman, James D. Green of Cambridge, left an account of this episode on the basis of information which Senator Sumner gave him: "The President [wrote Mr. Green], with his Secretaries, immediately put himself at the head of the troops then under the command of Gen. Macl, & at once proceeded to the capture of Norfolk, which was in no condition to defend itself, & of no importance in a military point of view; but, on the contrary, being surrendered, its garrison forthwith marched up to aid in the defence of Richmond. The President next dispatched three Gun Boats up the James River, ..."

Historians of this period will recognize at once that Chase and Stanton were the most violently anti-McClellan of the cabinet members, and Mr. Green saw in this episode an effort on the part of the President, by the sending of gunboats up the James, to "anticipate McClellan in the capture of Richmond." He quotes Sumner as saying that Lincoln and his cabinet, just before this, had unanimously decided to remove McClellan from the command of the army (which Mr. Green considered "madness"), but that on receiving news of the evacuation of Yorktown they decided to "let the matter stand for the present." As for the astounding suggestion of removing McClellan just as he had come in front of the enemy, the thought occurred to this Cambridge gentleman, though "it seemed too atrocious to be admitted," that opposition to McClellan was motivated by "a *political object*—the interest of a *political party*"; McClellan was to be sacrificed, and perhaps also his army, because "the politicians in control of the Government had an ulterior object in view, more important in their estimation than the restoration of the Union, viz. that, let what would come, *the war should not cease till slavery was abolished."*

Though Mr. Green in his perplexity (after talking with Sumner) questioned this astonishing theory, he considered it confirmed when he soon heard of Lincoln going with Chase and Stanton to Fort Monroe where the President took charge of operations, as he was led to believe, in the anti-McClellan sense.[20] This whole affair of Lincoln's presence at the front at the time of the capture of Norfolk is a bit hard to unravel in all its aspects, but confirming evidence does sustain the impression of the President serving as actual commander, expressing strong disapproval of what was being done under General Wool's

---

[20] James D. Green to Nahum Capen, Cambridge, Mass., Aug. 10, 1871, MS. copy in possession of Professor Frederick Green, Urbana, Ill. This letter, available through the kindness of Professor Green, is a remarkable document (see copy in Mass. Hist. Soc.). The substance of the letter, which loses somewhat of its force by not being strictly contemporary, is Mr. Green's recollection of an interview with Sumner, May 6, 1862, and his subsequent interpretation of events, especially in connection with the Lincoln-Chase-Stanton visit to Fort Monroe and the politically minded interference by the Washington government in the whole Peninsular campaign. Men in Washington, thought Green, did not want McClellan to capture Richmond, thereby becoming a popular idol and the next President.

direction, questioning subordinate officers, vehemently throwing his tall hat on the floor, and dictating military orders.[21]

IV

To give in detail all, or a major part, of the cross purpose behind the lines in the military planning for 1862 is quite impossible. There was basic difference as to the main strategic pattern and as to the fundamental organization and command of the army. McClellan had his plan, but Lincoln disapproved of it.[1] McClellan would move the army down the Chesapeake, up the Rappahannock to Urbanna, Virginia, thence across land to a railroad terminus (West Point) below Richmond on the York River; from there he would move to assault the Confederate capital. This may be designated as McClellan's "Urbanna plan." In contrast to this roundabout approach by water, Lincoln favored a direct land movement.

At this time the Union force was across the Potomac from Washington, at Alexandria; the Confederate force, under Joseph E. Johnston, was near by at Manassas. Lee, restless for action, was pinned down to staff duty in Richmond. As a military leader he had yet to be discovered. With logical modification McClellan's Urbanna plan developed into his Peninsular Campaign. This involved water transportation down the Potomac and Chesapeake to the Peninsula between the York and James Rivers, allowing from that point what McClellan considered a feasible and comparatively short advance against Richmond by the line of the James.

While McClellan pursued these plans in close consultation with Lincoln, there had developed a bitterly hostile and relentless intrigue behind the general's back. Perpetrators of this intrigue set traps to influence Lincoln with whom they sought private interviews, circulated falsehoods against McClellan, used the war committee to

---

[21] *Battles and Leaders of the Civil War*, II, 151–152.

[1] On June 18, 1862, O. H. Browning recorded a conversation with Lincoln on matters of strategy. He wrote: "During the conversation the President stated . . . that his opinion always had been that the great fight should have been at Manasses . . . —that McClellan was opposed to fighting at Manassas, and he, the President, then called a Council of twelve generals, . . . and that eight of them decided against him, and four concurred with him, ... The majority being so great . . . he yielded, but subsequent events had satisfied him he was right." Browning, *Diary*, I, 552.

defame the general, misrepresented his illness,[2] fomented jealousies among officers,[3] and plotted the commander's downfall. To replace him they favored Frémont, Pope, McDowell, or Banks. While shrieking "Onward to Richmond," these meddlers were accused by a newspaper correspondent of having defeated McClellan's projects to strike the enemy, while with their determination to know all of McClellan's secrets they were "aiding and assisting the rebels." [4] With entire confidence in their top general, according to this reporter, soldiers of the Army of the Potomac thought it "a pity that the Greeleys, Gurleys,[5] Chandlers, Wilkinsons, Garrisons and Lovejoys . . . [could not] be compelled either to close mouths which are perpetually vomiting forth slander and falsehood, or else be drafted . . . and made to wade through . . . thigh deep mud . . . ." [6]

There was evidence to indicate that McClellan's foes did not scruple to use that vilest of partisan tricks, the whispering campaign. A meeting of the Young Men's Republican Association of New York, according to the *Herald,* marked out a scheme to circulate rumors against McClellan and Mrs. Lincoln with the design of forcing McClellan to resign. It was further reported that private meetings were held in Wall Street, and that the campaign included an "editorial barrage," circulation of anti-McClellan literature among soldiers, and a hue and cry in religious publications.[7]

The motives of this conspiracy against the nation's chief commander were a mixture of partisanship, ambition, and honest abolitionism. Though far from pro-slavery, McClellan favored conducting the war on Congress's own platform of July 22, 1861, in which the nation's

---

[2] *McClellan's Own Story,* 155.

[3] Writing in this period to McClellan, Halleck mentioned a caucus of the abolition group in Congress which considered the question of high army ranks for their favorites, adding: "You . . . see the attempts of the abolition press to create jealousies between us." Halleck to McClellan ("Private"), Feb. 24, 1862, McClellan MSS.

[4] New York *Herald,* Jan. 14, 1862, p. 8, c. 1.

[5] John A. Gurley, Representative from Ohio, on January 29, 1862, had denounced the administration's inactive war policy, saying that the army had long been ready and the soldiers burning with a desire to strike at the traitors. He deplored the fact that the country had looked in vain for a commander in chief with enough enterprise to lead the forces to victory. Significantly he insinuated: "Did a general stand in the way to hold in check more than half a million of men? take him out of the way . . . ." *Ibid.,* Jan. 30, 1862, p. 8, c. 2. Next day, sarcastically denouncing the " 'On to Richmond' Orator," the *Herald* referred to Representative Gurley as "an 'onward' man before . . . Bull run, and . . . the same individual who ran twenty-seven miles without hat, coat or boots from that battle . . . ." *Ibid.,* Jan. 31, 1862, p. 5, c. 1.

[6] *Ibid.,* Feb. 1, 1862, p. 1, c. 2.   [7] *Ibid.,* Feb. 19, 1862, p. 5, c. 3.

war aim was officially declared to be not the eradication of slavery in the South against the will of the states, but preservation of the Union on the prewar constitutional basis.[8] He thought of Southerners as human beings, recognized the existence of diverse elements in a composite country, deplored the tendency to associate the abolition cause with vindictive radicalism, and, above all, looked forward to a genuine return of the Southern people, after military defeat, to a satisfactory instead of a hateful Union.[9]

There was much to support McClellan's belief that the radical clique were determined to ruin him,[10] first by forcing a premature and unsuccessful movement, and afterwards by withholding the means necessary to success. "The success of McClellan in 1862," wrote W. C. Prime (an early biographer), "would have been doubly fatal to the politicians. The old Union would have been restored and the general would command the political situation. . . . His popularity must be destroyed. . . . Above all, he must not be allowed to win a decisive victory. Neither a quick ending of the war nor a victorious campaign by McClellan would enure to party success." [11] To probe the minds of men is no easy historical task. It is sufficient to say that the deeds of McClellan's detractors were entirely in line with the motives just outlined.

One of the methods of this radical intrigue—which, if feasible, would have gone to the extent of congressional action to dismiss McClellan—was a plan to "reorganize" the Army of the Potomac. Known as the "army corps" plan, and impressively clothed with French phrases and references to continental practice, this was in truth a scheme to take away McClellan's authority as general in chief and put the army under several corps commanders who would take orders from the secretary of war. The plan was the subject of long conferences between Lincoln and radical leaders,[12] and was embodied in an order

---

8 See below, pp. 127–128.   9 *McClellan's Own Story*, 35.
10 *Ibid.*, 150.   11 *Ibid.*, 8.
12 ". . . the committee [on the conduct of the war] waited upon the President . . . , February 25. They made known . . . that . . . dividing the great army of the Potomac into *corps d'armée* had impressed the committee . . . [as] essential . . . . The President observed that he had never considered the organization . . . into army corps so essential as the committee seemed to represent it to be; still he had long been in favor of such an organization. . . The committee left without any conclusion having been reached . . . ." Journal of the Committee on the Conduct of the War, February 26, 1862, in their Report (*Sen. Rep. No. 108*, 37 Cong., 3 sess.), I, 86–87.

by Lincoln under date of March 8, 1862.[13] It was done over McClellan's head, without consulting him, and against his judgment.[14]

The main significance of the order was a matter of personnel; of the five corps commanders named (McDowell, Sumner, Heintzelman, Keyes, and Banks), only Keyes had agreed with McClellan on fundamental strategy and supported him in councils of war.[15] Officers close to McClellan, in whom he had highest confidence, such as W. B. Franklin, Andrew Porter, and Fitz-John Porter, were conspicuous by their absence in this order of reorganization. The order was a demotion for McClellan. He was now head of the Army of the Potomac and commander of the "Department of the Potomac," but was relieved of authority over other departments. The most serious aspect of the reorganization business was not that McClellan, about to take the field, was no longer general in chief. It was that the control of the army was inadequate, timid, and bungling, and that political influences were successfully at work to hamper, worry, and destroy the man who yet remained head of the main army, and upon whom the Lincoln government depended for victory and even for survival. Until March McClellan had planned as to all the eastern sectors, seeking to make them a unified front. For this he needed coördination of the divisions and "departments." But now the "President's Special War Order No. 3" (March 11, 1862),[16] relieved him of general command and required the various commanders to report "severally and directly" to the secretary of war at a time when that inexperienced official was not only unable to initiate and conduct strategic plans,[17] but was rapidly becoming a tool of the anti-McClellan cabal. Such an order was nothing less than a vote of no confidence in a commanding general about to launch upon his first major campaign.

V

Before the army moved there were yet other instances of groping and experimentation. One of the most curious and futile was the

---

[13] *Works*, VII, 116–117. The President was again consciously functioning as commander in chief. This order was designated as "President's General War Order No. 2."

[14] *McClellan's Own Story*, 222.   [15] Myers, *McClellan*, 256–257.

[16] *Works*, VII, 129–130.

[17] Stanton's peevish inadequacy and indecision appear in the Hitchcock episode which follows immediately.

Hitchcock episode. Ethan Allen Hitchcock was a Vermont soldier of long and varied record. He had instructed at West Point, served in the Seminole and Mexican Wars, held command on various western assignments, traveled widely, and made himself known as a man of experience, religious feeling, and learning. In tastes and aptitudes, however, he was "a scholar rather than a warrior," [1] and in 1862 he reached the age of sixty-four, having long before (1855) resigned from the army, which he seems to have entered because, being the grandson of Ethan Allen, it was expected of him. One can but imagine the feelings of this old soldier in March 1862 as he hastened to Washington on telegraphic summons, suffered a hemorrhage on the way and another on arrival, lay in bed while the secretary of war told him that he and Lincoln needed his services, and was soon after asked if he would take McClellan's place in command of the Army of the Potomac! According to Hitchcock's diary Lincoln received him civilly, mentioned how he was urged to remove "the traitor McClellan," stated that as President he was "the depository of the power of the government and had no military knowledge," and expressed the wish to have the benefit of the veteran's experience. After leaving the President, Hitchcock was in a mist as to what would come of it all. In his diary he wrote: "I want no command. I want no department. . . . I am uncomfortable. I am almost afraid that Secretary Stanton hardly knows what he wants, himself." [2] Declining the "high station" proffered, he accepted an ill-defined staff appointment as adviser to Stanton and Lincoln,[3] rendering such service as he was capable of, though in this capacity he was popularly held responsible for the very movements which he disapproved.[4]

In a scene of petulance and impatience (April 26, 1862) Stanton complained to Hitchcock that he had no one around him to give military opinions. " 'It is very extraordinary that I can find no military man to give opinions. *You* give me no opinions!' he added. The . . . subject . . . was the position of General Banks. Now I had given him a very definite opinion on that very point two or three days

1 W. A. Croffut, ed., *Fifty Years in Camp and Field: Diary of Major-General Ethan Allen Hitchcock, U. S. A.*, 437.

2 *Ibid.*, 439.

3 His signature in this period was: "E. A. Hitchcock, Maj. Gen. Vol. on duty in the War Dept." Memorandum, April 19, 1862, Hitchcock MSS.

4 Croffut, 443.

before . . . ." Thus reads the Hitchcock diary,[5] which proceeds to
record an extraordinary interview several days later when Hitchcock's
resignation reached Stanton's hands. What bothered Stanton on this
occasion to the point of humiliating lamentation and supplication
was the thought that he would be ruined by the general's resignation,
upon which Hitchcock destroyed the paper.[6] "His idea that my resignation would destroy him [wrote Hitchcock] was not from the loss of my
supposed services, but because he knows his reputation for acting on
impulse and . . . that my withdrawal would be construed to his
disadvantage."

Finding himself in a "painful situation" without ability to perform
his duties and denied even the boon of resignation, Hitchcock continued to struggle with his anomalous position until he was so weak
that he could scarcely reach his room from the lower story of his hotel.
With a twinge of conscience all too rare among men of the time he
wrote: "I feel my presence here as no other than a tax on the Treasury,
without being able to render any adequate service." [7] When he made
recommendations to Lincoln and Stanton they were "ignored," so
that he "insisted" on resigning rather than remaining "in a false position." [8] Though thrice offered, his resignation was not permitted.
With collapse of health, relief came by leave of absence from May
to November 1862; when he was again called for duty after recuperation, it was as commissioner of prisoners, "and for the next three years
this was his principal duty, though intermitted with that of counsellor
at headquarters [in the war department], and assignments to courts-
martial . . . ." [9] Though this Hitchcock episode has been all but forgotten, it offers an amazing revelation of the uncertainty and futility
of war administration under Stanton. The whole trend of Hitchcock's
advice had been in opposition to McClellan's plans; in this situation
neither Hitchcock nor McClellan, nor any general, was given a free

---

[5] *Ibid.*, 442.

[6] Hitchcock's diary records that he burned the letter of resignation in Stanton's presence (*ibid.*, 442). His own copy, preserved in his papers, bears the penciled endorsement: "This was presented—but recalled at the earnest request of Mr. Stanton." In
his letter to the secretary he frankly stated that he had tried his strength and found
it wanting. Hitchcock to Stanton, Washington, April 28, 1862, Hitchcock MSS.

[7] Hitchcock to Stanton ("Private"), Washington, May 13, 1862, *ibid.* In his diary of
May 21 Hitchcock wrote: "I told him [Stanton] . . . that I am positively ashamed to
be in receipt of the pay and emoluments of a major-general and render no adequate
service . . . ." Croffut, 443.

[8] Croffut, 443.   [9] *Ibid.*, 445.

hand and undivided support.

As a part of the whole confused situation, an equally curious assignment had been given to the secretary of the treasury. To relieve an
overburdened war department in 1861, problems of organization had
been put into Chase's hands. This applied to such matters as the three-
battalion organization for a regiment, the numbering of regiments,
the three-year term for volunteers, and the like. Fortunately, for the
working out of these details, Chase had the assistance of competent
officers—Lorenzo Thomas, Irwin McDowell, and W. B. Franklin—
but this was not all; beyond the tasks assigned to him, Chase showed
a degree of activity in military matters that was quite surprising in
a secretary of the treasury. Indeed much of his correspondence in
1861–62 reads like that of a secretary of war. To an Ohio friend he
wrote: ". . . I have urged the sending of an adequate force up the
James River to coöperate with the gunboats." [10] Writing to his friend
McDowell he mentioned that he had tried unsuccessfully to get Lincoln to direct a forward movement by that general; then he counseled:
"If I were you I would move forward with all the forces I
could . . . ." Realizing the ineffectiveness of central army direction, and anxious to build up McDowell's reputation in the public
mind, he added: "Only *act* on your judgment; do not wait for direc-
tions from Washington . . . do your own thinking, moving and
fighting—and when you accomplish anything report it . . . . You
know I believe in reports—by Generals." [11] It is unnecessary to add
that Chase's persistent zeal was directed toward the destruction of
McClellan, with whose radical opponents the secretary was in close
touch.

10 Chase to M. Halstead, May 24, 1862, copy in Chase MSS., Hist. Soc. of Pa.
11 Chase to McDowell, June 6, 1862, copy in *ibid.*

CHAPTER XIX

McCLELLAN'S DEMOTION ASSISTS LEE

I

SUCCESS for McClellan in his complicated undertaking against a powerful and brilliant defense required coöperation of the navy, availability of an adequate force, unity of command, and generous support at Washington. To say that these elements were lacking would be an understatement; back of the lines there was active obstruction and opposition to McClellan's campaign from its hampered start to its abrupt termination in mid-course. In contrast to the coöperation of Lee and Jackson which gave superiority of striking force to Confederate arms, the Union situation involved divided effort, political interference, and uncertainty of plan.

McClellan wanted more men.[1] Those who assail him for such a request may, if they wish, base their opinion upon the sage advice of the War Committee that "fighting, and *only* fighting" could end the rebellion [2] (what could be more simple!) or upon the expansive boast that if General Pope had been given McClellan's force and opportunity, nothing could have prevented him from marching promptly to New Orleans.[3] If, instead of this, one prefers the critical approach,

---

[1] In the voluminous literature that has grown up in criticism of McClellan there constantly recurs the stereotyped comment that he always overestimated the strength of the enemy and made excessive requests for a heavy force of his own. With this in view it is interesting to read the statement of Gideon Welles under date of August 31, 1862: "Halleck walked over with me from the War Department as far as my house, . . . ; [he] says that we overrate our own strength and underestimate the Rebels' . . . . This has been the talk of McClellan, which none of us have believed." Welles, *Diary*, I. 99.

[2] Report, Committee on the Conduct of the War (*Sen. Rep. No. 108*, Part I, 37. Cong., 3 sess.), p. 66.

[3] Pope's statement was in the form of brief assent to a leading question by Senator Chandler. *Ibid.*, 282. For another example in which Pope permitted bold words in criticism of McClellan to be put into his mouth, see below, pp. 99–100.

he may perceive hard realities not evident to a Zach Chandler or a
Ben Wade. Lee was one of those realities. So was the Confederate army.
McClellan had crack troops to oppose. The condition of the Union
cause when he took charge after Bull Run was pitiful. McDowell and
Scott had failed. To repeat that failure would have been to lay Washington open to enemy occupation.[4] Transition of the army from a
small-scale unmilitary aggregation to a colossal yet manageable or
ganism was McClellan's achievement. That transition had to be
accomplished amid the hazards of war and the interference of politicians. He had to "create a real army and its material out of nothing." [5]
There was justification for his statement that not a day of his preparation in camps of instruction had been wasted.[6]

Once he had his army, McClellan's task was not to move out and
take an enemy position or win a battle; it was *to force a military decision in the whole war.* It was not a sporting proposition of showing
what he could do on equal terms. It was a matter of overwhelming
the enemy with a heavy force in his own country, destroying his fighting power, making it impossible for him to strike again, and thus
forcing an end to the struggle. Whether McClellan could have done
this no one can say with absolute certainty. At least he saw what was
to be done; only a simple-minded person would have expected him
to do it without a huge army under unified command. Instead of such
unity the broad Virginia front was under six generals: Frémont, Banks,
McDowell, Wool, Burnside, and McClellan.[7]

Abandoning his Urbanna-West-Point scheme, McClellan launched
his Peninsular campaign with Fort Monroe as a base. Beginning in
March, the sailing of his troops carried over into the first days of
April. Before he embarked, the enemy had abandoned its position
at Manassas, leaving wooden guns which became the theme of anti-
McClellan sneers, though by their withdrawal the Confederates
showed their recognition both of McClellan's striking power and of
the importance of concentration near Richmond. Step by step as he
proceeded, McClellan found the area of his authority restricted and
his available force reduced. Contrary to previous understanding, his
base at Fort Monroe was removed from his control; it was ordered by

---

[4] *McClellan's Own Story,* 74.   [5] *Ibid.,* 72.   [6] *Ibid.,* 98.
[7] Statement of E. D. Keyes in McClellan, *Report on the* . . . *Army of the Potomac*
(1864), 168.

the President that troops were not to be detached from the Fort without General Wool's sanction.[8] Naval coöperation, necessary for control of the York and James Rivers, failed him; then a whole division— an important one—under General Blenker was detached from his command.[9] Though done with the promise that such a thing would not be repeated, this was immediately followed by a severe blow in the withholding of the First Army Corps under McDowell. Taken together, these dispositions meant a loss of nearly 60,000 men by McClellan's estimate, or more than a third of his force at the outset of a major campaign.[10] This blow "frustrated" McClellan's plans when he was "too deeply committed to withdraw" and forced the adoption of a less effective plan. He called it a "fatal error." [11]

After three and a half weeks of siege McClellan took Yorktown on May 4, 1862. Protecting Johnston's main force, Longstreet checked McClellan at Williamsburg (May 5), following which the Union fleet was stopped at Drewry's Bluff, so that McClellan lacked the flotilla support that had proved so essential in the West. With about 85,000 troops "for duty," [12] McClellan advanced to meet an enemy of approximately equal strength concentrating for a powerful stand in front of Richmond. The logical Union approach to Richmond was by the James, and it was so that McClellan intended it, planning that McDowell's force should join him by the best route—i. e., by water through Hampton Roads. Interference in Washington, however, put McDowell in independent command, kept his force back, and then tardily ordered it to join McClellan *by land,* a much more difficult matter.[13] It never did join him and was never effective in the campaign,

8 *Ibid.,* 156.   9 *Ibid.,* 160.   10 *Ibid.*   11 *Ibid.,* 161.

12 In letters to Washington McClellan stated on April 7 that his entire force for duty amounted to only 85,000, and on May 10 that he did not think he could bring more than 70,000 men upon the field of battle. *Report on the . . . Army of the Potomac,* 162, 191. Before Washington, in March, his command had embraced about 200,000. On the eve of Mechanicsville Lee hoped, with Jackson, to open battle "with about 85,500 soldiers of all arms" (Freeman, *Lee,* II, 116).

13 Illustrating the bad effect of the effort to manage things from Washington, McClellan wrote to Stanton showing how unsatisfactory was the secretary's plan for an overland march by which McDowell would join the main army on the Peninsula. Mentioning the destruction of railroad bridges and the delay (four weeks) before this could be remedied, all this at a time when the enemy was giving every indication of a fight McClellan pointed out the slowness of wagon transportation and the hazard of extending his own right to meet McDowell. The latter, he said, ought to be sent by water transports. McClellan to Stanton (autograph draft, signed), June 12, 1862. McClellan MSS.

but the effort to hook up with McDowell caused McClellan to expose his right, straddle and bridge the Chickahominy, operate in swampy country in a wet season, incur unnecessary delay and loss, and give battle under the difficult conditions of the Seven Days. A water movement of McDowell's force to join the main army on the James seemed to McClellan to offer better results; it was part of the considered and coördinated plan of the man who was in responsible command of the Army of the Potomac. Knowing this, political heads at Washington killed the plan, but they substituted nothing better.

II

Possible junction of McDowell and others with McClellan was deeply dreaded by Confederate leaders, and in Stonewall Jackson they found the answer. In the month between May 8 and June 9,[1] while McClellan was challenging Johnston and Lee on the Peninsula, Jackson was shifting, feinting, and striking in the Valley of the Shenandoah with the dash and mystifying cunning for which he has become famous. All the scattered and puzzled Union forces north of the Rappahannock—those of Frémont and Banks west of the Blue Ridge and of McDowell east of that barrier—were Jackson's game; part of them he engaged, managing to have superior force when he struck; others he baffled and neutralized. Near McDowell, [West] Virginia, he defeated units of Frémont's command under Milroy and Schenck; this engagement occurred on May 8. Disappearing, fooling Frémont, and keeping Union forces separated, Jackson next turned his attention to Banks, striking him at Front Royal (left defenseless by Stanton's bungling), racing him to Winchester, fighting him there, and sending his force in precipitate flight across the Potomac (May 23–25). In this period none of the maneuvers directed from Washington contributed to the timely reënforcement of Banks or the effective concentration of any Union force to meet Jackson when and where his blows fell. With far more than enough men to have disposed of Jackson, Federal leaders were now in a kind of panic for the safety

---

1 Prior to his famous May-June campaign Jackson's Valley operations had included the sharp battle of Kernstown near Winchester (March 23, 1862). Shields attacked him successfully while he was demonstrating against Winchester with a view to preventing Union concentration under McClellan; in the sense that he did prevent such a concentration, even this lost battle was no failure.

of Washington as reports came in that the enemy was about to descend upon the capital, this being the opposite of what Jackson was doing. As newsboys were shrieking "Washington in Danger" on the morrow of Banks's defeat, a badly worried government was intensifying the panic by measures taken to relieve it. The President took military possession of the railroads of the United States. The secretary of war summoned Northern governors to send all the militia and volunteer force they could muster. To create counter excitement, secessionists at Baltimore made a demonstration of rejoicing at Banks's defeat.[2]

Lincoln at this time, with his uninspired war minister, was taking a good deal to himself in the maneuvering and shifting of men, but his remote control did not work; the men did not shift as ordered. Frémont had been ordered to move toward Harrisonburg to put himself in Jackson's rear; instead of that he turned up at Moorfield. The usefulness of Frémont was to be assessed in terms of intercepting Jackson and relieving Banks; what happened was that Jackson swept Banks out of the Valley and eluded Frémont's pursuit. This bit of business may be a detail, but it is worth while to take a closer look at the records. When Banks was being hard pressed, Lincoln sent the following to Frémont:

> The exposed condition of General Banks makes his immediate relief a point of paramount importance. You are therefore directed by the President to move against Jackson at Harrisonburg . . . . This movement must be made immediately. You will acknowledge the receipt of this order, and specify the hour it is received by you.[3]

This was signed "A. Lincoln" and dated "War Department, May 24, 1862. 4 P. M." It was nothing if not a presidential order for the immediate movement of troops to a specified place for a stated purpose. That night at 7:15, having received Frémont's telegram of compliance, Lincoln wired:

> Many thanks for the promptness with which you have answered that you will execute the order. Much—perhaps all—depends upon the celerity with which you can execute it. Put the utmost speed into it. Do not lose a minute.[4]

To show what a jolt Lincoln received in his effort at remote control, he wired to Frémont on May 27: "I see that you are at Moorefield. You

---

2 Moore, *Rebellion Record* (Diary), V, 17.   3 *Works*, VII, 179 (May 24, 1862).
4 *Ibid.*

were expressly ordered to march to Harrisonburg. What does this mean?" [5] One could show by the records how that refrain "What does this mean?" ran through the war despatches from Washington in these days. Lincoln wanted to know whether or not the enemy were "north of Banks, moving on Winchester." For all he knew Banks might be "actually captured." He desired from Banks "more detailed information . . . respecting the force and position of the enemy" pressing upon him. He queried one of the lesser officers: "Are the [enemy] forces still moving through the gap at Front Royal and between you and there?" When Jackson was heading southward up the Valley Lincoln was fearing a general and concerted Confederate movement in large force northward, such as would menace Washington. He wanted to know what had happened to men sent to Harpers Ferry, and wondered if any of them had been cut off. He thought Banks's retreat was "probably" a "total rout." He feared Jackson was about to cross the Potomac. All the while he was puzzled as to why McDowell and Frémont did not get action in Jackson's rear. He was anxious to learn what Geary's scouts under Banks's command were doing. They found no enemy "this side of the Blue Ridge," but had they been to the Blue Ridge looking for them? Four days after Jackson's defeat of Banks he was uncertain "whether any considerable force of the enemy—Jackson or any one else— . . . [was] moving on to Harper's Ferry or vicinity." He wondered whether the enemy in force was "in or about Martinsburg, Charlestown, and Winchester, or any or all of them . . . ." "Where is your force?" he wired Frémont on May 30. "It ought this minute to be near Strasburg." That morning he had a despatch from Frémont, not telling where he was, but representing Jackson's force "at 30,000 to 60,000." (This was absurd; not more than about 15,000 or 16,000 would have been a fair guess.) Next day, referring to a rumor of more forces having entered the Valley, Lincoln commented: "This . . . may or may not be true." On June 3 he wired McDowell: "Anxious to know whether Shields can head or flank Jackson. Please tell about where Shields and Jackson . . . are at the time this reaches you." [6]

Much of this fog of war was inevitable; the remarkable thing was

---

[5] *Ibid.*, VII, 195.
[6] These bits are from Lincoln's telegrams in the confused days of Jackson's Valley maneuvers. *Works*, VII, 178–211, *passim.*

that in the Valley campaign the hampering obscurity of the fog worked almost entirely for the detriment of the Union side. With a small mobile force Jackson was keeping much larger Union forces jumping, wondering, pursuing, and backing. After Banks's defeat a force under Shields was shifted from the east side to the west side of the Blue Ridge to coöperate with Frémont and destroy Jackson, but Stonewall's God again "blessed his army" as he prevented the junction of these Union generals, and, in two more of his famous Valley battles (Cross Keys and Port Republic, June 8–9, 1862) defeated them separately.

So great was the Washington scare produced by Jackson's scant force that Lincoln even suggested to McClellan that he "give up the job" on the Peninsula and come back to defend Washington on the erroneous supposition that there was a "general and concerted" movement of the enemy against the Northern capital.[7] This spasm of alarm, known as the "great scare," [8] was short lived, but it weakened Lincoln's faith, never strong, in the Peninsular Campaign, while it confirmed his determination to hold back McDowell's forces.[9] When Union consternation was at the keenest Jackson was making a well calculated feint, not an attack, against Harpers Ferry and then withdrawing up the Valley. In a brilliant month he had marched 245 miles, won four "desperate battles," [10] and prevented Union forces several times his size from threatening Richmond. He had thwarted that Union concentration under McClellan which, since the Confederates feared it, must have been the reasonable line of Federal strategy. Then, when it was erroneously supposed that Lee would reënforce him, Jackson reënforced Lee and took part in the major campaign to save Richmond.

Stonewall was supporting Lee at the time that McDowell, to mention one among an array of generals, was supposed to be supporting McClellan, but in the manner of this support there was a marked difference. In Jackson's shifting about he accomplished much by the very shifting, but above all he did strike effectively in widely separate

---

[7] "I think the movement [of Jackson] is a general and concerted one, . . . not . . . a . . . defense of Richmond. I think the time is near when you must either attack Richmond or give up the job and come to the defense of Washington." *Ibid.*, VII, 183 (May 25, 1862). Confederate leaders were hoping that authorities in Washington would interpret Jackson's movement in precisely this manner.

[8] Rhodes, *Hist. of the U. S.*, IV, 19.   [9] *Works*, VII, 186–188 (May 25, 1862).

[10] *Battles and Leaders of the Civil War*, II, 297.

areas. On the other hand McDowell, one of three [11] corps commanders each of whom had a force much larger than Jackson's, did precisely the opposite. When Confederates were tensely anxious lest he march toward Richmond, he marched away from it.[12] He was poised uncertainly between two sectors without striking in either, and the manner of his poising and shifting was not such as to baffle or immobilize the enemy, but to relieve their fears.

III

It was Stanton's constant anxiety, and also Lincoln's, that Union forces even larger than McClellan's own be held back, north of the Rappahannock and in the Blue Ridge area, to "cover" the capital. On the other hand it was McClellan's contention that the Confederates would have to concentrate near Richmond and that the heavier his own attack the more likely such concentration would be. Any serious Southern effort to seize Washington, he judged, was out of the reckoning so long as the main Union army was not disposed of. In short, McClellan believed that offense constituted defense, that Washington was being defended on the Peninsula. Taking the whole situation in retrospect it is almost as if Lee and Jackson exercised a magic control over official minds at Washington. Union performance as hampered by these official minds was in precisely the terms which Lee and Jackson desired and foresaw.

On this point it is pertinent to note the well considered judgment of a Confederate officer: "McClellan had planned and organized a masterly movement to capture, hold, and occupy the Valley and the Piedmont region; and if his subordinates had been equal to the task, and there had been no interference from Washington, it is probable the Confederate army would have been driven out of Virginia and Richmond captured by midsummer, 1862." [1] After summarizing his own plans for holding the Valley and Piedmont areas (in the general region of Washington, Winchester, Warrenton, and Manassas), by which Jackson would have been held back and Washington "covered by a strong force well entrenched," McClellan wrote: "If these

---

[11] Frémont, Banks, and McDowell.   [12] Freeman, *Lee*, II, 66.
[1] Statement of General John D. Imboden, C. S. A., in *Battles and Leaders of the Civil War*, II, 283.

measures had been carried into effect Jackson's subsequent advance down the Shenandoah would have been impracticable; but, unfortunately, as soon as I started for the Peninsula this region was withdrawn from my command, and my instructions were wholly disregarded." [2]

It was not as though McClellan had neglected the Valley, nor the approaches to Washington. The main differences between his plans and those of the political leaders at Washington were on two points: (1) McClellan would send much the heavier force into the Peninsula, retaining smaller, yet adequate forces in the Winchester-Strasburg-Warrenton-Manassas region; (2) he would coördinate all fronts, planning that Banks's movement against Jackson in the Valley should coincide with his own against Richmond. He would not waste large bodies of troops by having them merely held back and scattered; he would plan movements to include the action of Banks and Frémont as well as himself and McDowell. Emphasis is upon the word *plan*. His Peninsular campaign constituted part of the plan, his disposition of Banks a complementary part. Always regarding his advance upon Richmond as the main business,[3] McClellan made arrangements for the more immediate defense of Washington without getting into a state of nerves about it. In the knowledge that Washington defenses were strong, his plan for dealing with Jackson was to throw that general "well back, and then to assume such a position as to . . . prevent his return"; this he thought could be done with a force of 25,000 or 30,000.[4] Rightly he regarded Jackson's move as "merely a feint." On that basis he wrote: ". . . if McDowell had joined me on the James the enemy would have drawn in every available man from every quarter to make head against me. A little of the nerve at Washington which the Romans displayed during the campaign against Hannibal would have settled the fate of Richmond in very few weeks." [5]

---

2 *McClellan's Own Story*, 240.

3 "I think that the time has arrived to bring all the troops in Eastern Virginia into perfect cooperation. I expect to fight another and very severe battle before reaching Richmond. . . . All the troops on the Rappahannock, & if possible those on the Shenandoah should take part in the approaching battle. We ought immediately to concentrate everything . . . . All minor considerations should be thrown to one side & all our . . . means directed towards the defeat of Johnston's army in front of Richmond." Rough signed draft of telegram. McClellan to Stanton, May 8, 1862, McClellan MSS.

4 McClellan, *Report*, 137–138.   5 *McClellan's Own Story*, 346.

IV

McClellan's first grapple (May 31-June 1) with Johnston's main force was at Seven Pines (Fair Oaks), several miles east of Richmond. The Union army was at a disadvantage on account of rains, high water on the Chickahominy, and dispersion of forces. Throwing a heavy force against exposed parts of McClellan's position, Johnston struck at the moment when McDowell, in obedience to orders from Washington, was marching the wrong way. Resisting stoutly, McClellan repulsed Johnston, whose severe wounding at this "desperate hour"[1] put Robert E. Lee in command of the main Confederate army. Twenty-five days passed, during which Jackson completed his Valley operations and headed toward Richmond. Then Lee fought his first battle (June 26), which was a Confederate failure.[2] Finding McClellan's forces scattered and divided by the Chickahominy, Lee attacked north of that river at Mechanicsville, hoping to turn McClellan's right, push down the Chickahominy, and threaten his base at White House on the Pamunkey. By preventing this, McClellan saved his army, deprived Lee of the element of surprise, and, after severe fighting, forced his enemy to retire.

Immediately came the second major battle of the Seven Days at Gaines's Mill, where Lee won a costly victory without dangerously shaking McClellan's army. Something of the proportions and intensity of this encounter is suggested by McClellan's comment just after it was fought that he believed it would "prove to be the most desperate battle of the war."[3]

In the face of a pursuing and attacking enemy, confident, powerful, and ably led, McClellan now accomplished the daring and difficult feat of changing his base from White House on the Pamunkey to Harrison's on the James. This involved moving "enormous trains and heavy artillery"[4] over swampy terrain, under such pressure that "there was not a night in which the men did not march almost continually, nor a day on which there was not a fight."[5] By this successful maneuver, which showed his ability to make quick decisions in field command, McClellan deflected Lee's next effort, kept his own forces

---

[1] Freeman, *Lee*, II, 72.   [2] *Ibid.*, II, 135.   [3] *McClellan's Own Story*, 424.
[4] *Battles and Leaders of the Civil War*, II, 376.   [5] *Ibid.*, II, 382.

intact, got away with slight loss of equipment,[6] and kept the cards for the next play. The armchair strategist could say that McClellan "should have" struck at Richmond, from which Lee had been drawn away, instead of withdrawing to a point fifteen miles below Richmond on the James. But the opposing army was the main objective. If McClellan had broken into Richmond, Lee might have crashed into his rear, severed his communications, nullified his chance for naval support, and isolated his army. Under such circumstances, even if "taken," Richmond might have been, not a Union triumph, but a death trap. In this connection anti-McClellan comment even goes to the point of stressing the lack of troops "in Richmond" as if McClellan had merely to march in and "take" the place. There were few troops there for the sufficient reason that Lee was managing his army by placing it where necessary for operation against his foe, watching for an opportunity to get on his flank or behind his lines.

The final phase of the bloody Seven Days was a matter of sharp rearguard fighting at White Oak Swamp and Savage's Station (June 29), then two more major battles, Frayser's Farm (Glendale) and Malvern Hill. At this point Jackson's coöperation with Lee was disappointing, and Frayser's Farm stands as "one of the great lost opportunities"[7] for the Confederates, in that they did not destroy McClellan's army while in the vulnerable process of hasty withdrawal. It was on the note of Confederate failure that the Seven Days ended when, at the terrific engagement of Malvern Hill (July 1, 1862), a series of Confederate assaults was stopped by McClellan's solidly placed army. In the sense that he had not yet "taken" Richmond, McClellan was alleged to have "failed." On the other hand, Lee had not won his objectives; McClellan had "escaped the destruction Lee had planned for him."[8] Union arms came through the Peninsular campaign well. With his army powerfully poised and well based at Harrison's Landing, McClellan was ready to continue the argument, while Lee, having lost 20,000 of the 85,000 he had at the beginning of the campaign,[9] concerned himself during the weeks after Malvern Hill with the recuperation and reënforcement of his troops.[10]

---

[6] *Ibid.*   [7] Freeman, *Lee*, II, 199.   [8] *Ibid.*, II, 219.   [9] *Ibid.*, II, 230.   [10] *Ibid.*, II, 256.

V

A period of confusion, perplexity, and political intrigue followed the Seven Days. The President's confidence in McClellan was slipping, he was looking elsewhere for captains, and the enemies of McClellan were taking advantage of the alleged "failure" of the Peninsular campaign to ruin that general and radically alter the whole strategic picture. On other than military fronts the President was hard pressed. A long session of Congress was drawing to a close, with radicals driving ahead with compelling force for laws that Lincoln did not want. The problem of emancipation was at a critical stage; coming weeks would see important developments in that explosive field. Foreign intervention was now a dread danger; never was this hazard more serious than in the summer and fall of '62. Should the military situation in the East show delay or defeat, a turn for the worse in international relations could be surely predicted. The campaign was about to begin for the election of a new Congress, and victories were keenly awaited for their effect on vote-getting prospects. Many Republicans, and these the most influential, were at odds with Lincoln in his basic political ideas of conducting the war. To placate these men, at least in part, might be a party necessity, however much it might be a national disadvantage. The war was in an early stage; the military leaders that were to see it through were yet to emerge; failures in military experimentation were yet to be made. Civil strife was not merely a matter of warring states. The North itself was badly divided; in presiding over a distraught nation Lincoln had to feel his way. Except for the briefest intervals he could not get away from Washington, and the atmosphere of the capital in the summer of '62 was not of the healthiest.

On the very day of Mechanicsville (June 26, 1862) Lincoln had taken a step which revealed a kind of discounting of McClellan's battles with Lee together with a persistent emphasis upon the Valley even after Jackson had left it, and upon covering Washington when it was not threatened. On that day John Pope, known for easy triumphs on the Mississippi and for favorable attention by Wade's officious war committee, was made commander of the "Army of Virginia," to be distinguished from the Army of the Potomac under McClellan.[1] Under

---

[1] *Offic. Rec.*, 1 ser., XII, pt. 2, 20.

Pope were the scattered forces of Frémont, Banks, and McDowell, together with minor units near Alexandria and in the intrenchments that guarded Washington. This was as if the administration was giving notice that it would not reënforce McClellan when the main business of the Peninsular campaign was well under way. Pope was anti-McClellan. He was a strong dissenter to McClellan's fundamental plans, and was expected to get results from opposite methods. That McClellan should be discredited was now a well formulated policy at Washington. Yet the new commander (Pope) was so uncomfortable and so full of "grave forebodings" that he asked at once to be relieved from command of the Army of Virginia and returned to the West.[2] On assuming command (July 14) Pope issued an address, as follows:

To the Officers and Soldiers of the Army of Virginia:
By special assignment of the President of the United States I have assumed the command of this army. I have spent two weeks in learning your whereabouts . . . and your wants . . . .
. . . I have come . . . from the West, where we have always seen the backs of our enemies; from an army whose business it has been to seek the adversary and to beat him when he was found; whose policy has been attack and not defense. . . . I presume that I have been called here to pursue the same system and to lead you against the enemy. It is my purpose to do so, and that speedily. . . . I hear constantly of "taking strong positions and holding them," of "lines of retreat," and of "bases of supplies." Let us discard such ideas. . . . Let us study the probable lines of retreat of our opponents, and leave our own to take care of themselves. Let us look before us, and not behind. Success and glory are in the advance, disaster and shame lurk in the rear. . . .[3]

Armchair pertness and amateur strategy [4] are implicit in this whole document as it casts slurs at "bases of supplies" and glibly promises to "lead . . . against the enemy" as if such a movement were a glorious parade. In army eyes on both sides this bragging was a matter of jest and ridicule. "I regret [wrote Fitz John Porter] . . . that Gen Pope

---

[2] "I . . . took the field in Virginia with grave forebodings of the result . . . ." Statement of Pope, *Offic. Rec.*, 1 ser., XII, pt. 2, 22.

[3] *Offic. Rec.*, 1 ser., XII, pt. 3, 473–474.

[4] That these were not the most grievous of Pope's defects was indicated in an amazing series of severe military orders at the time of taking his new command, in which he threatened destruction of homes, taking of supplies from enemy civilians without compensation, arrest of male non-combatants within his lines, expulsion of those refusing the Union oath, imposition of the death penalty for minor offenses, et cetera. See Freeman, *Lee*, II, 263–264.

has not improved since his youth and has now written himself down what the military world has long known, an ass. His address to his troops will make him ridiculous in the eyes of military men . . . , and will reflect no credit on Mr Lincoln who has just promoted him. If the theory he proclaims is practised you may look for disaster." [5] Confederate gibes against Pope were in much the same tone, various of his supposed expressions being Southern army jokes, as for instance that his headquarters were in the saddle and that he did not care for his rear.[6] Between the lines Pope's boastful address was a denunciation of McClellan and was so intended. According to General Jacob D. Cox the address was dictated by Stanton; [7] indeed, according to Gideon Welles, the whole episode of introducing Pope to high command in the East was "an intrigue of Stanton's and Chase's to get rid of McClellan." [8] Coming from Pope, when one remembers his trepidation and his wish to resign before he ever started moving, the loudly heralded words of this address are grimly amusing.

VI

In a quandary as to what to do after Malvern Hill, but under painful pressure for a change, Lincoln made a visit to Harrison's Landing (arriving on July 8) to see McClellan and view the army. Conferring at headquarters with McClellan and other generals, the President asked a series of questions as to the whereabouts of the enemy, the size of the army, and sanitary conditions in camp. The set questions, asked of one officer after another, suggest a lawyer who seeks in cross examination to produce a predetermined conclusion. More especially, Lincoln asked: "If it were desired to get the army away from here, could it be safely effected?" [1]

---

[5] Pencil copy of a letter from Fitz John Porter to Hon. J. C. G. Kennedy, dated Westover Landing, James River, July 17, 1862. In the same letter Porter also wrote: "I have heard that Gen McClellan has lost favor at Washington; a report which I hope is unfounded and that Gen Halleck is to be called to Washington as General-in-Chief." McClellan MSS.

[6] Statement of Gen. James Longstreet, C. S. A., in *Battles and Leaders of the Civil War*, II, 513.

[7] Jacob D. Cox, *Military Reminiscences of the Civil War*, I, 222.

[8] Welles, *Diary*, I, 108. Welles added: "A part of this intrigue has been the withdrawal of McClellan and the Army of the Potomac from before Richmond and turning it into the Army of Washington under Pope."

[1] "Memorandum of questions and answers . . . at Harrison's Landing," July 9, 1862, *Works*, VII, 262–266.

On this last point, Lincoln's chief question at the moment, only Keyes and Franklin would agree to a removal. McClellan opposed it. Sumner said "we give up the cause if we do it." Heintzelman said "it would be ruinous to the country." Porter said "Move the army and ruin the country." [2] All the circumstances of this interrogation of high officers indicate that Lincoln was personally taking a hand in strategic decisions, and was seeking to justify a contemplated withdrawal of the army from before Richmond. The note of retreat offers a strange contrast to Pope's bombastic address which came at nearly the same date.

The occasion of Lincoln's visit was used by McClellan to hand the President a document known as the "Harrison Bar Letter" in which he stated his ideas of broad policy in the conduct of the war. With great earnestness the general advised that the Union cause was the cause of free institutions and self government, and must never be abandoned. He would have the President consider war aims "covering the whole ground of our national trouble." The conflict had "assumed the character of war"; as such it should be conducted on the "highest principles," not with a view to "subjugation." It should not be a war upon populations, but upon armed forces. Instead of confiscating property (on which a bill was soon to be presented for the President's signature), executing persons for political reasons, reducing states to the territorial organization, and forcibly abolishing slavery, he would confine military action to the military sphere, avoiding all trespass upon the persons and property of the Southern people. Military government, he thought, should not be abused nor carried over into the regulation of domestic relations. He would appropriate slave labor where necessary but would compensate the owner. This might even require manumission for a whole state as in Missouri, "Western Virginia" and Maryland (on this aspect McClellan was not

---

[2] *Ibid.* In their biography of Lincoln (V, 453) Nicolay and Hay give a quite inadequate account of the President's visit to McClellan's army and his questioning of the generals. They briefly slur over the preponderant opinion of the generals which was strongly opposed to what became the next step from Washington—removal of the army from before Richmond. Furthermore, by putting all the stress on officer opinion concerning the slight extent to which the enemy was threatening McClellan, they give the wrong impression. If the enemy did not plan to attack at that time, that was evidence of McClellan's strength in his existing position, but the whole twisted context in Nicolay and Hay suggests that because the enemy was not planning to attack, therefore the army ought to be removed far to the rear and its commander reduced to a minor role.

a stickler for slavery interests), but any exploitation of the war to promote radical and vindictive views would, he feared, cause disintegration of the armies. With a sense of being on the brink of eternity, McClellan protested that this advice was given with love of country and with sincerity toward the President. "I am willing," he said, "to serve you in such position as you may assign me, and I will do so as faithfully as ever subordinate served superior." [3]

It is amazing how much abuse has been lavished upon McClellan apropos of this letter. Nicolay and Hay, writing (it is now known) with the studied purpose of tearing down McClellan while seeming to be fair to him,[4] treat the letter with stinging sarcasm. They refer to it as "mutinous," which it certainly was not, and mention the general's preference for the Democratic party as if to imply that partisanship offered the motive for the letter. As a kind of *post facto* comment they assert that the letter marked "the beginning of General McClellan's . . . political career." [5]

As for partisanship one can find that abundantly manifest in McClellan's contemporary opponents and historical critics. Rightly to judge the letter itself one must consider its occasion, content, and method. The occasion was one in which the President had to choose whether or not he would go along with the radicals in their drive for a vindictive war; the content was politico-military and was pertinent to problems at hand; the unpublicized method was that of a confidential communication for the President's consideration. It is even debatable whether McClellan was going outside his proper military sphere in this quiet personal advice to the President. In this connection two points should be remembered: (1) It was well known that many officers and men, keen to fight for the Union, would find their ardor seriously diminished if they felt that the war was directed by radicals bent upon punishing the Southern people. McClellan was properly concerned with the morale of his army. In this sense what was called political was of obvious military importance. (2) Instead of playing up the tendency of his soldiers to discuss politics in such a way as to sow disaffection against the administration, McClellan used his influence to discourage it, even though he might personally agree with the dissenters.[6] Remembering this, what better way was

---

[3] *McClellan's Own Story*, 487–489.   [4] See above, p. 68.
[5] Nicolay and Hay, *Lincoln*, V, 449–451.   [6] Cox, *Military Reminiscences*, I, 360–362.

there for him to convey this dissent to the President than by the respectful Harrison Bar letter? McClellan wanted the President to avoid the excesses of the radicals who were not merely interested in suppressing slavery but were out for punitive measures against the South. Such measures, he felt, were extraneous to the nation's military purpose and were calculated both to weaken the Northern war effort and to give the Southern people valid cause for resisting reunion. If in July 1862 "political" factors were linked with the military situation, which was painfully true, the radicals were as much to blame for it as McClellan.

By a strange error Nicolay and Hay refer to the language and tone of the letter as that of a "manifesto." [7] In truth it was a confidential document handed to the President; even the general's close friends did not see it until after McClellan's final removal from command.[8] To concede that the leading Union general, at a hard moment, may have failed in tact or political aptness is reasonable enough. The remarkable thing is that a purely confidential letter of advice handed in person to the President, addressing him with respect for his authority on topics of prime importance and timeliness, should have become the basis of the violent abuse which writers on Lincoln have traditionally emitted. It leads one to wonder why it is that a Lincoln writer may so obviously lack the Lincoln spirit. The letter was not a blast from a defiant Frémont nor a gaucherie from a blustering Butler. What was least likely was that the quiet handing of such a letter to the President in person could have promoted McClellan's fortunes in the "political" sense. If McClellan had intended his advice on the war as a means of promoting his political ambitions in opposition to the President, which critics broadly imply, he would hardly have handled the matter so inconspicuously as a communication for Lincoln's own personal attention. As for Lincoln, he read the letter in McClellan's presence as the general gave it to him; in doing so he showed no indignation and made no comment.[9]

There were, of course, things which McClellan did not say to Lin-

---

[7] Nicolay and Hay, *Lincoln*, V, 451.

[8] ". . . no one of McClellan's most intimate personal friends . . . knew . . . of this letter until rumors about it came from members of Mr. Lincoln's cabinet. None of them saw it until after the general was finally removed from command." Editorial note by W. C. Prime, *McClellan's Own Story*, 489–490.

[9] *Ibid.*, 487.

coln's face. These he said to his wife, or otherwise in private correspondence. Such correspondence is very revealing, and it shows that McClellan, while honestly serving the administration, had no faith in it. As for Stanton, he hated to think that humanity could sink so low. Referring to his political enemies, he feared they had "done all that cowardice and folly can do to ruin our poor country." Feeling so, as he told his wife, he had given the President the Harrison Bar letter to clear his conscience.[10]

So fully was McClellan convinced of the purpose of his foes to overthrow him that he wrote his friend Aspinwall, New York business leader, asking for assistance in obtaining some kind of employment in New York against the day when he might be forced to leave the army. He was receiving no reënforcements and he felt that the game was to deprive him of the means of moving and then cut off his head for not doing so, to weaken his command and then hold him responsible for results. He was weary of it; if he could no longer be of service he would rather resign his commission.[11]

VII

Lincoln returned to Washington where Chase, Stanton, and the radicals were intensifying their anti-McClellan drive. Then he attempted another bit of military experimentation on July 11 by ordering Halleck "to command the whole land forces of the United States," making him general in chief.[1] In his painful search for commanders other than McClellan it appears that Lincoln sought wisdom from that feeble old veteran, Winfield Scott. "The President [wrote Gideon Welles], without consulting any one, went about this time on a hasty visit to West Point, where he had a brief interview with General Scott, and immediately returned. A few days thereafter General Halleck was . . . ordered to Washington . . . as General-in-Chief, ..."[2] Another ineffective complication was now added to a confused military situation. Matters drifted till Halleck assumed com-

[10] *Ibid.*, 449.
[11] McClellan to Aspinwall, July 19, 1862, McClellan MSS., quoted in Myers, *McClellan,* 314.
[1] *Works,* VII, 266–267.
[2] Welles, *Diary,* I, 108–109; see also Charles W. Elliott, *Winfield Scott,* 755.

mand, which he did on July 23. They drifted further while the new general in chief visited Harrison's Landing. Then, having denied reënforcements to the Peninsular forces, Halleck on August 3 ordered McClellan to remove his whole army from before Richmond to Aquia Creek, south of Bull Run and close to Washington.[3] With military operations at a pause it was consistent with the existing situation and with unwritten practices in the American army to regard such an order as subject to consideration between brother officers. At any rate, McClellan could not let it pass without earnest protest. Withdrawal, said he, would be "disastrous in the extreme"; it would be a "fatal blow." His army was well placed twenty-five miles from Richmond, with conditions of transportation and supply in his favor. To move would demoralize the army, discourage the Northern people, and adversely affect the attitude of foreign powers. "Here," he said, "in front of this army is the heart of the rebellion. . . . It matters not what partial reverses we may meet with elsewhere; here is the true defense of Washington. It is here on the bank of the James River that the fate of the Union should be decided." "Clear in my convictions of right," he concluded, "actuated solely by love of my country, . . . I do now what I never did in my life before, I entreat that this order may be rescinded. If my counsel does not prevail I will with a sad heart obey your orders . . . whatever the result may be, and may God grant that I am mistaken . . . . I shall at least have the internal satisfaction that I have written . . . frankly, and have sought . . . to avert disaster from my country."[4]

Chapters could be written on this withdrawal of McClellan's army when that general, hampered though he was by orders from Washington, was planning a new advance against Lee. Two years were to follow before another such opportunity was to be presented, when Grant was to move in the same manner intended by McClellan. "All the lives [thought W. C. Prime] and all the agonies of the country which were expended in regaining that same position two years afterwards were wasted for the only purpose of getting rid of McClellan."[5] Leslie Combs considered that "nothing but Military madness or folly could have induced the withdrawing." "It was . . . fatal." What high officials, queried Combs, could have advised it? Then he added:

---

[3] *Offic. Rec.*, 1 ser., XII, pt. 2, 5.   [4] *Ibid.*, 8–9.   [5] *McClellan's Own Story*, 12.

"I presume one of them was . . . Stanton, whose administration of his high office has proved him to be an ass—if not a knave . . . ." [6]

The order for withdrawal was not rescinded and McClellan obeyed, getting "the army away from here," as Lincoln expressed it, and setting up new headquarters at that "wretched place," [7] Aquia Creek (August 24). There were now two main Union armies in Virginia— the Army of Virginia under Pope, and the Army of the Potomac under McClellan. In the strict sense the army was well nigh headless. Over all, not to mention Providence (on whose support Stonewall Jackson claimed priority), stood Henry W. Halleck. Behind the lines, with more power than wisdom, was the arrogant and intriguing Stanton, none too sure of his own place.[8] Mediating as best he could between conflicting factions,[9] with imperfect controls in his hands, was the buffeted Lincoln.

Pope was expected to stand on the defensive, holding the line of the Rappahannock until there could be a general Union concentration behind that river. Such concentration effected, it was expected that "Halleck, the General-in-Chief, was to take the field in command of the combined armies." [10] This, however, was a mere vague understanding; it was so indefinite that McClellan, retaining command of the Army of the Potomac, understood that he was to "direct . . . all the forces in Virginia, as soon as they should be united." [11] Still further vagueness was added when Pope received "information . . . of a secret character, afterwards suppressed" that a campaign was to be launched "without waiting for a union of all the forces, and under

---

[6] General Leslie Combs to McClellan, Dec. 4, 1862, McClellan MSS.

[7] *McClellan's Own Story*, 528. (Lincoln's reference to the desire "to get the army away from here" is found in his memorandum of questions and answers, July 9, 1862, cited above.)

[8] In midsummer of 1862 there were reports that Stanton was to be replaced by Banks. One of Banks's admirers wrote him: ". . . New England is looking to the change in the War Dept. & to you as the riseing man, all concede McClellans lack of capacity . . . & Stantons inability to fill so responsible a post . . . ." He added: "You . . . are the . . . riseing man . . . on whom we must rely as the successor of Lincoln. The War Dept. is the step to it. A successful administration of that Dept. puts you in the White House." John Fitch to N. P. Banks, July 7, 1862, Banks MSS.

[9] "The meddlers have tried to raise an issue between McLellan [sic] and Stanton. The President has overruled them firmly." John Ely to R. W. Thompson, New York, Aug. 8, 1862, MS., Lincoln National Life Foundation, Fort Wayne.

[10] *Offic. Rec.*, 1 ser., XII, pt. 2, 515. See also *Battles and Leaders of the Civil War*, II, 542 and n.

[11] *Offic. Rec.*, 1 ser., XII, pt. 2, 515.

some commander other than either of those before named." [12] For practical purposes McClellan was out of the picture. There was little point to recent dispositions except in the anti-McClellan sense, yet it was not until August 30 that he knew he had been deprived "of the command of all his troops then between the Potomac and the Rappahannock," remaining only in nominal command of the Army of the Potomac.[13] As revealing looseness in army management it is instructive to note McClellan's remarks in writing to his wife on the uncertainty of his own status, this on the eve of an important major battle. In this critical stage he had learned "nothing whatever of the state of affairs," did not see how he could "remain in the service if placed under Pope," could "hardly think that Halleck would permit" such a "disgrace," was without word from Washington as to where he stood, and was waiting "for something to turn up." "I presume [he wrote] they are discussing me now, to see whether they can get along without me." [14] These things he wrote on August 24. On August 29 he wrote: "I have a terrible task . . . . No means . . . , no authority, ... I find the soldiers all clinging to me; yet I am not permitted to go to the post of danger! . . . I have just telegraphed . . . to the President and Halleck what I think ought to be done. I expect merely a contemptuous silence. . . . I am heart-sick . . . . I see the evening paper states that I have been placed in command of all the troops in Virginia. This is not so. I have no command at present— . . . I have none of the Army of the Potomac with me, and have merely 'turned in' on my own account to straighten out whatever I catch hold of. . . . I have seen neither the President nor the secretary since I arrived here; [15] have been only once to Washington, and hope to see very little of the place. I abominate it terribly." [16]

---

[12] *Ibid.* This meant some commander other than McClellan or Pope. The reference was probably to Burnside.

[13] *Ibid.* See also *McClellan's Own Story*, 520.   [14] *McClellan's Own Story*, 528.

[15] The letter appears to have been written at his camp near Washington.

[16] *McClellan's Own Story*, 530–531.

CHAPTER XX

THE BREAKING OF McCLELLAN

I

EVENTS now moved with appalling swiftness to crisis and disaster. In a complicated campaign, whose details the reader may seek elsewhere, Pope and his subordinates got tangled up with Lee and Jackson. Operating separately from Lee, Jackson sped north through Thoroughfare Gap, struck Pope's rear, destroying supplies and communications, then shifted to a point where in two days of furious fighting (August 29 and 30) he acted powerfully with Lee to administer to Pope a smashing defeat on the unpropitious battleground of Bull Run.

To read the Union documents on Second Bull Run is to contemplate one of the saddest chapters of the war. "A terrific contest with great slaughter . . . , our men behaving with firmness and gallantry." The "enemy's dead and wounded were at least double our own." "The action raged furiously all day." "My cavalry was utterly broken down." "Our men, much worn down by . . . continuous fighting . . . and very short of provisions." "Kettle Run," "Manassas," "Centreville." "Hooker," "Sigel," "Reynolds," "Heintzelman," "Kearny," "Banks," "King," "McDowell," "Reno." "An unfortunate oversight." "I do not hesitate to say that if . . . Porter [1]

---

[1] Charged with disobedience of orders and failure to push forward his forces in co-operation with Pope in the campaign of Second Manassas, General Fitz John Porter, on court-martial trial, was cashiered and forever disqualified from holding office. In a long standing controversy, famous in American military history, Porter had strong support, uncertainty in high command being one of the factors in the case. Convicted in 1863, Porter was vindicated in 1886 when Congress passed a special act restoring him to army rank. With McClellan, Porter was one of the chief targets of the radicals; his court martial was regular, but in addition he was subjected to prejudiced "trial" by the committee on the conduct of the war. Accusations against Porter are given in *Offic.*

had attacked . . . we should have crushed Jackson before . . . Lee could have reached him." Night "must see us behind Bull Run." Confronting "a powerful enemy with greatly inferior forces." "All hope of being able to maintain my position . . . vanished." "The troops . . . I cannot say too much for them." "I am, . . . respectfully, your obedient servant." [2]

Such were the strokes and phrases of Pope's report. Only a part of the Army of the Potomac, as of Pope's own command, had been used. Superb fighting on the part of the men had gone for naught because of poor generalship. The idea had been to "save" Washington,[3] but Lee had been drawn north when McClellan's withdrawal relieved the pressure on Richmond,[4] had won a ringing victory, and confidently decided that his next move was to invade Maryland. The peninsular front, which occupied Lee at what McClellan called the "heart of the rebellion," had been stupidly given up. McClellan's contention that Washington was being defended on the Peninsula had now been impressively verified. Pope's grave forebodings had been fulfilled. His beaten army, in disorder and low morale, withdrew "within the defenses of Washington." [5] To look back at this point and quote the bombastic words put into his mouth on assuming eastern command, would be an excess of irony.

So complete and obvious was Pope's failure that he was relieved of command of the Army of Virginia and returned to the West. An incidental result of his brief occupation of a high military pinnacle had been the retirement of Frémont. This general, whose advancement to highest command had been sought by some of the anti-McClellan radicals, was to have become a corps commander in Pope's army. Feeling that he could not serve in that capacity, he was relieved of command at his own request.[6] This *"faux pas,"* as the *Herald* ex-

---

Rec., 1 ser., XII, pt. 2, 507–511. For his defense by an army board that made a full investigation after the war, see *ibid.,* 513 ff.

[2] *Offic. Rec.,* 1 ser., XII, pt. 2, 12–17 (especially 15–17).

[3] On August 29 McClellan wrote to his wife: "There was a terrible scare in Washington last night. A rumor got out that Lee was advancing rapidly on the Chain bridge with 150,000 men. And such a stampede!" *McClellan's Own Story,* 530–531.

[4] ". . . Lee did not move northward from Richmond with his army until assured that the Army of the Potomac was actually on the way to Fort Monroe, . . . so long as the Army of the Potomac was on the James, Washington and Maryland would have been entirely safe . . . ." *Ibid.,* 482.

[5] *Offic. Rec.,* 1 ser., XII, pt. 2, 8.

[6] Cox, *Military Reminiscences,* I, 202, 222. With Frémont's retirement his useless "Mountain Department" ceased to exist.

pressed it,[7] ended his military career. If in this gesture he was essaying the martyr's role, hoping to gain popular support over the President's head, he failed as completely as in other factious and disrupting efforts.

The Union cause had now reached a sorry pass. Pope wrote to Halleck: "You have hardly an idea of the demoralization among officers of high rank . . . , arising . . . from personal feeling in relation to changes of commander-in-chief and others. . . . When there is no heart in their leaders, . . . much cannot be expected from the men." [8] Feelings had been hurt, jealousies were running high, Pope was held in contempt, confidence in prevailing army direction was upset, Philip Kearny was dead, men were exhausted and broken in spirit, organization was badly impaired. Halleck was "utterly tired out." [9] The army, said Welles, had "no head." [10] Annoyance was caused by a "drunken rabble who came out as nurses by permission of the War Dept." [11] To McClellan's eyes there was a "total absence of brains" in army control from Washington.[12] Roads toward the capital were clogged with an "innumerable herd of stragglers,—mingled with an endless stream of wagons and ambulances, urged on by uncontrollable teamsters,—which presently poured into Washington, overflowed it, took possession . . . , and held high orgie." Such was the description by an eye-witnessing officer, who continued: "Disorder reigned unchecked and confusion was everywhere. The clerks in the departments . . . were now hastily formed into companies and battalions for defense; the Government ordered . . . arms and . . . money . . . to be shipped to New York, and the banks followed the example; a gun-boat, with steam up, lay in the river off the White House, as if to announce . . . the impending flight of the Administration." [13]

Even the President doubted that the capital city could be saved.[14] In this grave emergency, despite the radicals, Lincoln turned to

[7] New York *Herald*, June 29, 1862, p. 4, c. 6.
[8] Sep. 1, 1862, 8:50 a. m., at Centreville. *Offic. Rec.*, 1 ser., XII, pt. 2, 83.
[9] Halleck so described his condition in a telegram to McClellan, Aug. 31, 1862, 10:07 p. m., McClellan MSS.
[10] Welles, *Diary*, I, 107.
[11] H. Haupt to Gen. R. B. Marcy, Aug. 31, 1862, McClellan MSS.
[12] That McClellan used this language in writing "frankly" to Halleck, Aug. 31, 1862, is itself significant. *Ibid.*
[13] Richard B. Irwin, in *Battles and Leaders of the Civil War*, II, 541–542.
[14] *McClellan's Own Story*, 535.

McClellan, but the manner of calling him once more to highest field command was casual and somewhat grudging. On September 1, two days after Pope's defeat, Halleck personally asked McClellan to command the defenses of Washington, that and no more. Halleck's misreading of the situation was shown on this occasion when he specifically limited McClellan's authority to the works and garrisons guarding the capital, giving him no commission to step into Pope's shoes. This gave McClellan "no control over the active army." [15] In the inadequacy of Halleck the decision fell to Lincoln himself. An officer of Halleck's staff (J. C. Kelton) was sent to investigate the condition of Pope's army. "Next morning [wrote McClellan] while I was at breakfast, . . . the President and Gen. Halleck came to my house. The President informed me that Col. Kelton had returned and represented the condition of affairs as much worse than I had stated . . . ; that there were 30,000 stragglers on the roads; that the army was entirely defeated and falling back to Washington in confusion. He [Lincoln] then said that he regarded Washington as lost, and asked me if I would, . . . as a favor to him, resume command and do the best that could be done. . . . I at once said I would accept . . . . Both the President and Halleck again asserted that it was impossible to save the city, and I repeated my firm conviction that I could and would save it. They then left, the President verbally placing me in entire command of the city and of the troops falling back upon it . . . ." [16]

II

It was thus upon the President's informal and verbal request that McClellan assumed command at this desperate hour. The only published order in the premises was that of Halleck dated September 2, putting him in command "of the fortifications of Washington and of all the troops for the defence of the capital." [1] It took courage and

---

[15] *Ibid.*, 542.   [16] *Ibid.*, 535.

[1] *Offic. Rec.*, 1 ser., XII, pt. 3, 807. On September 2, 1862, Chase wrote as follows in his diary: ". . . the fact was stated . . . [in cabinet meeting] that McClellan had been placed in command of the forces to defend the Capital—or rather, to use the President's own words, he 'had set him to putting these troops into the fortifications about Washington,' . . . . I remarked that this could be done equally well by the Engineer who constructed the Forts . . . . The Secretary of War said that no one was now responsible for the defense of the Capital . . . ." *Annual Report*, Amer. Hist. Assoc., 1902, II, 64.

decision for Lincoln to act as he did. There were persistent efforts by McClellan's foes to make it appear that his refusal of coöperation had caused Pope's defeat, whereas in fact McClellan had chafed at the restraints which had held him detached from the main operation. At a time when the anti-McClellan drive had produced an appalling condition and threatened to make it worse, Lincoln quietly appealed to McClellan to step in and take over command.

This act was Lincoln's own. It was taken in opposition to his military advisers and his cabinet. The day it was done a meeting of the cabinet was held. The historian would give a good deal for an adequate report of that meeting; from the fragments we have, given by Chase and Welles, it is evident that Chase and Stanton vigorously took issue with Lincoln in his determination to restore McClellan. According to Chase there was considerable discussion as to the responsibility for the order, Stanton disclaiming responsibility for himself and Halleck, and Lincoln thinking that Halleck was as answerable as before. Chase used the occasion for a severe denunciation of McClellan, remarking upon his "series of failures," "omission to urge troops forward" to support Pope, and unworthiness of trust. The secretary of the treasury "could not but feel that giving the command to him was equivalent to giving Washington to the rebels." [2] Others in the cabinet, except Blair, agreed with Chase.

At this point one finds a cryptic statement in Chase's diary (September 2, 1862). As edited by Warden the diary reads: "The President said it distressed him exceedingly to find himself differing on such a point from the Secretary of War and the Secretary of the Treasury; that he would gladly resign his place; but he could not see who could do the work wanted as well as McClellan. I named Hooker, or Sumner, or Burnside, either of whom could do the work better." [3] Did Lincoln on this occasion express a wish to be relieved of the presidency? The words "resign his place" are not as clear as one could wish. They are so read by Warden, who prints this portion of the diary, and this is the reading which Carl Sandburg adopts.[4] In the

---

[2] *Ibid.*, 65.

[3] This is the version as given by R. B. Warden, in *Private Life and Public Services of Salmon Portland Chase,* 459–460. In the ms. diary the sentence concludes: ". . . either of whom, I thought, would be better." Warden's editing is careless.

[4] Carl Sandburg, *Abraham Lincoln: The War Years,* I, 543–544. Sandburg, of course, had basis for this reading by following Warden. It is a tricky point.

best published text of the diary, however, the reading is "resign his plan." [5] When one consults the manuscript he finds a passage written in a clerk's hand, not Chase's, in which the doubtful word looks like "place," but might also be "plan" considering this clerk's peculiar n's.[6] Since in any case the diary is not a verbatim recording, Lincoln's actual words are in doubt, but of his deep distress and his determination to reinstate McClellan despite almost unanimous cabinet opposition, there is no question.

Reading Welles's diary, one has further details. Those who had favored Pope were "disappointed" with his performance. Blair, who had known him intimately, called him "a braggart and a liar." Before the President came into the room Stanton, "trembling with excitement," announced that McClellan had been given command. Then Lincoln came in, confirmed the statement, and said that he was responsible, though he added that Halleck had agreed to it. "Much was said [wrote Welles]. There was a more disturbed and desponding feeling than I have ever witnessed in council; the President was greatly distressed. There was a general conversation as regarded the infirmities of McClellan, but it was claimed, by Blair and the President, he had beyond any officer the confidence of the army. . . . These, the President said, were General Halleck's views, as well as his own, and some who were dissatisfied . . . and had thought H. was the man for General-in-Chief, felt that there was nothing to do but to acquiesce, yet Chase . . . emphatically stated . . . that it would prove a national calamity." [7]

It was with such lack of war-department and cabinet support that McClellan led the army while Lee, shifting his forces from before Washington, launched upon the invasion of Maryland, threatening Baltimore, Philadelphia, and the capital. Conditions at Washington were pitiful. "The War Department [wrote Gideon Welles] is bewildered, knows . . . little, does nothing, proposes nothing." [8] Some days passed before Lee crossed the Potomac; at this moment there

---

[5] *Annual Report*, Amer. Hist. Assoc., 1902, II, 65.
[6] The ms. diary is available in the Library of Congress, and the author has a photostat of it before him as he writes. No record for this date in Chase's own hand has been found. The clerk's doubtful script seems the closest we can come to the original.
[7] Welles, *Diary*, I, 104–105. Welles also treats the subject in his *Lincoln and Seward*, 194 ff.
[8] Welles, *Diary*, I, 111.

was no telling whether the northward push was not a mere feint and Washington the immediate object of attack. As the Confederate columns advanced, McClellan interposed his army between Washington and the enemy, the timid Halleck meanwhile nagging him with querulous complaints that he was too precipitate and too neglectful of guarding the seat of government.

The pros and cons of the fearful Antietam campaign cannot be reviewed here, much less settled. Was McClellan too cautious? Did he err in not striking when Lee's forces were scattered? Was he to be censured for not immediately throwing all his troops into the front line? Was the lack of earlier and more effective assaults due to himself or to Burnside? Was he too timid in not pressing and striking his stunned foe immediately after the battle? Such questions may be left to the military writers. Sequences can at least be noted. In the passes of South Mountain (September 14) McClellan fought so effectively with Lee, and his forces were so disposed, that after the battle the Confederate commander contemplated immediate retreat into Virginia, this before Antietam was ever fought.[9] The battle along Antietam Creek, September 17, 1862, was up to that time the heaviest and bloodiest engagement of the Civil War; McClellan called it "the most severe ever fought on this continent." [10]

Lee was in a tight place. McClellan's maneuvering before and after South Mountain made it a desperate question whether the Southerner would be able to rush his scattered troops into concentration soon enough and in sufficient force to stop the Union assault. It was an aggressive McClellan with plenty of fight in him that the Confederates were facing. Maryland, whatever its sentimental attachment to the South, had not risen in practical response to Lee's proffer of "liberation." North of the Potomac the Confederates were in Union territory. Lee was the invader; yet at that moment, in a doubtful struggle,

---

[9] "Lee looked . . . at the facts: the day [of South Mountain] had been bad; the morrow might be worse. . . . The Army of Northern Virginia . . . must seek the friendly soil on the south side of the river, ... So reasoned Lee. . . . Then Longstreet and D. H. Hill arrived . . . . Hood came also. Their opinion was unanimously in concurrence with . . . Lee . . . : The army must retreat. It could not hold South Mountain the next day." Freeman, *Lee*, II, 372–373. (Further developments—e. g., Confederate capture of Harpers Ferry, and the expectation of reënforcement by Jackson—caused Lee almost immediately to reconsider, delay his retreat, and make a stand at Sharpsburg.)

[10] *McClellan's Own Story*, 613.

he was standing on the defensive against McClellan's attack. Since, however, McClellan was defending Washington, which Lee was threatening, the terms defense and offense seem almost interchangeable. As matters stood on September 17, Lee would not have attacked. It was indeed a question whether he could save his army from destruction. That he did save it despite Federal strength, stands as one of his biggest achievements, and authorities still dispute the issue as to which side was the victor in the tremendous battle that raged for fourteen hours and involved casualties of over twenty-three thousand.[11] When the "terrific" yet "superb" [12] fighting was over McClellan had not destroyed Lee's army. He had, however, turned the hopeful Confederate invasion into a complete failure; on September 20 Lee was back on the Southern side of the Potomac. The stereotyped statement that each side failed to accomplish its objective suggests an unrelieved checkmate. Yet the campaign was more than that; the advantages of South Mountain and Antietam were more on the Union than on the Confederate side. Union morale had been lifted from the morass into which it was plunged by Pope's disaster. The Confederate army's ambitious thrust into Union territory had been parried; its "dreams of 'invading Pennsylvania' dissipated." [13] Lincoln was provided with a favorable military situation without which the emancipation proclamation [14] would have fallen flat. "The efficacy of the President's proclamation," wrote the elder Frank Blair to McClellan, ". . . depends on the power that is to enforce it. You and the army you lead are relied on to make this measure fruitful of good results." [15] British observers, convinced until then that overthrow of the Union was inevitable, now harbored doubts as to the wisdom of intervention for, or even recognition of, the Confederacy. McClellan's objectives—defense of Washington, Baltimore, and Pennsylvania, driving the enemy out of Maryland—were accomplished. Tough fighting qualities in the Union army had been impressively demonstrated. Lee's men and generals had also fought superbly, but Confederate weaknesses had been exposed in the excessive number of Southern stragglers and in

11 Union losses (killed, wounded, captured, and missing), 12,410; Confederate, 11,172. Union dead, 2108, Confederate, 1512. Total losses on both sides: 23,582. *Battles and Leaders of the Civil War*, II, 603.

12 *McClellan's Own Story*, 612.   13 *McClellan's Own Story*, 613.

14 See below, p. 159.

15 F. P. Blair, Sr., to McClellan, Silver Spring, Sep. 30, 1862, McClellan MSS.

the failure to rally Maryland's support.

Less than his just meed of commendation was given by Lincoln to McClellan, yet the President considered South Mountain and Antietam significant victories. Of the first he said: ". . . General Mc-Clellan has gained a great victory over the great rebel army in Maryland. . . ." [16] Concerning the two engagements he remarked in brief reply to a serenade: "On the fourteenth and seventeenth . . . there have been battles bravely, skilfully, and successfully fought. . . . I only ask you . . . to give three hearty cheers for all . . . who fought those successful battles." [17] McClellan may be pardoned for "some little pride" (when writing in confidence to his wife) in having taken over a "beaten and demoralized army" and used it to defeat Lee and save the North.[18]

III

After Antietam the credit bestowed upon McClellan was in no proportion to the savage denunciation that would have descended had he failed to drive Lee back. Disparaging the service he had performed, the radical cabal against him was continuing its incessant attack, supported by McClellan's implacable cabinet enemies—Stanton and Chase. Against terrific pressure Lincoln had held an open mind toward McClellan while doubting the main pattern of his strategy, but the case that was being built up against the general was getting ever stronger than Lincoln's wavering favor. War weariness was an increasing psychological factor in the North as battle after battle brought frightful casualties with nothing settled. The North had not yet adjusted itself to the concept of a long, serious war with heavy sacrifices. People were impressed by facile assertions that Lee could have been easily crushed once for all; the failure of McClellan to pursue was made a more prominent thing than his checking of an invasion. There was no adequate appreciation of what was gained by McClellan's caution in face of Lee's formidable power; [1] and just

---

[16] *Works*, VIII, 34 (Sep. 15, 1862).   [17] *Ibid.*, VIII, 44 (Sep. 24, 1862).
[18] *McClellan's Own Story*, 613.
[1] ". . . Lee was still confident that he could resist successfully a Federal attack and he waited expectantly." Freeman, *Lee*, II, 405. ". . . I should have had a narrow view of the condition of the country had I been willing to hazard another battle . . . ." McClellan, in *McClellan's Own Story*, 618.

at this juncture it came to Lincoln's ears that a talkative officer, Major John J. Key, had expressed the view that Lee's army was not bagged after Sharpsburg because that "was not the game." Both sides were to be kept in the field till exhausted; fraternal relations were then to be restored with slavery saved; that was the "only way the Union could be preserved." [2] Fearing that this was "staff talk" and that it was indispensable to make a signal example of Key, Lincoln dismissed him from the service, though sending him a personal letter which contained more sympathy than rebuke.[3] On October 1 the President visited the army, viewing the camps, going over the battlefields, and holding "many and long consultations alone" with McClellan.[4] When the general explained his reasons for delay and for preparation before the next round, Lincoln said repeatedly that he was "entirely satisfied." "The President was very kind personally [wrote McClellan]; told me he was convinced I was the best general in the country, etc., etc." [5] "He told me that he regarded me as the only general in the service capable of organizing and commanding a large army, and that he would stand by me." [6]

Lincoln's main purpose in visiting the army was to get McClellan to move.[7] Returning to Washington, he made another of those efforts at presidential direction of the army which never quite amounted to positive command of operations. Through Halleck (October 6) he instructed McClellan to "cross the Potomac and give battle to the enemy, or drive him south." [8] Nothing happened. October days passed and McClellan lingered. Then Lincoln sent him a long, earnest letter.

---

[2] *Works*, VIII, 47.

[3] *Ibid.*, VIII, 48–49 (Nov. 24, 1862). See also Dennett, ed., *Lincoln . . . in the Diaries . . . of John Hay*, 219.

[4] *McClellan's Own Story*, 627. Lincoln spent the night at Harpers Ferry, which had fallen to the Confederates just before Antietam, but was once more in Union hands.

[5] *Ibid.*, 655. This was McClellan's statement in a letter to his wife, to whom he wrote with unstudied frankness of himself and others. For Lincoln's repeated expression of entire satisfaction with McClellan, see *ibid.*, 627–628.

[6] *Ibid.*, 627. Such a view of McClellan on Lincoln's part is amply confirmed by sources independent of that general; see Welles, *Diary*, I, 105; Chase's diary as quoted above, p. 112. The quintessence of Lincoln's judgment of McClellan seems to be contained in the following statement by O. H. Browning: "He [the President] again repeated to me what he had previously said about McClellan, that he could better organize, provide for and discipline an army, and handle it with more ability in a fight than any general we had, but that he was too slow." Browning, *Diary*, I, 591 (Dec. 2, 1862). See also *ibid.*, I, 525, 537–538, 552, 619.

[7] Dennett, *Lincoln . . . in the Diaries . . . of John Hay*, 218.

[8] *Works*, VIII, 53.

"Are you not over-cautious [he wrote] when you assume that you cannot do what the enemy is constantly doing? . . . Change positions with the enemy, and think you not he would break your communication with Richmond within the next twenty-four hours? . . . If he should . . . move toward Richmond, I would press closely to him, fight him if a favorable opportunity should present, and at least try to beat him to Richmond on the inside track. . . . If we cannot beat the enemy where he now is, we never can, he again being within the intrenchments of Richmond." [9]

It is easy to read this well written letter of Lincoln's, a long epistle whose substance is only briefly suggested here, and assume that it put McClellan completely in the wrong. To do so would be to forget that McClellan, in field command, knew what was needed in reconditioning and concentrating his army, that he already realized the need for checking and striking Lee, that the "true approach" [10] via the Peninsula had been barred by opposition in Washington, and that watchful delay when Lee was in no position to strike was less dangerous than ill-planned engagements which were the forte of McClellan's successors. It was not as if the general needed all this admonition. He had previously written to his wife (September 25) indicating a purpose to watch the Potomac and to attack Lee if he remained near Washington, or, if he retired toward Richmond, to follow and strike him.[11] With old regiments reduced to skeletons and new regiments in need of instruction, with a deficiency of officers and want of horses, McClellan would not then have maneuvered to bring on a battle unless necessary to protect Washington; yet all the evidence shows that he was actively building a stronger and larger force and was waiting to choose his moment for an effective blow when it should fall.[12] This, of course, was a matter of painful rebuilding. One can never estimate the full dimensions of the setback to McClellan's plans and to Union success produced by the incredible removal of his army in August 1862 from its strong position on the James River near Richmond.

Eager for an immediate knockout victory, Lincoln waited further, meanwhile reading a despatch in which McClellan, in an ill-chosen passage, referred to sore-tongued and fatigued horses. Then Lincoln

---

[9] *Ibid.*, VIII, 57–60 (Oct. 13, 1862).   [10] *McClellan's Own Story*, 642.
[11] *Ibid.*, 615.   [12] *Offic. Rec.*, 1 ser., XIX, pt. 1, 70–71.

burst out: "Will you pardon me for asking what the horses of your army have done since the battle of Antietam that fatigues anything?" [13] A few days later [14] the President admitted "something of impatience" in his despatch and assured McClellan of his deep regret if he had done him any injustice. Self control was becoming difficult. With momentous decisions in the balance nerves were frayed, tempers were rising, and trivial misunderstandings were in danger of producing ominous results.

Beginning on October 26 McClellan did cross the Potomac; a few days later his army was "massed near Warrenton, ready to act in any required direction, perfectly in hand, and in admirable condition and spirits." [15] He was now planning and expecting another battle. He was confident and ready. Then came the abrupt final blow against him. On November 7 General Buckingham [16] came by special train from Washington and turned up at Burnside's camp. Suspecting the purpose of this visit, McClellan kept his own counsel. Late at night, sitting alone in his tent writing to his wife, he heard a rap on his tent pole. Burnside and Buckingham then entered bearing an order "By direction of the President" relieving him of command of the Army of the Potomac and putting Burnside in his place.[17] There was immense resentment among soldiers and officers, so intense that many were in favor of McClellan's "refusing to obey the order, and of marching upon Washington to take possession of the government." [18] It was to quiet this restless feeling, and in compliance with Burnside's request, that McClellan remained with the army until November 10; then, with feelings beyond description and with "thousands of brave men . . . shedding tears like children," [19] he uncomplainingly turned his command over to Burnside and took his departure not only from the Army of the Potomac, but from active military service. Anger at his removal, felt keenly among raw recruits who had become

[13] *Works*, VIII, 67 (Oct. 24 [25?], 1862).   [14] *Ibid.*, VIII, 69 (Oct. 27, 1862).
[15] *McClellan's Own Story*, 648.
[16] Brigadier General C. P. Buckingham, "confidential assistant adjutant-general to the Secretary of War." *Battles and Leaders of the Civil War*, III, 104.
[17] In Lincoln's order that McClellan be relieved and that Burnside take the command, he included the statement that Halleck was authorized to issue an order to that effect; on the basis of this several war department orders were issued, all these under date of November 5, 1862. It was not until November 7, however, that these orders went into effect. *Offic. Rec.*, 1 ser., XIX, pt. 2, 545 ff.
[18] *McClellan's Own Story*, 652.   [19] *Ibid.*

veterans in his ranks, would have deepened into more bitter anguish of heart if these men had foreseen the sequel.

IV

The unhorsing of McClellan, with its disheartening of the Union army and its heightening of Confederate chances, was the result of a complex situation in which politician interference, congressional meddling, radical intrigue, amateurism, personal jealousy, McClellan's inattention to matters of tact, and a calculated campaign of misrepresentation were among the controlling factors. So far as the removal was Lincoln's responsibility it was an act of a buffeted President in whose mind there were enough doubts of McClellan's usefulness to give weight to heavy and unremitting attacks of a sort which any President would have found it hard to resist. Lincoln sometimes made mistakes, and it may be seriously questioned whether he had in military matters that unerring sureness of control which some of his eulogists claim. In McClellan's behalf it may be said that at least four serious errors were committed by authorities in Washington: (1) withholding McDowell's corps as well as other troops, and in a word giving less than its proper attention to the campaign against Richmond, while keeping forces ineffectively immobilized elsewhere; (2) relieving the pressure on Lee and inviting Union disaster by ordering withdrawal from the Peninsula; [1] (3) taking the army out of McClellan's hands and intrusting it to Pope, thus incurring defeat at Second Manassas; (4) finally removing McClellan when he was set with a reconditioned army for advance against Lee in November 1862, and substituting the incompetent Burnside.

Two cabinet men, Chase and Stanton, played important parts in McClellan's undoing. Wearing "two faces," [2] Stanton had professed friendship to McClellan, while intriguing to destroy him. In a long letter to Rev. H. Dyer, Stanton represented himself as the "sincere and devoted friend" of McClellan and justified his course toward him.[3] On July 5, 1862, Stanton wrote to the general: "Be assured you shall have the support of this department . . . ." [4] Three days later Mc-

---

[1] "The recall of the army from the vicinity of Richmond I thought wrong, ... But in this Stanton had a purpose . . . ." Welles, *Diary*, I, 113.

[2] Chase, *Diary (Annual Report*, Amer. Hist. Assoc., 1902, pt. II), 105.

[3] May 18, 1862, Stanton MSS., no. 51407–13.   [4] *McClellan's Own Story*, 475–476.

Clellan, smarting under the withholding of troops in his time of dire need, wrote a bluntly candid letter to Stanton mentioning the secretary's "deeply offensive" acts and "bitter personal prejudice" toward him, but accepting the assurance of friendship.[5] Despite his professions there is abundant evidence that Stanton talked McClellan down, intrigued against him, and actively sought his removal.[6]

With more of forthright honesty, Chase worked as persistently to the same end. He and Stanton concocted a paper denouncing McClellan and demanding his removal.[7] With this as a round robin, bearing, as they hoped, the signature of cabinet members, they proposed to put the matter up to Lincoln in such a way as to make it extremely difficult for him to refuse to act. When Chase circulated the paper it was signed by himself and Stanton, and also by Smith and Bates. Blair disapproved of it, while Welles thought the whole procedure underhand, factious, and disrespectful toward the President. Seward, who blithely dodged such controversies, was conveniently out of town. The plan was dropped and the paper not presented.

When little groups would meet there would be secret confabulations about McClellan. On the night of Pope's defeat (August 31) Caleb Smith, Stanton, and Welles had such a chat at the war department. Stanton held forth at great length recounting the whole history of McClellan, with emphasis upon his delay, the enemy's wooden guns, et cetera, all of which led up to a renewal of the demand that Welles join in the move to "get rid of him."[8] Welles expressed dislike of this "manner of proceeding" as being discourteous to the President. Then, as he records, "Stanton said, with some excitement, he knew of no particular obligations he was under to the President, who had called him to a difficult position and imposed upon him labors . . . which no man could carry, and which were greatly increased by fastening upon him a commander who was constantly striving to embarrass him in his administration of the Department. He could not and would not submit to a continuance of this state of things."[9] On further reflection Welles was yet more confirmed in his view that this method of

---

[5] McClellan MSS., July 8, 1862.

[6] Welles, *Diary*, I, 97, 104, 118–119; Browning, *Diary*, I, 538–539. In the interest of condensation further material on this matter in the writer's possession is omitted.

[7] For Welles's account of this intrigue by Chase and Stanton to force McClellan's removal, see his *Diary*, I, 93 ff. (Aug. 31, 1862).

[8] Welles, *Diary*, I, 95 ff.   [9] *Ibid.*, 98.

"conspiring" to control the President was "offensive." Stanton he characterized as "mad . . . and determined to destroy McClellan," and Chase as "credulous, and sometimes the victim of intrigue." [10] Chase's design, said Welles, was "to tell the President that the Administration must be broken up, or McC. dismissed." [11]

Mere removal was not the only object. Denouncing McClellan as a traitor, these men wanted to "disgrace" him.[12] So sorely was McClellan tried by Stanton's interference that, unwisely but with much truth, he wrote to him after Gaines's Mill: ". . . a few thousand more men would have changed this battle from a defeat to a victory. . . . If I save this army now, I tell you plainly that I owe no thanks to you or to any other persons in Washington. You have done your best to sacrifice this army." [13]

V

In the diary of John Hay under date of September 25, 1864, there occurs a remarkable passage concerning McClellan. Talking with Hay, Lincoln is said to have mentioned a "story" told him by J. Gregory Smith, governor of Vermont and brother of General William Farrar ("Baldy") Smith. According to this story the Democratic politician Fernando Wood, visiting McClellan's camp on the Peninsula, had urged him to become presidential candidate against Lincoln. McClellan, so the tale continued, had written a letter of acceptance, "Baldy" had protested that it looked "like treason," and McClellan had destroyed the letter in "Baldy's" presence. In this letter he had advocated such a method of conducting the war as would assure the people of the South that their rights were not endangered. Again, so the story went, after Antietam McClellan told "Baldy" that the same men had renewed the proposition, and that he had this time acceded, whereupon Smith at once applied for transference from McClellan's army.

It is to be noted that this story was used by Thurlow Weed to ruin McClellan in the presidential campaign of 1864.[1] The tale is very indirect; it comes from General Smith to Governor Smith, then to Lincoln, and through John Hay to the reader. Whatever may have

---

10 *Ibid.*, 101.   11 *Ibid.*, 102.   12 *Ibid.*   13 *McClellan's Own Story*, 425.
1 Dennett, *Lincoln . . . in the Diaries . . . of John Hay*, 217–218.

passed between Fernando Wood and the general, there was nothing in McClellan's actual conduct which showed anything like treachery against the Union or any deep-laid intrigue against Lincoln. What McClellan did as a candidate for the presidency, duly chosen by one of America's historic parties, was done nearly two years after his dismissal from command; it constitutes a separate and an honorable story. According to the very terms of "Baldy" Smith's narrative as indirectly transmitted, it was McClellan himself who told Smith whatever he knew about the whole episode. If McClellan had been plotting anything dark and disreputable after Antietam he would hardly have revealed it to the New England conscience of William Farrar Smith. In its implications of dishonorable intrigue on McClellan's part, the story, which Lincoln repeated to Hay without vouching for its authenticity, lacks that element of directness and corroboration which the realistic historian demands. So far as it bears upon Democratic efforts to use McClellan and upon the general's preference for a war that would not unduly invade the private rights of the Southern people, it offers nothing startling.

When the drive against McClellan was at its keenest in early September Lincoln resisted it, saying with emphasis: "I must have McClellan to reorganize the army and bring it out of chaos," adding "McClellan has the army with him." [2] Two months later he dismissed him. In trying to answer why he did so one is impressed with a growing impatience on Lincoln's part in the post-Antietam phase. After Antietam, said Lincoln in reminiscent mood in 1864, he had tried repeatedly to induce McClellan to move. There were nineteen days of delay before he began to cross the Potomac, nine further days before he crossed, then still further halting on what Lincoln called "pretexts." "I began to fear [said Lincoln as quoted by John Hay] he was playing false—that he did not want to hurt the enemy. I saw how he could intercept the enemy on the way to Richmond. I determined to make that the test. If he let them get away I would remove him. He did so & I relieved him.[3] Looking back from this reminiscence to the event, it will be remembered that there were in the spring and summer of 1862 furious accusations as to McClellan's alleged disloyalty, that the fabrication and spreading of such rumors was the deliberate business

[2] Welles, *Diary*, I, 113.
[3] Dennett, *Lincoln . . . in the Diaries . . . of John Hay*, 218–219.

of the war committee, that many weeks of such attacks had caused no Lincoln-McClellan break, and that some of the radicals considered it treasonable to advocate even so much as the preservation of Southern rights, which Congress was under pledge to recognize. While the smirching and whispering campaign against McClellan had raged in the spring of 1862 Lincoln had been unmoved by it,[4] though on one occasion, as O. H. Browning records, Stanton gave the President a long account of rumors which made it appear that McClellan, as an alleged member of the Knights of the Golden Circle, would "do nothing against the rebels" inconsistent with his obligations to that order.[5] McClellan's post-Antietam delay is explainable on military grounds, and it is somewhat curious to find Lincoln making army "delay" the basis for a suspicion that the general was "playing false," and then appointing Burnside, whose slowness had been recently demonstrated at Antietam and who waited five more weeks before making his disastrous and unsuccessful stroke. Taking this whole muddling period of 1862, the delay had resulted from what had been done at Washington over McClellan's head.

Knowing that Lincoln had thus referred to "playing false," Nicolay and Hay, bitter as they were against McClellan, took no stock in the accusation of treachery.[6] Against that charge, whatever may have been his defects otherwise, McClellan stands acquitted. Though his full vindication cannot be given in these pages, his record stands up in other respects. On the one hand, his soldiers adored and trusted him; on the other hand his opponents considered him a formidable antagonist. To give evidence that the soldiers wanted McClellan and followed him gladly would be to select from an abundant store of source material. General Cox, whose reminiscences contain many a severe criticism of McClellan, reports that in the pre-Antietam phase, when he was restored to command, the cheers of the soldiers "were given with wild delight."[7] In the anxious days before Gettysburg a soldier

---

[4] "I asked him [Lincoln] if he still had confidence in McClellands fidelity. He assured me he had, and that he had never had any reason to doubt it." Browning, *Diary*, I, 537.

[5] *Ibid.*, I, 538. According to Browning, Stanton told Lincoln he did not believe these imputations of disloyalty, but after they had parted from the President he told Browning virtually the opposite. For the hollowness of the charges of treason against McClellan (*apropos* of the K. G. C. and otherwise) and for their being disbelieved even by the commander's more intelligent critics—e. g., Bates—see *ibid.*, I, 538–539 n. See also Bates, *Diary*, 423 (Oct. 28, 1864).

[6] See above, p. 68.   [7] Cox, *Military Reminiscences*, I, 245.

in the Army of the Potomac wrote: "You . . . ask whom do they want to lead them? I answer the universal clamor is give us McClellan. . . . There is not a day but that you hear cheers for 'Little Mac' in the various camps in this command . . . ." [8] Friends of Senator Browning, having visited the army in January 1863, reported "that the soldiers are unanimous . . . for the return of Genl McClellan, believing that he is the only man competent for the command." [9] For a foe's appraisal one can point to a quoted statement in 1863 by a daughter of General Lee that "Genl. McClellan was the only Genl. Father dreaded." [10] Lee's biographer leaves no doubt on this subject. He writes:

"Who was the ablest Federal general he had opposed? He [Lee] did not hesitate . . . for the answer. 'McClellan, by all odds,' he said emphatically." [11]

[8] J. R. Blinn to R. W. Thompson, Thoroughfare Gap, Va., Army of the Potomac, June 24, 1863, MS., Lincoln National Life Foundation, Fort Wayne, Ind.

[9] Browning, *Diary*, I, 621. See also *ibid.*, I, 601, 619, for strong expressions of soldier confidence in McClellan.

[10] Quoted in a letter to McClellan signed "A Friend," Washington, Mar. 28, 1863 McClellan MSS. (no. 18141).

[11] Freeman, *Lee*, IV, 475.

CHAPTER XXI

A BLUEPRINT FOR FREEDOM

I

WHEN Lincoln said that he claimed not to have controlled events and confessed that events had controlled him,[1] his words might have fitted many episodes and policies of his presidency, but at the moment he was referring to the problem of the Negro slave. Lincoln never claimed that his emancipation proclamation was a matter of long-view planning, nor that it was a carefully calculated program, nor even that it was motivated by a moral judgment against slavery. Lincoln did in fact have a major plan of liberation, but it was not that of the proclamation, nor was it ever put into effect. Lincoln also had a strong moral judgment against slavery. Such a judgment was bred in the bone, for he said "I am naturally antislavery. If slavery is not wrong, nothing is wrong. I cannot remember when I did not so think and feel . . . ." Moral judgments of a leader, however, may be one thing, and his authorizations in office quite a different thing. John Quincy Adams, though antislavery in sentiment, had to bargain and argue for slave interests while secretary of state of the United States. It is sometimes forgotten that Lincoln was elected and inaugurated President of a slaveholding nation in 1861, and that, to use his own words, he did not understand "that the Presidency conferred . . . an unrestricted right to act officially upon . . . [his] judgment and feeling." It was his view that in civil administration his oath forbade him "to practically indulge . . . [his] abstract judgment on the moral question of slavery." [2]

Nor was slavery considered the main issue when trouble broke and disunion loomed. At the outset of Lincoln's administration the New

---

[1] *Works*, X, 68 (April 4, 1864).   [2] *Ibid.*, X, 65 (April 4, 1864).

York *Times* remarked: "The question which we have to meet *is precisely what it would be if there were not a negro slave on American soil.*" [3] Though the slavery question could not be so blithely muted, the statement of the *Times* correctly interpreted the attitude of the United States government when it was written (April 6, 1861); it also squared with a policy that persisted long after the abrupt shift from war to peace might have brought reorientation and discovery of new powers.

True to the platform of his party and to his previous declarations, Lincoln disclaimed in his first inaugural address (March 4, 1861) any "purpose, directly or indirectly, to interfere with the institution of slavery in the States where it exists." The lack of such official purpose was not all; he further declared that he had "no lawful right . . . and . . . no inclination to do so." [4] This was not a recanting of his "moral judgment" against slavery; it was a matter of using presidential authority. In making the declaration emphatic he sought to strip the slavery issue of its nuisance value, or rather of its explosive menace; he meant to assure the people of the South that their "property, peace, and security" were not "in any wise endangered by the now incoming administration."

Lincoln's next statement, addressed to the slaveholding section, was an assurance not merely of avoiding interference with the institutions of the dissatisfied states, but of extending "protection . . . consistently with the Constitution and the laws . . . as cheerfully to one section as to another." [5] Lincoln was no abolitionist President. According to an interpretation from which neither he nor the United States government ever swerved, he was from March 1861 the constitutional President of the whole country: deep South, upper South, border, and North. Nor did he consider himself merely President of the Republican party. As he faced the multitudes that honored or curiously viewed him on his way to Washington, he was well aware that the same honors would have been given to Douglas, or Bell, or Breckinridge, had one of these men been "constitutionally elected President of the United States."

The war came, Bull Run was fought and lost, and Congress echoed

---

[3] New York *Times*, editorial, April 6, 1861, p. 4, c. 2.
[4] *Works*, VI, 170. This passage was quoted from an earlier speech.
[5] Lincoln was choosing his words with meticulous care in this inaugural; he did not say "to one section as to *the* other." *Ibid.*, VI, 171.

Lincoln's disclaimer. On July 22, 1861, the House of Representatives resolved:

> That the . . . war has been forced . . . by the disunionists of the southern States, now in arms against the . . . Government . . . ; that . . . Congress, banishing . . . passion or resentment, will recollect only its duty to the whole country; that this war is not waged . . . for . . . conquest or subjugation, or purpose of overthrowing or interfering with the . . . established institutions of those States, but to . . . maintain . . . the Constitution, and to preserve the Union with all the . . . rights of the . . . States unimpaired; and that as soon as these objects are accomplished the war ought to cease.[6]

On July 25 the Senate passed a similar but more ably worded resolution sponsored by the senator from Tennessee, Andrew Johnson. In the House there were only two negative votes, in the Senate only five; seldom in the whole period of Lincoln could one find such an approach to unanimity.[7] Yet the unanimity was misleading. The vote was complex in that the resolution was a kind of catch-all. It was so worded as to contain, among other elements, an indictment of war guilt directed against the South (phrased as a statement of fact), a declaration for maintaining the old Union, and a renunciation of any purpose to subjugate the Southern states or interfere with their domestic institutions. It was essentially a moderate declaration of war aims. Radical extremists objected in debate because they felt that "traitors" ought to be subdued; at the opposite extreme such a man as Breckinridge objected because he thought that the purpose was in fact subjugation, and because he could not accept the imputation of Southern war guilt. A significant interpretation of what Congress was doing was given by Senator Willey of "Western Virginia" [8]

---

[6] *Cong. Globe*, 37 Cong., 1 sess., 222.

[7] The House voted twice on the resolution. There was a vote of 121 to 2 on the earlier part (approximately the first third), and a vote of 117 to 2 on the remainder (*ibid.*, 223). In the Senate the vote was 30 to 5 (*ibid.*, 265). The two who voted nay in the House, Henry C. Burnett of Kentucky and John W. Reid of Missouri, were both expelled in December 1861. The five who voted nay in the Senate were Lazarus W. Powell and John C. Breckinridge of Kentucky, Trusten Polk and Waldo P. Johnson of Missouri, and Lyman Trumbull of Illinois. Polk, Johnson, and Breckinridge were later expelled. The votes of certain prominent men are conspicuous by their absence—e. g., those of Thaddeus Stevens in the House and Charles Sumner in the Senate. It is safe to say that both these men dissented from the resolution. The affirmative votes of Senators Wade of Ohio and Chandler of Michigan seem hardly sincere except as to fastening war guilt upon the South.

[8] "Mr. Willey, of Western Virginia, stated [in the Senate] the views of the people of

who favored the resolution in order to quiet the fears of his own people that they would have to pass under the yoke, and who warned that if the war were directed against local institutions, "every loyal arm on the soil of the Old Dominion . . . [would] be . . . paralyzed." [9] On this point Senator Hale of New Hampshire assured him that the government had no more constitutional right to strike at slavery in the South than to deal with Russian serfs or English laborers.[10]

These disclaimers by President and Congress marked a stage in a rapidly shifting drama. It will not do to say that the President's disclaimer was insincere; [11] his inaugural assurance to the South was not an announcement of what might happen in case of a long civil war which he wished to avert. When ultimately Lincoln acted in the matter of slavery it was under circumstances vastly different from those of March 1861 and his action was not directed against areas adhering to the Union. As for Congress, there were indications that its members in July of 1861 were taking panicky counsel of their fears on the morrow of defeat; the resolution of that month was not reaffirmed when the question was reopened and put to vote in December 1861.[12]

II

The truth was that affairs could not remain static; the very fact of war was creating complications, posing slavery questions that could not be evaded, forcing piecemeal action, and presenting hard dilemmas. Slavery was, in Cleveland's famous words, a condition, not a theory. A resolution in Congress was one

---

the Old Dominion . . . ." (*Annual Cyclopaedia*, 1861, 242). In 1861 there was inexactness in referring to the governmental situation in Virginia (see above, pp. 11–14). The "reorganized" legislature at Wheeling, purporting to act as the legislature for all Virginia, had, in a special session of July 1861, chosen Waitman T. Willey and John S. Carlile as United States senators from Virginia (at a time when West Virginia had not yet been formed), to take the places of James M. Mason and R. M. T. Hunter, adherents of the Confederacy, whose seats had been declared vacant. *Journal of the House of Delegates of Virginia* (extra session commencing July 1, 1861, Wheeling), 32; *Journal of the Senate* (same session), 24. Thus, in Wheeling and Washington parlance Mr. Willey was United States senator from Virginia.

[9] *Cong. Globe*, 37 Cong., 1 sess., 259.   [10] *Ibid.*, 260.   [11] See below, p. 163.
[12] On December 4, 1861, the House refused to reaffirm the resolution by a vote of 65 to 71. *Cong. Globe*, 37 Cong., 2 sess., 15.

thing, a group of fugitive slaves fleeing enemy service quite another. The generalized question of emancipation might be deferred, but Negroes crowding into Union camps, though uninvited, could hardly be regarded as non-existent. A government conducting war with a slaveholding power over a vast and loosely held line could expect incidents aplenty involving fugitive slaves, and it was in this connection that some of the earliest issues concerning Negroes had to be met. In May 1861 General B. F. Butler, commanding at Fort Monroe, took a step in a small matter which opened up a wide problem when he detained three slaves who had appeared on his picket line. Acting on information that Negroes in the neighborhood were "employed in the erection of batteries and other works by the rebels," [1] Butler not only refused to return them but used their services, keeping an account of their labor and cost of maintenance for future settlement. As for the fugitive slave act, he treated that as applying only among states of the American Union, which would exclude Virginia by her own definition,[2] though he was ready to restore the Negroes if their owner would take oath to obey the laws of the United States.

As the number of such fugitives increased by hundreds, with whole families seeking protection, Butler dealt with the matter as a military problem, keeping and employing the slaves because of their enforced hostile service against the United States, and holding the women and children for "humanitarian" reasons.[3] His action was approved by the war department with the reservation that it was not to extend to interference with slavery as a state institution.[4] As with everything that Butler did, the incident acquired a sententious publicity, and "contraband" [5] was lifted from the code of war to become a slang term applying to Negroes.

If these Negroes, whose seizure was assumed to be roughly analogous to the taking of contraband property, had not acquired a new status, it could at least be said that their unsought appearance within Union army lines tended to push forward the complex question of war policy toward slavery. Refusing the return of so-called property that had been put to military use by the enemy, authorities had to decide whether these persons were in truth being held as property, or, in

---

[1] B. F. Butler, *Private and Official Correspondence of B. F. Butler*, I, 106.
[2] *Ibid.*, I, 107.   [3] *Ibid.*, I, 112–113.   [4] *Ibid.*, I, 119.
[5] For the use of the word "contraband" see Moore, *Rebellion Record* (Docs.), II, 437; Randall, *Constitutional Problems Under Lincoln*, 354–356.

Butler's words, as men, women, and children, "free, manumitted, . . . never to be reclaimed." [6]

It was only slowly that a general policy on this matter was worked out. In the earlier stages some generals acted as Butler did, while others, such as Williams at Baton Rouge and Halleck in Missouri,[7] refused to permit fugitive slaves to enter army camps or join a marching force. In some cases, to implement the exclusion order, fugitives were restored to their masters.[8] When, because of this, there arose the abolitionist outcry that the army was being employed as slave catchers, the subject became the theme of spirited debate in Congress. Exclusion of Negroes from Union lines was defended as a matter of withholding information from the enemy, and the return of those who escaped from slavery and entered such lines was held to be necessary in order to make exclusion effective. In reply it was remarked that generals arresting slaves and delivering them back to their masters ought to be stripped of their epaulets. Denunciation shifted from commanders to the President when it was charged that exclusion of refugees with the penalty of arrest and return to slavery was the policy of the Lincoln administration. At this point Kellogg of Illinois, speaking as one conversant with the purposes of the administration, denied the accusation and was stoutly joined in the denial by Owen Lovejoy, also of Lincoln's state.[9]

To remove what was regarded as the slave-catching stigma, Congress prohibited the use of the armed forces for the restoration of escaping slaves (March 13, 1862).[10] This was followed by a law (July 17, 1862) which was definitely a measure of emancipation; it declared that slaves whose owners were hostile to the United States, finding their way within Union lines, were free.[11] Only to a loyal owner could slaves be returned. Much later in the war the fugitive slave acts (the old measure of 1793 and the drastic law of 1850) were repealed.[12]

It was not so much that policy was shaping events. Events were shaping policy. The force of circumstances and the position of armies were having their emancipating effect. "We have entered Virginia," wrote Seward, "and already five thousand slaves, emancipated simply

[6] Moore, *Rebellion Record* (Docs.), II, 438.   [7] *Annual Cyclopaedia*, 1862, 754.
[8] *Ibid.*, 754–755.   [9] The debate is condensed in *ibid.*, 279 ff.
[10] *U. S. Stat. at Large*, XII, 354.   [11] *Ibid.*, XII, 591.
[12] *Ibid.*, act of June 28, 1864, XIII, 211.

by the appearance of our forces, are upon the hands of the Federal government there. We have landed upon the coast of South Carolina, and already nine thousand . . . hang upon our camps. Although the war has not been waged against slavery, yet the army acts . . . as an emancipating crusade. To proclaim the crusade is unnecessary, ..." [13] The New York *Herald* remarked that military and legislative action touching slavery had been "controlled by circumstances," [14] while the London *News* declared: "It has been understood . . . that this negro question was to be left *an open question . . . in order that events might decide* where rulars [*sic*] could not agree." [15]

III

On many a day in the long session of 1861–62 the grave and reverend in House and Senate directed their verbal fireworks as well as their laborious committee deliberations to this or that aspect of slavery. Under the head of confiscation, for instance, two emancipatory acts were passed. Under the first measure (the mild confiscation act of August 6, 1861) [1] slaves put to military or naval use against the United States were declared forfeit by a legalistic phrasing which did not declare them free. In the sweeping confiscation act of 1862 (July 17) the lawmakers went much farther; on the broad principle of punishing traitors and rebels, Congress enacted that slaves of traitors should be "declared and made free," and that rebel-owned [2] slaves were to be "forever free of their servitude, and not again held as slaves." [3]

There were other bits of emancipating legislation by Congress. If an enemy-owned slave rendered military service to the United States, he and his family (if they were enemy-owned) were declared free. [4] After national conscription had been adopted, drafted slaves as well

---

[13] Seward to Charles Francis Adams, Feb. 17, 1862, MSS., Dept. of State (Great Britain: Instructions, vol. 18, no. 187), Nat. Archives.

[14] Jan. 24, 1862, p. 1, c. 1.

[15] London *News*, Dec. 21, 1861, as copied in New York *Herald*, Jan. 4, 1862, p. 2, c. 2.

[1] *U. S. Stat. at Large*, XII, 319.

[2] Legally there seemed to be a distinction between traitors and those who engaged in or aided rebellion. Mere residence in what was called "rebel" territory, however, made one a "rebel." The subject is heavily encrusted with legalistic pronouncements, though in practical execution such legislation meant little. Randall, *Constitutional Problems Under Lincoln*, 358; *The Civil War and Reconstruction*, 482 and n.

[3] *U. S. Stat. at Large*, XII, 589–592.   [4] Militia Act of July 17, 1862, *ibid.*, XII, 599.

as colored volunteers were declared free, with compensation to loyal owners.[5]

Out-and-out emancipation by Congress, with no *if's* and *and's* about confiscation or enemy ownership or territorial restrictions, was urged by such men as Ashley [6] and Bingham of the House of Representatives, both from Ohio. "Pass your laws liberating the 4,000,000 slaves held by the rebels," said Bingham, ". . . and let the oppressed go free . . . . Do you say this is fanaticism? Do you say God was a fanatic when He commanded it, . . . ?" [7] If this were done, Steele of New York predicted that "this war would become one of extermination and death all over the country," [8] while Wadsworth of Kentucky declared that from the enactment of emancipation "the lines of the rebellion would advance; . . . its original pretense would be justified as truth." "Millions . . . now faithful," added Wadsworth, ". . . with one heart would join the foe. That instant . . . loyal men . . . from the free States . . . who have not gone into the war . . . to accomplish the Africanization of our society, will disband." [9]

Though support was not forthcoming for universal emancipation, Congress did abolish the institution in the District of Columbia and in the territories. In the debate on the District bill Senator Hale of New Hampshire deplored the fact that emancipation was rarely discussed as a measure of fundamental right or Christian humanity, but only in terms of the price of sugar or some such matter. Not confining itself, however, to economics, the discursive debate rambled among such topics as Haiti, Santo Domingo, Liberia, the torrid zone, the Caucasian race, the poet's dream, the Creator's design, the case of the *Antelope*,[10] the Chicago platform, the Constitution, the Supreme Court, habeas corpus, trial by jury, freedom of conscience, due proc-

---

[5] *Ibid.*, act of Feb. 24, 1864, XIII, 11.

[6] "The defeat of Mr. Ashley's Universal Emancipation bill to-day, under the cloak of providing provisional governments for the Territory recovered from the rebels, was a salutary lesson to the radicals. . . . This vote [to lay the bill on the table] was a . . . Bull Run . . . to the ultra faction, and has tamed them down considerably." New York *Herald*, March 13, 1862, p. 1, c. 1.

[7] *Cong. Globe*, 37 Cong., 2 sess., 348.   [8] *Ibid.*, 404.   [9] *Ibid.*, 355–356.

[10] In the case of the *Antelope* (1825) Chief Justice Marshall held that a foreign slave-trading ship, captured by an American warship in time of peace, should be restored. Legality of the capture was construed as depending upon the law of the country to which the vessel belonged. J. B. Moore, *Digest of International Law*, II, 917–918.

ess, liberty of the press, the nation's pledged word, the purpose of the war, social life at the capital, idolatry, cannibalism, and the dignity of the State of Maryland.[11] Through the oratorical maze Congress somehow focused upon the difficult problem, not only of *whether* to abolish, but *how* to abolish slavery in the capital. Of necessity the President's influence was important. There was doubt whether Lincoln would sign the District bill; [12] he was reported as opposing such a measure unless certain conditions were met. He wanted Maryland's consent, and insisted upon compensation to slaveholders and also upon adequate provision for removal and colonization of liberated blacks.[13] Radicals were accused of rushing the bill through so as to put the President in the uncomfortable dilemma of vetoing it or "signing it in direct opposition to all his hitherto expressed views on the subject." [14] Finally the bill was passed, incorporating Lincoln's provisions for colonization and compensation,[15] and the President signed it after holding it two days. Cross currents beating upon the harassed President were perfectly reflected in the conflicting reactions to his approval of this controversial bill. On the one hand the New York *Herald* found his signature disappointing to conservative men in Congress and depressing in its effect upon border-state feeling.[16] On the other hand Sumner "regretted that the Prest held the Bill back for two days—making himself as I told him, for the time being, the largest slaveholder in the country." [17] The *Herald,* having seriously doubted the expediency of the bill, looked on the matter in a different light when Lincoln appointed commissioners to administer the act, seeing in the appointments an honest intention to "deal fairly" with slaveowners.[18]

Some of those slaveholders, however, with their noisy supporters, were making it difficult for anyone in office to deal favorably with them. This was most evident in the capital city itself where there occurred in 1862 an amazing *opera bouffe* war between conflicting

---

[11] The debate is condensed in *Annual Cyclopaedia,* 1862, 333–344.

[12] New York *Herald,* April 15, 1862, p. 10, c. 3.

[13] *Ibid.,* April 6, 1862, p. 4, c. 6.   [14] *Ibid.*

[15] "I am gratified that the two principles of compensation and colonization are both recognized and practically applied in the act." Lincoln in message to Congress, April 16, 1862. *Works,* VII, 146–147.

[16] New York *Herald,* April 17, 1862, p. 10, c. 1.

[17] Sumner to Andrew, Senate Chamber, April 22, 1862, Andrew MSS., 16:41; see also Sumner, *Works,* VI, 393.

[18] New York *Herald,* April 17, 1862, p. 10, c. 1.

authorities. The combination of martial law, inefficient local government, and unsettled procedures offered the setting for this melodrama; its cast included Maryland slaveholders of doubtful loyalty, a pro-slavery circuit court in the District, a swashbuckler of a Federal marshal (Ward H. Lamon) whose hatred of abolitionists coexisted with a much-advertised intimacy with Lincoln, bands of rowdies seeking deviltry for its own sake, and on the other side a vigorous anti-slavery general, James S. Wadsworth, in command of United States troops as military governor of the District. It was a degrading spectacle, unworthy of a controlled democracy. Slaves pouring from Maryland into the District constituted a daily annoyance, and the laws on the subject were not clear. Slaveowners claimed that the fugitive slave law of 1850 applied to the District, but this was stoutly denied, and the question was so unsettled that Governor Bradford of Maryland wrote to Attorney General Bates to know where the law officers of the government stood. The governor wanted to know whether it was true that the United States government had forbidden the execution of warrants for the arrest of these alleged escaping slaves, not omitting to state that slaveowners and politicians were excited about it.[19] As for the Attorney General, he could give little satisfaction; he was himself struggling through a maze of puzzles concerning wartime legal aspects of the fugitive slave question.[20]

Appealing to the fugitive-slave law for the seizure and arrest of Negroes, many of whom were in fact free men kidnapped by rowdies, Marshal Lamon, with the support of the police and the circuit court, filled the jails of Washington with these unfortunates. At one point in the shifting drama Wadsworth's soldiers arrested the jailer, released the marshal's dark prisoners, and even seized some of his force as kidnappers. There followed spirited work on Lamon's part, as when his merry men turned out at two in the morning and regained the jail. When, late in 1862, Wadsworth was transferred from the military governorship of the District to the Army of the Potomac under Burnside, the issue was still unsettled. It disappeared only with the repeal of the fugitive-slave laws in 1864 and the progress of emancipation.[21]

---

[19] A. W. Bradford to Edward Bates, May 9, 1862, MSS., Attorney General's Office, Nat. Archives.

[20] Bates, *Diary,* 209–211.

[21] On this Wadsworth-Lamon imbroglio see Henry Greenleaf Pearson, *James S. Wadsworth of Geneseo,* 130–140.

Two months after having provided emancipation in the District, Congress abolished slavery in territories of the United States then existing or thereafter to be formed or acquired.[22] In this instance, as in the District case, Congress passed and Lincoln signed a bill which, by ruling law according to Supreme Court interpretation, was unconstitutional. This fact, as well as the legal extinction of that explosive territorial situation which had produced such prodigious prewar agitation, was allowed to pass over with little comment. Compensation to slaveholders was not included in the territorial bill, though there seems no logical reason why it should have been omitted there while applied in the District. Owing to the fewness of slaves the expense would have been negligible. To administer compensation in the District an evaluating commission was set up, the sum of one million dollars being appropriated with the proviso that the total sum paid out should not add up to more than $300 per slave.[23]

In this period several important steps looking toward Negro freedom were taken by the Lincoln government in the diplomatic field. Administrations prior to Lincoln's had avoided recognition of the Negro republics of Haiti and Liberia, but Lincoln was "unable to discern" any good reason why this recognition should be withheld.[24] Relations were established with the sanction of Congress, and negotiations were promptly instituted for treaties with these countries, with consequent commercial advantages.[25] Heretofore the United States had given unsatisfactory support to enlightened efforts of Great Britain to set up an international program for suppressing the slave trade. Certain limited steps had been taken at Washington in the 1840's toward the eradication of a practice which civilized nations were treating as piracy, but ships illegally flying the American flag, as well as American vessels, continued to engage in the hateful traffic.[26] It was therefore an important step when, in May 1862, a treaty was completed between the United States and England by which the two nations agreed to coöperate in an effective manner for suppressing the trade.[27] Though importation of slaves into the United States had been punishable by death under national law since 1820, the first

---

[22] Act of June 19, 1862, *U. S. Stat. at Large*, XII, 432.

[23] In 1860 census takers found 3185 slaves and 1229 slaveholders in the District of Columbia. *U. S. Census*, 1860, Agriculture, p. 246.

[24] *Works*, VII, 33 (Dec. 3, 1861). 　　　[25] *Ibid.*, VIII, 98 (Dec. 1, 1862).

[26] Randall, *Civil War and Reconstruction*, 44–46. 　　[27] *Ibid.*, 481.

enforcement of the law came in February 1862 when Nathaniel Gordon, captain of a slave ship, was executed in New York, having been denied presidential clemency. These details indicated that in its outlook on international problems the United States government was no longer conducting itself in the manner of a slave power.

IV

Viewing the increasing difficulties that emerged as liberating incidents inevitably arose out of the war, Lincoln seriously weighed the process of colonization. The idea was not new to him. While debating with Douglas he had shown an interest in Negro emigration, and in his first annual message to Congress (December 1861) he had advised that slaves presumably freed by the confiscation act of that year be colonized in some genial clime. If any of the states should adopt emancipation measures, Lincoln thought that their ex-slaves might be accepted by the United States in lieu of taxes—a rather curious idea—and that they might be included in a general colonizing scheme. He would also extend the process to those of the free colored who might desire a foreign home.[1]

With such preliminaries colonization came to be treated as an active policy, and Congress appropriated $100,000 for the purpose in the District emancipation act. This was later raised to a total of $600,000,[2] and in the second confiscation act the President was "authorized" to make arrangements for colonizing Negroes freed (on paper) by that enactment, again on a voluntary basis. This action by Congress may have been taken to assist in obtaining Lincoln's signature to a measure which he strongly disliked.

A curious scene in the White House in this period, and one which seems almost to have been forgotten, was a conference between the President and a committee of intelligent colored men who came by Lincoln's special request to confer regarding the departure of members of their race to Central America.[3] To one who thinks of the

---

[1] For these several suggestions see *Works*, VII, 49-50.

[2] By act of April 16, 1862 (the emancipation act for the District, *U. S. Stat. at Large*, XII, 378) Congress appropriated $100,000 for colonization. An additional $500,000 was appropriated by act of July 16, 1862 (*ibid.*, XII, 582).

[3] "The conference of the President, held last evening, at the Executive Mansion with . . . colored men in reference to . . . colonization . . . , is a noted . . . event. . . . He desires to see them . . . take their proper position as citizens in a separate

Emancipator in terms of abolitionist stereotypes the words of his remarkable address to this group, preserved in his published works,[4]
will come as something of a surprise. In this address Lincoln's thesis
was utterly different from the concepts of those to whom sudden and
complete abolition presented no obstacles in terms of post-liberation
adjustment. To Lincoln such adjustment, as well as the presence of
large numbers of Negroes long free, offered very serious difficulties,
and his words could have given little encouragement to his colored
auditors.

Whites and Negroes, he told them, are of different races. Your race,
he said, suffer greatly, and we of the white race suffer from your
presence. It affords a reason why we should be separated. Even "when
you cease to be slaves, you are yet far removed from being . . .
on an equality with the white race. . . . [O]n this broad continent
not a single man of your race is made the equal of a single man of
ours. . . . I cannot alter it if I would. It is a fact . . ." "But for
your race among us [said Lincoln] there could not be war, although
many men engaged on either side do not care for you one way or the
other. . . . It is better for us both . . . to be separated."

Continuing his unflattering advice, Lincoln told his dark friends
that there was an "unwillingness" on the part of whites to allow the
free colored to remain. He therefore appealed to intelligent free
colored men, as he could not appeal to the systematically oppressed, to
make sacrifices and endure hardships, as whites had done, for the sake
of a future day. Fearing that Liberia was too remote, he highly recom-
mended an area in Central America, mentioning its natural advantages, its nearness to the United States, its "very rich coal-mines,"
and its excellent ports on two great oceans. He was referring to
Chiriqui on the Panamanian isthmus; already Northern capitalists
were inquiring into the profits of a colonization scheme in that area.
Referring to the fact that men of the colored race had been "talked to"
concerning a speculation by gentlemen who had an "interest" in the
project, the President explained that "everybody you trade with
makes something," and that he would see to it that they would not be
wronged. As to success of the venture he wasn't sure. Having justified

---

Republic, and enjoy rights and privileges which the President tells them, they can
never receive in this country," Cincinnati *Daily Gazette*, August 20, 1862, p. 1, c. 1.
   4 *Works*, VIII, 1–9 (August 14, 1862).

the profit interest on the part of capitalists, Lincoln urged the Negro delegation to rally to the support of the project "not . . . for the present time, but . . . for the good of mankind . . . ." On this theme he burst into poetry:

> From age to age descends the lay
> To millions yet to be,
> Till far its echoes roll away
> Into eternity.

V

In favoring colonization Lincoln was promoting a scheme and a point of view violently opposed by nearly all abolitionists,[1] including notably Senator Sumner. Radical antislavery men were unready to admit that Negroes needed to be separated from whites, nor did they trouble themselves with practical consequences of emancipation. Garrison strongly opposed colonization. On the other hand there were Southerners who favored it, some of them paying from their own pockets to promote private emigration enterprises. This was not the only instance in which Lincoln was nearer to the Southern than to the average abolitionist viewpoint in regard to the Negro race.

Lincoln's efforts toward colonization would make a long story and a dismal one. He asked his cabinet for written advice, sought treaties with foreign nations,[2] and gave detailed attention to the two areas upon which actual efforts of the time were focusing. One of these was the Chiriqui location near Panama, a part of New Grenada (Colombia); the other was a Haitian island known as *Isle a' Vache*. Both ventures were abortive. The Chiriqui project was dropped when samples of the coal deposits failed in scientific tests. This disappointment of promising hopes [3] made it seem the more desirable to proceed

---

[1] There were a few exceptions. Governor Andrew favored colonization and Senator S. C. Pomeroy of Kansas became officially associated with the abortive attempt to establish a Negro colony in Central America. Cincinnati *Daily Gazette*, March 16, 1864, p. 3, c. 5; Browning, *Diary*, I, 577.

[2] Countries in the Western Hemisphere did not take avidly to these schemes. Diplomats from various Central and South American states remonstrated with Seward, urging that foreign colonies of this nature were not desired. Cincinnati *Daily Gazette*, August 29, 1862, p. 3, c. 3. For a rather lengthy comment on these treaties by the Attorney General, see Bates, *Diary*, 262–264.

[3] "The Chiriqui colonization scheme was discussed in a cabinet meeting today. . . . [I]t was . . . decided to abandon the whole scheme, ... It is understood, however,

with the Haitian experiment, and in an unguarded moment Lincoln became a party to a scheme promoted by one Bernard Kock, an alleged "business man" whom Edward Bates denounced as "an errant humbug" and "a charlatan adventurer." [4] In spite of Bates's denunciation, Lincoln and his secretary of the interior signed a contract with this Kock by which, at fifty dollars a head, five thousand Negroes were to be colonized. With government backing and predictions of colossal profits, Kock enlisted the financial support of certain New York capitalists, and the ill-fated Haitian venture was launched.

Over four hundred hapless Negroes were transported to the island at government expense, but the whole scheme, which, even if successful, could have been no more than "a tub to the whale," [5] collapsed from inadequate planning, want of essentials, poor housing, smallpox, unemployment, cupidity, Haitian opposition, and the strutting unpopularity of Kock. Midway in the venture Lincoln saw to it that the contract with Kock was canceled. When, on March 20, 1864, the government-chartered *Marcia C. Day* docked near Washington carrying back 368 of these colonists, about a hundred less than were sent, the Washington *Chronicle* reported the great joy of the returning survivors, while remarking upon "the folly of attempting to depopulate the country of its valuable labor." [6]

For Lincoln the idea died hard. This was partly because he considered it an important part of a comprehensive plan of emancipation, and it is interesting to note that Governor John A. Andrew of Massachusetts agreed with him. In February 1861 Andrew wrote: "If our . . . government would establish . . . a colony for the emancipated col'd people, . . . I think it wd. prove a blessing in a thousand ways, . . . would . . . help to . . . create a hereafter for the oppressed race, & would remove the prejudices of many . . . who now refuse to tolerate . . . liberty for the slaves. . . . I wish we might take some pains to prove that we are friends & not enemies to all classes of Southern society. A very strong anti-slavery man myself, I yet

---

that the President does not desire to have the matter abandoned . . . ." Cincinnati *Daily Gazette*, Aug. 30, 1862, p. 3, c. 3.

[4] Bates, *Diary*, 268.

[5] "As a tub to the whale, it may do to provide for voluntary colonization. But if Emancipation waits on colonization, that means eternal slavery . . . ." Alphonso Taft to S. P. Chase, Cincinnati, Ohio, Aug. 26, 1862, Chase MSS., Lib. of Cong.

[6] Washington *Chronicle*, Mar. 21, 1864, p. 2, c. 1. See also New York *Herald*, Mar. 22, 1864, p. 1, c. 2.

am conscious of only kind & fraternal feelings to our Southern people . . . ." [7]

Though colonization failed utterly as a solution,[8] so utterly that it is difficult to think of it as a serious undertaking, the motives of Lincoln in favoring it are worth remembering. These motives were much the same as those expressed by Governor Andrew. They did not, however, embrace the catch argument, as Lincoln called it, that the presence of the free colored would "injure and displace . . . white laborers." "Emancipation," he thought, "even without deportation, would probably enhance the wages of white labor, and very surely would not reduce them." Ex-slaves would do no more than their old proportion of the work to be done, and probably less. Having made his own rationalization to deal with the catch argument, Lincoln retained in December 1862 his strong interest in colonization, associating gradual emancipation with "deportation" and referring to a temporary adjustment after emancipation while awaiting the time when, for the colored people, "new homes . . . [could] be found . . . in congenial climes and with people of their own blood and race." [9]

VI

Where Lincoln gave thought to large-scale national planning in the matter of liberating the slaves, such thought was not embraced within the bounds of the emancipation proclamation. Speaking relatively and with a view to the President's main concept for solving the problem, it is correct to regard the proclamation as of minor importance. The famous edict was to Lincoln a war measure of limited scope, of doubtful legality, and of inadequate effect. In his reaching out for an adequate solution the President developed an elaborate blueprint for freedom in terms of gradual emancipation by voluntary action of

[7] John A. Andrew to Montgomery Blair, Feb. 23, 1861, Blair MSS.

[8] For these abortive colonization efforts, see W. L. Fleming, "Deportation and Colonization: An Attempted Solution of the Race Problem," in *Studies in Southern History . . . Inscribed to William Archibald Dunning,* 3–30; N. A. N. Cleven, "Some Plans for Colonizing Liberated Negro Slaves in Hispanic America," in *Journal of Negro History,* XI, 35–49. For the disappointing Liberian experiment, see E. L. Fox, *The American Colonization Society, 1817–1840 (Johns Hopkins Univ. Studies . . .* [etc.], series 37, no. 3).

[9] Lincoln's views as here condensed are found in his annual message to Congress, Dec. 1, 1862, *Works,* VIII, 126–128.

the slave states with Federal coöperation in two matters: foreign colonization of emancipated Negroes (already treated),[1] and compensation to slaveowners.

This blueprint was envisaged not merely with reference to the war, though its integration with a broad war policy was a vital factor; beyond the war the President's solution was projected into a peace-minded future with a view to the ultimate, statesmanlike elimination of an institution in which, as Lincoln felt, North and South had a common responsibility and a community of interest. Though the plan failed, a familiarity with it becomes necessary to an understanding of wartime currents and especially of Lincoln's manner of tackling a large problem. As one studies the President's pathetically earnest efforts to promote this "proposition," one is impressed with his conservatism, his sense of fair dealing, his lack of vindictiveness, his attention to legal adjustments, his respect for self-determination in government, his early vision of state-and-federal coöperation,[2] and his coördination of a domestic reform with the nation's paramount purpose to restore the Union and then to preserve it. The proposition is also significant as perhaps the major instance in which Lincoln tried manfully to enlist the support of Congress. On no other matter did he so far extend his presidential leadership in attempted legislation. The only other project of the period that compares with it is that of reconstruction, but in that case Lincoln did not rely upon congressional enactment of a presidentially sponsored measure.

Announced in a special message to Congress on March 6, 1862, and fully elaborated in his message of December 1 of that year, Lincoln's plan was unfolded as part of a grand concept of a large and growing people, a nation of untouched resources whose future, he hoped, would not be frustrated "by any political folly or mistake."[3]

---

[1] Correct sequences and relations cannot always be preserved as one topic after another is taken up. If it were possible to treat two topics simultaneously, the project for colonization ought to be studied step by step with that of voluntary compensated emancipation. Lincoln showed a tenderness for colonization largely because he held it to be part of his main comprehensive scheme of liberation.

[2] At the time such coöperation for peaceful projects was virtually an unused resource; its development, reaching the proportions of a new and enlarged federalism, remained for a distant future. Voluntary action by states in non-war enterprises, involving immense expenditures by the national government, is now such a commonplace that it takes something of an effort to realize the path-breaking nature of this kind of suggestion in Civil War days.

[3] *Works*, VIII, 113.

A long-term policy was envisaged, to be completed "at any time or times" before 1900.[4] Thirty-seven years did not seem too high a maximum for the consummation of such a reform. Though a broad solution was projected, the President was immediately concerned with initiatory steps. Emancipation was to be gradual. Both races were to be spared the "evils of sudden derangement."[5] No Federal claim of the right to impose emancipation upon a state was involved. Abolition was to be voluntary; "absolute control" of the matter by the states was recognized;[6] "perfectly free choice" was to govern their action.

Compensation was to be made to slaveholders, for, as Lincoln said, "the liberation of slaves is the destruction of property."[7] The Federal government was to bear the cost of such compensation but not to administer it. The states would emancipate with compensation; the Federal government would reimburse them "by installments" as abolition proceeded. This it would do by interest-bearing bonds. Freedmen were to be transported at Federal expense to new homes in some foreign land. In this connection the President used the strong word "deportation," though he intended no compulsion; only those freedmen who desired it would be colonized.[8]

Such in brief was Lincoln's emancipation plan. He proposed it first as a congressional resolution expressive of general approval of the whole concept, then as a bill which he himself drafted for applying the plan in Delaware,[9] later in more elaborate form as a constitutional amendment. Reactions at home and abroad reflected conflicting opinions on the merits of the project. To the *Herald* it appeared that no plan yet devised was "so simple, so just, so profound";[10] the President had taken "a sensible and conservative view."[11] The *Delaware State Journal* considered the proposal "one of the most important

---

[4] *Ibid.*, VIII, 116.   [5] *Ibid.*, VIII, 118–119.   [6] *Ibid.*, VII, 114.

[7] *Ibid.*, VIII, 119. Lincoln qualified this statement as to property by the words "In a certain sense."

[8] *Ibid.*, VIII, 128.

[9] There have come down to us two drafts of a bill prepared by Lincoln for compensated abolishment to be enacted by the State of Delaware; this was an experiment in state lawmaking by presidential sponsorship. The period of these Lincoln drafts was November 1861 (Paul M. Angle, *New Letters and Papers of Lincoln*, 285–286; Nicolay and Hay, *Works*, VII, 21–23). Support in Delaware was lacking and the project was dropped. See H. Clay Reed, "Lincoln's Compensated Emancipation Plan and Its Relation to Delaware," *Delaware Notes*, seventh series (Univ. of Del., 1931), 27–78.

[10] New York *Herald*, editorial, Mar. 8, 1862, p. 6, c. 3.

[11] *Ibid.*, Mar. 7, 1862, p. 4, c. 4.

[executive] documents . . . since the foundation of the Republic." [12] It seemed to the New York *Post* that the plan would bring its author "honorable fame" and "praise wherever civilized men dwell." [18] Though predicting that it would be "distorted and misconstrued by . . . politicians," the Chicago *Journal* regarded the plan as "in the highest degree sound." [14] If the slave states did it voluntarily, the Alton (Illinois) *Telegraph* felt that "the great majority of the people in the free States" would aid them.[15] A good deal of popular support for Lincoln's solution was suggested by the comment that many who privately denounced the plan were publicly supporting it. "Very soon [it was added] they . . . [would be] joining in the praises of General McClellan sounded by the . . . masses of the loyal people." Abolitionists, it was pointed out, would be trying to "make a merit of necessity" by joining in support of Lincoln's scheme.[16]

Yet these very abolitionists, many of them, were denying that the President was on their side. "I am afraid," wrote William Lloyd Garrison, "the President's message will prove 'a decoy duck' or 'a red herring,' so as to postpone that decisive action by Congress which we are so desirous of seeing." [17] A supporter of Frémont's Missouri policy thought it strange "that the President should ignore the sentiments of 18 millions [18] of men who elected him . . . and adopt the principles of the pro-slavery Union men & the 'West Point' aristocracy." [19] Expressing a middle-of-the-road sentiment, the New York *Times* doubted that the scheme would work, but rejoiced that the President had placed himself on the side of freedom.[20]

These varying comments show that Lincoln's program was one of those compromise schemes that are distasteful to widely diverse elements. Border-state moderates did not rise to it; on the other hand radical abolitionists were usually indignant at it, though some of them gave it reluctant support. "The Message," declared the *Herald*, "has taken all parties by surprise. A majority of the Senators and Repre-

[12] Issue of Mar. 11, 1862, as quoted in H. Clay Reed, as above cited, 47.

[13] As quoted in *Illinois State Journal* (weekly edition), Mar. 19, 1862, p. 1, c. 2.

[14] *Ibid.*, p. 2, c. 6.   [15] *Ibid.*   [16] New York *Herald*, March 21, 1862, p. 5, c. 1.

[17] Garrison to Oliver Johnson, Mar. 18, 1862, Garrison MSS.

[18] Actually, the popular vote for Lincoln in 1860 was only 1,866,000 in a total of more than four and a half million. The pro-Frémont writer was indulging in a tenfold exaggeration.

[19] W. M'Caulley to Charles Sumner, Wilmington, Del., Mar. 3, 1862, Sumner MSS.

[20] Mar. 7, 1862, editorial, p. 4, c. 3; Mar. 8, 1862, editorial, p. 4, c. 3.

sentatives are unprepared to express themselves upon it. All are afraid of it, and all are afraid to oppose it. The radicals look blank . . . . The conservatives . . . are anxious to sustain the policy . . . but they fear that they may be entrapped . . . from their chosen position." [21] To the London *Post* the message indicated Union despair in victory by arms; skeptical as to how it could be carried out, the *Post* ridiculed the plan as puerile and vain, the last resort of a government headed for ruin.[22] *The Times* of London considered it important, not for likelihood of acceptance, but as a bid toward ending the war; if raised, the bid might lead to something acceptable.[23]

VII

One can hardly find any subject on which Lincoln argued and pleaded more earnestly than on this. Sumner, who saw him frequently as he studied slavery matters, bore witness that "the invitation to Emancipation in the States" was "peculiarly his own" and that in furthering it his "whole soul was occupied." "In familiar intercourse with him," added Sumner, "I remember nothing more touching than the earnestness and completeness with which he embraced this idea." [1] Addressing border-state representatives at the White House Lincoln told them that they had more power for good than any other equal number in Congress. Let the border states adopt gradual emancipation and the war would be substantially ended. "Let the States . . . in rebellion see . . . that in no event will the [border] states . . . ever join their . . . confederacy, and they cannot much longer maintain the contest." The incidents of the war, said the President, could not be avoided. Slavery was doomed by "mere friction and abrasion." How much better to obtain compensation for a dying institution than to wait till both the institution and the power of compensation were forever sunk in the war. As President, he explained, he was constantly pressed for decisive measures of emancipation. It was an increasing pressure from an element whose support he could

21 New York *Herald*, Mar. 8, 1862, p. 3, c. 5.
22 Editorial, London *Post*, Mar. 21, 1862, in New York *Herald*, April 6, 1862, p. 8, c. 2.
23 Editorial, *The Times*, London, in New York *Herald*, April 1, 1862, p. 3, c. 4.
1 Charles Sumner to ———, June 5, 1862, Sumner, *Works*, VII, 117. This letter appeared in the Boston *Journal*, with editorial comment, June 13, 1862. See also McPherson, *Rebellion*, 233.

not afford to lose. With all the persuasion that he could muster he urged that border-state leaders take the patriotic view.

Before leaving the capital [he pleaded], . . . discuss it among yourselves. You are patriots and statesmen, and as such I pray you consider this proposition, and . . . commend it to . . . your States and people. As you would perpetuate popular government for the best people in the world, I beseech you that you do in no wise omit this. Our common country is in great peril, demanding the loftiest views and boldest action to bring it speedy relief. Once relieved, its form of government is saved to the world, its beloved history and cherished memories are vindicated, and its happy future fully assured and rendered inconceivably grand. To you, more than to any others, the privilege is given to assure that happiness and swell that grandeur, and to link your own names therewith forever.[2]

This fervid eloquence, contrasting as it did with Lincoln's habitual economy of crisply effective words, betokened unusual emotional earnestness. Returning to the subject at a later time the President addressed himself to some of its more practical aspects. He showed that the plan was a "compromise";[3] as such it took account of the slave interest within the Union. To those who considered the cost a conclusive objection, Lincoln explained that the scheme would in fact be "economical"; it would save money by shortening the war. He was proposing a long-time fiscal plan in a rapidly growing nation, giving bonds in future years as emancipation unfolded. Thus there would be the "great advantage of a policy by which we shall not have to pay, until we number a hundred millions, what by a different policy we would have to pay now, when we number but thirty-one millions." Each dollar for emancipation would be easier to pay than for the war, and it would "cost no blood, no precious life."[4] Far from the financial burden being fatal to the enterprise, Lincoln calculated that compensation at $400 each for all the slaves of Delaware could be paid and the total would amount to only one-half-day's cost of the war. Eighty-seven days' cost would pay for all the slaves in Delaware, Maryland, the District, Kentucky, and Missouri at the same price.[5]

[2] *Works*, VII, 270–274 (July 12, 1862).

[3] "This would be compromise; but it would be compromise among the friends, and not with the enemies of the Union." *Ibid.*, VIII, 118 (Dec. 1, 1862).

[4] *Ibid.*, VIII, 125 (Dec. 1, 1862).

[5] For the border area Lincoln calculated that the total emancipated cost at 173 millions of dollars ($400 per slave); the cost of eighty-seven days of war at two millions a day would be 174 millions. Lincoln to Henry J. Raymond, Mar. 9, 1862 (*ibid.*, VII, 119); Lincoln to Senator James A. McDougall, Mar. 14, 1862 (*ibid.*, VII, 132–134).

That the North should bear a heavy share of the money cost Lincoln considered entirely equitable. For the introduction of slavery he thought that the Northern people were as responsible as the Southern; considering the Northern use of cotton and sugar and "the profits of dealing in them," they were as responsible for its continuance.[6] Some might regard this as a considerable concession by a leader opposed to slavery, yet the statement is in entire harmony with Lincoln's main attitude toward the slave issue throughout his public career. He always spoke in measured tones and with wholesome respect for slaveholding friends. His was never the vocabulary of vituperative abolitionists intemperately denouncing Southerners and seeking their punishment. When Lincoln spoke of slavery, he treated it as a problem for statesmen to deal with, not as a theme for heaping blame upon Southern masters or putting a stigma upon the Southern people.

Lincoln's pleadings and his carefully figured schemes were of no avail. Border-state response was not forthcoming. There were objections to the cost as the President anticipated, questions of constitutionality, doubts as to procedure. Above all, there was indecision, and, as the *Herald* thought, the same dread of responsibility that had paralyzed the efforts of border-state men in Congress "when civil war first began to darken the horizon." It was a paralysis which emasculated their influence when they might have been leaders.[7]

It was not that the action of Congress was clear-cut in opposing Lincoln's plan; it was rather a matter of leaderless incompetence. The curious thing is that the plan was approved in principle, yet it came to nothing in practice. (Compensated emancipation was applied in the District, but this measure was separate from Lincoln's broad scheme for slave states.) The record of Congress was neither one thing nor the other; there was no consistent pattern. On April 10, 1862, Congress resolved that "the United States ought" to give pecuniary aid to any state that would adopt gradual emancipation.[8] A few days later it adopted the emancipation measure for the District (already treated) [9] which constituted the only bit of completed legislation in which actual compensation in a specified part of the country was provided. Proposals to apply the scheme in Missouri seemed early in 1863 to promise legislative success, and sizable sums were provided in

---

[6] *Ibid.*, VIII, 120 (Dec. 1, 1862).   [7] New York *Herald*, July 15, 1862, p. 5, c. 1.
[8] *Cong. Globe*, 37 Cong., 2 sess., appendix, p. 420.   [9] Above, pp. 133–134.

bills passed by the houses of Congress severally (ten million dollars in the House, twenty million in the Senate). When, however, the hectic short session ended in March 1863, the project had fallen down, despite majority votes of approval, because of the failure to pass the same bill through the two houses.[10] In this project for freedom Lincoln knew where he was going. As for Congress, the project went down by default. The war went on, and as its deadly toll increased Lincoln's attention was directed to other measures; yet late in the war his thought reverted in wistful contemplation to his "earnest and successive appeals to the border States to favor compensated emancipation."[11] As the war entered its last phase and terms of peace were under discussion Lincoln once more repeated his advocacy of a fair indemnity to Southern slaveowners, his willingness to be taxed for the purpose, and his belief that the people of the North were as responsible for the institution as those of the South.[12]

VIII

Slavery policy unfolded by changing phases, and by the middle of '62, with congressional action mounting and slave incidents multiplying, Lincoln was in the stage when anti-slavery pressure on the one side and border-state unresponsiveness on the other were driving him to a bold use of presidential power. Conservative as he was, and ready to put other questions above slavery, he was finding that on the complex issue of bondage he could not be neutral. Measures against slavery were being taken, and he had either to permit or repudiate them. Repudiation had been tried. Having overruled Frémont's emancipatory proclamation and suppressed Cameron's self-advertising pronouncement in 1861,[1] Lincoln had felt compelled in May 1862 to take similar action in overruling another order of military liberation which had attracted wide publicity. General David Hunter, with headquarters at Port Royal, South Carolina, had proclaimed that, as slavery and martial law were incompatible, persons held as slaves in the "Military Department of the South" (Georgia, Florida, and South

---

[10] Randall, *Constitutional Problems Under Lincoln*, 366.
[11] *Works*, X, 67 (letter to A. G. Hodges, April 4, 1864).
[12] Lincoln spoke in these terms at the Hampton Roads Conference, February 1865. Alexander H. Stephens, *A Constitutional View of the . . . War Between the States*, II, 617.
[1] Above, pp. 56–58.

Carolina) were "declared forever free." [2] When this sensational order
was issued Lincoln's slavery policy had not matured, his emphasis being
upon the proposal for compensated emancipation. Naturally, he felt
that if executive power were used on a great national problem, that
power ought to be wielded by the President. In a crisp endorsement
he wrote: "No commanding general shall do such a thing upon my
responsibility without consulting me." [3]

In these circumstances there was nothing for Lincoln to do but
repudiate and revoke Hunter's unauthorized order, and this he
promptly did. Declaring the general's proclamation of freedom "altogether void," the President made it known that such questions belonged to him as commander in chief and were not to be handled by
generals in the field as if they were matters of "police regulations in
armies and camps." He did not let the occasion slip, however, without reverting to the solemn resolution of Congress relating to compensated emancipation. For the slave states he had a special word:

> . . . To the people of those States I now earnestly appeal. . . . You
> cannot . . . be blind to the signs of the times. I beg of you a calm . . .
> consideration . . . , far above personal and partisan politics. This pro-
> posal makes common cause . . . , casting no reproaches upon any. It acts
> not the Pharisee. The change . . . would come gently as the dews of
> heaven, not rending or wrecking anything. Will you not embrace it? . . .
> May the vast future not have to lament that you have neglected it.[4]

Lincoln did not enjoy taking this action against Hunter, nor had
he gained much by it. Hunter, "an honest man," he said, was a "friend"
with whom he agreed "in the general wish that all men everywhere
could be free." In revoking the order the President had given "dissatisfaction, if not offense, to many" whose support could not be
spared.[5] Not only was the repudiating proclamation an embarrassment; it had the further defect of being inconclusive. Nothing was
settled. The pressure was increasing. Conservatives who agreed with
the President as to the Hunter affair [6] might include some whose praise

---

[2] *Offic. Rec.*, 1 ser., XIV, 341.   [3] *Works*, VII, 167 (May 17, 1862).
[4] These earnest words were part of a presidential proclamation, May 19, 1862 (*ibid.*,
VII, 172–173).
[5] *Ibid.*, VII, 272–273 (July 12, 1862).
[6] Among anti-abolitionists the President's squelching of Hunter's order was highly
approved. Thus the New York *Herald* (editorial, May 20, 1862, p. 6, c. 3) rejoiced that
the country had this conservative at the helm, adhering to rights under the Constitution rather than listening to radicals.

was of doubtful value; this would only increase the attacks of radicals who had no compunctions about causing him continual embarrassment.

On July 17, 1862, a none-too-helpful Congress brought a long and wordy session to a close, having passed a number of piecemeal laws, and one seemingly comprehensive one,[7] concerning slavery. Lincoln was indeed being pushed by the "signs of the times" and the pressure of events. He was buffeted by opposite forces. His own words show his dilemma. "As an anti-slavery man," he later wrote, "I have a motive to desire emancipation which pro-slavery men do not have . . . ."[8] As a check to this motive there was the whole border-state complex, with slavery entrenched as a legal institution within the Union, and on this very point there were Lincoln's repeated assurances that border-state sentiment and pro-slavery loyalty were to be respected. As long as he remained in the White House, he had told Representative Crisfield, "Maryland had nothing to fear . . . for her institutions or her interests."[9] As between the conflicting tendencies beating upon him, the President's assurances had been for the most part given to slaveholding interests. He was under no out-and-out pledge to abolish slavery, yet he was being uncomfortably forced to choose between the downright protection of slavery and some use of executive war power against the institution which he referred to as the "lever" of the Union's foes.[10] No one could accuse him of indulging his moral judgment or personal feeling. He was being assailed for exactly the opposite reason, as when he overruled Frémont and Hunter. He distrusted the radicals and disliked the pressure of the Greeley faction. He tried a long-range, statesmanlike solution on the basis of friendly recognition of slaveholding interests, and obtained no more than nominal support. His thoughts had been focused upon peaceful schemes of compensated abolition, with wishful eyes turned toward Central or South America. Yet these were not the measures fated to succeed. The day was fast approaching when blunt weapons of war would have to be used against human slavery by a leader whose legal sense and concepts of fairness preferred more considerate instruments.

---

[7] The treason act of July 17, 1862, also known as the second confiscation act. The seeming comprehensiveness of the slave clauses of the act contrasted strikingly with the utterly negligible effect of these clauses in actual practice.

[8] *Works*, IX, 57 (Aug. 5, 1863).   [9] *Ibid.*, VII, 125 (March 10, 1862).

[10] *Ibid.*, VII, 270–271 (July 12, 1862).

CHAPTER XXII

PRESIDENTIAL EMANCIPATION

I

THE painful and crowded summer of 1862 found Lincoln's slavery policy in a state of transition. As one gets the "feel" of the times through contemporary records one senses a rising demand that the President do something decisive for freedom, not through Lincoln's conservative plan, but as a dramatic wartime stroke. Abolitionists, of course, had been demanding this right along. Reporting a meeting in October 1861, an abolitionist leader mentioned that Gerrit Smith had "a grand hearing," that he was "really magnificent," and that the audience "gave Fremont three rousing cheers." [1] A similar response came when Frederick Douglass, distinguished Negro orator, addressed a large crowd in February 1862 at Cooper Institute.[2]

It was felt that the cancer had to be cauterized, and that Republicans could not sustain a wavering President.[3] Antislavery souls could not understand Lincoln's policy. They saw none of the complications that Lincoln saw; they saw only a clear-cut issue of right and wrong, with no shadings. They wanted the death of slavery, had voted for it (they thought), and were fighting for it; yet to their outraged eyes here was a President of their own choosing actually trying to preserve the institution. "A more ridiculous farce was never played," wrote one of them, than permitting slaveholders to keep their human property on taking oath of loyalty. Let the administration continue thus, and the Republican party would be forever broken and Lincoln the "most unpopular man in the nation." [4] "It strikes me," wrote an anxious

[1] Oliver Johnson to J. M. McKim, Oct. 31, 1861, MS., Boston Pub. Lib.
[2] New York *Times*, Feb. 13, 1862, p. 4, c. 2.
[3] W. Kitchell to Trumbull, Hillsboro, Ill., Dec. 10, 1861, Trumbull MSS.
[4] John Russell to Trumbull, Bluffdale, Greene Co., Ill., Dec. 17, 1861, *ibid.*

patriot, "that now is the time to emancipate the slaves . . . and that it is either emancipation *now* or . . . St. Domingo hereafter." [5] To end the war a blow had to be struck at the vital spot of the rebellion. When this was done, pious believers were sure that God would take the Union side.[6] To such persons it seemed that Trumbull had the right idea when he brought in his bill for the confiscation of rebel property.

To Salmon Chase's embattled view it was folly to think of winning the war while upholding or permitting slavery. "The government," he thought, could not succeed "in the attempt to put down this rebellion with the left hand while supporting slavery with the right hand." [7] When at the end of the Seven Days the "war cloud" loomed "blacker than ever," he felt that the way "to draw the lightning" was to "make . . . emancipation the conducting rod." [8] To an Ohioan writing to Chase it seemed that if the President saved slavery in the struggle, not only would he fail after all to save the Union, but he would "be ruined & forever disgraced." And, he added, "We all have too much invested in Mr Lincoln to wish to make him out a failure." [9] As to method, Chase would "declare free all Slaves of . . . [seceded] States and invite them to organize for the suppression of rebellion and the establishment of order." The border states, he thought, ought to be left free to choose whether to keep or abolish slavery.[10] Thus he would make forcible abolition a penalty for rebellion. Nor was Chase the man to keep these views to himself. In midsummer of '62, in cabinet meeting, he expressed the conviction just stated "for the tenth or twentieth time." [11]

Sumner wished to go farther than Chase. In an evening drive with the President in May 1861 he urged a blow for emancipation when the moment should come. Again, directly after first Bull Run, when Congress was proclaiming the opposite view, Sumner called on the President, repeating that he must strike at slavery and that the moment

---

[5] Bradford R. Wood to C. M. Clay, Copenhagen, Nov. 28, 1861, MS., Ill. St. Hist. Lib.
[6] D. T. Linegar to Trumbull, Cairo, Ill., Dec. 7, 1861, Trumbull MSS.
[7] Cyrus Pitt Grosvenor to S. P. Chase, London, July 28, 1862, Chase MSS., Lib. of Cong. (In this letter Grosvenor approvingly quoted the above words of Chase.)
[8] Chase to H. Barney, Washington, July 2, 1862, Chase MSS., Hist. Soc. of Pa.
[9] Alphonso Taft to Chase, Cincinnati, Ohio, Aug. 26, 1862, Chase MSS., Lib. of Cong.
[10] Typed copy of a long letter by Chase to an unspecified correspondent, Aug. 9, 1862, *ibid.*
[11] Diary of Chase, Aug. 3, 1862, as quoted in Warden, *Chase,* 445.

had come.[12] In December 1861 Sumner wrote: "He [Lincoln] tells me that I am ahead of him only a month or six weeks." [13] Interviewing Lincoln on July 4, 1862, Sumner told the President that he not only needed more men at the North, he needed them "at the South, in the rear of the Rebels." He needed the slaves. All he had to do was to say the word; by choosing July 4 as the day on which to say it he could outdo the Continental Congress in making the day sacred and historic.[14] According to Sumner's narrative of the interview Lincoln replied: " 'I would do it [issue an edict of emancipation] if I were not afraid that half the officers would fling down their arms and three more States would rise.' " [15] Yet Sumner was capable of more patience toward the President than other abolitionists. Criticism directed against him was "hasty," thought the Senator, who wrote: "Could you —as has been my privilege often—have seen the President, while considering . . . [these] great questions . . . , even your zeal would be satisfied . . . ." [16]

Though Sumner expected fulfillment of his heart's desire it must not be supposed that abolitionists were the President's most welcome callers. "Be sure that Lincoln is at heart with Slavery," growled Gurowski. "He considers that *emancipation is a job which will smother the free States. Such are his precise words.*" [17] When Wendell Phillips turned up at Washington early in '62 his presence "roused up proslavery spite and malice in every direction"; as for Garrison, he wrote in March of that year that he had not been invited to come to the capital.[18] At Cincinnati in March 1862 popular resentment against Phillips had been expressed with groans, hisses, and flying eggs.[19]

II

Lincoln's ending of delay and arrival at a decision are best told in the President's own words. "It had got to be midsummer, 1862," he

[12] Sumner, *Works*, VI, 31. [13] *Ibid.*, VI, 152.
[14] Speech at Faneuil Hall, Oct. 6, 1862, *ibid.*, VII, 215.
[15] Sumner to Bright, Boston, Aug. 5, 1862, Pierce, *Sumner*, IV, 83.
[16] Letter of Charles Sumner to unnamed correspondent, Senate Chamber, June 5, 1862, Sumner, *Works*, VII, 116–117.
[17] Gurowski to John A. Andrew, Washington, May 7, 1862, Andrew MSS., vol. 14, no. 32.
[18] W. L. Garrison to Oliver Johnson, Boston, March 30, 1862, MS., Boston Pub. Lib.
[19] Moore, *Rebellion Record* (Diary), IV, 67–68. The date was March 24, 1862. The meeting broke up in a fight.

said. "Things had gone . . . from bad to worse, until I felt that we had reached the end of our rope on the plan . . . we had been pursuing; that we . . . must change our tactics, or lose the game. I now determined upon the adoption of the emancipation policy; and without consultation with, or the knowledge of, the Cabinet, I prepared the original draft of the proclamation, and, after much anxious thought, called a Cabinet meeting upon the subject." [1]

On July 13, on a long carriage ride with Welles and Seward, Lincoln had informally broached the matter of a proclamation, that being "he said, the first occasion when he had mentioned the subject to any one." [2] "He dwelt earnestly [wrote Welles] on the gravity, importance, and delicacy of the movement, said he had given it much thought and had about come to the conclusion that it was a military necessity . . . for the salvation of the Union, ..." Welles emphasized that this "was a new departure for the President, for until this time, . . . whenever . . . emancipation . . . had been . . . alluded to, he had been prompt and emphatic in denouncing any interference by the General Government with the subject." [3]

Gloom rested heavily upon the Union cause. The Seven Days had passed, Southern defense had been strong before Richmond, the storm raged bitterly for McClellan's removal, a shake-up in military command and in operations was imminent, and, as to slaves, already "thousands . . . were in attendance upon the [enemy's] armies." [4] It was in this atmosphere of depression and frustration that Lincoln worked out alone the basic problem and the wording of his historic proclamation. His friend Eckert of the military telegraph service recalled that Lincoln wrote the first draft of the edict in the cipher room of the war department telegraph office. He began it, said Eckert, shortly after the Seven Days (this would put it about the beginning of July 1862). He would write a line or two on long foolscap sheets, study a while, look out of the window, and now and then stop to pass a remark with the operators. This continued for "several weeks," the sheets being locked up at the telegraph office and taken out "nearly every day" by Lincoln for careful composition and revision of every sentence. The President, added Eckert, told him that he had been

---

[1] *Works*, X, 1–2 (Feb. 6, 1864).   [2] Welles, *Diary*, I, 70–71.
[3] *Ibid.*   [4] *Ibid.*, I, 71.

able thus "to work . . . more quietly and . . . better than at the White House, where he was frequently interrupted." [5]

It was on July 22, 1862, that Lincoln broached the subject of his proclamation to the Cabinet. In his undramatic diary Chase gives incidental mention of the President's proposal to proclaim "the emancipation of all slaves within States remaining in insurrection on the first of January, 1863." This proposed proclamation, said Chase, was based on the confiscation bill (which had a clause concerning the freeing of slaves as a penalty for rebellion); yet as a kind of collateral approach to the slave problem it contained a renewed recommendation for compensation to slaveowners within the pattern of Lincoln's proposal for gradual abolition by state action.[6]

It is clear that Lincoln had made up his mind as to the proclamation; of his Cabinet he asked incidental rather than primary advice. His own statement, given in 1864 to F. B. Carpenter, the artist, was: "I said to the cabinet that I had resolved upon this step, and had not called them together to ask their advice, but to lay the subject-matter of a proclamation before them, suggestions as to which would be in order after they had heard it read." [7] Chase gave the proposal "entire support" chiefly because he considered it "much better than inaction on the subject." [8] Cabinet secretaries gave their suggestions, most of which had been anticipated,[9] but Seward came out with a bit of counsel that gave pause to the President. He doubted the expediency of a proclamation issued at a time of depression in the public mind, dreading the effect of such a step following so closely upon recent reverses. The government, he thought, would seem to be "stretching forth its hands to Ethiopia, instead of Ethiopia stretching forth her hands to the government." It "would be considered a last *shriek* on the retreat." The secretary approved the measure, but he said: ". . . I suggest, sir, that you postpone its issue until you can give it to the country

---

[5] Statement of Major Thomas T. Eckert of the war department telegraph staff, quoted in Bates, *Lincoln in the Telegraph Office*, 138–141.

[6] Diary of S. P. Chase, (*Annual Report*, Am. Hist. Assoc., 1902, II), 48.

[7] Statement of Lincoln to the artist F. B. Carpenter, Feb. 6, 1864, *Works*, X, 1–3. In his *Inner Life of Abraham Lincoln: Six Months at the White House* (20 ff.), Carpenter records these words of Lincoln. By including the passage in his *Works* the President's secretaries accept it as Lincoln's own account. Carpenter's enormous painting to represent the proclamation has hung for many years in the House wing of the Capitol at Washington.

[8] Diary of S. P. Chase (*Annual Report*, Amer. Hist. Assoc., 1902, II), 49 (July 22, 1862).

[9] *Works*, X, 2.

supported by military success . . . ." The "wisdom" of this view struck Lincoln "with very great force." "The result was," said Lincoln to the artist, "that I put the draft of the proclamation aside, as you do your sketch for a picture, waiting for a victory." [10]

Lincoln and those near him had a secret to keep the next two months; in keeping it the President was under the embarrassing necessity of seeming to be noncommittal or even hostile toward a policy upon which he was in fact determined. It is amusing to note the manner in which, with the draft proclamation in his desk drawer,[11] Lincoln gave out laborious and unsatisfactory answers on the subject of slavery while enduring severe taunts against his alleged proslavery attitude. It was in this period, for example, that he advocated separation of the races and colonization in a foreign country.[12] His embarrassment was increased in the anxious days of September when a delegation of Christian leaders descended upon him carrying a petition for national emancipation which had been adopted at a public meeting at Bryan Hall in Chicago. The President received these men courteously and listened "with fixed attention" while the memorial was read. Then he gave reply "in an earnest and . . . solemn manner, as one impressed with the weight of the theme, yet at times making a characteristically shrewd remark with a pleasant air" (such was the clumsy report of the delegation). [13]

The main tone of the President's answer was negative and disappointing. "What good would a proclamation of emancipation from me do, . . . ?" he asked. "I do not want to issue a document that the whole world will see must . . . be inoperative, like the Pope's bull against the comet." In the "rebel States" such a proclamation could no more be enforced, said Lincoln, than the recent ineffective law offering freedom to slaves coming within Union lines. And suppose they did throw themselves upon us in large numbers, what should we do with them? How could we "feed and care for such a multitude"? Much more the President gave them, impressively piling up doubts concerning the wisdom and feasibility of a liberating edict. Conceding that slavery was the *"sine qua non"* of the "rebellion," that emanci-

---

[10] *Ibid.,* X, 2–3.
[11] For this draft proclamation, dated July 22, 1862, see *ibid.,* VII, 289–290.
[12] Above, pp. 137–139.
[13] Report of the Christian delegation's interview with Lincoln, signed by W. W. Patton and John Dempster, Chicago, Sep. 21, 1862, MS., Chicago Hist. Soc.

pation would help the cause in Europe, and that it would weaken the enemy by drawing off their laborers, Lincoln would have the visiting committee consider the difficulties of freeing helpless thousands, the danger of their reënslavement, the impotence of the government to do anything about it if they were reënslaved, and the danger that arms put into Negro hands would be seized by the enemy. Especially he emphasized the importance of fifty thousand Union bayonets from the border slave states; if in consequence of a proclamation they should go over to the enemy, it would be a very serious matter.[14] He went on thus for "an hour of earnest and frank discussion." [15] Then, with the meeting about to break up, Lincoln remarked, as if giving a broad hint on a matter that could not go into the record: "Do not misunderstand me, ... I have not decided against a proclamation of liberty to the slaves, but hold the matter under advisement; and I can assure you that the subject is on my mind, by day and night, more than any other." He trusted that in freely canvassing their views, he had not injured his visitors' feelings.[16]

III

Among the commonest gibes against the President was the assertion that he had no policy. In a roundabout manner such a taunt came to him from New Orleans through the wealthy Democratic leader, August Belmont. Lincoln must take a decisive course, said this writer. Trying to please everybody would satisfy nobody. Let the North declare officially for restoration of the Union as it was. This complaint, with a motive opposite to that of the religious brethren from Chicago, drew from Lincoln the suggestion that if the objector would but read the President's speeches he would find "the substance of the very declaration he desires." [1] In a similar setting Lincoln

---

14 *Works*, VIII, 30 ff. (Sep. 13, 1862).   15 Patton and Dempster MS. (see note 13).

16 *Ibid.* Lincoln's reply appears in his *Works*, VIII, 28–33, and in the Patton and Dempster manuscript above cited. The statement as published in the *Works* reads like a state paper and seems more formalized than the President's actual utterance in the interview. One can only imagine Lincoln's feelings as he heard the delegation urge a proclamation which he had decided to issue, but against which he felt it necessary to give convincing objections. Late in the war, in a letter that seems a bit amusing, Governor Yates of Illinois wrote to Patton and Dempster (July 2, 1864) that their Bryan Hall meeting "must have had great influence upon the President" (MS., Chicago Hist. Soc.).

1 *Works*, VII, 299 (July 31, 1862).

158 LINCOLN THE PRESIDENT

wrote as to slavery that what was "done and omitted" was on military necessity, and that he was holding antislavery pressure "within bounds." [2]

With his mind full of anti-abolitionist complaints of a lack of policy, Lincoln now became the target for an editorial blast from the opposite direction. From Greeley's resounding sanctum there came the reproachful admonition that "attempts to put down the Rebellion and at the same time uphold its . . . cause . . . [were] preposterous and futile." In an editorial "Prayer of Twenty Millions" the *Tribune* pundit informed the President that an "immense majority of the Loyal Millions" of his countrymen required of him a frank execution of the- laws in the antislavery sense.[3] With bland equanimity for Greeley's fervor and with balanced, noncommittal phrases for his heated rhetoric, Lincoln replied in the famous "paramount object" letter which showed, among other things, that he was not swayed by abolitionist outcries. Calm down, and get off your dictatorial horse, would be an offhand paraphrase of his opening sentences. "I have just read yours of the 19th," wrote Lincoln to Greeley. ". . . If there be in it any inferences . . . falsely drawn, I do not . . . argue against them. If there be perceptible in it an impatient and dictatorial tone, I waive it in deference to an old friend . . . ." Having thus set the pitch for his even-toned reply, Lincoln wrote:

My paramount object in this struggle is to save the Union, and is not either to save or to destroy slavery. If I could save the Union without freeing any slave, I would do it; and if I could save it by freeing all the slaves, I would do it; and if I could save it by freeing some and leaving others alone, I would also do that. What I do about slavery and the colored race, I do because I believe it helps to save the Union; and what I forbear, I forbear because I do not believe it would help to save the Union. . . .

I have here stated my purpose according to my view of official duty; and I intend no modification of my oft-expressed personal wish that all men everywhere could be free.[4]

Antislavery folk did not like the calculated restraint of this famous letter. They wanted no such even balance between action and forbearance. They wanted a crusade. One of them sarcastically wrote: "From his policy hitherto, we must infer, that the way he applies it is,

[2] *Ibid.*, VII, 295 (July 28, 1862).   [3] New York *Tribune*, Aug. 20, 1862, p. 4, cc. 2-4.
[4] *Works*, VIII, 15–16 (Aug. 22, 1862).

to *save the Union with Slavery, if he can do it at whatever sacrifice of life & treasure.* If that is found impossible . . . [his policy is] *to save the Union without slavery,* unless it should be . . . too late. This is like the duel in which the terms . . . as prescribed by the challenged party were, that they should have but one sword between them, & that he should use it five minutes, & afterward the challenger should have it five minutes." [5]

Such complaints, many of them, Lincoln had to endure while all the time he was awaiting the appropriate public opportunity for launching the proclamation on which he had determined. To supply this much-to-be-desired opportunity rested with McClellan and his men. Major Union victories were not so frequent in '62; if McClellan had not checked Lee at Antietam, Lincoln's proclamation, withheld in hope of Federal triumph, would have been indefinitely delayed. From the day (July 22, 1862) when Lincoln put the famous paper aside on Seward's suggestion that it be not a shriek on the retreat, no important triumph for the United States came, except for Antietam, until July 1863. One appreciates the timeliness of this achievement by the much abused McClellan when one tries to speculate just where Lincoln and emancipation would have stood had the story of McClellan in Maryland been of a piece with that of Pope, Burnside, or Hooker.

It was in this very period of waiting for a victory that there came the word of Pope's disaster at Second Bull Run. "Things looked darker than ever." [6] McClellan was grudgingly reinstated. Further anxious days passed. On Wednesday, September 17, Antietam was fought. Lincoln, according to his own account, was then staying at the Soldiers' Home outside Washington. Here, determining to wait no longer, he finished the "second draft of the preliminary proclamation"; coming in on Saturday, he summoned his Cabinet for Monday. [7]

If contrary to custom there had been an observer at the President's cabinet meeting at the White House beginning at noon of Monday, September 22, 1862, he would have seen all the members in attendance. An important announcement was to come, but it was preceded by a trivial thing, frozen into recorded history as trivial things some-

[5] Alphonso Taft to S. P. Chase, Cincinnati, Ohio, Aug. 26, 1862, Chase MSS., Lib. of Cong.
[6] *Works,* X, 3 (Feb. 6, 1864).   [7] *Ibid.*

times are, the better to enable posterity to visualize the human aspects of a significant historic moment. Ready to enter upon the agenda, the Cabinet secretaries, whose formalized visages have been preserved on Carpenter's mammoth canvas, had first to give attention to something that was the antithesis of formal; Lincoln had an Artemus Ward book, sent him by the humorist, and he proposed "to read a chapter which he thought very funny." The "High handed Outrage at Utica" was the selected passage. Lincoln read it "and seemed to enjoy it very much." We are told that the "Heads" also enjoyed it, though Stanton, and (as the context shows) Chase, who recorded the trivial event, were exceptions. One can only picture them sitting with dour faces while the President sought to enliven a serious occasion with the leaven of humor.[8]

Assuming a "graver tone," the President made a statement. He had thought a great deal about the relation of the war to slavery. Ever since the former meeting when he had read an order on the subject, it had occupied his mind; now had arrived "the time for acting." He had determined, as soon as the enemy had been driven out of Maryland, to "issue a Proclamation of Emancipation." He had made the promise to himself and to his Maker; now he proposed to fulfill that promise. On the main matter he was not seeking counsel, his mind was made up; as to the expressions he used, or as to minor matters, he would be glad to have suggestions. He had one other observation to make. It pertained to himself as leader. He said:

. . . I know very well that many others might . . . do better than I can; and if I were satisfied that the public confidence was more fully possessed by any one of them than by me, and knew of any Constitutional way in which he could be put in my place, he should have it. I would gladly yield it to him. But though I believe that I have not so much of the confidence of the people as I had some time since, I do not know that . . . any other person has more; and, however this may be, there is no way in which I can have any other man put where I am. I am here. I must do the best I can, and bear the responsibility of taking the course which I feel I ought to take.[9]

Evidence is lacking on which to follow all the implications of this idea of Lincoln's that he would gladly yield his office to another if that procedure were possible and were demonstrably in the public

---

[8] Diary of S. P. Chase (*Annual Report,* Am. Hist. Assoc., 1902, II), 87.   [9] *Ibid.,* 88.

interest. It is clear that the whole subject of his relation to his high office, and the nature of his own personal responsibility to make and enforce a decision, had been traversed in his deliberations on the emancipation question. If these deliberations had given him humility, and a sense of association with Divine purpose (which was more than once indicated),[10] they had also given executive confidence. In reaching his important decision there is ample reason to believe that Lincoln had not only endured anxious hours, but had undergone a significant inner experience from which he emerged with quiet serenity.

The President read the proclamation through with running comments. In the Cabinet discussion that followed Chase agreed to take the document as written, though he would have charted a somewhat different course; Seward wanted it definitely stated that the government would maintain the freedom proclaimed; only Blair offered a substantial criticism. This was not an objection to emancipation *per se;* the party-minded secretary, whose position in the postal portfolio was peculiarly associated with "politics," was thinking of the coming elections; he feared the effect of the proclamation in the border area, and stated his apprehensions "at some length." [11]

IV

Lincoln's proclamation of emancipation is more often admired than read. Since there were two proclamations one hundred days apart, the first being monitory, one must read them both for a full understanding. In addition, one must read thousands of Lincoln's less formal words giving his own commentaries on the theme, to say nothing of elaborate contemporary statements and reminiscences by many who had a part in the historic act, or who, as in the case of the artist Carpenter, were in a position to hear and record Lincoln's asides and parentheses.

The preliminary proclamation of September 22, 1862, whose slow

---

10 ". . . I made the promise to myself, and . . . to my Maker" (*ibid.*); ". . . it is my earnest desire to know the will of Providence in this matter." *Works,* VIII, 29 (Sep. 13, 1862).

11 Diary of S. P. Chase (*Annual Report,* Amer. Hist. Assoc., 1902, II), 89. Blair seems at this time to have repeated the apprehensions which he had expressed in the meeting of July 22, to which Lincoln referred in the following words: "Mr. Blair, after he came in, deprecated the policy on the ground that it would cost the administration the fall elections." *Works,* X, 2 (statement to F. B. Carpenter, Feb. 6, 1864).

composition extended over anxious weeks, opened with a declaration that reunion (not abolition) was the object of the war. At the outset Lincoln designated himself as the "commander-in-chief of the army and navy," using a phrase which was not customary in presidential proclamations and which did not appear in the call for troops in April 1861. Thus Lincoln began his document with a military wording and a non-abolitionist flavor. Continuing, the President promised to renew his recommendation that Congress pass a "practical measure" (something beyond the paper declaration of April 10, 1862) tendering financial aid to such Union states as might adopt gradual abolition of slavery. In close association with this program, the "effort" toward foreign colonization of Negroes would, he said, be continued.

Then came the core of the proclamation: on the first day of 1863 "all persons held as slaves" in areas "in rebellion against the United States" were to be "then, thenceforward, and forever free." The Federal executive and the armed forces were to "recognize and maintain" this freedom, and not to "repress such persons . . . in . . . efforts . . . for their actual freedom." (A critic could cavil at this. He could note the President's announcement of a declared or constructive liberation that fell short of "actual freedom." Also, this declaration was open to violent objection as an encouragement of servile insurrection,[1] that hideous nightmare of Southern racial dread.) Particular states or areas in which the proclamation was to apply were to be designated "on the first day of January aforesaid." Congressional representation at Washington, by men chosen at an election wherein a majority of qualified voters participated,[2] would relieve a state from the liberation edict. Stay in the Union and you may keep your slaves, though you will be urged to free them on a voluntary, coöperative basis, was the meaning.

Measures of Congress were then quoted prohibiting the armed forces from returning fugitive slaves to their masters, denying such return in any case except to loyal owners, and liberating all slaves "of persons . . . hereafter . . . engaged in rebellion against the government of the United States."[3] Closing his edict on a note of friend-

---

[1] See below, pp. 195–197, where it is shown that such objection was unfounded.

[2] Next year (December 1863) Lincoln adopted the idea of ten per cent of the voters as a loyal nucleus for the reconstruction of state governments.

[3] This was section 9 of the second confiscation act of July 17, 1862, *U. S. Stat. at Large*, XII, 591.

liness to slaveholders rather than adherence to any abolitionist program, Lincoln promised that, on restoration of the Union, he would recommend that loyal citizens "be compensated for all losses by acts of the United States, including the loss of slaves." (Rather a sweeping promise of reparations to be paid by the victor.)

Turning to Lincoln's numerous comments on the subject one may acquire some sense of the motives and circumstances that prompted the act, as well as the patience with which the President answered his critics and reviewed the whole project in its relation to the war, to reunion, and to the future of American society. Despite his antislavery sentiment he had done no official act, he said, on the basis of abstract judgment on the moral wrong of slavery.[4] He had begun his administration with a pledge not to interfere with slavery within the states; the general government, he felt, had no lawful power so to interfere.[5] Some might have reasoned that such a pledge should not tie the future to the past. Lincoln took a different line; he had struggled nearly a year and a half to get along without touching the institution; when finally he "conditionally determined to touch it" he "gave a hundred days' fair notice . . . to all the States and people, within which . . . they could have turned it wholly aside by . . . becoming good citizens of the United States." [6] Lincoln by no means considered that he had violated a pledge or repudiated a disclaimer. The disclaimer was made within the pattern of the government of the United States to apply to adherents of the United States. It was made in time of peace and as an inducement for continuance of peace. It presupposed that non-interference was conditioned on loyalty. It did not amount to a prediction of future war policy toward areas that should have become enemies of the United States. When proclaiming conditional future emancipation in his September edict, Lincoln adhered to his disclaimer by announcing no interference except in the case of areas "in rebellion." Later, in a retrospective passage written in 1864, he reverted to his announcement to Greeley that the Union was paramount. Then he added: "All this I said in the utmost sincerity; and I am . . . true to the whole of it . . . . When I afterward proclaimed emancipation, and employed colored soldiers, I only followed the declaration . . . that 'I shall do more whenever . . . doing more will

---

[4] *Works*, IX, 57; X, 65–66.   [5] *Ibid.*, VI, 170; VII, 114; IX, 245–246.
[6] *Ibid.*, VIII, 182 (Jan. 8, 1863).

help the cause.' " [7]

Over and again Lincoln repeated that the Union, not abolition, was his main concern. When George Bancroft wrote him that civil war was the divine instrument to root out slavery, Lincoln, withholding agreement with this sentiment, suggested "caution." [8] "I have . . . thought it proper," he said, "to keep the . . . Union prominent as the primary object of the contest"; [9] yet constantly he felt that the necessity for unshackling and arming the blacks would come unless averted by the more normal and peaceable measures of compensated emancipation.[10]

By that earnestly advocated measure he would have eradicated slavery in conservative terms after the manner of the moderate liberal he was; by doing so he hoped in orderly manner to remove the main cause of the war,[11] and to deprive the disaffected leaders of all hope of winning over the more northern slave states.[12] So to deprive them, he thought, would substantially end the rebellion. When Congress nominally approved his conservative project, he could not think of it otherwise than as "an authentic, definite, and solemn proposal." "So much good . . . [had never] been done," he thought, as "in the providence of God" the border states could do by implementing the proposal.[13] Gradual emancipation he thought better than immediate; if temporary Federal protection for slaveholders' rights were needed in a transitional period, he was ready to brave abolitionist wrath by giving it.[14] He would not thwart efforts in the slave states to work out problems of emancipation.[15] Where slaves were returned to a loyal owner, Lincoln would withhold the full punishment permitted by law.[16] If a system of apprenticeships would ease the transition away

---

[7] *Ibid.*, X, 194 (Aug., 17, 1864).   [8] *Ibid.*, VII, 20–21 (Nov. 18, 1861).

[9] *Ibid.*, VII, 51 (Dec. 3, 1861); ". . . what is done and omitted about slaves is done and omitted on . . . military necessity" (*ibid.*, VII, 295, July 28, 1862).

[10] *Ibid.*, X, 67 (April 4, 1864).   [11] *Ibid.*, XI, 45 (Mar. 4, 1864).

[12] *Ibid.*, VII, 113 (Mar. 6, 1862).   [13] *Ibid.*, VII, 172–173 (May 19, 1862).

[14] *Ibid.*, VIII, 329 (June 22, 1863)   [15] *Ibid.*, VIII, 330.

[16] The reference here is to Lincoln's comment on the case of a man sentenced to five years at hard labor in the penitentiary for returning a slave to a loyal owner. Lincoln pointed out that the man was guilty under the law; he added, however, that what he did had been "perfectly lawful only a short while before," that the public mind had not fully accepted the change which made it unlawful, that the offense was not of frequent occurrence, and that the severe punishment indicated was "not at all necessary." *Ibid.*, X, 47 (Mar. 18, 1864).

from slavery, he would favor such a scheme.[17] He wanted "some practical system by which the two races could gradually live themselves out of the old relation . . . , and both come out . . . prepared for the new." [18] With this in view, he wanted due attention given to "the element of 'contract,' " to a probationary period, and to the education of young blacks.[19]

When Lincoln justified his long-delayed emancipation as an act of military necessity, he meant it as a kind of high political instrument which the President himself had to wield for military success; he did not favor emancipation by generals on their own authority.[20] He referred to this necessity sometimes to explain his delay (for he would not use the instrument till it was indispensable), sometimes to repel criticism by those who opposed abolition, sometimes to relieve himself of the charge of performing a dictatorial act.[21] He was striking at a constitutionally protected institution; this he justified on the ground that the restriction applied to "ordinary civil administration," that "a limb must be amputated to save a life," that "measures otherwise unconstitutional" might become lawful in a dire emergency, and that he had been "driven to the alternative of either surrendering the Union, and with it the Constitution, or of laying strong hand upon the colored element." [22]

Thus his executive oath to preserve the Constitution was constantly in his mind; when he did unusual things he stressed his function as military chief. The Constitution, he thought, "invests its commander-in-chief with the law of war in time of war." "Civilized belligerents," he added, "do all in their power to help themselves or hurt the enemy, except . . . things regarded as barbarous or cruel." [23] It was only as a matter of promoting Union success in the war that Lincoln cared to justify his course; the imputation that he most resented was that he was willfully seizing arbitrary power. He put the matter in a nut-

---

[17] *Ibid.*, VIII, 182 (Jan. 8, 1863); Dennett, *Lincoln . . . in the Diaries . . . of John Hay*, 73.

[18] *Works*, IX, 56 (Aug. 5, 1863).   [19] *Ibid.*, IX, 56–57.

[20] *Ibid.*, VI, 351, 358–359; VII, 171–172.   [21] *Ibid.*, VII, 113–114; IX, 245–246.

[22] *Ibid.*, X, 65–67 (April 4, 1864).

[23] *Ibid.*, IX, 98 (Aug. 26, 1863). This identifying of the military aspect with the constitutional is shown in Lincoln's statement: "The . . . proclamation has no constitutional or legal justification, except as a military measure." (*ibid.*, IX, 108–109, Sep. 2, 1863).

shell when, in the final edict, he characterized his measure not as a dictator's stroke, but as "a fit and necessary war measure." [24]

V

Taking a chronological liberty, we step forward a hundred days to January 1, 1863. It was then that the President promulgated the definitive edict without which the September document would have been useless. Curiously enough, there were doubts whether Lincoln would actually issue the January proclamation. In his annual message to Congress under date of December 1, 1862, he had indeed discussed emancipation elaborately, but not in terms of sweeping liberation by presidential act. Rather he treated it as a matter of compensated emancipation to be embodied in articles amendatory to the Constitution and implemented by uncoerced compliance on the part of such states as wished to adopt it. Furthermore, he presented it as a grave issue on which a program was yet to be framed, by no means as a problem already neatly solved by the President. More than two months after the preliminary proclamation had been issued, the Executive in addressing Congress was thus emphasizing a very different scheme of liberation. He did not say that proceedings under the proclamation would be stayed because of the "recommendation" of this more permanent solution, but its "timely adoption," he said, by bringing restoration, would stay both the war and presidential emancipation.[1] Thus even as late as December 1862 Lincoln was hinting that, under an assumed set of circumstances, forcible liberation by the executive might not actually go into effect. Though he meant this only in the sense of the warning proclamation as issued, and only toward areas that might return to allegiance (a dim prospect), it was possible to read, or misread, the December message as almost a relegation of the emancipation proclamation to a position of secondary importance.

Was it possible that the effective decree would not be issued at the New Year? There were friends of the edict who doubted it and opponents who wanted to avert it. Lincoln's Illinois adviser, Orville H. Browning, suggested to Judge Thomas of Massachusetts that the judge ought to try at the last minute to reason the President out of his an-

---

[24] *Ibid.*, VIII, 162.   [1] *Works*, VIII, 129.

nounced policy. ". . . I said to Judge Thomas [wrote Browning] that I thought he ought to go to the President and have a full, frank conversation with him in regard to the threatened proclamation of emancipation—that . . . it was fraught with evil, and evil only and would do much injury; and that . . . he might possibly induce him to withhold, or at least to modify it . . . . He informed me . . . that he had taken my advice, and had the talk [with Lincoln] but that it would avail nothing. The President was fatally bent upon his course, saying that if he should refuse to issue his proclamation there would be a rebellion in the north . . . . There is no hope. The proclamation will come . . . ." [2]

Misgivings of a different sort troubled those who differed with Browning and his doubting Thomas. A supporter of emancipation wrote to Sumner: "We feel no reliance that he [Lincoln] will [carry out the proclamation in full] while we see him guided by the baleful councils of Seward & the Border State men." [3] To J. M. Forbes the prospect seemed dubious. "The first of January is near at hand," he wrote, "and we see no signs of any measures for carrying into effect the Proclamation . . . . Before next April we ought to have 100,000 blacks under arms, ... Everything ought to be prepared on the 1st of January to *begin the war* in earnest." [4] To Sumner such doubts seemed unfounded. "The President is occupied on the Proclamation," he wrote on Christmas Day 1862. "He will stand firm. He said to me that it was hard to drive him from a position which he had once taken." [5] Soon afterward he wrote: "The President says he would not stop the Proclamation if he could, and he could not if he would. . . . Hallelujah!" [6]

With a lawyer-like "Whereas" and a resounding "Now, therefore,' the proclamation came on January 1. By virtue of military power in time of actual armed rebellion, so the document read,

. . . I, Abraham Lincoln . . . do, . . . in accordance with my pur- pose . . . publicly proclaimed for . . . 100 days . . . , order and des- ignate as . . . in rebellion, . . . the following . . . . [The designation

2 Browning, *Diary*, I, 606–607 (Dec. 31, 1862).
3 G. F. Williams to Charles Sumner, Boston, Dec. 19, 1862, Sumner MSS.
4 J. M. Forbes to Sumner, Boston, Dec. 18, 1862, *ibid.*
5 Sumner to George Livermore, Washington, Dec. 25, 1862, *Proceedings*, Mass. Hist. Soc., XLIV, 596.
6 Same to same, Washington, Dec. 28, 1862, *ibid.*

here given omitted the state of Tennessee altogether and made important territorial exceptions as to Virginia and Louisiana; otherwise it comprised the commonwealths of the Confederate States of America.]

And . . . I do order and declare that all persons held as slaves within said . . . States [etc.] . . . are, and henceforward shall be, free; and that the Executive Government . . . will recognize and maintain the freedom of said persons.

And I hereby enjoin upon the people so declared . . . free to abstain from all violence, unless in necessary self-defense; and I recommend . . . that . . . they labor faithfully for reasonable wages.

And I . . . declare . . . that such persons . . . will be received into the armed service of the United States . . . .

And upon this act, sincerely believed to be an act of justice, warranted by the Constitution upon military necessity, I invoke the considerate judgment of mankind and the gracious favor of Almighty God.

Rarely has a President signed so famous a document as this, but in the execution of the deed there was no fanfare. In disregard of the President's right hand the customary New Year's reception had been held, on which occasion, as often, the White House was open to any and all. Not till after three hours of wearisome handshaking did Lincoln sign the proclamation. According to Sumner the President "found that his hand trembled so that he held the pen with difficulty." [7]

It was at almost the last minute that the final touches had been placed on the document. On December 31, 1862, the proclamation had been discussed in special Cabinet meeting. There had been a few suggestions of emendations—e. g., Seward's suggestion that freedmen be enjoined, not merely appealed to, to avoid tumult.[8] The "felicitous closing sentence" [9] with its invocation of Divine favor, was the product of Chase's prompting and Lincoln's revision. To Chase's words "an act of justice, warranted by the constitution," Lincoln significantly added "upon military necessity." [10] It was Sumner's recollection,

---

[7] Charles Sumner to George Livermore, Senate Chamber, Jan. 9, 1863, *Proceedings,* Mass. Hist. Soc., XLIV, 597. For information on the pen itself, claimed by the Massachusetts Historical Society through the Livermore family, see *ibid.,* XLIV, 595–604. A conflicting claim as to the pen appeared in the catalogue of the Kolb Collection (auctioned by W. D. Morley of Philadelphia), item 204, where it is stated that the pen had been given by Sumner to James Wormley, colored, owner of the Wormley Hotel in Washington.

[8] Welles, *Diary,* I, 210.   [9] *Ibid.*

[10] For Chase's letter to the President, December 31, 1862, giving lengthy suggestions for revision of the final proclamation and enclosing a full draft as Chase would have worded it, see Warden, *Chase,* 513–515.

however, that the first suggestion for this passage had come from himself.[11]

Men of the time were not without a sense of the historic importance of the document. The learned George Livermore of Cambridge, Massachusetts, in whose essay on slavery [12] Lincoln had shown an interest,[13] had arranged that Sumner should procure a gold pen for the signing at Livermore's expense; the pen was then to become Livermore's valued treasure.[14]

VI

Repercussions from the proclamation were as complex as were social and political groups within and without the lines. The edict was jubilantly hailed; it was roundly cursed; it was exaggerated and twisted as to meaning both by supporters and opponents. "God bless President Lincoln. He may yet be the Moses to deliver the oppressed," [1] was the typical comment of Northern abolitionists. "All . . . trials . . . are swallowed up in the great deep joy of this emancipation." [2] By its dating on January 1, the edict captured the note of New Year bells ringing in an era of freedom.[3] "The . . . proclamation," wrote a Massachusetts Coolidge, "touches the key note of public expectation, and is universally acceptable to the people. For the good sense of the people . . . teaches them that this war cannot, & *ought not* to end until Slavery . . . is removed." [4] "President Lincoln has . . . hurled against rebellion the bolt which he has so long held suspended," declared Lincoln's home paper, the *Illinois State Journal*, which added: ". . . those who refuse to support the Government . . . are traitors and should be so treated . . . ." [5] Theodore Til-

---

[11] "The last sentence was actually framed by Chase, although I believe that I first suggested it both to him and to the President." Sumner to Livermore, Jan. 9, 1863, *Proceedings*, Mass. Hist. Soc., XLIV, 597.

[12] George Livermore, "An Historical Research Respecting the Opinions of the Founders . . . on Negroes as Slaves, as Citizens, and as Soldiers," read before the Massachusetts Historical Society, August 14, 1862. *Proceedings*, 1862–1863, 86–248.

[13] Livermore to Sumner, Dec. 29, 1862, Sumner MSS.

[14] *Ibid.*

[1] Joseph Emery to S. P. Chase, Cincinnati, O., Sept. 29, 1862, Chase MSS., Lib. of Cong.

[2] Rev. Charles E. Hodges to W. L. Garrison, Jan. 2, 1863, MS., Boston Pub. Lib.

[3] In the diary of John Wingate Thornton the first entry for 1863 reads: "The new year gloriously ushered in by Prest. Lincoln's proclamation of freedom" (Jan. 6, 1863). MS., Boston Athenaeum.

[4] B. Coolidge to Charles Sumner, Lawrence, Mass., Sumner MSS., vol. 57 (misdated).

[5] *Illinois State Journal* (weekly ed.), Oct. 1, 1862, p. 2, c. 4.

ton of the New York *Independent,* ardent abolitionist and reformer, avowed himself to be "in a bewilderment of joy"; the spirit of the edict he said, "is . . . so racing up and down and through my blood that I am half crazy with enthusiasm"; a friend, he said, had been down on his knees in prayer and praise.[6]

Where antislavery enthusiasm was joined, as it often was, with unstudied *naïveté,* the tendency to burst into emotional ecstasy took a tone of exaggerated burbling that may be illustrated by the following example: *"The Proclamation,* too! Isn't it glorious? . . . *Now* I am impatient to see our idolized *Fremont* . . . , Carrying that glorious Proclamation in his hand—bring Liberty . . . to thousands of oppressed ones." [7] To the Cincinnati *Gazette* it seemed that the proclamation would be received in the loyal states with a "perfect furor of acclamation," restoring old friends and uniting the "main portion" of the people.[8] From Concord, Massachusetts, E. R. Hoar congratulated Sumner, finding the military aspects of the measure even more important than the philanthropic, and concluding: "How this can do us any thing but good I cannot see." [9] Another of Sumner's friends was "overjoyed" that the President had created a "land of freedom" as he reflected that this "glorious result" was a compensation for all that had been suffered.[10]

Just after the proclamation was issued the President was serenaded; then the crowd rushed to Chase's residence, called loudly for the Secretary, and greeted him with resounding cheers as he appeared on the balcony. Referring amid cries of approval to the "great act of the President," Chase ventured the assertion that it was the "dawn of a new era." [11] Bostonians attended a carefully planned public assemblage to listen to stately and spirited oratory. The big meeting was held at noon on October 6, 1862, at Faneuil Hall. City and ward committees perfected the arrangements; Boston's best was represented in numerous vice-presidents and secretaries for the occasion; as for the speaker, he was none other than Charles Sumner, then seeking reëlection for

---

6 Theodore Tilton to W. L. Garrison, Sept. 24, 1862, Garrison MSS.
7 Lillie T. Atkinson to Anna E. Dickinson, Jan. 4, 1863, Anna E. Dickinson MSS.
8 Cincinnati *Daily Gazette,* Sept. 25, 1862, p. 3, c. 3.
9 E. R. Hoar to Sumner, Concord, Dec. 29, 1862, Sumner MSS.
10 T. Gilbert to Sumner, Boston, Sept. 23, 1862, *ibid.*
11 Cincinnati *Daily Gazette,* Sept. 26, 1862, p. 3, c. 4.

a third term in the United States Senate.[12] Waving hats and flutter-
ing handkerchiefs greeted the senator as he stepped upon the platform; the demonstration was said to have been unsurpassed since
Webster had been greeted in the same historic hall. The orator began
with ancient Athens, took note of the Mohammedans in Africa and
Spain, paid vote-getting respects to embattled sons of Erin, and touched
every throbbing New England chord as he voiced his impressive support of the policy of the Lincoln administration, for which he claimed
sponsorship and credit.[13] In its double character as an electioneering
occasion and a ratification of the proclamation, the meeting boosted
Sumner while conferring a kind of reflected glory upon the President.

Even among abolitionists, however, enthusiasm for the proclamation was somewhat dampened by doubts and dissatisfaction. Neither
Lincoln's preliminary nor his final edict met their wishes. To Oliver
Johnson, friend of William Lloyd Garrison, the President's decree
was "not all that justice requires, nor all that we would wish." [14] The
proclamation, croaked Gurowski, was issued "without a fixed, broad,
positive plan what to do & at once with the emancipated." [15] Some who
accepted the Emancipator's act at even more than face value nevertheless withheld praise from Lincoln himself; among such the tendency was to give "thanks for the Proclamation of Emancipation coming from a reluctant govt. trembling beneath the retributions of
justice." [16] Wendell Phillips, out for blood and bursting with hor-
rendous rhetoric as he denounced "bedeviled Southerners," thought
it "childish" for the President "to hide himself in the White House and
launch a proclamation at us on a first of January." As shipways are
oiled before a vessel is launched, he would have preferred to see
preparations made "for the reception of three million bondmen into
the civil state." [17] Admitting that the proclamation was "a great step
onward," Lydia Maria Child wrote that it excited "no glow of enthusi-

[12] Sumner was renominated for the Senate by the Republican state convention of
Massachusetts on September 10, 1862, and overwhelmingly reëlected by the legislature
on January 15, 1863. Public discussion of the emancipation was intimately associated
with his campaign for this post. Sumner, *Works*, VII, 240, 245.

[13] For the ratification meeting and the Sumner speech see *ibid.*, VII, 194-236.

[14] Oliver Johnson to Garrison, Sept. 25, 1862, Garrison MSS.

[15] Gurowski to John A. Andrew, Washington, Oct. 27, 1862, Andrew MSS.

[16] Mary Grew to W. L. Garrison, Philadelphia, Oct. 2, 1862, Garrison MSS.

[17] Phillips, *Speeches, Lectures, and Letters,* 547.

asm"; she could not "get rid of misgivings" as to what might occur before the edict went "into effect." [18] Despite his above-noted exuberance, Tilton had to take a fling at the defects of the proclamation, with "its . . . imperfect statesmanship, . . . its . . . delay of . . . operation, . . . [and] its rheumatic and stiff-jointed English." [19]

Though a number of antislavery reformers took credit for the edict, and though the fame of Garrison was advanced by its issuance, there was a tendency to award the palm to Chase, as when a New York lawyer noted that the government was on his (Chase's) "platform" and that the President had "adopted" the secretary's views.[20] By his own statement, Chase preferred a more vigorous act, but, said he: "As the President did not concur . . . , I was willing, and indeed very glad, to accept the Proclamation as the next best mode of dealing with the subject." [21] Associating a prolongation of the war with the freeing of the slaves, Chase saw in all this the judgment of Providence upon the North "for having so long shared the guilt of slavery." [22] In Garrison's mixed feelings on the proclamation one can see both the joy and the dissatisfaction of abolitionist reformers. In a letter to his daughter about the time he received the news, Garrison wrote: "The President's Proclamation is certainly matter for great rejoicing, as far as it goes . . . , but it leaves slavery, as a system . . . , still to exist in all the so-called loyal Slave States . . . . What . . . is still needed, is a proclamation distinctly announcing the total abolition of slavery." [23] After the final proclamation the Boston agitator wrote with his old bitterness toward the Lincoln government: "The policy of the Administration is singularly paradoxical and self-defeating. Think of . . . Fremont, Butler, Sigel and Phelps laid upon the shelf, to propitiate the 'copperhead' element . . . !" Reflecting upon the weakness of abolitionism, Garrison could only lament: "How vulgar and brutal, and yet how fearfully prevalent, is . . . colorphobia at the North." [24]

---

18 Lydia Maria Child to Sumner, Wayland, Mass., Oct. 3, 1862, Sumner MSS.
19 Theodore Tilton to W. L. Garrison, Sept. 24, 1862, Garrison MSS.
20 John Livingston to S. P. Chase, New York, Oct. 1, 1862, Chase MSS., Lib. of Cong.
21 Chase to N. B. Buford, Oct. 11, 1862 (copy), Chase MSS., Hist. Soc. of Pa.
22 S. P. Chase to Elihu Burritt, Oct. 6, 1862 (copy), *ibid.*
23 W. L. Garrison to Fanny Garrison, Boston, Sept. 25, 1862, Garrison MSS.
24 Garrison to "Dear Friend May" (probably Samuel J. May), Boston, April 6, 1863, *ibid.*

VII

Lincoln was never in fact hostile, as were the Jacobins, to the Southern people; yet the Richmond *Whig* treated his measure of emancipation as "a dash of the pen to destroy four thousand millions of our property." [1] In this stinging comment one finds the epitome of Southern interpretation. The Richmond *Examiner* stigmatized the act as the "most startling political crime . . . in American history." [2] Referring to the savagery and "darkest excesses" of the Negro in the Nat Turner insurrection (which, as the paper omitted to state, was altogether exceptional for the United States), the Richmond *Enquirer* asserted: "This is the sort of work Lincoln desires to see." [3] To the embittered E. A. Pollard the proclamation seemed "the permanent triumph of fanaticism under a false pretense." [4] To President Jefferson Davis it offered "but one of three . . . consequences—the extermination of the slaves, the exile of the whole white population from the Confederacy, or absolute and total separation of these States from the United States." [5] The bogey of slave insurrection, which had intense emotional value, was the chief motif of Southern criticism, but the economic factor was not neglected, as when a Louisianian, urging that agriculture could not exist without slaves, lamented that the proclamation would effect "the ruin of the State." [6]

With almost equal vehemence the proclamation was denounced at the North, both by Lincoln's opponents and by some of his more moderate friends. The subject was entangled with the heated campaign for the state and congressional elections of 1862, as in New York where General James S. Wadsworth, Republican candidate for governor, stood firmly for the President's policy, while Wadsworth's opponents, supporting Seymour, denounced emancipation

[1] Richmond *Whig*, Oct. 1, 1862, quoted in Moore, *Rebellion Record* (Diary), V, 89. The reference to "four thousand millions" (of dollars) was an exaggeration. (The readiness of Lincoln to give compensation for emancipated slaves in the South is well known.)

[2] Jan. 7, 1863, *ibid.* (Diary), VI, 32.

[3] Richmond *Enquirer*, Oct. 1, 1862, quoted in Cincinnati *Daily Gazette*, Oct. 8, 1862, p. 1, c. 4.

[4] E. A. Pollard, *The Lost Cause*, 360.

[5] Message of President Davis, Jan. 12, 1863, *Journal*, Confederate Congress (Jan. 14), III, 14.

[6] Letter from unnamed correspondent to Lincoln, New Orleans, Sept. 29, 1863, MS., N. Y. Hist. Soc.

as the butchery of women and children.[7] The September edict, it must be remembered, had synchronized with another presidential proclamation suspending the habeas corpus privilege and legitimizing arbitrary arrests; often the two executive acts were linked in the same denunciation. The case of Browning, whose wish to avert the edict has been noted, serves as an illustration of misgivings among Northern conservatives. To Browning it seemed that the "useless and . . . mischievous" proclamations served only "to unite and exasperate . . . the South, and divide and distract us in the North."[8] Thomas Ewing thought these proclamations "had ruined the Republican party in Ohio,"[9] while another doubter feared that in his brief service as pilot Lincoln might "drive the ship of state on the shoals of *proclamations*, or the snags of '*Habeas Corpus*.' "[10] Senator W. P. Fessenden of Maine expressed surprise that the proclamation was ever issued. It was, he thought, "very unfortunately worded, and was, at best, but *brutem* [sic] *fulmen*."[11]

Northern criticism of Lincoln's decree appeared in the vigorous pamphlet literature of the day. In a brochure that appeared in New York in 1863 it was asserted that "freed negroes of the North were a standing monument to the folly of Abolitionism," and that the "idea of working for pay never entered in black nature." After exhibiting deplorable conditions resulting from emancipation in the West Indies, the author concluded: "Practically the link is broken—the blacks are pushed off the plank, and we of the North, who are not in office [a fling at the Lincoln government], are rolling in the dirt."[12]

---

[7] Pearson, *Wadsworth*, 156.   [8] Browning, *Diary*, I, 609 (Jan. 2, 1863).
[9] *Ibid.*, I, 592 (Dec. 5, 1862).
[10] Hugh Campbell to Joseph Holt, St. Louis, Nov. 15, 1862. In an earlier letter (Sept. 26, 1862) Mr. Campbell, a merchant at St. Louis of Irish birth and Southern connections, had written to Holt: "Stop him! Hold him!—is all I can say by way of advice to you, as the friend of the President. Beg him to write no more letters to newspapers, and never to publish a proclamation. . . . His proclamations have paralized [sic] our armies . . . . We must retrocede—but let us do so . . . with dignity." On July 24, 1862 Campbell had written to Holt: "The *rump* Congress has ruined the country. The President has yielded to . . . the most destructive party [the radical Republicans] that the country has ever known, and we now find ourselves fighting for emancipation & confiscation." Holt MSS.
[11] Browning, *Diary*, I, 587–588 (Nov. 28, 1862).
[12] *Emancipation and Its Results*, Papers from the Society for the Diffusion of Political Knowledge, No. 6, (N.Y., 1863), 5, 15, 30. The president of this society was S. F. B. Morse; the copy used by the author bears the inscription of a gentleman (Shepard Devereux Gilbert) who lived in Beaufort District, S. C. Here was a bit of Northern propaganda which found an appreciative reception in the South.

In Kentucky there was excitement, dissatisfaction among army men, demand for a change of dynasty, conservative wrath, and genuine alarm as to Lincoln's course even among his friends. One of these friends, the clear-headed George D. Prentice who had predicted in his Louisville *Journal* that sectional war would spell the doom of slavery, and who had sought to dissuade the South from what he deemed the madness of secession, still considered slavery doomed, but preferred that it be destroyed "by the . . . inevitable operations of the war [rather] than by emancipation proclamations and Congressional legislation." [13] Another patriotic Kentuckian wrote: "There are vast numbers . . . who feel that there are two wars against the integrity of the Government, one by Secessionism and the other by Abolitionism." He thought abolitionism had to be prostrated; that done, the rebellion might be settled.[14] When it was suggested that Emerson Etheridge, Tennessee Unionist, be named for a Federal judgeship, he declared he could not accept it, for, said he, ". . . since his Proclamation of the 22d of Sept. last, and his treachery to the Union men of the South, any Southern man would be disgraced to accept any appointment under the President unless in . . . military service . . . ." He added that on the restoration of peace he wished to live in Tennessee, which he "could not do wearing his [Lincoln's] official livery." [15]

From an unexpected quarter came vigorous opposition in the outspoken criticism of Benjamin R. Curtis of Massachusetts, former member of the Supreme Court of the United States. Curtis's public and forensic utterances had not justified the antislavery approval that had greeted his famous dissenting opinion in the Dred Scott case.[16] In a pamphlet whose effect was regretted by friends of the proclamation,[17] Curtis argued against "subserviency to a man." Deploring

13 George D. Prentice to John Hancock, Louisville, Ky., Feb. 25, 1864, MS., Ill. State Hist. Lib.

14 Charles G. Wintersmith to Horatio Seymour, Elizabethtown, Ky., Feb. 23, 1863, *ibid.*

15 Emerson Etheridge to R. W. Thompson, Washington, D.C., Mar. 23, 1863, MS., Lincoln National Life Foundation, Ft. Wayne, Ind.

16 For Curtis's attitude, which by no means presented a clear-cut antislavery record, see F. H. Hodder, in *Miss. Vall. Hist. Rev.*, XVI, 3-22 (June, 1929).

17 Having written a pamphlet in Lincoln's defense, G. P. Lowrey, a New York lawyer, wrote to S. P. Chase (December 1, 1862): "I wished . . . to undo . . . the bad effect of Judge Curtis' pamphlet on the popular mind, ..." Chase MSS., Lib. of Cong.

that "every citizen" was placed "under the direct military command and control of the President" (here he referred to arbitrary arrests), he assailed the proclamation of emancipation as a misuse of executive power.[18] Such a denunciation by Curtis, with its impressiveness of legal phrasing, leads one to wonder what would have been his role had he remained a member of the United States Supreme Court in a day when the very legality of the President's wartime acts was tested by that Court and approved (in the *Prize Cases*)[19] by a five-to-four decision. Every statement such as that of Curtis came as an increment to the vast body of less dignified opposition typified by Bennett's mordant *Herald,* to whose editorial mind the January proclamation, besides being "practically a dead letter," was "unwise and ill-timed, impracticable, and outside of the constitution."[20]

VIII

Reception of the proclamation in England varied according to economic or social patterns. Sophisticated and aristocratic elements were unfavorable and sarcastic, while popular mass meetings were jubilantly enthusiastic, being usually linked with demonstrations for workingmen's rights and with liberal agitation at home. To Earl Russell the edict appeared to be "of a very strange nature," for, said he: "It professes to emancipate all slaves in places where the United States' authorities cannot . . . now make emancipation a reality, but . . . not . . . where . . . emancipation, if decreed, might have been carried into effect." Pointing out that "friends of abolition" expected "total and impartial freedom for the slave," Russell stated that the proclamation made slavery "at once legal and illegal," and that it lacked altogether any "declaration of a principle adverse to

---

[18] Benjamin R. Curtis, *Executive Power* (29 pp., Boston, 1862).

[19] When the President's proclamation of a blockade at the beginning of the conflict (in the absence of a congressional declaration of war) was challenged in the *Prize Cases,* decided in 1863 (67 U. S. 635), the majority of the Court (five members) decided in favor of the legality of Lincoln's acts, but four, including the Chief Justice, dissented. Of those who sustained the President, three (Swayne, Miller, and Davis) were Lincoln's appointees, while another of the five (Wayne of Georgia) came from the deep South. Had Wayne decided differently, as he might well have been expected to do, this vitally important case would have gone against the President. In such a close situation the presence of Curtis on the Court might have made a great difference. Randall, *Constitutional Problems Under Lincoln,* 51–59.

[20] New York *Herald,* Jan. 3, 1863 (editorial), p. 4, cc. 2–3.

slavery." [1] In a memorandum intended for his cabinet Russell wrote: "There is surely a total want of consistency in this measure [the proclamation of September 22]. . . . If it were a measure of Emancipation it should be extended to all the States of the Union . . . ." He added: ". . . emancipation . . . is not granted to the claims of humanity but inflicted as a punishment . . . . Mr. Lincoln openly professed his indifference as to the . . . fate of the four millions of blacks who inhabit the Republic. He declared that if their freedom would help to restore the Union, he was willing they should be free; if their continued slavery would tend to that end he was willing they should remain slaves." [2]

In a "leader" the *Times* of London referred to the preliminary proclamation as the President's "last card," adding that if anything could induce the South to continue the war to the "last extremity," it was this decree. While not pretending to attack slavery, declared the *Times*, the decree launched the threat of servile insurrection as a means of war against certain states.[3] The "harmlessness of the proclamation," said the pro-Confederate Manchester *Guardian*, did "not excuse its utter want of principle." [4] Agreeing as to the ineffectiveness of Lincoln's act, Francis W. Newman wrote from London in 1864: ". . . what is one to make of his [Lincoln's] . . . speeches, & his . . . shilly shallying about slave property, . . . ?" [5]

These complaints were overwhelmingly offset, at least as to numbers, by spontaneous demonstrations in a series of remarkable meetings in British cities at the turn of the year, 1862–63. Held at York, Bolton, Halifax, Sheffield, Birmingham, Leicester, Preston, Coventry, Manchester, and at the Great Exeter Hall in London, these meetings issued declarations which, for Englishmen, had both international and domestic significance. In the National Archives at Washington one finds the original "Address of the Inhabitants of Birmingham to

---

[1] Earl Russell to Lord Lyons, Jan. 17, 1863, *Annual Cyclopaedia*, 1863, 834.

[2] "Original draft of Memorandum respecting interposition in American contest," Oct. 13, 1862. (Such "interposition," of course, did not materialize.) The above quotations were taken by the author from the memorandum, which was confidentially circulated in the British Cabinet. For brief references to the document, see E. D. Adams, *Great Britain and the American Civil War*, II, 49, 101–102; Spencer Walpole, *Life of Lord John Russell*, II, 351.

[3] *The Times*, Oct. 6, 1862, p. 6, cc. 2–3; Oct. 7, 1862, p. 8, cc. 2–4.

[4] Manchester *Guardian*, Oct. 7, 1862.

[5] Francis W. Newman to Epes Sargent, London, Sept. 10, 1864, MS., Boston Pub. Lib.

His Excellency Abraham Lincoln, President of the United States of America." This gigantic document is an unbroken scroll, an amazingly long roll of paper carrying at least ten thousand signatures, headed by that of Charles Sturge, Mayor, and including such names as Burgoyne, Wallington, Pownall, Wilkes, Butler, Heseldine, Lambert, Morgan, Cadwalader, Smallwood, Derrington, Bowden, Bates, Royston, Pollock, Heath, Harris, Thompson, and Partridge. These Birmingham friends conveyed to Lincoln their "deep and heartfelt sympathy" and assured him of the "good wishes of all Men who love liberty." [6]

Home of the "Manchester school" and seat of economic liberalism associated with Cobden and Bright, the city of Manchester was a center for agitation in favor of labor rights as well as for free trade and other reforms; as such it was the target of Tory scorn.[7] This must be borne in mind in reading of the notable meeting at the Free Trade Hall in Manchester on the night of December 31, 1862. Called by a committee of laborers to enable the working classes to express their sympathy with the United States and their endorsement of the President's emancipation proclamation, the meeting opened about seven o'clock and lasted till nearly eleven. The mayor presided, John Stuart Mill sent a letter, speeches in the liberal tone were delivered, and a glowing "Address to President Lincoln by the Citizens of Manchester, England" was issued. Honoring the President for his acts for human liberation, and striking the chord of common "blood and language," the citizens ventured to "implore" the President "not to faint" in his "providential mission," and hailed the "mighty task" of reorganizing "the industry not only of four millions of the colored race, but of five millions of whites." [8]

In reply Lincoln sent his famous letter *To the Working-Men of Manchester.* Referring to the "integrity of the . . . Republic" as

---

[6] MS., Dep. of State, Nat. Archives.

[7] The opponents of the Cobden and Bright school, wrote Henry W. Lord, United States consul at Manchester, "under the leadership of the *Times* now point with derision to . . . 'a nation in the pangs of dissolution, from the . . . very agencies sought to be introduced into England.'" Lord to Seward, Manchester, Aug. 20, 1862, MSS., Dept. of State (Consular Letters, Manchester, vol. 1), Nat. Archives.

[8] The text of the address is given in Moore, *Rebellion Record* (Docs.), VI, 344–345. Meetings in Manchester and elsewhere are described as "assemblies of the largest dimensions" evincing "absolute unanimity and enthusiasm" in the *Morning Star*, London, Jan. 2, 1863. The author has consulted numerous documents on the subject among the MSS. of the U. S. Department of State in the National Archives (Consular Letters, Manchester, vol. 1; Diplomatic Despatches, Britain, vol. 81).

the "key" to all his measures, the President pointed out that he could not always "enlarge or restrict the scope of moral results" arising from public policies. Though he considered that the duty of "self-preservation" rested solely with the American people, he warmly welcomed foreign favor, and found it pleasant to acknowledge the demonstration at Manchester of a desire "that a spirit of amity and peace toward this country may prevail in the councils of your Queen, . . . respected and esteemed . . . by the kindred nation . . . on this side of the Atlantic." He continued:

I . . . deeply deplore the sufferings which the working-men at Manchester, and in all Europe, are called to endure in this crisis. It has been . . . represented that the attempt to overthrow this government, . . . built upon . . . human rights, and to substitute . . . one which should rest . . . on . . . human slavery, was likely to obtain the favor of Europe. Through the action of our disloyal citizens, the working-men of Europe have been subjected to severe trials, for the purpose of forcing their sanction to that attempt. Under the circumstances, I cannot but regard your decisive utterances . . . as an instance of sublime Christian heroism . . . not . . . surpassed . . . in any country. . . . I do not doubt that . . . [these] sentiments . . . will be sustained by your great nation; and . . . I have no hesitation in assuring you they will excite . . . reciprocal feelings of friendship among the American people. I hail this interchange . . . as an augury that . . . the peace and friendship which now exist between the two nations will be, as it shall be my desire to make them, perpetual.[9]

In a similar though briefer address to the working-men of London (February 2, 1863) Lincoln gave eloquent thanks for their "exalted and humane sentiments," which he interpreted as manifestations in support of "free institutions throughout the world." He asked them to accept his best wishes for their individual welfare, "and for the welfare and happiness of the whole British people." [10]

British popular demonstrations and the President's graceful response constituted a pleasing chapter in Anglo-American relations. Charles Francis Adams wrote of "signs of extensive reaction in the popular feeling toward the United States" as shown in many meetings and addresses to the President.[11] "The President's proclamation," thought Adams, "has had a great effect here, if not in America. It has

9 *Works*, VIII, 194–197 (Jan. 19, 1863).

10 *Ibid.*, VIII, 211–212.

11 C. F. Adams to Edward Everett, London, Jan. 23, 1863, Everett MSS.

rallied all the sympathies of the working classes, and has produced meetings the like of which, I am told, have not been seen since the days of reform and the corn laws." [12] Nor was reaction less favorable on the continent of Europe. It was reported that France was "unanimously for emancipation," [13] while in Spain the "entire press, the Clerical and reactionary not excluded, was loudly in our favor." [14] In general the foreign outlook was so influenced by emancipation as to be deeply disappointing to the architects of Confederate international policy. Judah Benjamin was soon to concede that spades were trumps.[15]

---

[12] Adams to Everett, London, Feb. 27, 1863, *ibid.* "The . . . proclamation has had a remarkable effect here. It has consolidated the popular sentiment friendly to us, which had before lain dormant, whilst it has equally developed the alienation of the higher classes. The meeting at Exeter Hall [London] was a phenomenon which surprised even those who understood it." Adams to Everett, London, Feb. 13, 1863, *ibid.* Such crowds had sought entrance at the Exeter Hall meeting (January 29) that a second and third meeting were held to accommodate the overflow.

[13] John Bigelow to Seward, Oct. 10, 1862, Bancroft, *Seward*, II, 340.

[14] Gustave Koerner to I. Baker, Belleville, Ill., Feb. 5, 1868, MS., Ill. State Hist. Lib. Koerner was United States minister to Spain, 1862–1865.

[15] Owsley, *King Cotton Diplomacy*, 552.

CHAPTER XXIII

A LIMPING FREEDOM

NOT only was Lincoln's emancipation of limited scope; where applied, it was beset with difficulty and delay. Indeed it was but a limping freedom that was launched by virtue of the war power, to be followed by political disappointment and by that Union military defeat which came after McClellan's removal. To manage the transition from a stabilized order of society into an untried system could never be easy. To attempt it on a colossal scale involving millions of human beings would be a major problem at its best, but the attempt was made at its worst, for the new regime was proclaimed during war, was imposed by military force, and was promoted in the absence of that governmental and civilian planning which such an ambitious social, economic, and agricultural program rightly demanded. In its initial stages the new dispensation was haphazard, casual, utopian in some of its aspects, and unable to proceed under its own social and economic power.

As a measure to be some day imposed upon an enemy not yet conquered, the dispensation of freedom lacked immediateness and partook of the nature of a paper pronouncement. In the North many did not favor it, but among those that did, it was greeted with rhetorical burbling; to the lowly blacks in the South it was only in part the theme of kingdom-come shoutings, for even within their bewildered ranks there were deep-seated Southern loyalties, as there were prejudices against Yankees. To suppose that the sense of being part of a definite Southern way of life existed only in white skins is to harbor an erroneous assumption. As the act of a far-away government at war with the South, the edict of emancipation was denied that home coöperation and that local support which so extensive and so intimate a program required. In the absence of that voluntary effort which Lincoln

181

desired as he unsuccessfully sought peaceable liberation in the midst of war, there was little reason to hope for everyday friendly assistance and wise guidance being extended to millions of dependents who were soon to realize that erstwhile owners had been protecting guardians as well as taskmasters, and that incoming employers might have as much of an eye to money-getting as to Negro welfare. As a questionable assumption of executive power the proclamation was bound in legal shallows. Launched as a punishment for rebellion, it lacked even that moral denunciation of slavery for which friends of freedom earnestly, though often abstractly, yearned. Programs to deal with hard facts of Southern economy were of less concern to sentimental abolitionists than sonorous pronouncements; the satisfaction of such persons came from reading into the proclamation a moral quality which its hard-headed critics failed to see. Justified by Lincoln as a measure of war, the edict had the disadvantage of close association with the military arm and with that "martial law" by which John Quincy Adams had declared that liberation could some day be imposed.[1] Coming at a stage when the government at Washington was on crutches (in the period of the election of 1862, of Fredericksburg, and of Lincoln's cabinet crisis) [2] it was open to criticism as a kind of last resort. Such were the conditions under which the embattled sections labored in the early phases of Lincoln's regime of emancipation. Before glancing at the realities of that regime, attention must be given to the policy of organizing Negroes for service in the Union army.

I

The question of Negro troops was among the unsought but inevitable problems laid upon Lincoln's doorstep. Just as general recruiting was largely by haphazard popular effort, so the raising of colored soldiers arose spontaneously as a matter of civilian agitation and as a concomitant of emancipation. First results were unpromising, as in the abortive efforts of General David Hunter, whose premature organization of a black regiment (the first South Carolina) in April 1862 proved a bad beginning and an unkindness to ill-treated

---

[1] Randall, *Constitutional Problems Under Lincoln*, 343–347, 374–376. Ex-President Adams argued thus while a member of Congress.

[2] See below, pp. 242–249.

Negroes.[1] Champions of the colored man persisted, however, until they formed under Colonel Thomas Wentworth Higginson the "first slave regiment mustered into the service of the United States during the . . . civil war." [2] Though an invitation to command "a regiment of Kalmuck Tartars" would have been no more unexpected,[3] Higginson trained and led his colored force, whose minor service in an area near Charleston seemed almost a flaunting of Negro fighters in the faces of proud Carolinians. In his vivid account of his experience with these "perpetual children," the colonel emphasized the blackness of his men, with hardly a mulatto among them, their innocence of vandalism, and their fine military qualities.[4] The youthful Robert Gould Shaw, commanding "the first colored regiment of the North to go to the war," [5] lost his life when leading his colored troops as they assaulted Battery Wagner in the harbor of Charleston (July 18, 1863); the artistry of St. Gaudens has given him sculptural immortality on Boston Common. Another commander who ardently favored the recruitment of Negro troops was J. W. Phelps, in command near New Orleans. Out of these efforts there grew a quarrel between Phelps and B. F. Butler, culminating in Phelps's resignation.[6] Following this, Butler himself organized several colored regiments, comparing their complexion to that of "the late Mr. Webster." [7] It was asserted that one of these regiments had been in Confederate service.[8] Some of the advocates of Negro troops proposed Frémont as organizer and chief commander.[9] Urged by an impressive memorial on the subject, Lincoln gave consent, but in a lengthy letter the inactive general

---

1 "The trouble is in the legacy of . . . distrust bequeathed by the abortive regiment of General Hunter,—into which they [the Negroes] were driven like cattle, kept for several months in camp, and then turned off without a shilling, by order of the War Department." T. W. Higginson, *Army Life in a Black Regiment,* 15. See also Fred A. Shannon, in *Jour. of Negro Hist.,* XI, 563–583 (Oct., 1926).

2 Higginson, 1.   3 *Ibid.,* 2.   4 *Ibid.,* 10, 29, 127–128.

5 J. F. Rhodes, *Hist. of the United States,* IV, 332.

6 Nicolay and Hay, *Lincoln,* VI, 447 ff.   7 *Ibid.,* 450.

8 "By accepting a regiment which had . . . been in Confederate service, he [Butler] left no room for complaint . . . ." George S. Denison to S. P. Chase, New Orleans, Sep. 9, 1862, Chase MSS., Lib. of Cong. Mentioning that Southern authorities were quietly arming the Negroes, a friend of Chase wrote: "Their plea is, 'Lincoln offers you freedom but with colonization. We will give it you & you stay here.'" B. Rush Plumbley to S. P. Chase, Philadelphia, Pa., Sep. 30, 1862, *ibid.*

9 "I learned from the President . . . that he was about to offer to the General the command of the Negro Army . . . . I hope Fremont may accept it, and beat all the white troops . . . , and thereby acquire glory." Letter by Thaddeus Stevens, Lancaster, [Pa.], June 9, 1863, Thaddeus Stevens MSS., no. 52749.

dissociated himself from the enterprise.[10]

In the recruitment of these Negro units, which were always commanded by white officers, much of the activity was outside of, or in opposition to, the war department. From the first the strongest impulse for the whole movement had come from Massachusetts, and when Secretary Stanton authorized Governor John A. Andrew to organize volunteer units to include "persons of African descent," the task "cut out for Andrew [was] a piece of work after his own heart." [11] Under Andrew's leadership the work was done by a committee of private citizens headed by the wealthy George L. Stearns, who had done so much to encourage John Brown. Among other distinguished names on the committee were Amos A. Lawrence (prominent capitalist), LeBaron Russell, William I. Bowditch, and John M. Forbes. One of the tasks of the committee was to promote the recruiting of colored men; another was to raise a large sum of money by private subscription to defray recruiting expenses beyond those which could be borne by the government.[12] It was in this manner that the men for Robert Gould Shaw's famous Fifty-Fourth Massachusetts were found. A curious feature of the whole scheme was that Negro recruiting for Massachusetts was conducted mainly in other states, with complications that can readily be imagined.[13] Enough Boston Negroes could be brought together to form a company, and a few more might be found in New Bedford. "Elsewhere in the State the negro population, small and scattering, could not possibly supply eight hundred able-bodied men." [14] On the morning of May 28, 1863, however, these difficulties were forgotten as the colored regiment marched down Beacon Street and paraded on the Common, while public officials including Governor Andrew gave dignity to the grand review.[15]

---

[10] Nicolay and Hay, *Lincoln*, VI, 457–459.

[11] H. G. Pearson, *Life of John A. Andrew*, II, 73.

[12] On this point the author has consulted the papers of Amos Lawrence (vol. 25), MSS., Mass. Hist. Soc. See also Pearson, *Andrew*, II, 81 ff.

[13] Pearson, *Andrew*, II, 82 ff.

[14] Pearson, *Andrew*, II, 81. (The total number of free Negroes of all ages and sexes in Massachusetts was reported as 9602 in 1860.)

[15] Pearson, *Andrew*, II, 88. Andrew complained to Lincoln that a hundred Negroes in Alexandria, Virginia, eager to go to Massachusetts and enlist, were hindered by Stanton's orders, whereupon the President is reported to have ordered: *"Let them go!* A. Lincoln." There seems to have been a prodigious gubernatorial ado over this rather absurd incident. *Ibid.,* II, 93.

II

The use of colored soldiers produced a crop of legal complications.[1] The attorney general of Massachusetts concluded that he could not legally refuse to enroll black men,[2] while the attorney general of the United States declared that native-born colored persons were citizens of the United States despite the contrary dictum of the Supreme Court in the Dred Scott case.[3] Though urged to insert the word "white" in the conscription law of 1863, thereby eliminating colored conscripts, Congress refused to do so,[4] and in the law as passed all able-bodied male citizens were made liable to service.

As to other legal matters, slave-soldiers, with their families, became free as above noted;[5] compensation up to $300 was provided for their owners;[6] persons of color in the District of Columbia were given the same legal standing as whites;[7] colored soldiers, late in the war, were declared entitled to the same uniform, clothing, arms, rations, medical attendance, pay, and emoluments as "other soldiers";[8] where a slave of a loyal master should be drafted (this was long after the emancipation proclamation), the slave becoming free, the hundred-dollar bounty was to be paid to the master.[9]

There were numerous emphatic protests against the raising and employment of Negro soldiers.[10] Governor Andrew of Massachusetts, enthusiast for Negro recruitment, must have been rudely shocked when a friend in the sea island area of South Carolina informed him of army brokers' scandals by which the raising of colored fighters had

---

[1] Legal matters concerning the use of Negro troops are treated at length in William Whiting, *War Powers Under the Constitution of the United States* (Boston, 1871), 478–511. Written first as wartime pamphlets, this volume is by the solicitor of the war department.

[2] *New York Herald*, Aug. 19, 1862, p. 4, c. 5. On the other hand the circuit court sitting in Montgomery county, Illinois, ruled that Negroes were not citizens; this obscure decision revealed how much anti-Negro law there was in Lincoln's own state in 1862. The court pointed out that Negroes were forbidden to migrate into and settle in the state; they were further denied the right to vote, hold office, do jury service, or testify where whites were parties. *Annual Cyclopaedia*, 1862, 752–753.

[3] *Ibid.*, 752. The Cincinnati *Gazette* (Dec. 27, 1862, p. 3, c. 3) deemed this "the ablest, as it is the most important, legal paper drawn up by him since he assumed . . . office."

[4] *Annual Cyclopaedia*, 1863, 289.   [5] Above, p. 132; *U. S. Stat. at Large*, XII, 599.

[6] *Ibid.*, XIII, 11.   [7] *Ibid.*, XII, 407.   [8] *Ibid.*, XIII, 129.

[9] *Ibid.*, XIII, 11 (act of Feb. 24, 1864).

[10] For a debate in Congress in which the use of colored troops was severely denounced, see *Annual Cyclopaedia*, 1863, 289.

become a "disgrace to all concerned." The governor was told that the "poor negroes" were "hunted like wild beasts," that very few able ones were found, that there was money in it, and that "outrageous frauds" had been practiced.[11] It was feared that the border would be offended,[12] that a "war of races" would result, and that "white men . . . [would] not rally to . . . the Union if . . . mixed . . . with negro battalions."[13] There was "prejudice in the [Union] army against the military employment of the blacks," and there was trouble in the war department with the result that payment of colored troops was held up.[14] Unwillingness among white officers to recognize colored men as soldiers raised serious questions of army discipline, and it was found advisable to avoid the mixture of the races in a given army unit.[15]

In addition to Northern white prejudice, serious aspects of the question were encountered in the angry resentment of Southerners, the bitter policy of retaliation pursued by the Confederacy, and the embarrassment attendant upon the Northern demand for counter retaliation. Lincoln's answer to that demand was two-fold: he issued on July 30, 1863, a seemingly severe order directing that penalties be inflicted in retaliation for the killing of Union soldiers "in violation of the laws of war"; next April, when precisely this kind of retaliation was demanded of him in a specific instance (the so-called Fort Pillow "massacre"),[16] he gave out a restrained and cautious statement explaining his avoidance of retribution in practice. That retribution, which would have been the execution of captured Confederate sol-

11 Pearson, *Andrew*, II, 144-145; Andrew MSS., vol. 28, no. 70. This was in connection with the recruiting of Negroes in South Carolina, with credit to the quota of Massachusetts. The New York *Semi-Weekly Tribune* (Jan. 1, 1864, p. 1, c. 1), referred to frauds perpetrated by sharpers upon colored men entering the Union army.

12 For the ferment in Kentucky over the bill to make slaves liable to military service on the same basis as whites, see New York *Times*, Mar. 17, 1864, p. 4, cc. 3-4.

13 J. S. Gallagher to R. W. Thompson, Washington, D. C., Aug. 4, 1862, MSS., Lincoln National Life Foundation, Ft. Wayne, Ind.

14 S. P. Chase to Maj. Gen. O. M. Mitchel, Washington, D. C., Oct. 4, 1862 (copy), Chase MSS., Hist. Soc. of Pa.

15 Boston *Daily Advertiser*, Feb. 25, 1863.

16 This affair occurred on April 12, 1864, when Confederate soldiers killed hundreds of Negroes in a garrison at Fort Pillow, Tennessee. In accusations that shook the North with indignation an investigating committee charged that about three hundred Negro soldiers were deliberately massacred in cold blood; the Confederate statement was that the men were killed in warfare, not slaughtered after surrender. In spite of strenuous urgings Lincoln saw to it that there was no retaliation by the Union government. Randall, *Civil War and Reconstruction*, 506-507.

diers, was not in fact applied. The key to the July 30 order was Lincoln's reference to "the usages and customs of war, as carried on by civilized powers," and his insistence on the "duty of every government to give protection to its citizens of whatever . . . color . . . , and especially to those . . . organized as soldiers." [17] In his Fort Pillow statement he referred to the fact that the colored soldier, being used, must have protection, but he also made a clear-cut distinction between "stating the principle" and "practically applying it." On the matter of practical application he said: "To take the life of one of their prisoners on the assumption that they murder ours, . . . might be too serious, . . . [too] cruel, a mistake." [18] A study of all the factors in this complicated subject, and not merely the harsher words of the retaliatory order, leads to the conclusion that Lincoln's purpose was not retaliation. On the contrary, his aim was to avert trouble and to restrain enemy action in dealing with a sensitive and vexing problem. In a word he intended to avoid unjustifiable severity on the part of his own government without forgoing protection to Negro soldiers who had been put into uniform by the law of the land.

In keeping with his habit of facing the realities of a subject and viewing all its sides, Lincoln proceeded circumspectly in handling the problem of Negro troops. At the first broaching of his emancipation decree to his Cabinet he had shown himself "unwilling to adopt" a measure for "arming slaves" which Chase "warmly" advocated.[19] Even after Congress had authorized the President to "employ" Negroes for the war purpose,[20] Lincoln "felt constrained to postpone a systematic organization of negro troops for active campaigns." [21] "The President's great difficulty," wrote Sumner, "is as to arming the blacks. He invites them as laborers, but . . . holds back from the last step to which everything . . . tends." [22] Though as a practical issue the movement for raising colored soldiers had gone far by September 1862, having been discussed in the Cabinet, the subject was omitted

---

[17] *Works*, IX, 48–49.

[18] Address at Sanitary Fair in Baltimore, Apr. 18, 1864, *ibid.*, X, 78–80.

[19] Diary of S. P. Chase (*Annual Report*, Am. Hist. Assoc., 1902, II), 48. Chase reported Lincoln as thinking in July 1862 that using Negroes as soldiers would be "productive of more evil than good" (*ibid.*, 49).

[20] Section 11 of the second confiscation act of July 17, 1862, *U. S. Stat. at Large*, XII, 592.

[21] Nicolay and Hay, *Lincoln*, VI, 441.   [22] Pierce, *Sumner*, IV, 84.

in the emancipation proclamation of September 22. When it was briefly mentioned in the January proclamation, the cautious reference to "forts, positions, stations, and other places" seemed to suggest a limited army use of Negroes. By March 1863, however, the President was speaking emphatically in favor of promoting a Negro military force. Advising Governor Andrew Johnson of Tennessee to raise such a force, he said: "The colored population is the great available and yet unavailed force for restoring the Union." [23] In the summer of 1864 he remarked to Governor Randall of Wisconsin: "Abandon all the posts now garrisoned by black men . . . and we would be compelled to abandon the war in three weeks." [24] Generalizing as to Lincoln's treatment of the whole matter, his secretaries, after noting with favor the tangible results, point out that he would have wrecked his administration if he had rushed to adopt the policy when enthusiasts first urged it, but that by restraint and delay and by playing the card at the opportune moment, he made it both a "military overweight . . . to crush . . . rebellion" and a "lever to effect emancipation." [25]

As the months passed people of the North became accustomed to the concept of Negro troops; in March 1864 a colored regiment was given a genuine ovation in New York City. In the words of the *Times:* "A thousand men, with black skins, and . . . with the uniforms and arms of the United States . . . , marched . . . through the most aristocratic . . . streets, received a grand ovation . . . , and then moved down Broadway to the steamer which bears them to their destination—all amid the . . . cheers, . . . plaudits, . . . waving handkerchiefs, . . . showering bouquets, and other approving manifestations of a hundred thousand of the most loyal of our people." [26] Dark-skinned warriors were used in a number of operations; many gave their lives to the cause; in time even the bitter New York *Herald* reported a "change . . . in . . . opinion" concerning colored fighters. Captured guns, declared the *Herald,* "spoke in eloquent terms of the bravery of the colored troops." [27] Covering only the late phases of the war, a writer in 1865 stated that in "battles be-

---

[23] *Works*, VIII, 233 (Mar. 26, 1863).   [24] *Ibid.*, X, 190 (Aug. [15?], 1864).
[25] Nicolay and Hay, *Lincoln*, VI, 469.
[26] New York *Times*, Mar. 6, 1864. p. 8, c. 1. This was in striking contrast to anti-Negro riots in New York City the previous July.
[27] New York *Herald*, June 27, 1864, p. 1, c. 4.

fore Nashville, the capture of Fort Fisher, the final operations around Richmond, and numerous minor engagements, [colored troops] sustained their previous well-earned reputation for bravery and soldierly qualities." [28] Their numbers were impressive; the war department's postwar summary showed colored troops to the total of 186,000 in Union service. [29]

III

Of the stereotypes concerning Lincoln one of the most unhistorical is the stock picture of the Emancipator sitting in the White House and suddenly striking the shackles from millions of bondmen at a stroke of the presidential pen. The fact is that Lincoln issued his proclamation and nothing happened in the immediate or prompt freeing of slaves by virtue thereof. The September proclamation was only a warning and a prediction, while the January proclamation had the curious feature of making declarations which applied only to areas where Lincoln's arm could not reach. With occupied portions of Louisiana and Virginia, as well as the whole state of Tennessee, excepted, the only regions to which the proclamation extended were those in which the Confederacy was still in control. The measure did not touch slavery in Kentucky, Maryland, Delaware, or Missouri, these being slave states adhering to the Union. Though such a situation was most unlikely, any other slave state could have avoided its emancipatory effect by return to Union allegiance.

Writing six days after the September proclamation, Lincoln confessed that the situation was "not very satisfactory," and that his expectations for the edict were "not as sanguine as . . . those of some friends." [1] What the government was doing, according to Seward, was to emancipate slaves where it could not reach them and to hold them in bondage where it could have set them free. [2] Horace White considered it doubtful whether the edict "freed anybody anywhere." [3]

---

[28] *Annual Cyclopaedia*, 1865, 32.
[29] *Offic. Rec.*, 3 ser., V, 661–662. Many of these were recruited or drafted within the states of the Confederacy—e. g., 17,869 from Mississippi, and 24,052 from Louisiana. Massachusetts was credited with 3,966, of whom probably no more than one fourth came from the state itself.
[1] *Works*, VIII, 49–50 (Sep. 28, 1862).
[2] Donn Piatt, *Memories of the Men Who Saved the Union*, 150.
[3] Horace White, *Life of Lyman Trumbull*, 222.

"The efficacy of the proclamation," declared a contemporary writer, "was probably very imperfectly manifested during 1863. On the one hand, it did not appear to make free any slave by its own operation during the year. . . . On the other hand it tended to awaken . . . sympathy among the slaves for the Union cause, which held out . . . the promise of certain freedom by its success . . . ." [4] "No wonder the Proclamation of January 1st has produced so little effect at the South," wrote William Lloyd Garrison in April 1863.[5] Abolitionist work, thought Garrison, was yet unfinished. "If slavery were really abolished," he declared, "I should care very little about continuance of the Liberator . . . ." [6]

In 1864 an earnest antislavery group headed by Robert Dale Owen, known as the American Freedmen's Inquiry Commission, submitted a voluminous report which treated emancipation as a task unachieved. Created by order of the war department to study methods that might contribute to the protection and improvement of freedmen, the commission doubted whether its object could be accomplished under existing conditions, and raised the question "whether the protecting freedom of these people is reliably founded," and whether it could endure, unless emancipation became "universal throughout the Union." [7] As to the proclamation of 1863, the commissioners declared: "It cannot free a single slave." [8]

Something more was needed than a proclamation; how much more only a detailed study could reveal. Directly after the preliminary edict General O. M. Mitchel wrote of the "mighty work which now lies before us." [9] Men of the time had yet to determine how to make emancipation legally effective, how to integrate Federal liberation with state laws, how to set freedmen to work at wages, how to give them training, education, and perchance some land of their own, how to instruct ignorant thousands as to their new status, how to avoid social disorder, how to mitigate the handicap of unequal opportunity, and how to deal with the problem of civil and political rights for the submerged race. Problems of the freedman had to be solved on the

[4] *Annual Cyclopaedia,* 1863, 835.

[5] W. L. Garrison to "Dear Friend May" (probably Samuel J. May), Boston, April 6, 1863, Garrison MSS.

[6] Garrison to Oliver Johnson, Boston, Dec. 14, 1862, *ibid.*

[7] *Offic. Rec.,* 3 ser., IV, 290.   [8] *Ibid.,* 361.

[9] Having been in western service, Gen. O. M. Mitchel was at Hilton Head, S. C. when this letter was written (Sep. 28, 1862), Chase MSS., Lib. of Cong.

basis of hard facts, not of doctrinaire opinions. Among these facts were the ineradicable instinct for racial separateness, the slight desire of Southern Negroes to go North, the vulnerability of the dark race to exploitation, the sterility of paper freedom if unaccompanied by economic security, and the risk that "under the guise of guardianship, slavery, in a modified form, . . . [might] be practically restored." [10]

As the problem presented itself under Lincoln it posed the almost unsolvable puzzle of trying to promote liberation in some states, and those the more Southern, while keeping slavery in others. As to the seceded area, slavery was declared abolished in Alabama and Mississippi, for example, but not in neighboring Tennessee. Even within the Union itself, where the border states differed considerably as to future policy, the institution appeared to have a greater life-expectancy in some states than in others. The proclamation of emancipation did not apply to either Missouri or Kentucky; in Missouri, however, emancipation was well under way as a matter of state polity in 1863, while conservation of slavery was still the persistent purpose in Kentucky. Such a situation offered a chance for gain that was not likely to be overlooked in that profiteering age. Since slavery was to be still active even after the January proclamation, and since the value of slaves in Missouri depended chiefly upon the prospect of selling them in Kentucky at several hundred dollars a head, there existed "a system of kidnapping constantly practiced . . . by slave traders—a kidnapping of both fugitive slaves and . . . emancipated *contrabands*—freed by the Proclamation." It was reported that this occurred "almost daily, & the villains evade[d] punishment by . . . laws which exclude[d] negro evidence & by the sympathisers who . . . [held] offices . . . ." [11]

In the records of the time one finds, even among friends of the proclamation, extensive doubts as to its law-worthiness. "In thinking of the future," wrote George Bancroft, "I feel unwilling to rely on the President's proclamation for the termination of slavery . . . ." [12] When in 1864 Lincoln sought to inaugurate loyal state governments in the South on the basis of individual oath-taking, Secretary Chase suspected that many in Louisiana might take the oath who were not

[10] *Offic. Rec.*, 3 ser., IV, 381.

[11] Lucien Eaton to Richard Yates, Oct. 16, 1863, Reavis MSS., Chicago Hist. Soc.

[12] George Bancroft to Gen. Robert C. Schenck, New York, Nov. 18, 1863, Bancroft MSS., Mass. Hist. Soc.

loyal at heart; such persons, he thought, might consider the oath merely conditional—e. g., "binding in case the emancipation clauses of the Proclamation" should not be "annulled by the Supreme Court or modified or abrogated by Congress." [13] There was the possibility that Lincoln's successor might "repudiate, and declare null and void the proclamation . . . emancipating slaves, and all acts and doings under it." [14] A learned legal writer who upheld its validity regarded the proclamation as a "mere command, which . . . could work no change . . . until executed by the hand of war . . . ." [15] Though he considered slavery a "rotten" and disappearing institution, Gideon Welles doubted the "ultimate effect" of the proclamation as to the "exact status of the slaves and the slave-owners"; for solution of the problem he looked to the courts and to legislation by Congress and by the states. He expressed a general questioning in which he did not share as he said: "I do not trouble myself about the Emancipation Proclamation, which disturbs so many." [16]

If there had been no other factor, such questioning would have arisen from many declarations by Lincoln himself as to the limits of emancipatory power on the part of the Federal government. Lincoln was frank in admitting legal doubts concerning the proclamation which he had once compared to "the Pope's bull against the comet." [17] No one saw more clearly the need of a constitutional amendment to clear up the subject. "I think it is valid in law," wrote the President in July 1863, "and will be so held by the courts"; yet in the same letter he voiced a preference for "gradual emancipation" as "better" for both races.[18] Next year, when a petition of youngsters besought him to "free all slave children," he confessed that he had not "the power to grant all they ask[ed]." [19]

The proof of legal effectiveness is in specific cases, but there is a dearth of material as to the application of the emancipation proclamation by legal process in the liberation of particular individuals. As late as July 1863 a Missouri sheriff was "arresting slaves of rebels

13 S. P. Chase to Col. Frank E. Howe, Feb. 20, 1864, Chase MSS., Lib. of Cong.

14 Hiram Ketchum to Horatio Seymour, New York City, Jan. 27, 1863, MS., Ill. State Hist. Lib. (Ketchum advocated such repudiation to the man who in 1868 became the Democratic candidate for President.)

15 J. I. C. Hare, *American Constitutional Law* (1st ed., Boston, 1889), 946.

16 Welles, *Diary*, I, 415, 429–430.   17 *Works*, VIII, 30 (Sep. 13, 1862).

18 *Ibid.*, IX, 52 (July 31, 1863).

19 Letter to Mrs. Horace Mann, April 5, 1864, *ibid.*, X, 68–69.

inside . . . [Union] lines, and returning them in great numbers." [20]
Contrarywise, a magistrate at St. Louis, using a trivial case as text for
an ambitious decision, passed favorably upon the legality and constitutionality of the emancipation proclamation. One Williams, a
Negro convicted of grand larceny in the criminal court of the city, was
a slave who had escaped from Arkansas, to which the emancipation
proclamation applied. Holding that the proclamation was valid, the
judge ruled that the offender was punishable by imprisonment in the
penitentiary, this being the penalty for grand larceny committed by
a free person, instead of by lashes on the bare back, as in the case of a
slave. This obscure decision upholding the constitutional validity of
the proclamation became the target of a sarcastic editorial in the
New York *World,* in which the "St. Louis functionary" was represented
as "conscious that his position was untenable, yet desirous to stand
well with the administration at Washington." As a legal basis the
judge had cited an inapplicable passage from Vattel, as well as hasty
remarks by John Quincy Adams which were in opposition to the
official position which Adams had taken when conducting American
diplomatic affairs. [21] The unimportance and uniqueness of the case
serve only to emphasize the scarcity of contemporary judicial action
giving effect to the proclamation.

Imperfections in the self-sufficiency of the proclamation were revealed in suggestions put forth for implementing it. A distinguished
New Englander suggested an emancipation bureau. [22] William Whiting, solicitor of the war department, suggested the creation of a
separate executive department of emancipation whose head should
have a place in the President's Cabinet. [23] Another inventive citizen,
noting the vague ideas of the Negroes concerning the boon that had
come to them, and wishing to get hold of their minds, proposed some
"token" that would make liberation seem real. He suggested a cheap
pewter medal bearing the words "Free Negro, January 1, 1863," with

---

[20] *Ibid.,* IX, 40 (July 21, 1863).

[21] New York *World,* Feb. 6, 1863, p. 4, c. 3 (editorial).

[22] In a letter to Secretary Chase (Nov. 19, 1862) S. G. Howe advocated such a bureau
because of the need "for the possible political birth of millions on the first January,"
arguing that it would have "potent moral effect South as well as North." Chase MSS.,
Lib. of Cong. Howe later became a member, with Robert Dale Owen and J. McKaye,
of the organization known as the American Freedmen's Inquiry Commission, forerunner
of the Freedmen's Bureau. See above, p. 190.

[23] Whiting, *War Powers Under the Constitution,* 466.

a quotation from Scripture. Such a medal, he thought, ought to be about the size of a quarter dollar, so that it could be concealed if necessary. The words *"omne ignotum pro mirifico"* he considered appropriate; if its owner could not read, so much the better. Every man possessing such a medal would believe himself free by law and would be encouraged to seek practical realization of that freedom. For the difficult and tricky work of distributing such medals, he would employ picked contrabands who knew the by-paths through woods and swamps better than the whites.[24]

There were various proposals that Congress should add its legal sanction to the proclamation. On February 9, 1863, Charles Sumner presented a mammoth petition of a hundred thousand men and women praying that Congress pass "an act emancipating all persons of African descent held to involuntary service or labor in the United States." [25] George Bancroft, who knew history and statecraft, asked: "Could not Congress enact, that henceforward every one born in our common country should be born free?" [26] For putting the proclamation "into more complete and immediate execution" Representative Isaac Arnold of Illinois presented a bill prohibiting the reënslavement of freedmen; [27] in 1864, when the Wade-Davis reconstruction bill was taking shape, Sumner moved an amendment in the Senate providing that the proclamation "is hereby . . . enacted as a statute of the United States," the senator being unwilling that emancipation be "left to float on a presidential proclamation." [28] None of these proposals was enacted. Congress refused to pass the ones mentioned, and when in 1864 it did provide in the Wade-Davis bill for the emancipation of slaves and their posterity in the seceded states, the measure fell before Lincoln's veto.[29]

---

[24] B. C. Tilghman to W. M. Tilghman, Camp near Falmouth, Va., Dec. 27, 1862, Stanton MSS.

[25] The petition, examined by the author, was promoted by the Loyal National Woman's League, Susan B. Anthony, Secretary. Papers of the House of Representatives, 37 Cong. (Misc., Box 6), MSS., Lib. of Cong.

[26] George Bancroft to Gen. Robert C. Schenck, N. Y., Nov. 18, 1863, Bancroft MSS., Mass. Hist. Soc.

[27] *Cong. Globe*, 38 Cong., 1 sess., 20 (Dec. 14, 1863).

[28] Senator Saulsbury of Delaware was quick to use Sumner's suggestion as a confession by Lincoln's friends that his proclamation was without validity. *Ibid.*, 3460. See also Randall, *Constitutional Problems Under Lincoln*, 383.

[29] In explaining this veto, Lincoln stated that he was unprepared "to declare a constitutional competency in Congress to abolish slavery in States," thus denying to Congress a power which he had exercised as President. *Works*, X, 153 (July 8, 1864).

IV

The story of how freedom actually came to Negroes in camp, home, or plantation is one of the imperfectly understood chapters of the Lincoln administration. It is not merely a matter of groups, classes, and categories, of legal declarations and governmental pronouncements. It is a question of dark-skinned human beings in person, millions of them. To tell the story would be to locate these human beings where they were, which was for the most part beyond the reach of the proclamation, to know their feelings, their long-standing loyalties, and their faithful records in servitude. It is a truism that to do this they must be viewed in association with their white folk; on that matter the two facts that stand out most clearly are the dependence of Negroes upon their masters for sustenance and all that goes with everyday living, and their prideful habit of identifying themselves with their white families. It was only in association with a white household that a slave had any social status. Within that pattern of service he had importance; at least he had a place (as a slave, to be sure) in the social order. He had a more secure social status than the free Negro of the South. This is not to argue that slavery was justifiable; it is merely to note the fact that the Southern slave was part of an all-enveloping system of society. He could not suddenly jump out of his skin or transport himself to a new order of existence. This was the more impossible since freedom was proclaimed not by his own protectors and rulers but by an alien and an enemy. To say this is to speak in the Southern sense, but that is precisely the point; one cannot understand the subject at all unless he treats these people in terms of the locale and the regime in which they lived, not in a hypothetical setting imagined by a distant abolitionist.

The first fact to note is the absence of servile insurrections. To stir up such insurrections was no part of Lincoln's purpose; Southern accusations of such a purpose were in the nature of propaganda, though doubtless to a large extent such was the Southern belief. Lincoln was not the man to promote uncivilized methods of warfare. Though in the September proclamation the President predicted, perhaps unfortunately, that the Federal executive would not repress Negroes in efforts "for their actual freedom," he meant no sanction of domestic violence, having in mind rather the fact that if freedom was proclaimed it must, under proper procedures and only so, be substantively recognized. His disapproval of slave insurrections had been expressed in his Cooper Union address of February 1860, where he emphatically disclaimed Republican responsibility for such uprisings.[1] In the January proclamation the matter was left in no doubt; the President enjoined those declared free to abstain from violence and to "labor faithfully for wages."

It is true that Lincoln spoke of "arming the blacks," and approved the raising of Negro troops, which at the South was accounted the equivalent of stirring up insurrection. No soldier, however, is supposed to strike except within the pattern of army command. If it was legitimate to use Negroes as soldiers under army discipline, their service in that capacity was no more inhuman or uncivilized than that of the white men. If one is dealing with the whole wretched subject of war itself, the matter is more than a question of Negro troops; one hardly touches fundamentals when he supposes that whites may go into authorized armies but Negroes may not. As to guerrilla warfare and all those hidden irregular activities that accompanied the war, including much that was criminal, it was the whites that were chiefly at fault.

Colored servants in the South did not feel themselves called upon to rise against their masters; the absence of such uprising is one of the attested facts of the period.[2] The "devotion and faithfulness" of Southern Negroes in war time has been mentioned as "one of the beautiful aspects of slavery." Though slaves, except those deep in the interior, had "every opportunity to desert to the Federals, . . . desertions were infrequent until near the close of the war." "On the whole," writes W. L. Fleming, "the behavior of the slaves during the war . . . was most excellent."[3] Confederate authorities had naturally made use of slaves as "teamsters, cooks, nurses, and . . .

---

[1] *Works*, V, 315 ff. In this passage Lincoln showed how insubstantial was the actual danger of slave insurrection and how unfounded was the "elastic fancy" by which it was imagined that the Republican party was engaged in promoting Negro uprisings.

[2] The famous diarist of the Confederate war department wrote on July 3, 1864: ". . . there has been no instance of an attempt on the part of the slaves to rise in insurrection." J. B. Jones, *A Rebel War Clerk's Diary* (Phila., 1866), II, 244. See also Randall, *Civil War and Reconstruction*, 496.

[3] Walter L. Fleming, *Civil War and Reconstruction in Alabama*, 210, 212.

laborers." [4] Soldiers of the South did not care to dig trenches, cook, or split wood. As body servants of Confederate officers many a Southern slave performed a war service in which he was faithful unto death; in after years those who survived showed a truly Southern pride in recalling their records in "Virginny" or "Ilun 10." [5] If some of the Negroes hailed "Linkum's" freedom as the sound of Gabriel's trumpet or an occasion for a barbecue, others, especially in the deep South, thought of a Yankee as a thing with horns.[6] They were more inclined to save "massa's" property from Yankee plunder than to perpetrate an insurrection for which they lacked both the impulse and the organization. "To the last day of bondage the great majority were true against all temptations. With their white people they wept for the Confederate slain, were sad at defeat, and rejoiced in [Southern] victory." [7]

How did that last day of bondage and first day of freedom come? Not as a rule with fanfare nor with much of drama; certainly not by any universal pattern. Even among Higginson's dark soldiers the celebration of the proclamation was more like a solemn religious service than a dramatic event.[8] In Florida, where raiding for the recruitment of Higginson's and Saxton's men was active, a Federal recruiting agent might offer the first uninviting contact with the new regime. In occupied parts of Louisiana conditions of free labor were first experienced by ex-slaves on "abandoned" plantations administered by Union authorities, not under the emancipation proclamation but under a law of Congress known as the captured and abandoned property act. In displacement of their Southern owners, these estates were operated by "loyal" lessees, put there by the United States treasury department. Negroes in such a situation, unused to conditions of free labor, had little concept of a contract and were likely to suppose that they were under no obligation to remain at one place any longer than they pleased. Hands were easily seduced from one plantation to another by promises of higher wages, which in the existing scarcity of laborers was a serious annoyance; furthermore, they claimed the right to plant cotton or anything else on their respective patches regardless of the overseer's requirements. Unfaith-

---

[4] *Ibid.*, 205.   [5] *Ibid.*, 207.   [6] *Ibid.*, 211.   [7] *Ibid.*, 212.
[8] Higginson, *Army Life in a Black Regiment*, 40–41.

fulness to contract, however, was not alone the fault of laborers; lessees fell down in the matter of rations, clothing, and care of the wives and children of plantation workers. Discontent led to mutiny; military force was in some cases necessary to settle difficulties between emancipated workers and their bosses. Such military intervention might produce an order to the overseer to conform to what the Negroes were used to—i. e., to issue rations to all hands whether working or not —after which the crop would look after itself, for the Negroes would have little incentive to work.[9]

To refugee Negroes who flocked by the thousands to Union camps or joined the Federal line of march, first contacts with freedom came under distressing circumstances. Forsaking tradition, "garbed in rags," bleeding, urged by terror or "blind hope," "often nearly naked," they stumbled forward in a planless exodus, with "no Moses to lead it."[10] Such, at least, is the description of Chaplain (and Brigadier General) John Eaton, who under Grant assumed the difficult initial work of dealing with "these hordes" by forming Negro camps, caring for the sick, and striving amid tragedy and travail to bring order, systematic labor, and relief to masses of helpless blacks. Union commanders in general had this problem thrust upon them; the usual policy was to urge the colored people to stay "where they were," as Sherman said, "not to load us down with useless mouths, which would eat up the food needed for our fighting-men."[11] In Virginia and North Carolina B. F. Butler organized an elaborate system of Negro rehabilitation as a phase of army control. Perhaps the best known episode of this sort is that of General Rufus Saxton, Higginson's chief, who, with headquarters at Beaufort, South Carolina, promoted the tasks of organizing colored soldiers and giving relief to thousands of refugees, setting up courts, superintending property interests, initiating agricultural efforts, directing labor contract systems, protecting his wards from fraud, and seeking to develop in

---

9 Records of these transactions are among the papers of the treasury department, being for many years in charge of the "miscellaneous division," but now in the National Archives. They consist of plantation lists, accounts of inspection, treasury agents' reports, inventories of estates, records of the "plantation bureau" at New Orleans, et cetera. A doctoral dissertation (in manuscript) by the author, "The Confiscation of Property during the Civil War" (Univ. of Chicago, 1911), and an article based thereon (*Am. Hist. Rev.* XIX, 65–79) have been drawn upon for the above account.

10 John Eaton, *Grant, Lincoln and the Freedmen*, 2.

11 *Memoirs of General William T. Sherman*, II, 181

them "habits of carefulness and prudence." [12]

Guardianship, however, had to be exercised with discretion and restraint. Exploitation of the blacks, sometimes by their new bosses, sometimes by Union army pickets who returned them to former masters and pocketed the reward,[13] was distressingly prevalent. One reads with disgust the statement of a government report: "To cheat a negro by a private citizen or by a public officer is too much of a pastime. To plunder him of all he has seems little of a crime, because he has so little. To . . . starve his family, while he fights to maintain a government which supports the plunderers, is the . . . business of too many who wear the nation's livery." [14] Lurking evils of freedom were suggested in a Union general's special order in 1863 near Vicksburg referring to injurious results of Negroes coming under Union protection and advising prospective wards of Uncle Sam to remain on their plantations.[15] Mistreatment was the easier because wages were an indeterminant entity; they might be monthly but were more likely to be yearly; often compensation was on a crude share-crop basis. Incoming bosses were less likely than former masters to care for "non-productive" members of Negro families. According to a competent observer, Negroes preferred a Southern to a Northern employer. Even at his best, the Northerner was energetic, economical, and determined to exact a full day's labor, while the Southerner, "accustomed to the ways of slaves from his youth up," was "languidly and good-naturedly indifferent." Left to his own choice, the freedman preferred to "return to the service of the southerner." [16]

As the Union armies proceeded to occupy one area after another in their Southern march, military contact with the population enabled more and more slaves to find freedom in the shadow of the army and thus to taste the results, not always very exciting, of Lincoln's proclamation. For the vast majority of Southern slaves, however, liberation came with defeat of the Confederacy, the close of the war, and Union occupation of the South. Such occupation in its earlier phases was not as harsh as it might have been (the worst excesses began with about the

12 *Offic. Rec.*, 3 ser., IV., 1022 ff.   13 *Sen. Exec. Doc. No. 53*, 38 Cong., 1 sess., 12.
14 *Sen. Exec. Doc. No. 28*, 38 Cong., 2 sess., 20.
15 Special Order No. 45, Vicksburg, Miss., Aug. 18, 1863, *Offic. Rec.*, 3 ser., III, 686–687. See also *ibid.*, 917–918, in which it is emphasized that camps for freed Negroes were to be considered simply as places of temporary refuge.
16 Report of Benjamin C. Truman, April 9, 1866, *Sen. Exec. Doc. No. 43*, 39 Cong., 1 sess., 10–11.

year 1868); harsh or not, the new regime made no revolutionary difference in the daily lives of ex-slaves. The governmental pattern as it applied generally was illustrated in the order of General John M. Schofield directly after Appomattox in North Carolina, in which he declared that former slaves were free by virtue of Lincoln's proclamation, but advised that freedmen remain with former masters working for wages, and that they avoid congregating about towns or camps. They were told that they would not be supported in idleness.[17] In a typical Southern home the domestic pattern was that described as follows by W. L. Fleming: "For several weeks before the master came home from the army the negroes knew that, as a result of the war, they were free. They, however, worked on, somewhat restless, . . . until he arrived and called them up and informed them that they were free. This was the usual way in which the negro was informed of his freedom. The great majority of the blacks . . . waited to hear from their masters the confirmation of . . . freedom. And the first thing the returning slaveholder did was to assemble his negroes and make known to them their condition with its privileges and responsibilities." [18]

In an elaborately documented study Mr. Bell Irvin Wiley has given us a composite picture of the emerging freeman.[19] With the coming of the Yankees, as Mr. Wiley shows, there were two opposite kinds of refugee movements: a flow of slaves toward Union camps, and, to counteract this, an effort of Southern masters to move their slaves toward the interior, in which there was some Confederate compulsion. Since a longing for freedom was a general motive among Southern Negroes,[20] the emancipation proclamation was commonly hailed with elation. The cause of this, however, was the shining lure of liberty rather than defection toward masters. There were those who felt the lure and yet refused when freedom knocked at the door. The high record of loyalty among Southern Negroes to their masters is in the main confirmed by Mr. Wiley, though he finds it impossible to accept all the familiar encomiums on the subject. He emphasizes the slightness of any tendency toward insurrection, the nonviolent nature of

17 John M. Schofield, *Forty-Six Years in the Army*, 368.
18 Fleming, *Civil War and Reconstruction in Alabama*, 270.
19 Bell Irvin Wiley, *Southern Negroes, 1861–1865*.
20 *Ibid.*, 19–21. Mr. Wiley writes: ". . . many of them, had they known what freedom entailed, would have recoiled from it" (p. 19).

the dark race, and the fact that a Negro seldom betrays a trust.[21] He finds more disorder (falling short of insurrection) than Southern writers usually admit, but emphasizes that such disorder was more common in invaded areas than in the interior.[22] Though he finds that by 1865 it was recognized in the South that slavery was a "dying institution," he shows the dissatisfaction felt by such a man as Robert Barnwell Rhett because of the provision in the Confederate constitution that permitted the admission of new states. Rhett had no wish to admit the people of the Northwest who were "fundamentally unsound on the question of slavery."[23] Noting conditions of hardship that came with liberation, Mr. Wiley finds enthusiasm and elation giving way to disillusion; when war ended in 1865 it was obvious that "the fight for real freedom had just begun."[24]

V

There remained, of course, the inspirational aspect and slogan value of Lincoln's proclamation. There were overtones of the edict which a literal examination of its words would not reveal. In the popular mind the document was dramatized as the opening of a new phase of the war. From the moment of its issuance the conflict took on, in the emotional sense, a new meaning. It "made emancipation the policy of the Administration," wrote a contemporary writer, "and encouraged the friends of that great cause to make every exertion to secure its speedy accomplishment."[1] Beginning with January 1863 the conflict was both a war for the Union and a crusade against slavery. Legalistic arguments might refute this, but factors other than the legal word were coming into play. Gaps in the antislavery front were now more easily closed, as in the border states where the proclamation gave impetus to the movement for state laws to sweep away the institution of slavery as it remained within Union lines. One step led to another. The doctrine of "contraband" had come first; then preparatory acts of Congress; then the preliminary proclamation; in due course the definitive proclamation with its reverberations over the civilized world; then Negro troops; later on, state laws to stop the chinks; finally, by a movement well launched while Lincoln was yet

---

[21] *Ibid.*, 65.   [22] *Ibid.*, 66, 83–84.   [23] *Ibid.*, 164.   [24] *Ibid.*, 344.
[1] *Annual Cyclopaedia*, 1863, 835.

President, the "king's cure all" of a constitutional amendment prohibiting slavery. All this except the slow enactment of the amendment had come to pass by the end of the war.[2] It was a cumulative process in which the President's edict was the central element, but to which many factors, not the least being popular opinion and world approval, made a contribution.

In the minds of many earnest people at the North emancipation was a greater stimulus and a loftier challenge than even the preservation of the Union. If it were to be a Union with slavery, many considered it not worth fighting for, or at best an inadequate goal. That the hand of war was working its liberating effect in part outside the pattern of governmental intent was to many minds a source of strength. This movement for human liberation seemed a bigger thing than Lincoln, a mightier force than that of constituted rulers. A sense of destiny and of providential intervention gave to the movement a spiritual element of evangelistic fervor which can in no wise be left out of the account. With the uplifting sense that God was taking a hand in human affairs there came an increment of power to meet the new challenge. War aims now had to be recast. The Crittenden resolution of July 1861 was outmoded. The Union was not to be reconstructed except on the basis of abolition of slavery in the Southern states. "The problem . . . to be solved was . . . the re-appearance of the slave-holding . . . States in the Union, with the shackles of their slaves knocked off, with their bondmen and women and children sent forth as free." [3] If this seemed to require a fuller subjugation than otherwise, if it tended to prolong the war, it offered a higher challenge than statesmen of the time realized, for with greater control there would need to be greater generosity if a sorry postwar bitterness were to be avoided.

Men of the time were quick to adopt the view that the emancipation

---

[2] The constitutional amendment abolishing slavery, not treated in the present volume, was introduced by Senator Trumbull in February 1864. On December 18, 1865, Secretary Seward proclaimed that its ratification by state legislatures had been completed and that it was from that date a part of the Constitution. By that time emancipation had been loyally accepted in the South. Ratification of the amendment by eight of the seceded states was counted in estimating the three-fourths necessary for adoption. Congress subsequently refused to recognize the validity of "Johnson's reorganized states," which had thus participated in amending the United States Constitution, but this non-recognition was not construed as invalidating the amendment.

[3] *Annual Cyclopaedia*, 1863, 836.

proclamation was the "crowning act" of Lincoln's administration.[4]
Lincoln himself caught the spirit and remarked to John Hay that he
considered this problem "the greatest question ever presented to
practical statesmanship." Hay added: "While the rest are grinding
their . . . organs for their own glorification the old man is working with the strength of a giant . . . to do this great work." [5]

For a down-trodden and submerged race the Negroes made a worthy
and honorable war record. Some of them in their daily associations
came close to the Lincolns, such as Elizabeth Keckley, modiste to the
First Lady, or William Slade, messenger to the President; their stories
have recently been recovered.[6] Some of them, otherwise forgotten,
have come down to us in the rhetorical pages of Thomas Wentworth
Higginson,[7] who did not fail to record the picturesque and the comical
among these capering brothers while noting the "minor-key pathos"
of their responsive natures. In guffawing antics they added a welcome
touch of comedy to the army scene. In their tugging and chorusing
gangs heavy labor became a pastime; in drill their rhythm and love
of swank made for snap and style; when off duty their whirling and
frolicking made camp a delight; in grim action, where many paid the
supreme sacrifice, they proved themselves real soldiers. Deep in the
South the great majority not only avoided insurrection but gave their
all in faithful service to mistress and master.

---

[4] Seward was reported to have protested against such a concept, saying that "the
formation of the Republican Party destroyed slavery," and that the bigger work of
Lincoln's government was preserving the Union and thereby saving popular government for the world. Thus wrote John Hay in his diary, June 24, 1864. Dennett, ed.,
Lincoln . . . in the . . . Diaries of John Hay, 197.

[5] Diary of John Hay, July 31, 1863, *ibid.*, 73.

[6] John E. Washington, *They Knew Lincoln*. Dr. Washington conveys the broad race
memories of his people and their folk thoughts of the Emancipator as he recovers the
stories of those few who knew and served the Lincolns, whom they devotedly loved.

[7] *Army Life in a Black Regiment.*

CHAPTER XXIV

POLITICS AS USUAL

THAT Lincoln had a war to fight, a country to save, and, as he believed, a contribution to make to the abiding cause of free government in the world, is but a partial statement of his task. He had to endure inefficiency, factional bickering, and some of the sorriest "politics" that this party-ridden country has ever witnessed. Ideologically Lincoln was an ardent democrat, an enthusiast for popular rule, an enemy of tyranny; yet he was always wary of revolutionary or too drastic methods. Working for human progress in conservative terms, he was essentially a moderate liberal. Cautious reform, stability combined with enlightened change, was his ideal. As President he was less of an intense party man than he had been in earlier days. The muting of politics for the higher unity of a nation struggling for survival was his aim, but this aim was not achieved by the American people in Civil War times; they did not even achieve unity within either of the major parties. Petty men kept grinding their little axes; Congress made life miserable for the President; politicians jostled for favor and prominence; rocking-chair strategists won battles on paper; editors emitted streams of advice or denunciation. If in some respects the war effort brought exaltation, party politics remained on its regular uninspired plane.

I

It would be pleasant, if true, to record that Lincoln's voice was the dominant note, or that he rode the storm to his own destined port; the disturbing fact was the growing dominance of that group of hard-driving Radicals whom Hay dubbed "Jacobins," and who have also been designated as "vindictives." A more unlovely knot of politicians would be hard to find. Self important, humorless, itching for power, and scornful of ethical scruple, they sold their wares at their own valuation and paraded behind a front of crusading zeal.[1] Unmerciful in their pressure upon Lincoln, they used the stratagems of patronage, party trickery, and propaganda to impose their pattern upon all phases of war effort. With a technique of intimidation that moderates found hard to resist, they made it their business to take over problems of army command, conduct of campaigns, composition of the Cabinet, formulation of war aims, and reconstruction of a shattered nation in proscriptive and punitive terms. Their assaults upon McClellan have already been seen; they actually dreaded Union success if achieved under McClellan's leadership. If a general did not wear their livery, especially if he were a Democrat, they set out to destroy him by inquisitorial investigations and unfair publicity; if commanders spoke their glib language, they were petted or promoted, though the outcome might be defeat of Union arms. With all their emphasis upon action and efficiency they were capable of obstructing the effective prosecution of the war, or even of deliberately protracting it in order to promote their political purposes.[2]

The reason usually mentioned to explain this—i. e., the determination that the war must become the lever for dislodging slavery—was only part of a complex bill of goods which involved sectional supremacy, social revolution, capitalistic exploitation, and such a program of future party ascendancy as would make the Radicals the controlling element in the whole country. A Yankee colonel in the South stated the case in exaggerated form. "Do we fight them to avenge . . . insult, . . . ?" he asked. "No! The thing we seek is *permanent* dominion; & what instance is there of a permanent dominion without changing, revolutionizing, absorbing, the institutions, life, and manners of the conquered peoples? . . . They think we mean to take their *Slaves*. Bah! We must take their *ports,* their *mines,* their *water powers,* the *very soil* they plough, and develop them by the hands of our *artisan* armies. . . . We are to be a regenerating, colonizing

---

[1] In T. Harry Williams, *Lincoln and the Radicals,* one finds a competent and readable account of this influential group.

[2] "They believed that if the struggle continued long enough, public opinion would force the government to resort to emancipation and the arming of the slaves. Hence they favored a policy that would prolong the war until they . . . [could] force the radical program upon the reluctant Lincoln." *Ibid.,* 12–13.

power, or we are to be whipped. Schoolmasters, with howitzers, must instruct our Southern brethren that they are a set of d—d fools in everything, that relates to . . . modern civilization. . . . *This army must not come back.* Settlement, migration must put the seal on battle, or we gain nothing." [3] In terms that would have shocked the majority of his fellow-soldiers, this sizzling colonel declared: "Vindicating the majesty of an insulted Government, by extirpating all *rebels,* & fumigating their nests with the brimstone of unmitigated Hell, I conceive to be the holy purpose of our further efforts. I hope I shall . . . do something . . . in 'The Great Fumigation,' before the sulphur gives out." [4]

This extirpator and fumigator was too drastic to be typical; certainly his tone was altogether exceptional in the army. Nevertheless the increasing amount of such clamor outside the army is a recognized factor of the war which explains Lincoln's wholesome dislike of the "ultra" element. "We are growing more radical . . . every day," wrote a friend of Trumbull. "The people are ripe for extreme measures." [5] "We have been too angelic to rebels both north and south," wrote another, "& I think we have got to be more severe with them." [6] Having visited St. Louis, Theodore Tilton was dissatisfied with western men, finding them "not sufficiently actuated by *moral* convictions to make them safe . . . leaders in a good cause." [7] In a lengthy diatribe Jonathan B. Turner of Illinois College at Jacksonville deplored too much forgiveness and wanted the divine power of the sword exerted upon offenders. "Mr. Lincoln," wrote Turner, "seems to imagine that he is a sort of half way clergyman . . . . Mr. Lincoln has nothing whatever, as commander of the army & navy to do with the N.T. [New Testament]; He never ought to read it . . . . Let him turn to the O.T." Referring to a coming "traitor conclave" in Louisville, Kentucky, Turner wanted the President "to surround . . . and take every dog of them, . . . and either *hang them on the spot,* or imprison them till the war is over." He mentioned that loyal men wanted him to write either to Trumbull or the President. "But as

---

[3] Lt. Col. Sargent to Gov. John A. Andrew, Annapolis, Jan. 14, 1862, Andrew MSS.

[4] Sargent to Andrew (again), Camp Williams, Beaufort, S. C., Mar. 3, 1862, *ibid.*

[5] P. P. Enos to Lyman Trumbull, Springfield, Ill., July 14. 1862, Trumbull MSS.

[6] T. J. Moore to Lyman Trumbull, Stanfield, Ill., May 26, 1862, *ibid.*

[7] Theodore Tilton to Horace Greeley, Chicago, Jan. 6, 1865, Greeley MSS., New York Pub. Lib.

I have been thorning the President about McClellan, Fits John Porter
. . . & other cursed West Point fools & traitors, ever since I was in
Washington in September, I dont like to write him . . . now." [8]

While some of the above-quoted expressions of radical doctrine are
vitriolic to excess, one can hardly give a mere record of their position
that is not emphatic and extreme. In that restrained and factual year-
book, the *American Annual Cyclopaedia*, one finds the following
characterization: "Their bitter and unsparing denunciation of all
Northern citizens who stood aloof . . . from . . . strictly antislavery views . . . [gave] another turn to the screws under which
the President was writhing." [9]

II

Foremost among the Radicals in the House was Thaddeus Stevens,
whose dour countenance, protruding lower lip, limping clubfoot, and
sarcastic invective made him the perfect type of vindictive ugliness.
Though chairman of the ways and means committee he paid comparatively little attention to finance; it was as leader of Republicans in
the lower house that his overbearing power was exerted. Proscriptive
measures against Southerners were a veritable obsession with him.
With a blunt forthrightness that had in it a certain terrible honesty
he blurted out his searing passages, scorning to find excuse for them
either in ethics or the Constitution. It was natural for him to join in
the Radical sport of "thorning" Mr. Lincoln. "Mr. Thaddeus Stevens," wrote a Boston journalist, "has never been sparing of his
insinuations against the administration, for which he is nominally
the leader in the House of Representatives," adding: "he has attacked
it openly, with the vehemence, and . . . ferocity, which is apt to
characterize his action in moments of deep excitement." [1] The quality
of his stinging tongue can be judged from one of his personal flings
at an opponent: "Mr. Speaker, it will not be expected of me to notice
the thing which has crawled into this House and adheres to one of
the seats by its own slime." [2]

[8] The contents of this bristling epistle have only been faintly suggested here. Jonathan
B. Turner to Lyman Trumbull, Jacksonville, Ill., Feb. 1, 1863, Trumbull MSS.

[9] *Annual Cyclopaedia*, 1862, 792.

[1] Boston *Daily Advertiser*, Feb. 26, 1863.

[2] Quoted in Thomas Frederick Woodley, *Great Leveler: The Life of Thaddeus Stevens*, 10.

In the Senate Charles Sumner had impressiveness and prominence rather than practical leadership. Tall and massive, with distinguished head rising from stuffy cravat, complete with side whiskers and Latin phrases, he moved with a pompous superiority which told the world that he expected to be admired. To him the war was not the battlefield nor the garrison; it was the Senate Chamber. Its supreme product was the *Congressional Globe* in which his grandiloquent speeches were embalmed. There were those who spoke highly of him. Emerson referred to his "singularly pure character," [3] but Emerson also praised John Brown with equal extravagance. A greater tribute was that of L. Q. C. Lamar whose address in the Senate after Sumner's death in 1874 served double duty as an official encomium and a handsome gesture of postwar friendship from the South to the North. It was said that the general upper class of Boston regarded Sumner "as a renegade and a menace." [4] This might be far from a condemnation, but contemporary statements from men who personally knew the man (as Lamar did not) were often unfavorable. Hugh McCulloch considered him prejudiced, "open to flattery" and "too lofty to descend to persons." [5] Carlyle's verdict was: "the most completely nothin' of a mon that ever crossed my threshold,—naught . . . in him or of him but wind and vanity." [6] The confidential estimate of senatorial colleagues was recorded by Browning who mentioned a train ride in which the Bay State solon was the topic of conversation which he had with Foote, Fessenden, and Collamer, who concurred "in characterizing him as cowardly, mean, malignant, . . . hypocritical, . . . cringing and toadyish to every thing, and every body that had the odor of aristocracy." [7] Sumner's learning tended toward pedantry; his constitutional reasoning was clumsy and bookish; his opposition to slavery—the main emphasis of his life—left him cold to "appeals by needy colored people." [8] It was a day, however, when senators were expected to spread themselves, and the Websterian prominence of the man makes it impossible to dismiss him with a deprecation. It is significant of Lincoln's shrewdness that he not only treated the humorless statesman with respect, but got on well with him and gained much in the process.

[3] Emerson, *Miscellanies (Complete Works*, XI), 234.
[4] Carl Sandburg, *Abraham Lincoln: The War Years*, I, 100.
[5] Hugh McCulloch, *Men and Measures of Half A Century*, 234.
[6] M. A. DeWolfe Howe, ed., *Letters of Charles Eliot Norton*, I, 422.
[7] Browning, *Diary*, I, 588.   [8] McCulloch, *Men and Measures*, 234.

It may be said of Sumner that his anti-Southern radicalism did not often, as in the case of Wade and Chandler, take an anti-Lincoln turn, nor did he descend to partyism of the coarser kind. In 1872, for example, he withheld support from Grant. Nor can one forget the vast importance of Sumner's relation to John Bright, and the specific focusing of this historic Bright-Sumner friendship in terms of Anglo-American amity, especially with reference to the *Trent* affair. Much might have been done with Sumner if his contact had been less with books and more with life.

Between Sumner and Henry Wilson, his colleague from Massachusetts, there was little to choose. Lacking Sumner's ornate façade, Wilson was like him as to basic policies. Count Gurowski, though himself a radical, could not abide either of them. "Oh what an infernal nu[i]sance," he wrote, "are your Wilsons or Sumners, without brains the one, without a heart the other." [9] Two westerners, Bluff Ben Wade of Ohio and Zachariah Chandler of Michigan, were at the very front of the radical movement; they were alike in their insolence, coarseness of method, and vulgarity. Referring to a day when both these seigniors had spoken, the *Herald* declared: "Ben. Wade, the stupid old pug dog, and silly Chandler, the cowardly and impertinent puppy, of the abolition faction of traitors, distinguished themselves in the . . . Senate . . . ." [10] That Wade was anti-Lincoln was well known. Giddings of Ohio attributed his ill will to bad humor because of defeat for the presidential nomination in 1860. Wade, said Giddings, "denounced the President as a *failure* from the moment of his election and began to lay his plans for his own advancement. . . . The truth is that . . . the congress has been the theatre for making Presidents and not to carry on the war. . . . Wade proclaimed that no party could succeed on *moral principle*. That if we intended ever to elect a President we must cease to avow immutable truth as the basis of our party and get every man to vote with [us] who objected to the democracy [i. e. the Democratic party]. He was a candidate for nomination at Chicago, and his friends were anxious to strike from our [Republican] platform all allusion to principle. They were acting as he dictated. By . . . wireworking . . . I was kept from the Committee on platforms . . . and the Committee reported a plat-

9 Gurowski to Gov. Andrew, Feb. 1, 1864, Andrew MSS.
10 New York *Herald*, July 18, 1862, editorial, p. 4, c. 3.

form . . . without reference to any doctrine or moral or political
principal [*sic*]. . . . [T]hen and there the party was disbanded and
our *principles abandoned* . . . ." [11] At another time Giddings wrote
to Julian of Indiana: "The probability is that Wade will be blown up
with the explosion he has kindled. He ought to be, for he has demoralized the party which you and I had spent our political lives in
building. It was by the influence of that party that he was elected to
the Senate; but having ascended to that chamber he kicked away the
ladder to prevent other republicans from ascending it." [12]

Zach Chandler, "that Xantippe in pants," [13] was as firmly set against
Lincoln and as ruthless in politics as Wade. Mustering a powerful
publicity campaign and carrying "the Republican organization in
his breeches' pockets," [14] Chandler sought power and domination by
pressure, intimidation, spoils, wealth, and the blunter instruments
of politics. Welles found him "steeped & steamed in whisky . . .
coarse, vulgar, and reckless." [15]

In Lyman Trumbull of Illinois the radicals had a senatorial leader
of finer fiber who nevertheless served their purpose on many wartime
occasions. His authorship and sponsorship of the bill for the confiscation of Southern property was the most prominent of his activities in
the earlier half of the war. A stickler for the Constitution "rightly interpreted," more regardful of civil rights than most Jacobins, he was
a caustic and able critic of the Lincoln administration. His competence on the Senate floor made him a formidable antagonist.

Revolving around these major stars of the Jacobinical world were
satellites, secondary bodies, and briefly flaming meteors whose main
function was voting and whose place among the political constella-
tions was a matter of party conformity. To enumerate them would be

---

[11] Joshua R. Giddings to G. W. Julian, Montreal, Jan. 28, 1862, Giddings-Julian MSS.,
marked "Private." This indignant letter is full of disillusionment as to party politics.

[12] Giddings to Julian, Montreal, Jan. 18, 1863, *ibid.*

[13] The characterization is that of Senator Graham N. Fitch of Indiana. *Cong. Globe*,
36 Cong., 1 sess., 2403.

[14] Wilmer C. Harris, *Public Life of Zachariah Chandler, 1851–1875*, 66. Dr. Harris
states (65–66): "Mr. Chandler's agents had been busy in . . . caucuses and . . . con-
ventions. . . . By 1862 Mr. Chandler owned the Republican organization [in Michi-
gan] . . . . His power was due in part to . . . patronage and to a judicious use of
money, ..."

[15] MS. Diary of Gideon Welles, Dec. 5, 1866, quoted in Howard K. Beale, *The Critical
Year*, 14.

to give a catalogue of the unknown, but one should not overlook such men of the lower house as Lovejoy of Illinois, Colfax and Julian of Indiana, Ashley and Bingham of Ohio, Roscoe Conkling of New York, Henry Winter Davis of Maryland (after 1863), and Covode of Pennsylvania. In the Senate, in addition to those mentioned, the radical ranks were filled out with John Sherman of Ohio, Henry S. Lane of Indiana, James H. Lane of Kansas, and Pomeroy of Kansas.

III

Of the Democrats it may be said that in general they failed to perceive the distinction between genuine service by an opposition party in a democracy and exploitation of the nation's misfortune for party advantage. Yet this was not all. Much of their criticism was directed against leaders who were foes not only of the Democrats but also of Lincoln. Where their darts were directed against Lincoln this was often on points concerning which the administration was vulnerable, as in the matter of arbitrary arrests. No one generalization covers all the Democrats of the period; they were of varying shades and hues. Between the solid Reverdy Johnson of Maryland and the sensational Vallandigham of Ohio there were as great a gulf as between Lincoln and Ben Wade.

Democrats had a longer history than the Republicans. Theirs was the party of tradition and ancient strength. Seldom indeed had it been a party of opposition. As the year 1860 had opened the Democratic party had had what seemed a promising chance to continue as a national organization uniting North and South. The loss, or throwing away, of that opportunity had signified the removal of the only important party that was national in scope. It was not mere claptrap for them to hope for their restoration as a reëstablishment of stability and unity in the nation. It was logical for those who thought in terms of the old Union and who noted the utter sectionalism of the Republican movement, to place their stakes on the time-honored party of Jefferson, Jackson, Calhoun, and Douglas. On the wide border, which reached far up into Ohio, Indiana, and Illinois, the Democrats were the only promising party. In the free West theirs was the tradition of that "progressive western democracy" of which H. C. Hubbart has written.[1] This was the term attached to a vigorous group which formed in the buoyant forties, championed Jeffersonian liberty and the rights of man, opposed soulless capitalism, took up for the farmer, and carried high the banner of free institutions. Much of their wartime feeling against the Republicans is explainable on the ground of deep disappointment that the war had to interrupt their hopes of reform. It was due also to sympathy with Southern brothers, 'and resentment against Lincoln's party for, as they thought, causing the war. If the South was ever to be won back, they naturally considered themselves better fitted to do the winning and holding than the party of Wade and Chandler.

Meeting at their state capital in January 1862 the Democrats of Indiana resolved that only Democrats could preserve the Union, that the war was the result of the formation of a sectional party with consequent Southern reaction, and that Republicans in Congress were to blame for the failure of peace proposals. With a sarcastic quip at the affair of Mason and Slidell, the convention declared that the war could have been avoided if the controlling party's desire for peace with the South had been equal to its leniency toward England in the *Trent* case.[2] In their public address the Democratic state convention of Wisconsin denounced abolition in the District and assailed the presidential policy of arbitrary arrests and of suppression of newspapers.[3] These examples serve to give the tone of Democratic declarations.

Unionism was no monopoly of the Republicans. The "war Democrats" were for greater solidarity in support of the existing war administration than the "peace Democrats," but even the latter looked ultimately to an integrated United States rather than a dismembered nation. This quality of Unionism, however, should not be understood as an adjournment of politics. Being out, and wanting to get in, and also being honestly convinced that their party could best promote peace and welfare in the country, the Democrats found no lack of honest reasons for opposing the Lincoln administration. In the convention at Indianapolis above mentioned (January 1862) there was manifest "a determination amongst the leading Democrats . . . of Ind & Illinois to crush the present administration and with it the

---

[1] H. C. Hubbart, " 'Pro-Southern' Influences in the Free West, 1840–1865," *Miss. Vall. Hist. Rev.*, XX, 45–62. See also H. C. Hubbart, *The Older Middle West, 1840–1880.*
[2] New York *Herald*, Jan. 10, 1862, p. 8, c. 2.   [3] *Ibid.*, Sep. 10, 1862, p. 4, c. 1.

republican party . . . ." At this meeting Joseph Holt of Kentucky was "privately agreed upon as the next President." [4]

Democratic declarations often gave a pronounced proslavery impression. The party was assuredly critical of abolitionist agitation and of various antislavery measures including the emancipation proclamation. It was nevertheless true that by the summer of 1862 prominent Democrats were prepared to admit that slavery "must go down if necessary to save the union." [5] Both parties were sick of the political nuisance of slavery. Young Democrats in New York wished to sidestep the Negro question; in inviting Samuel J. Tilden to join them in a meeting they declared themselves "opposed to the further agitation of the Negro question and in favor of the prosecution of the War for the restoration of the Union as it was and the . . . Constitution as it is . . . ." [6] In a "largely attended" state convention the Democrats of New Hampshire were "firm and uncompromising in favor of sustaining the Union and constitution." [7] An address to the nation issued by combined Democrats of various states (May 8, 1862) invited all men without distinction of party "who are for the constitution as it is, and the Union as it was" to unite with them in preserving both these principles. This, they agreed, was the "great issue." [8]

Gloom and defeat, of which there was plenty, tended to help the Democrats and embarrass the Republicans. That Lincoln's opponents should fail to capitalize this gloom was too much to expect. In state convention at Columbus, Ohio, in August 1861 some (not all) of the Democratic delegates "were rejoicing at the defeat at Bull Run, and were ready to make political capital out of the mismanagement of the War Department." [9] This did not mean, however, that the convention was anything but overwhelmingly pro-Union. The prevailing sentiment was not rejoicing at defeat, but indignation at corruption and mismanagement combined with a strong and optimistic purpose to appeal to Union-minded Southerners to return to the fold. It would be a mistake to regard as typical the few, if any, Democrats who would

[4] E. T. Bainbridge (prominent Democrat) to Joseph Holt, Louisville, Ky., Jan. 20, 1862, Holt MSS.

[5] H. S. Bundy to S. P. Chase, Reid's Mills, Ohio, Aug. 1, 1862, Chase MSS., Lib. of Cong.

[6] C. F. Averill, Chairman, to Samuel J. Tilden, New York, June 21, 1862, Tilden MSS.

[7] News item from Concord, N. H., New York Herald, Jan. 10, 1862, p. 3, c. 1.

[8] Ibid., May 9, 1862, p. 5, c. 3.

[9] G. H. Porter, Ohio Politics during the Civil War Period, 83.

actually have sold their country short. The men who perhaps went farthest in capitalizing Union defeat, for which they were largely responsible, were the anti-Lincoln radicals in the Republican party.

Of the Democrats in the House the most prominent were Pendleton of Ohio, Vallandigham of Ohio (he being more extreme than the Democratic norm), S. S. Cox of Ohio, Corning of New York, Crittenden and Grider of Kentucky, W. J. Allen of Illinois (beginning with 1863), and Voorhees of Indiana. Among the Democratic senators were Bayard and Saulsbury of Delaware, Pearce and Hicks of Maryland, Davis and Powell of Kentucky, McDougall of California, and, from 1863, Richardson of Illinois and Hendricks of Indiana. Taking the last-mentioned leader, a man above the Civil War average, it is safe to say that, though a Democrat, he was closer to Lincoln's genuine views than were the Jacobins.

There are certain persisting misconceptions regarding the "War Democrats" as contrasted with the "peace Democrats" of the period. There is the concept that, while a very large element of the Democratic party as such supported the Lincoln administration, those who did not do so formed a separate party group (of "peace" or anti-Lincoln Democrats) distinct from the main Democratic party. The only way to become clear on the matter is to study it by states; to do so here would be too long a story, but some examples may be briefly noted. In Ohio, for the state and congressional elections of 1862, the contest was between the Union party and the Democratic party. The Union party was the Republican party (for the moment held together by the conservative element) and a small minority of the Democrats. The Democratic party in that election was the regular organization which carried on a vigorous anti-Lincoln campaign. The Democrats won the election.[10] In Indiana, as J. A. Woodburn has pointed out, there were three Democratic groups: war Democrats, constitutional Union Democrats, and "anti-war" Democrats. The war Democrats came into such "close harmony, if not identification, with the Republicans" that they may be "eliminated as a part of the Democratic opposition."[11] The constitutional union Democrats comprised the

---

10 *Ibid.*, 100–109.
11 James A. Woodburn, "Party Politics in Indiana during the Civil War," *Annual Report*, Am. Hist. Assoc., 1902, I, 231. See also Winfred A. Harbison, "Lincoln and Indiana Republicans, 1861–1862," *Ind. Mag. of Hist.*, XXXIII, 301.

main bulk of the party and held it together. They were strong for the union and civil rights, but took a firm stand against the administration. They favored compromise with the South, opposed the abolitionists, whom they blamed (with the Republicans) for the war, and referred to the Republican appeal for all-party support as the "no-party dodge." "In their eyes this 'no-party party' . . . was merely . . . [a] pretense of the Republicans by which they hoped to take to themselves the spoils of office and perpetuate their own power." [12]

As for the third group, the minor faction of anti-war Democrats, they worked within the main Democratic party, but with far less importance than the regular or constitutional union element. The so-called Copperhead faction, in other words, "did not determine the official utterances and leadership of the party." As to the "great body of the party," writes Woodburn, "We have no sufficient reason to doubt . . . their loyalty to the Union or . . . to . . . the Constitution, ..." [13] In a brief treatment of an elaborate situation these points as to Ohio and Indiana give the general pattern. There were still two main parties. The Republicans, seeking to make the nation's cause a party possession, added some Democrats to their own group by using the name "Union" party; despite this the main bulk of the Democrats remained in their own organization, keeping it as an opposition party, but claiming withal as much loyalty, pro-Unionism, and determination to prosecute the war, as the Republicans. Indeed they claimed that they could do better in administering the government and restoring the Union. Their opposition was not directed against the Union cause, but against the abolitionists, the Republicans, and the existing administration.

The use of the name Union party by the Republicans implied that the moderate element was in command, and this was emphasized by the fact that radicals found it hard to go along with the movement. The fact is, however, that the dominant party as a whole might gain by the "union" feature, giving an impression of conservative control, and yet the Democrats who joined them might have insufficient guarantee that "radicalism," by which is meant intolerant excess, would not in time prevail. In order to get votes there was the tendency to give the Republican party a conservative coloration at election time. The radicals would support the party anyhow because they had no-

---

[12] Woodburn, "Party Politics in Indiana," 242.   [13] *Ibid.*, 232.

where else to go; they hoped that after election theirs would be the controlling party voice. In Ohio, for instance, it was by the influence of conservative Republicans that some Democrats went into the Union party with the Republicans in 1862; this, however, did not prevent the reëlection of the super-radical Wade to the United States Senate. If one thing was clear above others in the Ohio election of 1862 it was that the people of that state had declared themselves against all that Wade and his policies involved. Not only had both the state and congressional elections gone Democratic; it was also true that the Republican party, with its "Union" appeal, was professing moderation. It is unnecessary to note the factors that brought about Wade's reëlection by the Ohio legislature in January 1863; it is sufficient to note that genuine popular choice did not determine the selection of a man who, by reason of his position in the Senate, was to come within an inch of succeeding to the presidency in 1868.[14]

IV

Conservatives of the time found their great point of difference with the radicals on the basic purpose of the war. With Lincoln, they wanted the South to be spared the horrors of a conflict directed against civilian homes and to be genuinely satisfied when the Union should be remade. They did not want Union victory to be understood as subjugation. They stood at the opposite pole from the Jacobins, to whom suffering on the part of wicked slaveholders was a much relished expression of divine vengeance, and to whom continuing domination over the South offered the indispensable weapon of power politics. For the Union the conservatives had burning zeal, but they felt, as a sturdy Bostonian put it, that "the best fighting material in the New England ranks . . . [was] inspired not by *negrophilism,* . . . but by the spirit of the political grandfathers." [1] It was not that they were friendly to slavery; one of them urged making "short shrift of slavery"

---

[14] Being president pro tempore of the Senate, Wade would have become President if Andrew Johnson had been removed on impeachment charges in 1868. With this personal interest at stake, Wade himself voted for Johnson's conviction, which failed by only one vote.

[1] Elizur Wright to Abraham Lincoln, Boston, May 23, 1862, photostat of MS., Lib. of Cong.

for the very reason that "Jacobins . . . would be unhorsed but for this hobby." [2] Sympathizing with border Unionists and even with men of the upper South, these conservatives opposed proscriptive schemes, objected to confiscation, and preferred to avoid a war of legislation against individuals. They were ready to treat the South fairly, and were mindful of equitable and constitutional procedures. If they differed markedly with Lincoln on any point it was in the matter of civil rights, for they did not favor arbitrary arrests. Among the conservative, nonvindictive Republicans may be found some of the ablest men of the Senate: Edgar Cowan of Pennsylvania, Orville H. Browning of Illinois, James W. Grimes and James Harlan of Iowa, Jacob Collamer of Vermont, John B. Henderson of Missouri, and that "enthusiastic Jeffersonian Republican," [3] James R. Doolittle of Wisconsin.

In the House such men as Owen Lovejoy and Isaac Arnold of Illinois and A. G. Riddle of Ohio, though definitely on the Stevens side because of opposition to slavery, were innocent of the anti-Lincoln tone that was so common among radicals. They even rose to the support of Lincoln when attacked; in this they were exceptional. Francis P. Blair, Jr. of Missouri was another Republican in the House who supported the President, but his combativeness, factional tendency, desire for military distinction, and readiness to attack persons with whom Lincoln had to deal—e. g., Chase—made him a somewhat doubtful champion.

Being of the cultured, milder variety, conservatives in Congress had less boldness and dominant force than the radicals; they differed from them also in the possession of scruples and the lack of fighting organization. This situation worried men who had the welfare of the Lincoln administration at heart. Joshua Fry Speed of Kentucky, old friend of Lincoln, was "persuaded" that there was "mischief brewing." A "large and powerful party of . . . ultra men," he wrote, was "being formed to make war upon the President and upon his conservative policy." He feared that while the "other party" was

---

[2] F. P. Blair, Sr., to Montgomery Blair, Silver Spring, Md., Dec. 28, 1863, Blair MSS.

[3] James L. Sellers, "James R. Doolittle," reprinted from *Wis. Mag. of Hist.*, (vols. XVII and XVIII), p. 18 of reprint. (Henderson was a Republican, though a former Democrat; in 1868 he was to become one of the seven Republicans who voted not to convict President Johnson on impeachment charges.)

"rapidly organizing, coaxing & driving," Lincoln's friends were drifting with no concert of action.[4]

Noticing and regretting the superiority of the radicals over conservatives in the matter of organization, Speed wanted the situation
corrected: he wanted the few Southern men in Congress, the Northern
Democrats, and the conservative Republicans to form a union under
some competent leader. If necessary Speed thought the President
ought to "go before the country on the next congressional election
[of 1862] upon the issue," but he preferred it should not go that far;
conservatives ought "to beat them at every point from the picket
skirmish to the grand charge," in "parliamentary movements as in
the field." He continued: "We need a cool, active young man—one
capable of forming combinations—and our friends should be willing
to give the leadership to some conservative republican . . . . I have
talked to all of our Ky delegation on the subject. They all agree with
me—but they don't go to work." [5]

This statement by Speed touched a fundamental matter in the party
situation under Lincoln. The unnatural development by which the
radicals constituted an increasingly influential portion of a party that
also included Lincoln and the moderates was a matter of tactics, drive,
and organization. Suspicious of vengeful reform, and wary of disruptive tendencies, milder Republicans would seem to have been
more at home with the Democrats than with the Jacobins; the most
distinguished of the Democratic leaders, Douglas, had supported Lincoln on the war issue. The true party alignment, if there had to be
parties, would have been moderate liberals on one side (non-vindictive
Republicans together with the main body of the Democrats), and
on the other side Republican Jacobins mustering under such a
leader as Stevens or Wade. This would have left the more bitter
Democrats of the Fernando Wood or Vallandigham school with no
place to go except in a hopeless group to themselves, which is where
they might well have been left. The Northeast would thus have had
less directing influence, big business would have had smaller opportunity in the exploitive sense, and the party associated with Lincoln
would have had larger influence in his own section, the Middle West.
Such a group would have been antislavery in the constructive, not
punitive, sense.

---

[4] J. F. Speed to Joseph Holt, Washington, D.C., Dec. 8, 1861, Holt MSS.   [5] *Ibid.*

Such a consolidation of political forces was actually discussed and attempted. After the adjournment of the House of Representatives on May 9, 1862, there was read from the clerk's desk a call for "a meeting of the conservative members of Congress in this hall to-morrow, Saturday, May 10, at two o'clock, P. M." Conservatives from all states were invited to attend and "counsel . . . as to the best means to defeat the schemes of the abolitionists and secessionists." [6] The purpose, according to the *Herald*, was "to rally the democratic [this probably meant democratically minded] party" by inviting the co-operation of those who "go for the constitution as it is, and the Union as it was" in the congressional campaign.[7] The meeting was held at the scheduled time with the venerable Crittenden in the chair and forty-three members from both houses of Congress in attendance. Agreeing that they were not forming a political party, they announced that they were trying to get their views before the people; for this purpose a committee of one member from each state was designated to promote the good work. The possible result, as stated by the *Herald*, was "an organization of the conservative majority in the House for a systematic resistance to the radical revolutionary measures of the abolition disunionists . . . ." [8] The group was reported as containing twenty-seven Unionists, thirteen Democrats, and two Republicans.[9] As a similar sign of the times it was reported that a "new political party" was forming in New Hampshire, to be "composed of the conservative elements of both the old democratic and republican organizations, or rather of the honest supporters of the administration of Mr. Lincoln." [10] Connecticut was doing likewise; there was held at Hartford on January 8, 1862, a convention "participated in by Union democrats and republicans, representing each county in the State." [11]

Here there appears at first glance an effort to offer moderate and tolerant men a *modus vivendi* of coöperation for national, constructive measures. For one reason and another, however, the movement collapsed. Lack of leadership was an important element, but perhaps the chief reason was the ingrained tendency of American party men toward politics as usual. When another of the congressional group meetings was held on June 28, 1862, only thirty-five members attended; not

6 New York *Herald*, May 10, 1862, p. 6, c. 5.   7 *Ibid.*, May 7, 1862, p. 7, c. 1.
8 *Ibid.*, May 11, 1862, p. 4, cc. 5–6.   9 *Ibid.*, May 14, 1862, p. 6, c. 2.
10 *Ibid.*, Feb. 2, 1862, p. 4, c. 2.   11 *Ibid.*, Jan. 9, 1862, p. 1, c. 5.

all the border-state men were there, and there were no Republicans by that name. It was feared that the movement would have forced some of the conservative Republicans, the more party-minded ones, back into the arms of the radicals because of their strong influence in the party. Resolutions passed at this meeting of June 28 expressed belief in war for the Union only, conservatism as to property and slaves, observance of the Constitution, and adherence to the Crittenden resolution of July 22, 1861.[12]

Throughout this discussion of conservatism there was a frequent recurrence of two themes: that radicals were intent on seizing power, and that, as Lincoln belonged among the conservatives, the danger of such a seizure was a real challenge to his leadership. A Cabinet member wrote to the President: "I am apprehensive that you do not realize the truth of your own words . . . to the effect that the Radicals are planning a new war to maintain themselves in power." [13] The New York *Herald* in the summer and fall of 1862 harped continually on the contrast between Lincoln's conservatism and radical excess, lauding the President to the skies whenever he took a step to check the radicals. Apropos of his veto message on the confiscation bill the *Herald* declared that the President had "immortalized himself"; he had performed the "crowning act of his career." [14] "The President," declared the *Herald,* "is sustained in this [moderate] policy by Secretary Seward and the conservative members of the Cabinet, by most of the generals and by the great mass of the people." [15] Mentioning radicalism as "the only danger . . . we have now to fear," the *Herald* said: ". . . in President Lincoln we have found the man who has thus far been able to grapple it successfully," then added: "The time has come . . . when the conservative Union men of Congress and the country should rally . . . to his support . . . ." [16]

Lincoln's moderation versus radical fury—such was the recurring theme. David Davis, Illinois friend of Lincoln, destined for the Supreme Court, wrote: "The abolitionists not only intend to ostracise

---

[12] *Ibid.,* June 29, 1862, p. 5, c. 2.

[13] Rough draft of letter, Montgomery Blair to Lincoln, undated, probably 1862 or 1863, Blair MSS.

[14] New York *Herald,* July 18, 1862, editorial, p. 4, c. 4. As it turned out, however, Lincoln did not veto the confiscation bill. See below, pp. 228–229.

[15] *Ibid.,* June 16, 1862, editorial, p. 4, c. 3.

[16] *Ibid.,* June 17, 1862, editorial, p. 6, c. 3.

every Southern man, but all in the free States, who do not think with them." "[I]f he [Lincoln] preserves his conservatism inflexibly [added Davis] & makes himself the breakwater agt the radicalism that is rampant—then his fame will be undying . . . & his deeds of omission & commission will be buried out of sight." [17]

V

One is struck with the lack of significance (in terms of public service) attaching to parties in Lincoln's day of power. It was in the narrow and uninspired sense that parties functioned—i. e., as organizations or machines owned and operated by politicians for winning elections and seizing or retaining government offices, not as groupings of citizens for civic-minded betterment. It was in the party sense that Republican and Democratic organizations carried on. This suited the politicians; in their view the party sense was dominant. There was little regrouping according to principle; existing party models were perpetuated as instruments for gaining political power. Had parties been made over for the emergency each group would have been composed of like-minded men. Instead of that, each of the major parties was made up of diverse elements, in keeping with the practice of party managers whose object is not to create a clear-cut division for deciding a public issue, but rather to garner the votes of all kinds of citizens, whether they agree or not.

Thus it cannot be said that one of the two major parties stood for a particular thing, and that the other party stood for the opposite thing. A friend of Lincoln said that "there would be as much propriety in saying that Mr. Lincoln was an anti-war Republican as [that] Samuel J. Tilden was an anti-war Democrat." [1] The course of John A. Dix illustrates the flexibility of party principle together with the persistence of party solidarity; he was urged as Democratic candidate for governor, but his name was also presented to the Republican Union convention in New York for the same office. [2] Neither party chose him, however, preferring more regular party men: Seymour for the Demo-

---

[17] David Davis to Joseph Holt, Bloomington, Ill., Mar. 27, 1862, Holt MSS.
[1] Statement of J. D. Caton, quoted in A. C. Flick, *Samuel Jones Tilden: A Study in Political Sagacity*, 138.
[2] *Ibid.*, 135, 136.

crats, Wadsworth for the Republicans.

Divisions as to sentiment were more evident among factions within a given party than between one major party and another. The Democrats had factions which did not break up the party; they had their Vallandighams on the one hand and their Belmonts or Tildens on the other. As to the Republican party there were factions all the way through. In Indiana Schuyler Colfax was a rival of Caleb Smith; Henry S. Lane, "resenting the charge of Abolitionism," [3] was an Indiana Republican of a very different type than George W. Julian. Rivalry was exceedingly keen in Ohio between Wade and Chase; neither faction was friendly toward Lincoln. Touching on one of the rising young Republicans in Ohio, John Hay referred to Whitelaw Reid as "outrageously unfair to the President and . . . servilely devoted to Mr. Chase." [4] In New York it was the Greeley faction versus the Weed-Seward group; in Pennsylvania it was the McClure-Curtin element versus the Cameron clan. Delahay of Kansas had no use for Pomeroy of Kansas. The Howard group in Michigan went down as the Chandler group in Michigan went up. In Massachusetts the outgoing Republican governor, N. P. Banks, spoke a different language in 1861 than the incoming Republican governor, John A. Andrew. [5] In Missouri the Bates following was vastly different from the pro-Frémont element, and so keen was the agitation on the part of Republican antislavery Germans that, as a conservative Republican said at the time, there was "no freedom of discussion" in Missouri; it did no good to refer anything to popular vote. [6] "These . . . Radicals," he wrote, "are of the class that in any well ordered state would either be hanged or sent to the penitentiary." No one can rival them, he added, "unless he is willing, as Aubrey said in the time of Charles I 'to risk a term in Purgatory.'" To enter this rivalry, he asserted, one would have "to burn, rob, lay waste . . . , pillage for gain, and

[3] Woodburn, "Party Politics in Indiana," 227–228.

[4] Diary of John Hay, Dec. 13, 1863 (Dennett, *Lincoln . . . in the Diaries . . . of John Hay*, 138). That Reid was the Washington correspondent of the Cincinnati *Gazette* and also of the western Associated Press, made his anti-Lincoln animus the more dangerous.

[5] Pearson, *Andrew*, I, 137. Banks's conservative valedictory was challenged two days later by Andrew's anti-slavery inaugural. Andrew considered Banks's performance "execrable"; Andrew's biographer characterized it as "distinctly outside the proprieties" (*ibid.*).

[6] Thomas T. Gantt to Montgomery Blair, April 25, 1863, Blair MSS.

murder . . . ."⁷ All this is merely a suggestion of what some Republicans thought of other Republicans in Missouri. In Illinois there was Trumbull who thwarted Lincoln, and there was Browning who voted against confiscation while Illinois radicals voted for it. In the nation at large it was the moderate element against the Jacobins; in each community it was Republican Smith versus Republican Jones.

This meant that the trend in public questions would be determined, not so much by straightforward and untrammeled expressions of opinion in popular balloting, but by a process of jostling and maneuvering among rival and antagonistic groups. It was not that a party as such had a clear-cut policy reducible to yes-and-no voting at election time; the shaping of affairs was more a reflection of the skill, one might almost say the effrontery, of politicians in playing their vote-getting tricks. Over and above the question as to which party won an election was the important issue as to which element would dominate the party. It is remarkable how seldom this turned out to be the Lincoln element.

Republican factionalism meant that the President might lose, no matter which "party" won an election to Congress. Americans had parties and believed in them, yet their political tradition was a bit fogged as to the party role, if any, that a President ought to play. If parties had statesmanlike, not merely politicianlike, significance, if (for example) Republican success had great public importance, it is hard to see the harm in a Republican President taking the lead in a party appeal. To deny the propriety of such a presidential role is to suppose that a President ought to be "above" parties—in other words, that parties are something other than clean and genuine public instruments. The result was that Republican leadership slipped into coarser hands than Lincoln's; even where his party had success his moderate purposes were often frustrated. An editor of the time wrote thus: ". . . it is our great desire to sustain the President, and we deplore the opportunity he has let go by, to sustain himself. . . .

---

⁷ Gantt to Montgomery Blair (again), May 12, 1863, *ibid*. Going from state to state the account of these disagreements among Republicans could be greatly extended. In Maine W. P. Fessenden thought poorly of Hannibal Hamlin (letter to J. Washburn, Jr., Nov. 18, 1864, W. P. Fessenden MSS.). In Illinois David Davis was distrustful of Trumbull and his followers. Considering the Chicago *Tribune* friendly to Trumbull, Davis was of the opinion that this newspaper was doing "infinite harm" to the Lincoln cause. (Davis to Simon Cameron, Oct. 13, 1861, Cameron MSS.).

[We] regard the fact of his being . . . isolated from his party, as the greatest danger of the State. . . . Supported by a great branch of the American people, . . . the President remains an object of power and respect, but Tylerized and alienated, he becomes merely Abraham Lincoln, who cannot be supported . . . merely because he is filled with good intentions. If he lose the support of his own party, he cannot . . . guide the Nation through these stormy times." [8]

In the temper of the time there was hardly an episode not colored by "politics." A move to remake the constitution of Illinois, for example, was used by the Democrats for party advantage. Using a partisan constitutional convention for the purpose, the Democratic managers framed (and nearly established) a new constitution for Illinois which contained provisions excluding Negroes from settling in the state and denying them the vote and the right to hold office. The "anti-administration complexion of the convention" was unmistakable. [9]

On the Republican side one of the party stratagems was the expulsion from the Senate of Jesse Bright of Indiana in February of 1862 on the excessive charge of disloyalty against the United States. Accused of having written a letter to Jefferson Davis recommending a man interested in firearms, the senator replied that the letter had been written in March 1861 when, like many others, he did not expect war, and that it was a mere device for getting rid of a man who had become a nuisance. It was as a party measure that Bright was expelled. The judiciary committee had found the basis for expulsion insufficient. Had the man been guilty of treason he should have been judicially prosecuted as well as expelled. No such prosecution took place. One misses in the political contests of that era those informing elements that are designed to enlighten the people as they exercise their sovereign rights of democratic suffrage. In Michigan, for instance, where political results were manipulated by Chandler, the campaign

---

[8] *Wilkes's Spirit of the Times*, Sep. 13, 1862, p. 25, c. 1. This editorial continued in the pro-Hooker and pro-Burnside sense. The above passage is quoted for itself rather than for approval of the tone and policy of this rather racy sheet, owned and edited by George Wilkes, whose political editorials served a purpose not unlike that of later-day columnists.

[9] Jasper W. Cross, Jr., *Divided Loyalties in Southern Illinois during the Civil War* (abstract of doctoral thesis, Univ. of Ill., 1942), 7. Dr. Cross points out that the anti-Negro sections received a good majority in the whole popular vote, but "the body of the constitution (on whose passage the addition of the anti-Negro sections was contingent) was rejected."

of 1862 was far from "educative." "Ridicule and abuse were greatly relied upon by both sides." [10]

Contemplating the futility of existing instruments in the political field, David Davis of Illinois wrote in October 1861: "Parties are dead. The Republican party . . . accomplished the object of its being, and it cannot exist as a party organization any more. No matter what may be the result of this contest [the war], when it is over, other organizations must arise . . . ." [11] On the same day J. M. Palmer wrote to Trumbull as one Republican to another: "I think . . . like you that parties are dead in Illinois . . . ." [12]

VI

Radical-conservative jousts of the period were evident on many a weary day in the long congressional session of 1861–62. It was typical of this session that it began with a refusal of the House to reaffirm its former moderate (anti-radical) statement of war aims, and ended with enactment of the radical confiscation act. A glance at these two developments, both unfavorable to Lincoln, will suggest something of the reason why the President welcomed every recess of Congress. It was on December 4, 1861, that a vote came in the House of Representatives on the important resolution of William S. Holman (Democrat of Indiana) to reaffirm the conservative Crittenden resolution that the war was being waged for the Union with "rights of the . . . States unimpaired," and not for conquest or subjugation. In a maneuver which has been characterized as "a direct repudiation of Lincoln's message and . . . concept" [1] the House voted, 71 to 65, to lay the reaffirming resolution on the table. All the votes against reaffirming, except one, were Republican. The rear guard of conservatism in the dominant party, however, was shown by the fact that twenty-six Republicans voted with thirty-nine Democrats in favor of the reaffirmation—i. e., against laying the Holman resolution on the table. [2]

---

[10] Harris, *Zachariah Chandler*, 66.

[11] David Davis to Cameron, Lincoln, Ill., Oct. 13, 1861, Cameron MSS.

[12] J. M. Palmer to Lyman Trumbull, Camp near Tipton, Mo., Oct. 13, 1861, Trumbull MSS.

[1] Williams, *Lincoln and the Radicals*, 60.

[2] *Cong. Globe*, 37 Cong., 2 sess., 15; McPherson, *Rebellion*, 287. As usual in McPherson, Republicans appear in roman type, Democrats in italic.

A similar situation was revealed in the proceedings on the radical bill for the confiscation of Southern property. Sponsored by Senator Trumbull and presented in December 1861, the bill wended its stormy and devious way through House and Senate, coming up repeatedly for spirited and voluminous debate and finally achieving passage on the last day of the session, July 17, 1862. To steer the measure through Congress was something of a trick. Not only was it difficult to get a bill on which a majority would agree; it took parliamentary maneuvering to weed out extraneous matter and to insert features that might avert a presidential veto. After months of complicated debate, during which Trumbull frequently urged that deliberation cease and a decision be reached, the Senate voted (May 6, 1862) to refer the matter to a select committee of nine to shape a measure for further consideration. Meanwhile the House had built up its own bill presented by Eliot of Massachusetts; it was passed on May 26, by a vote of 82 to 68.[3] An analysis of this vote throws considerable light on the political situation. All but two [4] of the voting Democrats opposed the bill. No such solidarity appeared in the majority party, for twenty Republicans or Unionists voted nay. Of the 82 who voted for the bill, 78 were Republicans representing constituencies north of the Ohio. The Senate substituted its own measure, prepared by the committee of nine, for the House bill, and for a time there was deadlock, neither house receding. In the closing week, a conference committee reported a measure which was mainly that of the lower house. Finally the bill as thus shaped drew a vote of 82 to 42,[5] the notable shrinking in the negative vote probably signifying that moderate Republicans had ceased to struggle. In the Senate the bill drew 27 yeas and 12 nays.[6] All but three of the affirmative votes were Republican. In both houses the proceedings showed that confiscation was a Republican measure, but with a goodly number of Republicans dissenting.

Declarations for vindictive seizure of property were blunt and crude. "Rebels" had no constitutional rights, so the argument ran; "if their whole country must be . . . made a desert . . . to save this

---

[3] *Cong. Globe*, 37 Cong., 2 sess., 2361.

[4] The two Democrats who voted for the confiscation bill were William G. Brown, from the unionist portion of Virginia, and John W. Noell, Union Democrat of Missouri. They were highly exceptional; most border men were solidly against the bill.

[5] *Cong. Globe*, 37 Cong., 2 sess., 3267.   [6] *Ibid.*, 3276.

union . . . , so let it be." [7] Wholesale confiscations had taken place
in England and by American states in the Revolution; Northern confiscation was a necessary retaliation against Confederate sequestration;
Southerners in rebellion should pay the cost of the war; penalties
should be imposed upon traitors, and so on. Opposite arguments were
presented by Browning, Henderson, Collamer, and others. Conciliation toward erring brothers, they said, was better than stripping millions of their property; partisanship should be sunk "in one universal
. . . service by every Union man to the cause of the country." [8] The
measure, said its opponents, was in effect a bill of attainder; it violated
the fifth amendment as well as the constitutional prohibition against
forfeiture beyond the offender's life; lawmakers should not take
counsel of their resentments; punitive measures would only aggravate
a confusion already bad enough; the path of confiscation was not the
road to peace. Conservatives in the confiscation debate talked in the
Lincolnian sense; radicals, on the other hand, assaulted the President.
An example was the outburst of Representative John Hickman of
Pennsylvania, who denounced the "refusal on the part of the President
. . . to discharge . . . a plain duty . . . ." Referring to the
President's tendency to "shirk," he spoke of Congress being forced
into discord and disagreement because of the Chief's "lack of . . .
traits of character necessary to the discharge of grave responsibilities." [9]

Emerging from the legislative hopper the confiscation bill decreed
judicial forfeiture of all the property of specified classes of "rebels."
Several of its clauses related to slaves and have been considered in another connection.[10] The inclusion of antislavery provisions drew more
votes than straight confiscation would have done; many, in fact, regarded it as an antislavery bill. It was known that Lincoln opposed
confiscation, as had McClellan, also that men of Lincoln's party in
Congress had deliberately ridden roughshod over his expressed wishes.
It was further known that the President found Congress an embarrass-

---

[7] Though this statement was made by Thaddeus Stevens in support of the confiscation bill of 1861, it expressed his view also as to the much stronger measure of 1862.
Ibid., 37 Cong., 1 sess., 414–415.

[8] Statement of Garret Davis of Kentucky, a Democrat proud of his loyalty. *Ibid.*,
37 Cong., 2 sess., 1757.

[9] *Cong. Globe*, 37 Cong., 2 sess., 1801 (April 23, 1862).

[10] See above, p. 132.

ment and did not desire the prolongation of its session.[11] The bill had supposedly been made more palatable to the presidential mind by unnecessarily declaring that the pardoning power applied to confiscation and by including an appropriation for colonization of Negroes, which Lincoln favored. Nevertheless the President's veto was considered likely and radicals were wondering whether they could muster two-thirds to override it.

With courage in opposing legislators of his own party and with lawyerlike comprehension of constitutional questions, Lincoln did prepare a veto message expressing his disapproval of the bill. It is one of his ablest state papers. Some sections he could approve, since loyal men, he understood, were not touched, civil trials were provided, and "especially" since offenders were "within the . . . pardoning power." As to the slave provisions he raised no objections, though he noted a defect as to determining "whether a particular . . . slave does or does not fall within the classes defined." As was natural with an executive, the President's mind went forward to the problem of enforcement, on which he significantly remarked that there ought to be a "power of remission" and that the "severest justice may not always be the best policy." What the President chiefly objected to was that the bill declared "forfeiture extending beyond the lives of the guilty parties"; this, he thought, violated a plain clause of the Constitution. Also, as in admiralty cases, the bill permitted forfeiture by proceedings *in rem* (against the property) "without a conviction of the supposed criminal, or a personal hearing given him in any proceeding." [12]

Had Lincoln so far challenged the radicals as to veto their pet measure? Not quite. In the knowledge that the veto message was in preparation, an "explanatory joint resolution" was rushed through both houses which declared that the bill should not be construed to apply to acts prior to its passage, nor "to work a forfeiture of the real estate of the offender beyond his natural life." Though this did not touch the President's objection concerning the lack of a personal hearing in court, he approved the bill and joint resolution as substantially one. Curiously, however, and perhaps irregularly, he did something further; though signing the bill, he sent to Congress the

[11] New York *Herald*, July 13, 1862, p. 4, c. 6.
[12] *Works*, VII, 280 ff. (July 17, 1862).

executive veto message to become part of the record. It was read in both houses "amid the sneers and laughter of the abolitionists." [13]

VII

Lincoln had his technique in meeting the radical challenge, which was in all conscience a serious threat to his leadership. He avoided an open break or explosion, but did what he could to prevent the vindictives from seizing the reins. When it was evident that Cameron had been converted to radicalism for political reasons, Lincoln removed him, yet kept him on the reservation, so to speak, by an appointment to Russia. He overruled Hunter's emancipating order, but combined the incident with a warning to those who were obstructing the President's moderate solution of the slavery problem. In answering Greeley he suggested that preservation of the Union was paramount to abolitionism. He exposed and partly corrected the injustice of the confiscation bill; then he signed it, but submitted a veto message as a check to the radicals. He seized an interval when Congress was not in session to issue his emancipation proclamation, stealing the radicals' own thunder at a point where they could not but agree with him. He showed enough antislavery zeal to work along with Sumner and Chase, while holding the Negro sufficiently in the background to mollify Seward. At times he yielded to radicals on military matters, though his regret in doing so sometimes reached the point of acute pain.[1] In recalling McClellan after Pope's defeat, however, he stood up to the radicals, and the general justified his confidence at Antietam. Visiting committees unexpectedly found themselves taking Lincoln's cue. He would politely listen to them, thank them for their advice, tell them an amusing anecdote to ease the termination of the interview, bow them out, and then follow his own judgment.

When he had a conference of indignant governors on his hands in 1862, he turned an embarrassing situation entirely to his own advantage. Under the lead of Governor Curtin of Pennsylvania such a conference had been called to meet at Altoona in September 1862.

---

[13] New York *Herald,* July 18, 1862, p. 1, c. 1.

[1] In withdrawing Blenker's division from McClellan's force and sending it to Frémont, Lincoln wrote to McClellan: ". . . I did so with great pain, understanding that you would wish it otherwise. If you could know the full pressure of the case, . . . [etc.]" *Works,* VII, 138 (March 21, 1862).

In the sequel the evidence as to the original purpose of the gathering was obscured and conflicting statements have been made; this was partly because of a change of outlook between the calling and the holding of the conference, and partly because some of the participants had a purpose which they did not wish publicly to avow. It was just after Pope's defeat, when the Union cause looked very dark, that the call was issued; when the conference was held (September 24) the situation had been radically changed by Antietam and the emancipation proclamation.

The conference as planned had a double basis: desire for action against slavery, and distrust of the President because of military defeat. It was felt that the President should become both more radical and more efficient. This was illogical, since radicalism produced military inefficiency, but consistency was no part of the movement. Whatever the inner purpose of the conclave, the talk that floated about at the time associated it with some kind of a drive against the President, at least a move to admonish him or tell him his duty, at most an effort to supplant him. "The governors may declare," wrote Count Gurowski, "that the country is in danger, . . . that if he Lincoln sees not the . . . danger, the people & the governors see it, . . . that it is the duty of the governors to save the country's cause in spite of the faults & the predilections of the president . . . ." [2] It was suggested that the purpose of the state executives was "to dictate a policy for the president"; an adviser of Governor Yates thought that "such a course . . . would be fatal" as it would give "unnatural authority" to inferiors.[3] The conferring governors were understood to be anti-McClellan; it was cynically stated that their hope was "to extort from the President, by fair means or foul, . . . submission to their dictation as to . . . generals," and that they were working "to have McClellan removed and Frémont installed in his place." [4] To the Washington correspondent of the *Herald* it seemed that "a vast conspiracy has been set on foot by the radicals . . . to depose the present administration, and place Frémont at the head of a provisional gov-

---

[2] Gurowski to Governor Andrew, Aug. 2, 1862, Andrew MSS. (This may have been associated with an earlier gubernatorial combination to promote a new call for troops, but it also fits the Altoona incident.)

[3] L. U. Reavis to Governor Richard Yates, Beardstown, Ill., Sep. 19, 1862, MS., Chicago Hist. Soc.

[4] New York *Herald*, Sep. 27, 1862 (editorial), p. 4, c. 4.

ernment; in other words, to make him military dictator." It was reported on the authority of prominent politicians that one of the
features of the conspiracy was the proposed meeting of Northern
governors whose purpose was "to request President Lincoln to resign,
to enable them to carry out their scheme." [5]

What the state executives would have done if events had not stolen
their thunder is a question. What is certain is that two days after the
conference, when some of the governors met Lincoln personally at
Washington (September 26), the President held the trumps. By that
time he had clipped the gubernatorial wings by publicly associating
himself with their effort, giving it his own emphasis, and the governors
found themselves with nothing to do but to endorse the President's
policy, which they did in a laudatory public statement.[6] Lincoln
smilingly thanked the visiting magistrates for their support and indicated that no fact had so thoroughly confirmed to him the justice of
the emancipation proclamation as the approval of the executives of
the loyal states. On some aspects he would not answer them specifically
at the time, he said, but he would give these matters his most favorable
consideration, carrying them out "so far as possible."

After the formal proceedings there followed an informal interview
of some length, but the historian can give no detailed report of it.
According to the *Tribune* a "phonographic [stenographic] reporter"
belonging to that paper appeared in the anteroom at the White House
while the Cabinet was in session upstairs, the ante-room being alive
with "the Governors in waiting." When the Cabinet departed, the
reporter requested Lincoln's permission to attend the conference; the
request was granted by the President and he entered with the rest.
Curtin of Pennsylvania, however, protested at the presence of the
news writer and stated that according to his understanding the interview was not public, whereupon the *Tribune* man mentioned Lincoln's permission and Lincoln himself added (as reported) that "he
was . . . willing to have the results of the interview go . . . to the
people if the Governors did not object." Yates and others, however,
rejoined "that the interview was . . . strictly confidential," and
the reporter retired.[7] This incident suggests that the governors meant
to have it out with Lincoln on matters of disagreement or complaint,

[5] *Ibid.*, Sep. 17, 1862, p. 4, c. 5.   [6] *Annual Cyclopaedia*, 1862, 793–794.
[7] New York *Tribune,* Sep. 29, 1862, p. 3, cc. 1–2.

but that the President was entirely confident of his ability to command the situation, and even to use the occasion for his own purpose.
According to one account the governors found the President doing the
talking, then ushering them out before their complaints had been
presented.[8] The public statements that issued from the White House
interview were favorable to the President; it was in that sense that
the Altoona incident took its place in history.

VIII

In the fall of 1862 the American electorate performed the solemn
duty of choosing representatives in Congress to hold until 1865. Or-
ators, agitators, and editors belabored the people with catchwords and
arguments. Military deadlock, new calls for troops, compulsory
military service (in a mild form), emancipation, arbitrary arrests, internal blockade, negrophilism, abolitionism—such elements on the
Republican side were denounced by the Democrats who advocated
the Union, the Constitution, suppression of corruption, respect for
civil rights, readiness to deal with Southern unionists, and sane reconstruction. People were asked whether they wanted their communities Africanized and whether the Petition of Right and Magna Charta
were forgotten. Editors spoke out and were arrested; then their
friends raised the issue of freedom of the press. Examples were Dennis
Mahoney of Iowa and Edson B. Olds of Ohio; especially in Ohio,
where Olds was not the only victim, the effect on popular feeling was
acutely felt.

When Republicans met in secret congressional caucus on July
12, 1862, they became involved in a protracted discussion that re
vealed differences within the ranks on current issues. In a meeting
that lasted till nearly midnight they rejected an address that had
been carefully prepared by a committee and contented themselves
with a colorless resolution which in resounding rhetoric asked all
loyal men to stand by the Union and to support the prosecution of
the war. It was remarked by the *Herald* that points of Republican
policy were not particularized in any way; radicals had been "shrieking against the President, and demanding some more specific an-
nunciation of policy"; there had evidently been "trouble in their

---

[8] Williams, *Lincoln and the Radicals*, 185–186.

POLITICS AS USUAL 233

camp," with "irreconcilable divisions" throughout the party; as a result they had found it "easier to demand a policy than to adopt one." [1]

Naturally the problem of supporting the administration was an issue in the congressional campaign, and on that issue the Republicans suffered, not an overthrow, but a setback of such seriousness that "Mr. Lincoln was . . . very uneasy." [2] The former Congress may be usefully compared with the new one in connection with the election for speaker. In the case of the old Congress, the Thirty-Seventh, 111 out of 159 votes had been cast for Republican candidates for Speaker (71 for Galusha A. Grow and 40 for Frank P. Blair, Jr.) In the Thirty-Eighth Congress Schuyler Colfax received a vote for speaker which James G. Blaine mentioned as "the distinctive Republican strength," but it amounted to only 101 out of a total of 182.[3] From nearly 70 per cent of the speakership vote, the Republicans thus slipped to 55 per cent. Casting up party totals of membership in the lower house one finds the following result: In the Thirty-Seventh Congress there were 106 Republicans, 42 Democrats, and 26 Unionists, nearly all the "Unionists" being from the border states; in the Thirty-Eighth Congress there were 102 Republicans and Unionists, 9 border-state men, and 75 Democrats. The Senate did not change much. The old Senate had 35 Republicans and Unionists out of a total of 48 (subtracting vacancies and omitting seceded states); the new one had 36 Republicans and Unconditional Unionists out of a total of 50.[4]

Five important states which had given their full electoral vote to Lincoln in 1860 now chose Democratic majorities for Congress: New York, Pennsylvania, Ohio, Indiana, and Illinois. In Indiana Lincoln "received the equivalent of a vote of want of confidence." [5] New Jersey, which had given Lincoln four of its seven electoral votes in 1860, went Democratic; Wisconsin, a Lincoln state in 1860, chose an evenly divided delegation. Prominent Republicans of the preceding Congress did not return; among these were Roscoe Conkling and

---

1 New York *Herald*, July 13, 1862, p. 4, c. 6.
2 A. G. Riddle, *Recollections of War Times*, 249.
3 Blaine, *Twenty Years of Congress*, I, 324, 497.
4 New York *Tribune Almanac*, 1862, pp. 17–18; 1864, p. 24.
5 W. A. Harbison, "Lincoln and Indiana Republicans, 1861–1862," *Ind. Mag. of Hist.*, XXXIII, 301. A Republican majority of 10,000 in 1860 in Indiana was "replaced by a Democratic majority of approximately the same size" (*ibid.*).

E. G. Spaulding of New York, John A. Bingham of Ohio, and the Republican speaker, Galusha A. Grow of Pennsylvania. It was a serious "political re-action," wrote James G. Blaine; there were "radical changes," and "the narrow escape of the Administration from total defeat" was evident when the roll was called.[6]

One of the features of the congressional election was the failure of Lincoln's own state to sustain him, for there was no doubt that the President was on trial in the balloting for Congress. Of the fourteen congressmen returned from Illinois, five were Republicans and nine Democrats. What made the defeat particularly poignant for the President was that in his home district his old friend and first law partner, John Todd Stuart, being the Democratic nominee, was chosen to Congress in opposition to another friend, Leonard Swett. As a Whig, Stuart had been a party associate of Lincoln in the old days; now he had carried on an active campaign against his former partner's presidential policies, while Swett, carrying the Republican banner, had announced himself as champion of the President. Swett's defeat showed that, with Lincoln's administration as the unmistakable issue, the President's home district gave a verdict of thumbs down.[7]

On the western map the party division showed Lincoln's opponents in command in southern and central Illinois, southern Indiana, some of northern Indiana, and most of Ohio. H. C. Hubbart, in a close analysis, treats the election under the title "The Free West Repudiates Abraham Lincoln, 1862." [8] Though in Ohio Vallandigham went down in this election, a southern Illinois equivalent in the person of W. J. Allen was chosen to represent "Egypt." Of Southern antecedents, this one-time partner of John A. Logan was a vigorous critic of Lincoln's policies; he opposed the emancipation proclamation, arbitrary arrests, use of Negro troops, and conscription. Men of Southern Illinois, he said, were fighting to bring the South back into the Union, not to free the Negroes.[9] The Republican governors of Illinois and Indiana found themselves greatly embarrassed by the election of

---

[6] Blaine, *Twenty Years of Congress*, I, 498.

[7] Harry E. Pratt, "The Repudiation of Lincoln's War Policy in 1862 . . . ," *Journal*, Ill. State Hist. Soc., XXIV, 129–140.

[8] Hubbart, *Older Middle West*, chap. xi.

[9] These matters, with many other divisive factors in Illinois, are ably treated in Jasper W. Cross, Jr., "Divided Loyalties in Southern Illinois during the Civil War" (ms. doctoral dissertation, Univ. of Ill., 1942).

Democratic legislatures in 1862; deadlock resulted in each case between the executive and the lawmaking branch. Yates solved it by
proroguing his legislature, Morton by a kind of budgetary miracle
which enabled him to finance the state's war effort (with support from
Washington and from friendly banks) without a regular appropriation. When William A. Richardson, elect of the "copperhead" legislature of Illinois, succeeded Orville Browning in the Senate of the
United States in 1863, the President had to face a bitter opponent in
the place of a former part-time supporter.

Agreeing with the *Herald* that the Republican party was "defeated"
because it had changed the war into an abolition crusade,[10] Browning
wrote in his diary: "Badly beaten by the Democrats. Just what was to
be expected from the insane ravings of the Chicago Tribune, Quincy
Whig, [etc.] . . . ." Considering that Browning had been a prominent Republican, his attitude is especially significant. Convinced
that Lincoln had gone over to the radicals, and displeased with
emancipation, arrests, and confiscations, he went about "denouncing
leading Republicans as traitors and enemies to the country," and
entirely omitted to endorse the President's policy in a public speech
on the eve of the election.[11]

Browning was virtually a man without a party. Not only had he
lost confidence in Lincoln; he was also out of tune with anti-Lincoln
trends which were growing in intensity. His disappointment with
Lincoln, whom he considered "fatally bent upon his course," [12] was
that he had not successfully resisted these trends. From late 1862 to
his death in 1881 he was to withhold support from Republican candidates.[13] Browning's case was that of a disillusioned friend of the Lincoln
administration giving way to a bitter opponent. Facing home with a
sense of utter frustration, he wrote: ". . . I feel that I can do no
good here— The counsels of myself and those who sympathize with
me are no longer heeded. I am despondent, and have but little hope
left for the Republic." [14]

It was a common Republican assertion that absence of soldiers from
the polls determined the result; this implied that Democrats were at

---

10 Nov. 8, 1862, editorial, p. 4, c. 3.
11 Quincy (Ill.) *Whig*, Nov. 10, 1862, quoted in Browning, *Diary*, I, 582 n.
12 Browning, *Diary*, I, 607 (Dec. 31, 1862).   13 *Ibid.*, II, xxi.
14 *Ibid.*, I, 621 (Jan. 30, 1863).

home voting while Republicans were at the front.[15] In general, state
laws of the time did not give soldiers the privilege of absent voting,[16]
and it was assumed that the lack of their votes explained Democratic
success, especially in such states as Ohio, Indiana, and Illinois. Various
writers have shown the assumption to be unfounded. George H.
Porter writes that "the facts . . . do not support this charge";
J. F. Rhodes finds that this factor had "little to do with the result."[17]
There is no historical basis for the partisan assertion that Democrats
lagged behind Republicans in military service for the Union. Records
do not exist to show the party affiliations of individual volunteers, but
one can take election figures by counties in Illinois and compare them
with county statistics in the state adjutant-general's reports giving
the number of volunteers and also the number properly liable to
military service. Calculations based on such records show that the
ratio of volunteers to the total of men subject to military duty was in
fact higher in Democratic than in Republican counties.[18] Though the
soldier-vote argument brought Republicans the comfort of wishful
thinking, there were enough other factors to determine the result—
imprisonments, factional disputes within the Republican party, corruption, the draft, taxes, and dissatisfaction with radicalism. Most
potent of all was "failure of the army to accomplish decisive results." [19]

The President had not actively participated in the drive for congressional votes. Where it was a contest between Republicans seeking
nomination, he was especially careful to avoid interference. Yet his
name and his policies could not be dissociated from the campaign;
indeed it is characteristic of congressional contests in the United
States that they have as much to do with executive as with lawmaking

---

[15] Blaine, *Twenty Years of Congress*, I, 443.

[16] In Iowa, Wisconsin, and Pennsylvania voting in the field by the soldiers was
permitted in 1862, soldier preferences being heavily weighted on the Republican side.
In Illinois, soldiers were not allowed to vote in the general election of 1862, but on the
proposed new state constitution their votes were taken by commissioners who, under the
provisions of the proposed constitution, visited camps, barracks, hospitals, etc., for that
purpose. The soldier vote was unfavorable to the constitution by 10,151 to 1,687, this
being deemed a Republican victory. For Illinois, information has been obtained from
Margaret C. Norton, Archivist, Illinois State Library; see also Benton, *Voting in the
Field*, 51, 66, 203, 253.

[17] George H. Porter, *Ohio Politics During the Civil War Period*, 109; J. F. Rhodes,
Hist. of the U. S., IV, 166.

[18] In this connection the author has used elaborate notes and calculations prepared
by one of his students, Mr. A. R. Hoeflin of Peoria, Illinois.

[19] Harbison, "Lincoln and Indiana Republicans," 302.

matters. The voting in 1862 was as much for or against Lincoln's administration as it was a judgment upon congressmen for their purely legislative records. Had the election gone against the President's party in an absolute, instead of a relative, sense, the further course of his administration would have been seriously hampered. In the actual sequel the Democrats took a bolder tone in assailing some of the more vulnerable measures of the government, but the Republicans retained control of the House and Senate, and with the crude force of Stevens's domination, which tended to scare any dissenting Republican out of his skin,[20] they were able to pass their measures. More often than not, these were non-Lincoln or anti-Lincoln measures.

To one of its Ohio members who left a frank record, service in the wartime Congress was "irksome" and distasteful. Noting with relief that he had at least escaped personal injury, he considered congressional service a kind of dissipation. A retiring congressman, he said, loathes the word "Honorable" affixed to his name, this being his only emolument, "save personal and political animosities and alienated friends." The Capitol, "its passage-ways and odors," had grown "offensive." This Republican had found Cox, Pendleton, and Vallandigham among his "assured friends." "Indeed," he added, "I have always found disinterested friends among the Democrats, and have observed among politicians that the warmest personal ties are usually across party lines."[21]

---

[20] Referring to Stevens's "iron will and relentless mastery," A. K. McClure tells how he received a protest from a Republican congressman against a particular measure, then ordered the member to vote for it or be branded as a coward. The quaking legislator complied. Had he refused obedience, the "Commoner" would have ruined him. *Abraham Lincoln and Men of War-Times*, 280–281.

[21] A. G. Riddle, *Recollections of War Times*, 225–227.

CHAPTER XXV

GENERALS, SECRETARIES, AND
"SOME SENATORS"

AT the turn of the year 1862–1863 Lincoln was approaching the mid-point of his administration. As President in a democracy he occupied an office of great power, but it was a power that had to be exercised with deference. He could govern, but only if his governing voice was not too bluntly audible. There were those who wanted to take the power of government out of his hands. Men of such intent were not confined to the opposite party whose increased strength had just been demonstrated at the polls; in his own party were men of extreme views who were determined to seize dominant influence out of all proportion to the number of their popular supporters. Moderates were making so little fuss that their influence was in danger of being dissipated; radicals were intensifying the tempo of their drive. News from the military fronts was to tell of disaster and disappointment before it took a turn for the better. Disaster could be politically exploited, and if a steady hand were not at the helm, confusion and worse disaster might be the direct result. There were forces of morale which made it possible that defeat might produce a tightening of the belt and a courage for renewed effort, but these forces had to be brought into play; they had to have a focus. Without that focus, defeat could mean defeatism and divided counsel. To produce a concentration which could overcome the evident tendencies toward dissipation, to prevent disruptive elements from playing havoc with the machinery of government and with the military management, and to do it with the tact of a moderator instead of the scowl of a dictator, was Lincoln's task.

I

The poorly based hope of victory which came with Burnside's displacement of McClellan was dashed to pieces on the line of the Rappahannock in mid-December 1862. Under conditions that were due
precisely to poor generalship the army which had repelled Lee at
Antietam obeyed the death order of its commander in a bravely hopeless encounter at Fredericksburg on December 13. Courage the men
had in abundance, but every factor of battle planning, of terrain and
position, was unfavorable to Union triumph. Massed with artillery
support on Mayre's Heights behind the city of Fredericksburg or
crowded within the protection of the "sunken road" just ahead, Lee's
troops stood unshaken as repeated charges were launched against them,
only to be broken in sickening slaughter. Having "persisted in crossing the river after all hope of a surprise had faded away," and having
been restrained by supporting generals from repetition of suicidal
assaults, Burnside could only recross to the north side of the river,
where the best hope for the army under its "dazed . . . and grief-
stricken" commander was a period of inaction.[1]

In reporting the "truthful and terrible panorama of that bloody day"
a New Hampshire colonel wrote of "brave legions . . . struggling
against the terrible combination of the enemy's artillery and infantry, whose unremitting fire shook the earth," of crowded Union
hospitals that had "no note of triumph," of the enemy's "unyielding
resistance," of "direct and enfilading batteries," of "death-dealing
artillery," of "one startling crash, . . . one simultaneous sheet of
fire and flame." "The arrangement of the enemy's guns," wrote this
officer, "was such that they could pour their concentrated and incessant fire upon any point occupied by our assailing troops . . . ."[2]
"It was impossible the result should be otherwise," wrote an observing
journalist, "as the converging fire of the enemy was plainly crushing.
. . . [T]heir bellowing batteries . . . and the swarm of sharp-
shooters, secure . . . behind a stone wall, and in a sunken road, like
that Victor Hugo finds on the field of Waterloo, were too much for

---

[1] *Battles and Leaders of the Civil War*, III, 133, 138.
[2] Moore, *Rebellion Record* (Docs.), VI, 84-85. Realistic and rhetorically vivid accounts of the battle by a number of minor officers appear in this volume, pp. 80 ff.

the naked valor of our infantry." [3]

This maddening defeat was the second major disaster on the Virginia front in 1862. Both unhappy events had resulted from factors emanating from Washington, the most alarming of which was radical interference. For twenty months the war had been raging. Not only was it beginning to seem interminable; its toll of dead and mutilated men and of treasure seemed a useless sacrifice under existing leadership. People in the North were still loyal, but their loyalty to functionaries at Washington was being sorely tried. Credit slumped; gold took a dive; government censorship, never effective, was tightened; indignation meetings were planned; radicals "searched frantically for some device which would lift from their party the onus of Fredericksburg." [4]

McClellan's reinstatement was urged; [5] scapegoats were demanded; European repercussions were feared; citizens generally were losing confidence in those who guided and commanded. Civil morale was one with military elan and force. If the existing army went down, some doubted whether it would be replaced.[6] The army is melting away, it was said; "we cannot get another, except by using the blacks." [7] The people were not yet conditioned for a long and desperate war. While they were thinking of past and present contributions and puzzled to know why they were not of greater avail, the government was demanding additional sacrifices. Suppose those further burdens and losses were endured, what assurance was there that they would not again be wasted?

It was upon Lincoln that much of the popular wrath descended. Ironically the most wrathful were the radicals, who did not scruple to abuse Lincoln for unhappy results which they themselves had produced. "May the Lord hold to rigid account the fool that is set over us," wrote an abolitionist who had begun to think that Higginson's black troops were the country's "only real hope." He continued: "What suicide the Administration is guilty of! What a weak pattern of

---

[3] *Ibid.*, VI, 100.   [4] Williams, *Lincoln and the Radicals*, 201–202.
[5] Bates, *Diary*, 270.
[6] ". . . I find that the South is more united . . . than we . . . . What then. Shall we stop fighting. . . . We must go on . . . . But the armies now in the field must do the work. . . . [T]his army destroyed, cannot be replaced—at least [it] wont be." Willard Warner to S. P. Chase, Columbus, Ohio, Nov. 27, 1862, Chase MSS., Lib. of Cong.
[7] Grant Goodrich to Trumbull, Chicago, Jan. 31, 1862, Trumbull MSS.

Old Pharaoh! What a goose!" [8] "My opinion of Mr. Lincoln," wrote a friend of Sumner, "is that nothing can be done with him . . . . He would damp the ardor of the bravest . . . & neutralize the efforts of the ablest . . . . He is wrong-headed, . . . the petty politician not the statesman, & . . . ill-deserving the *sobriquet* of Honest. I am out of all patience with him." [9] "I am losing confidence in the *executive* capacity of Mr. Lincoln's administration," wrote a perplexed New Englander. "I see plainly that doubt and discouragement are spreading among the people . . . ." This downcast citizen feared a demand for termination of the war with the Union objective unattained, not because of incapacity or unwillingness of the people to fight and crush the enemy, but because of "a fixed belief that the managers . . . at Washington are incompetent . . . ." [10]

II

Dissatisfaction now focused on the question of secretarial change. If only the President could have a reorganized ministry, perhaps something could be done. "Reorganization" of the cabinet was the talk; this being interpreted meant getting rid of Seward. A Pennsylvanian who foregathered with Stevens, Pomeroy, and other radicals accused Seward of doubling the proportions of the rebellion, promoting party opposition to the administration, inviting "insult" from abroad, and being bullied by Palmerston and Russell. Deploring Seward's ascendancy to the cabinet, he denounced the nation's secretary of state as "a thorough, ingrained, moral and physical coward." [1] This was not one man's opinion. It was the Jacobin theme.

Thus again were anti-Lincoln radicals using a time of national disaster to promote factional attacks, and that too directly after an election in which the Republican appeal had been made in "Union" or conservative terms, and in which distrust of Jacobin influence had produced Democratic popular gains. If Seward were dropped, radicals felt that Montgomery Blair and possibly Bates should go down with

[8] James Sloan Gibbons to W. L. Garrison, N. Y., Dec. 3, 1862, MS., Boston Pub. Lib. This was written before Fredericksburg; after that defeat the feeling was yet more intense.

[9] O. A. Brownson to Charles Sumner, Dec. 26, 1862, Sumner MSS.

[10] John D. Baldwin to Sumner, *Daily Spy* Office, Worcester, Mass., Dec. 30, 1862, *ibid.*

[1] Amasa McCoy to Joseph Holt, Harrisburg, Pa., Dec. 14, 1862, Holt MSS. McCoy was circulating a petition, asking a change of cabinet.

him. Smith, as revealed by Welles, was tired of the cabinet and ready to serve his country in the pleasanter life-office of judge. [2] Various men were mentioned as suitable cabinet members. On the conservative side there were suggestions of Thomas Ewing of Ohio, who had served in the cabinets of Harrison, Taylor, and Fillmore; of Banks, who had been associated with the Democratic, American, and Republican parties; or of James Guthrie of Kentucky, who had been in the Pierce cabinet. Preston King of New York was also suggested.[3] It was from the radicals, however, that suggestions flowed most freely: their favorites were such men as Sumner, Holt, Fessenden (in Seward's place), Grow (to be moved from the speakership), Henry Winter Davis, and B. F. Butler. Architects of military ruin were demanding that theirs be the controlling voice. Demands for cabinet reorganization came with greatest emphasis from those who had vociferously demanded the overthrow of McClellan, whose demotion on two occasions had been followed by two major defeats.

While rumors spread and people wondered what was afoot, the Republican senators assumed a kind of informal cabinet-making function. On December 16 and 17 they held lengthy caucus deliberations, debating, complaining, almost adopting a resolution denouncing Seward by name, and finally coming through with a decision to call upon the President for a "re-organization" of the cabinet. In these senatorial wranglings the air was thick with denunciations of Lincoln and Seward. Wilkinson of Minnesota assailed the President and his secretary of state; Grimes spoke in the same sense; Fessenden alluded to the "back stairs & malign influence which controlled the President"; Wade outdid all of them, declaring that the Senate should go in a body and demand Seward's dismissal. What Wade wanted was a Lieutenant General "with absolute and despotic powers." He would never be satisfied "until there was a Republican at the head of our armies." [4] "Many speeches were made," wrote Browning, some of

---

[2] Welles, *Diary*, I, 193.   [3] Browning, *Diary*, I, 601, 603.

[4] *Ibid.*, I, 597. The military judgment of Wade, so coarse in his opposition to Lincoln and so dominant in the partisan proceedings of the congressional committee on the conduct of the war, may be measured by the generals he sought to destroy and by those he favored. Besides McClellan, he vigorously opposed Grant, Meade, and Sherman; he favored Frémont, Pope, Burnside, Hooker, and Butler. See T. Harry Williams, *Lincoln and the Radicals* (index under Wade). On the question of Frémont he "scathingly assailed" Lincoln, declaring that only a man sprung from "poor white trash" (by which he meant the President) could have acted as he did. *Ibid.*, 40–41, 108.

them "denouncing the President and expressing a willingness to vote for a resolution asking him to resign." [5]

Hearing of these doings, Seward and his son Frederick, assistant secretary of state, presented their resignations to Lincoln and packed their private papers for departure from Washington.[6] This raised the question of other resignations. Some thought the whole cabinet should resign.[7] Stanton became alarmed. Fearing that Seward's resignation might be a signal for a general reorganization in which he might be left out, he tried to induce Seward to return, several "weak-kneed Senators" (in the words of the Cincinnati *Gazette*) working to the same end.[8] This only added to the complication; Stanton's conduct proved one of the difficulties of the whole movement.

In great distress the President questioned his friend Browning about the caucus. What did these men want? he asked. Browning could only reply that they were "exceedingly violent towards the administration." The Browning diary continues: "Said he [Lincoln] 'They wish to get rid of me, and I am sometimes half disposed to gratify them.' I replied Some of them do wish to get rid of you, but the fortunes of the Country are bound up with your fortunes, . . . stand firmly at your post . . . . Said he 'We are now on the brink of destruction. . . . I can hardly see a ray of hope.' . . . He then added 'the Committee [of Republican senators] is to be up to see me at 7 O'clock. Since I heard last night of the proceedings of the caucus I have been more distressed than by any event of my life.' " [9]

Bates and others attested Lincoln's acute distress.[10] An old friend who saw the President described him as "perplexed to death nearly," adding: "It certainly is enough to make a man crazy." [11] So "haggard and care-worn" did the President appear to another friend that he was reluctant to spread the story.[12]

---

[5] Browning, *Diary*, I, 598–599.

[6] The resignations were personally presented to the President by Senator Preston King of New York on the night of the 17th. Bates, *Diary*, 269; Cincinnati *Daily Gazette*, Dec. 22, 1862, p. 1.

[7] Such was the view of Reverdy Johnson, who said "we would go [to] the Devil unless a new cabinet was formed." Browning, *Diary*, I, 601.

[8] Cincinnati *Gazette*, Dec. 22, 1862. p. 1.   [9] Browning, *Diary*, I, 600–601.

[10] Bates, *Diary*, 269.

[11] S. Noble to E. B. Washburne, Washington, Dec. 25, 1862, Washburne MSS.

[12] "[Joshua F.] Speed tells me that the President looked haggard and care-worn beyond what he expected . . . . I have mentioned it to no one except to you and one other personal friend. I wish he could show a . . . cheerful look, and let the world

Lincoln's upright and puritanical secretary of the treasury bore a peculiar relation to the whole embarrassing movement. This is not to say that Chase pulled all the strings himself, nor that one should believe in full the bald statement of Tom Ewing in conversation with Browning that "Chase was at the bottom of all the mischief, and was setting the radicals on to assail Seward." [13] That Chase was the main instigator of an underhand intrigue seems hardly likely. It was rather that the radicals themselves wanted to exalt Chase, that a cabinet of the "ultra" type was in contemplation, and that Chase had given unfavorable accounts of the President and his cabinet in conversation with disaffected senators. While gunning for Seward, these men intended that Chase should come through with increased influence. This was the point and purpose of the reorganization. Chase was the type of man who, with entire sincerity, could have lent support to the senatorial onslaught.

The distrust of Seward on the part of radicals and antislavery men was deep and profound. Sensing that he had more influence over the President than any other secretary, they knew that this influence was a moderate factor at the time when they wanted extreme measures. They even found occasion to complain bitterly of some of the secretary's diplomatic despatches. A great objection was raised, for example, to a published note from Seward to Charles Francis Adams (July 5, 1862) criticizing vehement opponents of slavery for helping to precipitate servile war by demanding universal emancipation as a way of saving the Union. The comment may have been unfortunate and it would presumably not have been made, much less published, if submitted to Lincoln. Nevertheless it was but an expression of opinion to Adams and it would probably have done no harm except for the antislavery dither made over it.[14]

III

Lincoln was presented with no mere tempest in a teapot. He was face to face with a challenge to his position and leadership, but this

---

see that disaster cannot make him quail. There are many . . . expressing doubts of his ability and I grieve over the feeling that such an idea . . . should take possession of the Union men." T. S. Bell to Joseph Holt, Dec. 22, 1862, Holt MSS.

13 Browning, *Diary*, I, 602.

14 Bancroft, *Seward*, II, 365; Pierce, *Sumner*, IV, 110; Nicolay and Hay, *Lincoln*, VI, 263–264.

was not all. He was at a crisis which involved the success of the government and the fate of the nation. Even if, in response to selfless prompting, he should step out, what of the country and of the cause he was serving? The President's unhappy state of mind was not merely personal. Already the question of his own leadership had been canvassed in his mind. He had pondered dispassionately whether he ought to yield to another, supposing that were constitutionally possible,[1] and had decided that such action was not indicated as the solution of the nation's difficulties. Yet he must stay in office as a real and not a merely nominal leader. If senators could push him around, his effectiveness would be seriously weakened, with the possibility of further disaster to the Union cause. He could not forget that in the minds of conservative men it was the radicals who had been responsible for the unhappy outcome of Fredericksburg.[2] The men who were using the caucus of Republican senators as their instrument were, as Browning said, the President's "bitterest enemies"; they were "doing all in their power to break him down." They were the "ultra, radical, unreasoning men who raised the insane cry of on to Richmond in July 1861, and have kept up a war on our generals ever since—who forced thro the confiscation bills, and extorted from the President the proclamations and lost him the confidence of the country . . . ." Fearing that popular indignation would fall upon their heads, thought Browning, they were "intent upon giving it another direction." [3]

The art of governing was put to the test. For a leader to fail in skill and finesse at such a time might be productive of irreparable injury. It would take careful steering to prevent division at home, with consequent comfort to the enemy. If the President was to come out of the episode without an impairment of his own leadership and a cracking of the governmental structure, a high degree of tact was indicated. "There should be harmony," Browning told his colleagues, "and unity of . . . action between all the departments of government . . . ." The plan of the complaining senators, he thought, "would be war between Congress and the President, and the knowledge of this antagonism would injure our cause greatly in the Country. It would produce strife here, and strife among the peo-

---

[1] *Diary of S. P. Chase*, Sep. 22, 1862, *Annual Report*, Am. Hist. Assoc., 1902, II, 88.
[2] Bancroft, *Seward*, II, 364.   [3] Browning, *Diary*, I, 598 (Dec. 16, 1862).

ple . . . ." [4] Lincoln had to keep the machine running. Soon he would have to prepare a new military advance, probably with a new commander. At such a time he could not permit senatorial interference nor allow a "party or faction" to "dictate to the President in regard to his Cabinet." [5] Yet it was equally imperative that the assertion of presidential leadership be not too abrupt. Willingness to talk things over must be shown, yet nothing vital could be yielded. The President must see to the outcome, yet the issue must not be in terms of explosion or unseemly combat.

Lincoln's technique, or diplomacy if that is the word, rose to the occasion. It was arranged that a committee of the senators should call on the President on the evening of Thursday, December 18, and state their demands. Patiently the nation's Executive listened while senators presented the case against Seward—his lukewarmness and responsibility for failure. "To use the P[r]est's quaint language, while they believed in the Prest's honesty, they seemed to think that when he had in him any good purposes, Mr. S.[eward] contrived *to suck them out of him unperceived.*" [6]

Lincoln arranged that the senatorial committee (nine men selected to represent the Republican caucus) should meet him again on the evening of Friday, December 19. That morning, beginning at 10:30, he had a long and earnest session of his cabinet. Enjoining secrecy, he reported the resignation of the two Sewards and the conference with the senators. The President stated how "shocked and grieved" he was to hear the senators' objections to Seward, knowing as he did how there had never been any disagreements in the cabinet "though there had been differences," and how their confidence and zeal had "sustained and consoled" him. [7]

Having given the cue for the cabinet's attitude—coöperation with the President and among themselves—Lincoln made an adroit move which disarmed the critics and doubters. He contrived it so that when the senatorial committee of nine [8] came again they found themselves

---

[4] *Ibid.*, I, 597–598.   [5] Welles, *Diary*, I, 199.
[6] Bates, *Diary*, 269.   [7] Welles, *Diary*, I, 195.
[8] The committee of nine Republican senators consisted of Collamer of Vermont as spokesman, Wade of Ohio, Fessenden of Maine, Harris of New York, Grimes of Iowa, Sumner of Massachusetts, Trumbull of Illinois, Howard of Michigan, and Pomeroy of Kansas. The committee had an obvious majority of radicals. Wade seems not to have attended the conferences at the White House.

confronted by the whole cabinet except Seward. One effect of this was that Chase, who had talked with some of the senators in the anti-Seward sense, found himself in a situation in which he could not do otherwise than confirm the President's statement of essential harmony in the cabinet. The mere confronting of the legislators with the cabinet, in a meeting of which Lincoln was moderator, gave the President a notable advantage. It was one thing for senators to use strong language in a caucus; it was quite another to do it face to face with President and cabinet. When questioned directly by the President, only four of the solons stuck to their guns in insisting upon Seward's removal.[9]

As with the senators, so with the secretaries. For any cabinet member to associate himself with a senatorial drive against a colleague would put him clearly in the wrong. "This Cabinet," said Stanton, "is like yonder window. Suppose you allow it to be understood that passers-by might knock out one pane of glass—just one at a time—how long do you think any panes would be left in it?" [10] At length the meeting of President, cabinet, and senators broke up "in a milder spirit" than when it met.[11] The senators had shot their bolt, yet no explosion had occurred.

Thus ended Friday. Next day Washington buzzed with rumors that the whole cabinet had resigned and the President was in receipt of a number of new slates.[12] Holding another cabinet meeting, Lincoln found himself in possession of another resignation. What happened is best told in the language of Gideon Welles: "Chase said he had been painfully affected by the meeting last evening, . . . and . . . informed the President he had prepared his resignation . . . . 'Where is it?' said the President quickly, his eye lighting up in a moment. 'I brought it with me,' said Chase, ... 'Let me have it,' said the President, reaching his long arm and fingers toward C., who held on, . . . reluctant to part with the letter, . . . Something further he wished to say, but the President . . . did not perceive it, but took and hastily opened the letter. 'This,' said he, . . . 'cuts the

9 Collamer, spokesman of the senators, expressed the view that there should be more general consultation of secretaries and President. Fessenden "felt . . . more than he cared to say"; Grimes, Sumner, Trumbull, and Pomeroy urged Seward's withdrawal. Harris wanted Seward to remain. (Wade did not attend.) Welles, *Diary*, I, 196–198.
10 Bancroft, *Seward*, II, 367.   11 Bates, *Diary*, 270.   12 *Ibid.*

Gordian knot.' . . . 'I see my way clear.' " [13] In his prairie phrase, Lincoln could ride; "I have got a pumpkin in each end of my bag," he said.[14]

Having maneuvered the situation to precisely the point which he desired, and having arranged it so that both secretaries stayed in town, Lincoln now addressed to Seward and Chase identical notes mentioning their resignations and adding that the public interest would not admit of their acceptance. He therefore requested each to resume his duties.[15] Seward promptly complied; Chase, not forgetting the President's gratified look at the cabinet meeting, asked leave to "sleep on it." On the same day that his resignation was presented (Saturday, December 20) he wrote out a letter asking that the resignation be accepted and advancing the view that both he and Seward could serve better as private citizens. He gave the matter further thought over a painful Sunday; then on Monday, December 22, he sent the President two letters. Enclosing the Saturday letter, he stated that he had changed his mind and would resume his post.[16]

It was a fortunate week-end for Lincoln. He had kept the game in his hands and had adjusted a menacing crisis; moreover, he had so managed the incident that neither secretary was humiliated in the public eye. As on other occasions Lincoln sustained himself by a self-less attitude. In taking on his own shoulders the blame that had descended upon secretaries, he had warded off a threat to presidential as well as secretarial prestige. If he could not gain positive coöperation from senators, he could serve a high purpose by avoiding open hostility with them. As the committee of the caucus returned to Capitol Hill and the secretaries to their offices, both groups and both factions bore less of disruptive force on Monday than on Friday. Looking back over recent proceedings they could not fail to realize that the steering had been Lincoln's and that the quiet outcome had been of his determining. Lincoln's inmost thoughts of the affair can only be guessed. Though his severe mental suffering is well attested, he had not fallen prey to distress of mind. He had retained his equipoise and even his power to joke. If one may lift a phrase from a Gilbert and Sullivan lyric, he may have longed for an upper house that

13 Welles, *Diary*, I, 201–202.   14 Nicolay and Hay, *Lincoln*, VI, 271.
15 *Works*, VIII, 148 (Dec. 20, 1862).   16 Warden, *Chase*, 509–510.

Did nothing in particular,
And did it very well.

There were some conditions that the President could control, but
there were others he simply had to live with. He had to work with
senators. He could not make over the Senate, but he could study the
best method of approaching its members. With luck, and with attention to the human art of government, he might turn a senatorial
upheaval into a triumph of presidential prestige. Whatever happened,
he could not afford an open break. In addition to all his other complications, he had to deal with what he once called the objections of
"some Senators." [17] In using the phrase the President was referring
to a minor matter, the Senate's rejection of a lesser general; yet in
Lincoln's mind the expression could easily have had a larger meaning.
To give the sum of Lincoln's difficulties with "some Senators" would
indeed be a large order.

---

[17] *Works*, VIII, 233 (Mar. 25, 1863).

CHAPTER XXVI

EXIT BURNSIDE

I

THE army was Lincoln's main anxiety. Morale after Fredericksburg was low and desertions numerous. The men were "disheartened and almost sulky." [1] The President is said to have remarked that a marching Union army "dwindled . . . like a shovelfull of fleas pitched from one place to another." [2] Having been in a ferment on the subject of cabinet change, the North was now demanding such a shuffle of commanders as would "give more vigor to our armies.". [3] Prominent generals—McClellan, Porter, Stone, Buell, McDowell, Frémont, and others—were without commands. In some cases this was fortunate; in others it was a wasted resource and a cause of resentment. With radicals insisting on greater legislative control of army movements, with urgent demands that conservative men should force the administration "to a change of measures and men," [4] with army affairs in a tangle and a conscription act in the making, the civilian mind was deep in the gloom of defeat while the soldier mind was in a state of "savage" dissatisfaction that "tended strongly to mutiny." [5]

This unhealthful state in the army was due to a combination of factors: delay in pay, jealousy among generals, prejudiced proceedings of military courts and of the congressional war committee, "politicians

[1] *Battles and Leaders of the Civil War*, III, 154.

[2] Random notes in 1863 of John Hay, Dennett, *Lincoln . . . in the Diaries . . . of John Hay*, 53.

[3] Lyman Trumbull to Norman G. Flagg, Washington, Jan. 21, 1863, MS., Ill. State Hist. Lib.

[4] August Belmont to S. J. Tilden, Jan. 27, 1863, Tilden MSS.

[5] Isaac M. Brown to R. W. Thompson, Burnside Barracks, Indianapolis, Feb. 8, 1863, MS., Lincoln National Life Foundation, Ft. Wayne. Nicolay (*Short Life of Abraham Lincoln*, 365) also speaks of a "spirit akin to mutiny" in the army.

seeking to influence military movements in favor of their own partisan
and selfish schemes," [6] legislative patronage in military appointments,[7]
and, most of all, a pervading sense of hopelessness under existing
command. To mention the three men who had the highest military
functions at the time, Lincoln had Burnside, he had Stanton, and
he had Halleck. Stanton was as unstable as he was arrogant and stub-
born. Some of his decisions were reversed by himself, often from
"mere caprice"; "there . . . was none with whom men found it
more difficult to deal." [8] "The extent to which Lincoln interposed
his tact and patience between Stanton and generals of the army, . . .
preventing injustice and insuring . . . continuity, is a commonplace of history." [9] At times it appeared that the President and his
minister of war were at loggerheads; at other times it seemed that
Lincoln knew Stanton to be "unprincipled" but felt he had to retain
him to get the country's business done.[10] The best of men found it impossible to get along with the secretary. Henry W. Bellows, promoting the fine work of the sanitary commission, sought secretarial co-
operation in vain.[11] Welles referred to Stanton as "unreliable" and
impatient toward Lincoln; [12] Bates described him as "brusque—not
to say uncivil." [13]

Lincoln would give an order and Stanton would undo it.[14] The
secretary had allied himself with radicals, had withheld coöperation
from McClellan, and had been one of the chief agents in the ruin of
that general. Defeats of 1862 were largely of his making.

---

[6] "Extracts from the Journal of Henry J. Raymond," ed. by his son, *Scribner's Monthly*, XIX, 703 (1880).

[7] Cox, *Military Reminiscences*, I, 433.   [8] Pearson, *Andrew*, II, 95.   [9] *Ibid.*

[10] Draft of letter by Montgomery Blair to unnamed correspondent, undated (probably summer of 1865), box marked "Various," Blair MSS. (Internal evidence shows this
to have been written after Lincoln's death.)

[11] ". . . I believe the Secy of War allows himself to speak of our Commission with
contempt, ..." Henry W. Bellows to S. P. Chase, N. Y., Nov. 25, 1862, Chase MSS.,
Lib. of Cong. In the Bellows MSS. there is ample evidence of disappointment with
Stanton on the part of Bellows.

[12] Welles, *Diary*, 1, 98; II, 293.

[13] Bates, *Diary*, 280.

[14] When the vice-regent of the Mount Vernon Association asked that a vessel be
allowed to run from Washington to Mount Vernon, Lincoln approved it, but Stanton
did not "deem it expedient." Letter from vice-regent to Lincoln, Feb. 26, 1864, MS.,
N. Y. Hist. Soc. When J. P. Usher tried to get something done (on a matter not fully
stated), he wrote a friend: ". . . the President made the order & . . . it is withheld
in the War Department." J. P. Usher to R. W. Thompson, Mar. 31, 1864, MS., Lincoln
National Life Foundation, Ft. Wayne.

Halleck's task was no easy berth. Condemnation should be tempered by a realization of his difficulties, yet it was the prevailing view of contemporaries that his performance after taking up his duties in Washington was unsatisfactory. Bates wrote of his "bad judgment," his "cunning and evasive" manner; he summed it up by referring to "that poor thing—*Halleck*," and again to the "improvidence (not to say imbecility) of . . . Stanton and Halleck." [15] One of the keenest of military observers, General Jacob D. Cox, a man of measured words, referred to the general in chief as "unequal to his responsibility" and as "in no true sense a commander of the armies." [16] In the opinion of Nicolay and Hay, as a nominal general in chief "his genius fell short of the high duties of that great station." [17]

The count against Burnside is simply that of failure. He was a man of courage, of fine military bearing, of "single-hearted honesty and unselfishness." [18] As a defeated general, however, he could not have been expected to retain the confidence of his men and officers; this was the less possible in view of his post-Fredericksburg attitude and intentions. Having determined upon a move across the Rappahannock in the face of almost unanimous opposition by his generals, Burnside created a further difficulty for a buffeted President by putting the responsibility for a decision on Lincoln's shoulders; this he did by a letter stating his purpose, with an offer to resign if his plan should not be approved.

The plan of Burnside seemed to smack of reckless blundering, and under these circumstances the President turned for advice to "Old Brains" (Halleck); yet in the very act of doing so he revealed his lack of faith in that general. "If in such a difficulty . . . you do not help," wrote Lincoln, "you fail me precisely in the point for which I sought your assistance." He wanted the general in chief to go over the ground, gather all the elements for forming a judgment, and then come through with an approval or disapproval. "Your military skill," he said, "is useless to me if you do not do this." [19]

This was written on January 1, 1863, the day of Lincoln's definitive proclamation of emancipation and of a protracted public reception. It was a crowded day, one incident of which was a painful conference

---

[15] Bates, *Diary*, 304, 389, 398.   [16] Cox, *Military Reminiscences*, I, 257; II, 2.
[17] Nicolay and Hay, *Lincoln*, V, 357.   [18] Cox, *Military Reminiscences*, I, 390.
[19] *Works*, VIII, 165.

with Burnside, as a result of which that commander submitted his resignation. On receiving Lincoln's New Year's Day letter through Stanton, Halleck promptly wrote out his resignation.[20] At a time of hazard and anxiety the President was thus presented with the resignations of the general in chief and of the commander of the principal army. The immediate difficulty as to the resignations was patched up. Halleck's was at once withdrawn on the President agreeing to withdraw his January first letter.[21] Burnside also for the time remained. The case of each was that of an offer of resignation rather than a definite withdrawal.

The President still had his generals, but what of the army's plans? Against the objections of competent officers, Burnside's project of the crossing of the Rappahannock was approved by Halleck, and (with a note of caution) by Lincoln. Its result was the "mud march" of the Army of the Potomac which failed so completely in its hopeless floundering that it became a by-word in military tradition.[22]

As if the mud episode were not enough, Burnside now took another step which made it utterly impossible to retain him. On January 23 he prepared an order dishonorably dismissing an impressive list of generals, including Joseph Hooker, W. T. H. Brooks, John Newton, John Cochrane, W. B. Franklin, and William Farrar Smith. This sensational order declared that Hooker was "dismissed the service of the United States as a man unfit [etc.]"; he had been "guilty," said the order, of making criticisms, creating distrust, producing incorrect impressions, and "habitually speaking in disparaging terms of other officers." Newton and Cochrane were declared dismissed "for going to the President . . . with criticisms . . . of their commanding officer."[23] These orders, being published in the newspapers, added to the existing demoralization, but they never went into effect; Lincoln saw to that. Burnside had unintentionally made Lincoln's task of decision easier. He had made his own incapacity for command so unmistakable that his removal was no longer open to question. There

<hr/>

[20] *Ibid.*, VIII, 165–166. [21] *Ibid.*, VIII, 166, n. 1.

[22] In late January 1863 several grand divisions of the Army of the Potomac were caught south of the Rappahannock by rains which made the roads impassable; stuck in the mud, the dejected army had to abandon the whole enterprise. It was Burnside's hopeless attempt to redeem himself. *Battles and Leaders of the Civil War*, III, 118–119, 239 n.

[23] *Ibid.*, III, 216 n.

was nothing to do but relieve the luckless general of his command of the Army of the Potomac. This the President did on January 26, 1863, giving that post to Joseph Hooker.

What went on behind the lines as this bit of business took place would make a sorry story: officers leaving the field for Washington where they poured criticisms in the ears of the President; congressional inquisitors plotting which generals to besmirch and which to whitewash; journalists becoming the depositaries of information that should have remained confidential. When matters were at the sharpest crisis Burnside, with Raymond of the *Times,* had darted back in a sensational night ride from army headquarters at Falmouth to Washington (January 24–25). Both of them saw Lincoln: Burnside handed the President his bold order, tendering his resignation if the order should not be approved; the announcement hit Lincoln like "a clap of thunder." Having delivered the bolt, the general sped back to the army; obviously he was thinking more of disciplining certain generals, especially Hooker, than of accepting the alternative of resignation. Raymond sought out Chase, poured into his ears the "whole story," then drew Lincoln aside at a White House reception and told him of Burnside's difficulties with Hooker and other subordinates.[24] If Burnside's purpose, with Raymond's support, was to force the issue, they succeeded, but not in the sense intended. It was directly after these intrigues and conferences that Hooker's displacement of Burnside was announced.

The new commander was not the choice of Stanton and Halleck. Rosecrans, operating effectively in the West, would have suited them.[25] Those who like to ponder the "ifs" of history may speculate as to how far and how high Rosecrans "might have" gone if appointed. Would he have been another failure, or would his have been the triumph and postwar fame that came to Grant? Lincoln's appointment of Hooker, which was his own decision, showed how little value he placed upon the counsel of his high military advisers. As it turned out, the President had picked another failure, but that could not be

---

[24] "Extracts from the Journal of Henry J. Raymond," *Scribner's Monthly,* XIX, 704–705 (1880). See also Williams, *Lincoln and the Radicals,* 266.

[25] "Both Stanton and Halleck were dissatisfied with the choice. They had set their hearts upon General Rosecrans." Statement by the editors (Nicolay and Hay), in *Works,* VIII, 206.

known in advance. In January 1863 Hooker had a fightng reputation; he exuded confidence; he had been with the Army of the Potomac through hard campaigns and battles; he had the experience and prestige of a corps commander. On the other hand were factors that made the appointment doubtful: he had been part of the intrigue against Burnside, had "talked blatantly to the reporters about the new regime that would prevail if Joe Hooker were in command," [26] had violently denounced McClellan, and, perhaps worst of all, had played the game of the radicals—e. g., in his testimony before the war committee—so that the "bosses of the Jacobin machine were delighted" [27] with his appointment.

That the President was uncertain as to Hooker at the moment of appointing him is revealed in an admonishing letter which he wrote to the new chieftain. It is one of the most remarkable of Lincoln's epistles, being of the kind that he sometimes wrote and did not send; this time he sent it. "General," he wrote, "I have placed you at the head of the Army of the Potomac. . . . I have done this upon what appear to me . . . sufficient reasons. And yet . . . ." Then the President explained that he was "not quite satisfied" with the general, that he considered him ambitious, and that in thwarting Burnside he had done "a great wrong to the country." He continued:

I have heard . . . of your . . . saying that both the Army and the Government needed a Dictator. Of course it was not *for* this, but in spite of it, that I have given you the command. . . . What I now ask of you is military success, and I will risk the dictatorship. . . . I much fear that the spirit which you have aided to infuse into the Army, of criticising their Commander, and withholding confidence from him, will now turn upon you. I shall assist you . . . to put it down. Neither you, nor Napoleon, if he were alive . . . , could get any good out of an army, while such a spirit prevails in it. And now, beware of rashness. Beware of rashness, but with energy, and sleepless vigilance, go forward, and give us victories.[28]

There have been various commentaries on this letter, including the conjecture that Lincoln paced the floor after writing it before

[26] Williams, *Lincoln and the Radicals*, 265.

[27] *Ibid.*, 266.

[28] In *Works*, VIII, 206–207, this letter appears with numerous errors of punctuation, capitalization and the like. Quotations here have been checked with the superb Caxton Club facsimile mentioned in the following note.

adding his signature.[29] For an understanding of the epistle one must remember the buzz and intrigue that had been going on for weeks in military circles, the recent conferences Lincoln had held with various generals, the realization of low morale in the army, the President's pathetic sense of the urgency of victory, and his troubled misgiving as to whether he had chosen the man who could deliver it. To attach any particular significance to Lincoln's comment on dictatorship as applying to himself, would be an error.

II

It is no part of the purpose of this book to include the elaborate and complex history of military operations. George Bancroft refers to "six hundred and twenty-five battles and severe skirmishes" fought in the Civil War.[1] Everyone has heard of Bull Run and Gettysburg; the action at Carnifex Ferry, West Virginia, has been forgotten, except by the families of those killed and wounded. The same may be said of literally hundreds of incidents such as the action at Big Creek Gap, Tennessee, the skirmish on the Purdy Road (near Adamsville, Tennessee), or the affair at Cave City, Kentucky. A man killed at Wartrace, Tennessee, was as much of a casualty as those who fell at Antietam; such incidents, however minor they were, loomed large to thousands of participants. Though the impossibility of a complete account is obvious, the military literature of the conflict is stupendous. The merely statistical aspect is formidable, and a writer learns to think twice before he mentions the number of troops under a general's command at a given time, the number available for duty, the active and reserve forces, the number engaged in a particular combat, and the losses in killed, wounded, captured, and missing.

If one takes the period of April 1863 he finds the doubtful struggle at its midway phase with honors approximately even, except that the naval advantage was with the Union. Both sides had seen political interference with armies; in each case there had been a plummeting of

---

29 William E. Barton, *Abraham Lincoln and the Hooker Letter*, address before the Pennell Club, Philadelphia; Paul M. Angle, *Abraham Lincoln's Letter to Major General Joseph Hooker . . . a Facsimile . . . with Explanatory Text* (printed by Caxton Club, Chicago, 1942).

1 Memorial address, joint session of the houses of Congress, Feb. 12, 1866, reprinted in *Works* [of Lincoln], VIII, xxxvii.

some reputations and a soaring of others. In high placed commanders the Confederacy had the edge in the fine adjustment of Lee and Jackson to their specific tasks. Over-all factors in the war were the indecisiveness of leading campaigns, the rapid shifting of battle areas, the inexperience of troops and officers, the frequent turnover of army command, and the ineffectiveness of centralized direction. Gallantry, courage, and individual fighting power was shown on both sides; nevertheless it was plain that Americans were not a military people. Whatever may have been the talk of irrepressible conflict, the element of preparation was utterly lacking in the North and only somewhat less so in the South. To look squarely at a situation which is seldom correctly stated, the United States prior to 1861 had not seen its destiny in terms of an intensive program of militarization to deal with an internal war to destroy the Union. Preparedness for dissolution would have been an absurdity; on the other hand, preparedness that would have given a distinct advantage to a Union-preserving North was hardly conceivable in the anxious fifties when Presidents were of Southern sympathies and secretaries of war were Southerners. The lack of a compact nation had been illustrated in the unchallenged resignation and withdrawal of Southern officers trained at West Point. It had been for the service of the United States that they had been trained, but the army of the United States made no point of holding them.

Then as always the statesmanlike way to deal with war was to prevent its breaking out by promoting reason in the adjustment of disputes and by keeping predominant military power in the hands of those who meant to keep the peace; the power being there, it would not have had to be used. In this high purpose statesmanship had failed. Divisive forces and irrational movements had been allowed to rise; they had been so little restrained that a war was now raging to tear the nation apart. For Americans North and South to be slaughtering each other was unthinkable; yet here the fratricidal conflict was and it had to be fought to the death. It could not be stopped halfway. If there was not victory for the Union, the result was disunion. Once war had been allowed to develop, compromise was not in the cards. If for no other reason, men would continue to fight in order not to be beaten; they would be fighting because there was a war; it was no longer a matter of war aims according to the original calculation. Men might consider the war senseless; yet there seemed no way of terminating it short of a military decision. Solutions that had been easy in 1860 appeared now as a wistful mirage; a backward look at that far-off year could only bring remorse; it could not restore a lost peace. Many a time history has revealed that a war cannot be controlled nor its uses appropriated in terms of the intentions of rulers. The American war had changed its character. It was a monster let loose, not an instrument to be applied for a predetermined object.

On the eastern front the year 1861 had witnessed near panic in the brief isolation of Washington, minor campaigns in western Virginia, one major campaign with its indecisive Union defeat at Manassas close to Washington, and Confederate failure to press the advantage at the moment of Union demoralization. With a change of commanders on each side the year 1862 had seen the ambitious Peninsular campaign, the placing of a Federal army in a position of great striking power near Richmond, the Valley diversion, the indecisive Seven Days between Lee and McClellan, the amazing cross purpose between Washington and the army, and the releasing of Lee's forces by the foolish removal of McClellan from the Peninsula. Having been pinned down by McClellan to the close defense of Richmond, the army of Lee was invited to shift north and threaten Washington; it was then able to inflict a smashing defeat on McClellan's successor (Pope). In a time of great desperation on the Union side McClellan was grudgingly reinstated and was able to save Washington by the defensive victory of Antietam. Lee's first offensive was thus stopped. Weeks passed and McClellan was finally dropped. Burnside was put in and the heartbreaking defeat of Fredericksburg showed how a superb fighting force could be wasted by faulty generalship. After further floundering Burnside gave way to Hooker. Facing the Northern foe on the line of the Rappahannock, Lee's army was not only a mighty obstacle on the path to Richmond; it was a reminder that Washington was in danger, that the Confederacy was still potent for offense, and that Hooker's "finest army on the planet" had grim business ahead.

Meanwhile in the West the war had been waged first in Union territory—Kentucky and Missouri; then it shifted south as important river positions were taken by the Federals. This inland river war, favorable to the North, yet disappointing when compared with its large possibilities, was one of the main aspects of the struggle. Transports and gunboats assisted the Union armies; the South was made to

regret its naval inferiority. Activity, however, was spasmodic; battles
were not followed up; the checking of an army in one sector meant that
it would turn up in another. Results of river operations were seen in
the capture of Fort Henry on the Tennessee and the more significant
capitulation of Fort Donelson on the Cumberland (February 1862).
This "unconditional surrender" episode was Grant's first big victory;
to make it possible the coöperation of Foote's naval force had been an
indispensable element. Consolidating the results of Donelson, Union
forces soon occupied Nashville, Tennessee, and Columbus, Kentucky.
Southern armies were being pushed back to internal lines of defense.
Further land-and-water operations at New Madrid and Island Number Ten produced another formal Confederate surrender, produced
also the exaltation of Pope and his transfer to the East.

On April 6–7, 1862, occurred the main western military event of
the year in the battle of Shiloh, another incident in the river war. In
this fierce but uncoördinated battle the combined forces of Beauregard and Albert Sidney Johnston were able to deliver a surprise attack
upon Grant's unready army before it could be joined by Buell. On
the first day the Federals were driven back in confusion. With the
arrival of Buell on the second day, however, the tide was turned and
the Confederates were pushed back to Corinth, Mississippi. The river
war now shifted to the lower Mississippi as the shining prize of New
Orleans, largest city and greatest port of the South, fell into Union
hands following a great naval battle (April 1862) under Farragut and
Porter. B. F. Butler stepped in and the hated Federal occupation of
the proud city and much of Louisiana began. Butler's rule continued for seven and a half months, bringing such odium to the Union
cause that Lincoln removed him in December 1862. On the upper Mississippi Forts Pillow and Randolph were evacuated by the Confederates. Memphis was taken after a naval battle (June 6, 1862), but
the efforts of Farragut and Porter against the next big prize, Vicksburg,
were unavailing. This well defended Southern city could be passed,
but another year was required before it fell, and then only after repeated failures and as a result of an elaborate and arduous campaign.

These advances had been the work of Halleck, or, more accurately,
the work under Halleck. In the earlier phases of his western command,
by contrast with the chaos, futile effort, and corruption under Frémont,
Halleck had made a good impression. With headquarters at St. Louis,

he, or the commanders and forces under him (Pope, Foote, Grant, Sherman, Buell, etc.), had shown real achievement. This, however, was while Halleck was in desk command at St. Louis. When he took the field after Shiloh his performance was so slow and cautious that, as Sherman remarked, an army carrying a hundred thousand bayonets moved (if it could be called moving) toward Corinth "with pick and shovel." [2] Crawling at a snail's pace, and encountering little opposition, the army "fortified almost every camp at night"; its advance was "provokingly slow." [3] The twenty-three miles from Pittsburg Landing to Corinth, with negligible fighting, took over a month, the whole of May 1862 being occupied in this enterprise. Misreading the capacities of his generals, Halleck had reorganized his command, leaving Grant "without any apparent authority." Uncomplaining as he was, Grant felt keenly the "indignity, if not insult, heaped upon him." [4] Such had been the complaints against him directly after his victory at Donelson that his arrest had been authorized by McClellan on the basis of advices from Halleck; fortunately the arrest was not effected.[5] The fact that it could have been seriously planned showed how little the controlling military minds in March 1862 appreciated the qualities of the man who was later to emerge as the North's chief army hero. Pope's army, fresh from its accomplishments at New Madrid and Island Number Ten, had been brought on river transports to the Shiloh-Corinth area; yet the combined Union forces did not come to grips with Beauregard. They merely occupied the empty prize of Corinth after Beauregard evacuated it. Meanwhile Halleck had disappointed Lincoln's wish that something be done in eastern Tennessee and withheld coöperation from Farragut at Vicksburg; he had chosen virtually to "go into summer quarters." [6]

In his report to Washington Halleck had managed to cause his

---

[2] *Offic. Rec.*, I ser., XVII, pt. 2, 83. Sherman to Halleck, July 8, 1862.
[3] Sherman, *Memoirs* (1875 ed.), I, 251.   [4] *Ibid.*, I, 250.
[5] The complaints were that Grant had neglected his duty, had resumed his "bad habits," and had gone off to Nashville, leaving his troops, without authority. His arrest, which was not carried out, was authorized for the sake of military discipline. Halleck had written: "It is hard to censure a successful general . . . , but I think he richly deserves it." McClellan authorized the general's arrest on what seemed adequate basis; later the matter was explained and adjusted satisfactorily. *Offic. Rec.*, I ser., VII, 679–680, 682–684.
[6] Nicolay and Hay, *Lincoln*, V, 350.

occupation of Corinth to appear as a supreme achievement. In a statement that was almost entirely hearsay and boasting he quoted Pope as claiming the capture of 10,000 prisoners and deserters, and referred to a farmer's statement that Beauregard had become "frantic, and told his men to save themselves the best they could." [7] From Halleck's report, published in various newspapers, one may turn to Beauregard's statement that the Confederate evacuation of Corinth was a "complete surprise" by which the foe was "utterly foiled," that Union reports were "inaccurate, reckless, and unworthy," and that Halleck's dispatch of June 4 (the one about the farmer and the ten thousand captives) was "disgracefully untrue." [8] The Federal general's statement was said to have contained "as many lies as lines." [9] When confronted with this refutation Halleck made no reaffirmation of his expansive statements. Instead, he weakly stated that he was "not responsible for the truth" of the statements he communicated, that the report of prisoners was taken from Pope, and that any error was Pope's responsibility.[10] One could find a far better basis for complaint concerning Halleck's performance from April to July of 1862 than concerning McClellan's. Yet McClellan was demoted and ordered to withdraw his whole army from its position before Richmond, while Halleck was called to Washington and lifted to the surprising eminence of general in chief.

When Halleck stepped out of the western picture, so did Beauregard; the argument was now between their successors—Buell and Bragg. (Later it would be between Grant and Pemberton; still later, between Grant and Bragg.) Buell's task was to shift his force to eastern Tennessee and take Chattanooga and Knoxville. His movement (through northern Alabama) was painfully slow and all his calculations for an offensive on his own part were upset by harassing Confederate raids and by the Southern enemy seizing the initiative and launching an ambitious invasion of Kentucky by two armies under Bragg and Kirby Smith. This was no mere diversion. It was a serious effort to occupy, "liberate," and hold Kentucky, whose people were expected to join in a pro-Confederate uprising. The political motive of the invasion was not permitted to wait upon the military; rather, for a time the political factor took precedence as Bragg diverted a

---

[7] *Offic. Rec.*, 1 ser., X, pt. 1, 669.   [8] *Ibid.*, 764–765.   [9] *Ibid.*, 671.   [10] *Ibid.*

considerable force of men to conduct a ceremony at Frankfort where Richard Hawes, with questionable legal right, was inaugurated as secessionist governor of Kentucky. The popular uprising did not materialize; [11] Hawes's day was brief; he was soon in flight from the state; the episode of the inauguration had but enabled the Union forces to occupy Louisville and make other defensive dispositions. Finally, Bragg's Kentucky thrust ended in the battle of Perryville (October 8, 1862). This hard fought struggle was indecisive in that it was an incomplete testing of strength. Since it resulted in the abandonment of the Confederate invasion, however, the advantage was with the Federal side, as Bragg withdrew to Nashville and Buell to eastern Tennessee, soon to give way to Rosecrans.

While this Confederate offensive in Kentucky had been in progress, there had been waged an important campaign between Rosecrans and two Confederate generals (Price and Van Dorn) who had been shifted from trans-Mississippi operations to the area of Corinth. By the battles of Iuka and Corinth (September 19 and October 3–4, 1862) western Tennessee had been kept clear of Confederate forces and the coöperation of Price and Van Dorn with Bragg had been prevented. The Southern way of putting it, however, was that Rosecrans had been hindered from joining Buell.

The success of Rosecrans had synchronized with what was regarded as the failure of Buell. That general had not mastered eastern Tennessee; he had not anticipated Bragg's invasion of Kentucky; after checking the invasion he had not pressed the retiring enemy. For political reasons he was a target of the Jacobins and a suspect of their war committee. He had also incurred the wrath of midwestern governors (Morton, Yates, and Tod) whose troops from Indiana, Illinois, and Ohio were under his command. He was a Democrat and it was customary for Republicans to associate him with McClellan. The result of it all was that on October 30, 1862, a few days before McClellan's dismissal, Buell was removed from command of the Army of the Ohio whose organization and fighting power he had done so much to develop. His command, involving the Department of the Cumberland,

---

11 It had been Bragg's hope that the people of Kentucky would "rise in mass to assert their independence," but he was "distressed to add" that there was "little or no disposition" to make any such effort. Report of General Bragg, Oct. 12, 1862, *ibid.*, 1 ser., XVI, pt. 1, 1088.

was turned over to Rosecrans.[12] Months passed; then at the turn of the year (1862–1863) Bragg and Rosecrans clashed in bloody but indecisive combat at Murfreesboro (Stone's River). As the battle ended Bragg retired from the field. For a long time, however, he blocked the Federals from the next objective of Rosecrans, which was Chattanooga.

Heading the Army of the Tennessee, and commanding the important area of western Tennessee and northern Mississippi, was Ulysses S. Grant.[13] He and Sherman, with the loyal coöperation of Porter and the jealous interference of McClernand, were to be occupied for months with bravely conceived and hard-fought failures in the earlier stages of their complex efforts against Vicksburg. At the mid-point in the war (April 1863) this river stronghold was a center of stout Southern resistance, a point of Confederate contact with the trans-Mississippi, a challenge to Union strategy, and a test of strength between powerful antagonists.

III

There were, of course, many other factors in the vast war at this midway point. Political allegiance was rather well stabilized. The Confederacy still had eleven states as in June of '61. Their efforts to add Kentucky and Missouri had failed, though they still kept up a paper claim to these commonwealths. West Virginia had its full birth as one of the United States in 1863.[1] Whether or not the South wanted to add the Northwest, which was debatable with them, that great area was holding fast to the Union, though not without irritation; it was sending its hundreds of thousands to the front while also producing those huge quantities of grain that meant so much in the feeding of

---

[12] Buell was not only removed from his western command but was subjected to a harrowing trial by a military commission which reported no charges against the general but severely condemned his operations. In testimony before the commission and in various writings Buell put up a strong defense, remarking upon the "irregularities" of its proceedings and the "spirit" of its members. *Offic. Rec.*, 1 ser., XVI, pt. 1, 65. For the opinion of the commission, see *ibid.*, 8 ff.

[13] It had been under Grant that the operations of Rosecrans against Price and Van Dorn were conducted. Grant's command had been comparable with that of Buell, but in a different area. He had sought a greater coördination of western command than had been put into effect.

[1] See above, p. 13.

the Federal armies. Social and economic dislocations at the North were being endured, adjustments being made. There were mighty loans, all-inclusive taxes, a new national banking system, and a flood of paper money. There was great economic expansion, not all of which was healthful, in the extension of railroads, the opening up of new lands, and the manifold activities of wartime manufacturing. Social controls were feeble; unsocial practices rampant. Greed, profiteering, cheating, and fraud were prevalent. On the other hand there were enlightened humanitarian enterprises afoot in the work of the sanitary commission, the mustering of brave nurses, and sundry measures of relief and stimulus intended to keep life going on the home front. In spite of this, perhaps the greatest lack at home was national social and economic planning. This was to be evident in the small gains made by labor during the war and in the coming aftermath of panic, greed, and depression. Local and voluntary effort and state activity were not adequate to the problems at hand.

In the naval war the superior achievement was on the Union side, though there had been disappointments to offset this advantage. Welles and Fox, secretary and able assistant secretary of the navy, had virtually produced a navy *de novo,* having increased Lincoln's warships tenfold, from forty-two in March 1861 to 427 in December 1862. The gigantic blockade of Southern coasts was ineffective if judged by Confederate reports and measured only by those swift specialized vessels of limited tonnage that slipped through as blockade runners (often with more of a selfish than civic-minded motive), but it was powerful if seen in terms of larger ocean-going vessels that did not even try to enter Southern ports. Perhaps the best proof of the potency of the blockade was the fact that none of the Confederacy's few cruisers enjoyed access to Southern harbors. As Welles reported in December 1862, "in no previous war had the ports of an enemy's country been so effectually closed by a naval force." [2]

In both inland and coastal operations the influence of sea power upon history was being confirmed; a youthful officer, Alfred T. Mahan, was even then gaining in combat service under the Union flag the experience that would later enable him to master the history of modern sea power and marshal it in those epoch-making studies that

[2] Report of the Sec. of the Navy. Dec. 1, 1862, *House Exec. Doc. No. 1,* 37 Cong., 3 sess., vol. III, p. 3. See also Randall, *Civil War and Reconstruction,* 575.

were to become so potent a factor in world politics.[3] In March 1862 had occurred that battle of the ironclads in Hampton Roads which put a brake upon the brief threat of Southern floating power while it also marked the transition from old methods of wooden sailing ships to steam-driven, iron-plated craft. By April 1863 the Union navy had seized important coastal positions: Hampton Roads (commanded by Norfolk), Roanoke Island (conquered by Admiral Goldsborough and General Burnside, February-March 1862), the sea-island area of Beaufort, and Port Royal, South Carolina (Du Pont's achievement, November 1861), Fort Pulaski (guarding Savannah), and New Orleans. The ocean gateways of Virginia, Georgia, Florida, and Louisiana, were in Union possession. Not so Charleston, which was to resist a series of determined assaults upon its land and sea defenses. In April 1863 Du Pont conducted an ambitious effort with a fleet of monitors and an army force under Hunter, against the proud Carolinian city. The result was a failure which produced the greater psychological shock at the North because ironclads were considered an invincible innovation that would insure unbroken Northern superiority. These operations, as those of April 1861, found Beauregard in command of forces centering in Charleston. This general, mistreated by the Confederate President, was as popular there as his immediate predecessor, Pemberton, had been unpopular. There were other failures.[4] The Union navy had been checked on the James. It had not yet mastered the Mississippi Maritime commerce of the United States was still a prey to the roving *Alabama*. Wilmington, Mobile, and Galveston remained in Confederate hands.

IV

With military and naval fortunes at the focus of his thought, Lincoln was made to realize the complications of remote control from Washington and the hazards of interference by civil officials, not to

---

[3] Alfred T. Mahan, *The Influence of Sea Power Upon History, 1660–1783* (1890). *The Influence of Sea Power upon the French Revolution and Empire, 1793–1812* (2 vols., 1892).

[4] Another army-navy failure on the Union side occurred in August 1863 when Admiral Dahlgren and General Gillmore bombarded the city (this was suspended after Confederate protest) and reduced Fort Sumter to ruins without winning the coveted prize. It was not until near the very end of the war (February 1865) that Charleston was evacuated by its defenders and put under Federal occupation.

say politicians, in the operations of his warriors. In general terms, or at times in considerable detail, he would make known his wish for a particular operation; he would even plead with his generals to bring it about, only to meet with frustration or to see enacted the very result he wished to avoid. In the pre-Shiloh phase he wanted Halleck to prevent the junction of A. S. Johnston with Beauregard. They were permitted to join. He strongly desired, almost as a kind of specialty, that eastern Tennessee, because of its Unionist sympathies, should be occupied and possessed. He urged that efforts be made against Chattanooga; [1] he wanted to know how the expedition for that purpose was progressing; [2] he studied closely the almost unsolvable problem of sending western troops east, yet launching successful offensives in the West. He kept asking Halleck for reënforcements to be sent to Virginia [3] (this at a time when reënforcements for Halleck himself were being urged),[4] yet insisted that the movement against Chattanooga and eastern Tennessee must not be interfered with,[5] and "must not on any account be given up." [6] "To take and hold the railroad . . . in East Tennessee," he considered "fully as important as the taking and holding of Richmond." [7] Noting in mid-October 1862 that Buell's "main object"—i. e., capture of eastern Tennessee—was unattained, the President, through Halleck, wanted to know why the Union army could not do as the Confederate—"live as he lives, and fight as he fights." [8] This implied that in Lincoln's thought the people of that mountain region would be as ready to avoid harassment of the Union as of the Confederate army. The activities of guerrilla bands and of bold Confederate raiders in Tennessee and Kentucky were a matter of concern to the President, who advised that vigorous counter measures be taken.[9]

---

1 *Works*, VII, 214 (June 8, 1862).   2 *Ibid.*, VII, 228 (June 18, 1862).

3 *Ibid.*, VII, 238, 255, 260, 261.   4 *Ibid.*, VII, 179–180 (May 24, 1862).

5 *Ibid.*, VII, 238 (June 28, 1862).   6 *Ibid.*, VII, 247 (June 30, 1862).

7 *Ibid.*, VII, 248 (June 30, 1862).   8 *Ibid.*, VIII, 63–64.

9 Not only guerrilla bands, but also the most famous of Confederate raiders, N. B. Forrest and J. H. Morgan, were highly active in 1862 in Tennessee and Kentucky. (*Battles and Leaders*, III, 3, 28, 37, 451; Comte de Paris, *Civil War in America*, II, 365; John A. Wyeth, *Life of General Nathan Bedford Forrest*; Robert Selph Henry, "*First with the Most*" *Forrest*; Offic. Rec., 1 ser., XVI, pt. 1, 731–784, 815–819, 871–882.) The frequency and daring of such raids bothered Lincoln. In no other way, he said, did the enemy give "so much trouble at so little expense." He wanted counter-raids organized and suggested getting up a corps for the purpose. Yet he wanted this done "without any or many additional troops." *Works*, VIII, 215–216 (Feb. 17, 1863).

The President's hopes for eastern Tennessee, however, were again and again deferred. After the time of his strong urging upon Halleck in the spring of 1862 it was to take a year and a half before that area was brought under Federal mastery. In Halleck's slow conduct before Corinth Lincoln found equal disappointment. Halleck was doing next to nothing, yet asking for more men. Patiently and with only an oblique hint of his dissatisfaction, Lincoln wrote the general that he was doing the best he could, that commanders all along the line wanted more men, and that lines were being thinned with heavy loss. The men who were needed, he said, were not at hand. Then, with the gentlest possible hint that the general had better bestir himself, Lincoln closed the letter: "My dear general, I feel justified to rely very much on you. I believe you and the brave officers and men with you can and will get the victory . . . ." [10]

Lincoln had constantly to contend with the fog of war, the imperfect state of military intelligence, and the hazardous difficulty of operational direction at a distance. It is seldom indeed that one finds the imperative mood in his communications to generals, but the interrogation point was typical. On September 8, 1862, with Bragg's invasion of Kentucky in full swing, he asked Buell how he could be certain that Bragg, with his command, was not at that time in the Valley of Virginia. [11] Four days later he asked General Boyle at Louisville: "Where is the enemy which you dread in Louisville? How near to you? What is General Gilbert's opinion? With all . . . respect for you, I must think General [Horatio G.] Wright's military opinion is the better. . . . Where do you understand Buell to be, and what is he doing?" In the same letter Lincoln showed his concept of remote control. Referring to the same General Wright, in command in Kentucky, he said: ". . . for us here to control him there . . . would be a babel of confusion which would be utterly ruinous." [12]

No part of Lincoln's military task was more vital than the making of appointments, and at no time was this function more difficult than in the summer and fall of 1862, when also the questions of foreign policy and of emancipation were at their most acute stage. The transfer and elevation of Halleck and Pope, the removal of Buell, and the assigning of important new commands to Rosecrans, Grant, and Schofield—all these western matters had to be studied, argued over,

[10] *Ibid.*, VII, 180 (May 24, 1862).   [11] *Ibid.*, VIII, 22.   [12] *Ibid.*, VIII, 26–27.

and decided under pressure in the very period when the affairs of the Army of the Potomac and the problem of McClellan were at the stage of greatest anxiety. He even had to write to an aggrieved colonel explaining that he could not "conjecture what junior of yours you suppose I contemplate promoting over you." [13] To another disgruntled officer he wrote that he had "too many family controversies" already on his hands "to voluntarily . . . take up another." [14] The feelings of Rosecrans had to be soothed by the President's assurance that the general had "not a single enemy" in Washington.[15] When Fitz John Porter was convicted in the military trial above mentioned,[16] it was Lincoln's painful duty to issue the order that he be "cashiered and dismissed from the service . . . , and forever disqualified from holding any office of trust or profit under the . . . United States." [17] This matter of military appointment rested heavily upon Lincoln's shoulders. Taking it along with many other military aspects, it shows that the President's task as Commander in Chief was not merely nominal. Every time an appointment, change of rank, or shift of command was made, the President had to study alternatives; he had to deal with military men as persons, as fallible and sensitive human beings; he had to consider not only this or that army or campaign involving perhaps the fate of the nation, but the traditions and attachments of men in the service, the often unknowable capabilities of leaders, the delays of reorientation when a new command was assumed, the numerous pressures and interferences behind his back, and the sometimes difficult questions of senatorial confirmation or congressional attack. Of all the many duties that weighed upon Lincoln in the crowded war years, the function of Commander in Chief of the army and navy was the most serious as well as the most harassing and burdensome.

---

13 *Ibid.*, VIII, 72 (Nov. 5, 1862).
15 *Ibid.*, VIII, 226 (Mar. 17, 1863).
17 *Works*, VIII, 199 (Jan. 21, 1863).

14 *Ibid.*, VIII, 201 (Jan. 22, 1863).
16 See above, p. 108 n.

CHAPTER XXVII

WAR AT ITS PEAK

I

"ELATED and depressed. Cheered and chagrined. Exultant and desponding. The rebels were between two fires. Hooker had them just where he wanted them. They could not retreat. They would be annihilated. The Rebellion was nearly at an end. Such was the talk—the feeling. All is now changed. The army is back in its camp. The victory that was to be is not." [1] Such were the opening lines of the Boston *Journal* account of Hooker's frustrated effort at Chancellorsville in May 1863. Men thought that Hooker could not fail: his numbers were greatly superior (about 130,000 to Lee's 60,000); his army was in fine condition; his strategy seemed faultless; his manner exuded confidence; his fighting reputation promised successful attack.

Holding Lee's threatening line by a powerful demonstration under Sedgwick near Fredericksburg (making the Confederates think this was the main operation), the Union commander would push a strong force across the upper Rappahannock and the Rapidan, pass by forced marches around Lee's left, and deliver a crushing attack on his rear. So confident was Hooker of his scheme that he sent off all his cavalry on the wide flanking movement (under Stoneman), leaving his right in the air, with insufficient reserves and no protecting terrain. He conceived of the coming battle in his own terms; the idea that his right would be assaulted had not entered his mind. Not fully aware of the Federal trap, but boldly resolving to take risks against a superior enemy, Lee had divided his forces, already small because of the detachment of Longstreet to a distant venture against Suffolk. For

[1] Moore, *Rebellion Record* (Docs.), VI, 593.

the operation against Hooker Lee's army was in three parts: Early disputed Sedgwick in the Fredericksburg area; Lee took care of the center near Chancellorsville; Jackson was to deal with the enemy's right. The main feature of the battle, whose details must be omitted, was a terrific surprise blow by Jackson who swung a heavy force into action against Howard's men of the Eleventh Corps on the Union right, catching them off guard at supper (May 3, 1863), and driving them into hasty retreat. Superior Confederate numbers were brought to bear upon the sector selected for attack, despite over-all superiority on the Union side.

The bold audacity of Jackson's maneuver brought Southern triumph at Lee's zenith; it was not, however, as crushing a stroke as Lee had hoped, and the Confederates paid heavily for their victory by the disaster of Jackson's death. Hooker had been stunned by a minor injury and when the fighting was over he did not know that a general engagement had been fought. It was as if he had been bluffing. Not only had he sent his cavalry on the unsuccessful flanking movement; he had deliberately withdrawn his forces on the main line of the two armies, and had left huge portions, by far the major part, of his army out of the conflict altogether. Nevertheless, the action had not reached the proportions of a Union disaster; it was rather a maddening setback at a moment when fate seemed to offer conspicuous success.

In painful deferment of his hopes Lincoln had watched Hooker's operations while also keenly interested in western developments. His watching was none too hopeful. Two weeks before the battle he feared Stoneman's flanking expedition was too slow and was "another failure already." [2] Those who thought only of Baltimore, or of Pennsylvania, or of General Schurz, asked him to weaken Hooker for a supposed benefit elsewhere, but he saw that this was precisely what the enemy wanted.[3] On the day of the main fighting in the Chancellorsville battle the obscurity of the operation as viewed from Washington was shown by Lincoln's questions: "Where is General Hooker? Where is Sedgwick? Where is Stoneman?" [4] When the battle was over and it was learned that Hooker had failed—this on top of so many failures—and had withdrawn behind the Rappahannock, Lincoln, according to his secretaries, "was for a moment in despair." [5] Reacting

---

2 *Works*, VIII, 249 (April 15, 1863).   3 *Ibid.*, VIII, 244, 261.
4 *Ibid.*, VIII, 262 (May 3, 1863).   5 *Ibid.*, VIII, 263 n.

promptly, however, he conferred with Halleck, visited Hooker's headquarters, and urged another "early movement," pointing out that it
would "help to supersede the bad moral effect of the recent one." [6]
In its immediate sequel the Chancellorsville chapter of accidents had
no such depressing effect as that at Fredericksburg. Realizing that
Hooker's main purpose had been frustrated, the President and his
chiefs took satisfaction in Stoneman's damaging of Lee's communications [7] and in the fact that no disorganizing blow had been dealt to
the structure and effectiveness of the Union army, whose power for
further fighting, considered relatively to that of the enemy, had not
diminished.

II

The peak of the furious war was now at hand. With a tempered and
confident army Lee struck north in the most ambitious undertaking
of the whole Southern effort. Invasion of the Yankee realm held out
high prospects to Confederate eyes. How far Lee could seriously expect his northward thrust to cause a depletion of Grant's strength before Vicksburg is a question, but he could reasonably hope that a
successful Confederate invasion might bring a decisive turn of the tide
against the cause of Lincoln and of the United States. Hooker might
be caught at a disadvantage as the terms of service of thousands of his
men were about to expire. Confederate needs of supply and food might
be satisfied. Virginia might be given a welcome respite. Dissension
and defeatism might be fomented behind Union lines. Perhaps Baltimore, Philadelphia, or Washington could be captured. If these things
were done, foreign powers might recognize the Confederacy; this
would be a major blow to the Union.

At any rate, to remain at Fredericksburg waiting for Hooker to
strike south, was of no use. Even failure in an offensive move, with
successful withdrawal, might have defensive importance. The summer was going to witness heavy fighting in any case, and if the
enemy's country could be invaded, his devices and strategic plans
could be disrupted and a good deal of time consumed before another
Virginia campaign could be launched. Above all, in the Southern view
the main consideration was that never again could the Confederate

---

[6] *Ibid.*, VIII, 265 (May 7, 1863).   [7] Moore, *Rebellion Record* (Diary), VI, 72.

chieftain hope for a better chance than in the post-Chancellorsville phase. If ever the cause of secession was to gain the victory, a fighting offensive was a necessity. Added to all this was Lee's low opinion of the Army of the Potomac under the kind of generals that had led it since the displacement of McClellan.

Pushing north in three great army corps under Longstreet, Ewell, and A. P. Hill, Lee was paralleled by Hooker's grand army, whose obvious business was to cover Washington and seek the advantage of favorable position when the foe should strike. On June 27 Hooker was near Frederick, Maryland, when a flare-up of antagonism between himself and Halleck occasioned his removal from command of the Army of the Potomac. Doubts as to support by authorities at the capital had been troubling the Union commander for some days; in a request for more definite orders he added the comment: ". . . outside of the Army of the Potomac I don't know whether I am standing on my head or feet." [1] Correctly enough, Hooker had requested the abandonment of Maryland Heights (at Harpers Ferry), where he said that the garrison of ten thousand was "of no earthly account," [2] so that these troops could be added to his army. Halleck, with the old obsession for guarding Washington by a scattering and immobilizing of Union forces, replied that he could not approve the abandonment.[3] Hooker then impatiently requested that he be unburdened of his command.[4]

A strategic difference and a clash of feeling between his general in chief and commander in the field were thus laid upon Lincoln's doorstep at a time when a false move would bring disaster. A momentous decision was called for and Lincoln made it. With what seemed like breathtaking promptness he accepted Hooker's resignation and appointed George Gordon Meade as commander of the Army of the Potomac.

This important bit of executive business requires explaining. It is not to be naïvely supposed that Hooker's asking to be relieved offered a sufficient reason for a change of command at so hazardous a moment. To swap horses while crossing a river was contrary to Lincoln's famous aphorism.[5] As for Hooker, his maneuvering of the army

---

[1] *Offic. Rec.*, 1 ser., XXVII, pt. 1, 56.   [2] *Ibid.*, 60 (see also p. 58).
[3] *Ibid.*, 59.   [4] *Ibid.*, 60.
[5] It was later, in the presidential campaign of 1864, that the aphorism was uttered.

as a foil for Lee had caused his stock to rise and it is altogether likely that he expected to be retained, his gesture of resignation being intended to bring a showdown with Halleck. According to an inside story of the episode as given by Charles F. Benjamin of the war department, the removal of Hooker and the appointment of Meade had been ordained weeks before it occurred. Just after Chancellorsville, according to this account, when Lincoln, taking Halleck with him, had hastened to the front in disgust at Hooker's retirement behind the Rappahannock, an investigation on the spot had virtually sealed the decision so far as Hooker was concerned. On return to Washington Lincoln and Halleck had agreed that Chancellorsville was "inexcusable," and that "Hooker must not be intrusted with the conduct of another battle." [6] Having checked Hooker on more than one occasion, Lincoln had come to be watchful of mistakes in his strategy. When in early June it seemed that the general might cross to the south of the Rappahannock on finding Lee to the north of that stream, Lincoln picturesquely advised against "being entangled upon the river, like an ox jumped half over a fence and liable to be torn by dogs front and rear without a fair chance to gore one way or kick the other." [7]

The advance decision to dismiss Hooker may help to explain the rising tension between that general and Halleck, a tension which led Lincoln to write to Hooker an admonition which applied equally to both men: "If you and he [Halleck] would use the same frankness to one another, and to me, that I use to both of you, there would be no difficulty. I . . . must have the . . . skill of both, and yet these suspicions tend to deprive me of both." [8] When Hooker questioned Halleck's right to control him, Lincoln, exercising the supreme power of commander in chief, again took Halleck's side as he peremptorily wired to Hooker: "I shall direct him [Halleck] to give you orders, and you to obey them." [9] These "family quarrels" [10] should probably be regarded as an unholy nuisance and annoyance to Lincoln, of the sort

Speaking to a delegation of the Union League just after his renomination, Lincoln attributed his selection not so much to his own merit as to the view that "it is not best to swap horses while crossing the river." *Works*, X, 123 (June 9, 1864).

[6] Charles F. Benjamin, in *Battles and Leaders of the Civil War*, III, 241.

[7] Lincoln offered the advice gently, as a mere suggestion. *Works*, VIII, 291–292 (June 5, 1863).

[8] *Ibid.*, VIII, 321 (June 16, 1863).   [9] *Ibid.*, VIII, 323 (June 16, 1863).

[10] *Ibid.*, 320 n.

that he had often to endure, rather than as the full cause of Hooker's dismissal.

A complicating factor in the episode was the attitude of Chase and his friends. As they were known to be partisans of Hooker, a "temporizing" policy had to be followed to avoid rupture with the "Treasury faction." [11] Matters were allowed to drift as weeks passed, Stanton being meanwhile determined to push the dismissal of Hooker. The drifting went so far, with Hooker growing stronger, that, according to Mr. Benjamin, "severe measures had to be resorted to in order to wring from him . . . [a] tender of resignation . . . ." [12]

Final details of the transfer of command seem nothing less than melodramatic. Meade had been slated for appointment when Hooker's sought-for resignation finally came, but impending battle was then so close that Stanton was alarmed lest "by accident or design" the transfer could not be effected. Never in the war was the Army of the Potomac at a more critical point: the North invaded, Philadelphians shaken by the rumor that Harrisburg was being bombarded, the railroad broken between Baltimore and Harrisburg, business suspended, gold taking a tell-tale leap, militia and thirty-day men mustering in haste, farmers aghast at the loss of harvests and stock, men and women of the North trembling [13] as they read their newspapers or peered at bulletins. In a proclamation that suggested the crack of doom Governor Curtin of Pennsylvania asked for sixty thousand men; appealing to "the patriotism and pride of every Marylander," Governor Bradford asked for ten thousand. [14] All the fighting potentialities of the Army of the Potomac were undimmed; yet there was danger that these potentialities might again be thrown away. [15]

As fateful moments passed there was a conference at the war department, Lincoln participating, and the transfer of command was agreed upon. [16] General James A. Hardie was ordered to start for the

---

[11] Charles F. Benjamin, in *Battles and Leaders of the Civil War*, III, 241. Mr. Benjamin explains (p. 240) that Hooker's influence had been enlisted in the movement to make Chase President.

[12] *Ibid.*, 241.   [13] Rhodes, *Hist. of the U. S.*, IV, 279.

[14] *Offic. Rec.*, 1 ser. XXVII, pt. 3, 169–170, 347–348.

[15] Ten days before Hooker's removal an observer in Washington had written: "Hooker does not know Lee's position. Halleck does not know what Schenck, or Hooker is doing or where Hooker is, ... We are adrift . . . ." Richard H. Rush to McClellan, Washington, June 18, 1863, McClellan MSS.

[16] Details are given by Charles F. Benjamin, in *Battles and Leaders*, III, 239–243.

front. As the personal representative of Lincoln, he was directed to deliver carefully prepared and authenticated duplicate orders to Hooker and Meade, with a previous personal word to Meade. Risking capture by Stuart's raiders and obstruction by whiskey-filled Union soldiers, Hardie reached Meade's tent at night and roused him from sleep. Feeling that the command ought to go to Reynolds, Meade could not be induced to accept until it was made clear that he had no choice and that, by orders from Washington, "it should be done immediately." There was a meeting next day (June 28) between Meade and Hooker, made painful by "Hooker's chagrin and Meade's overstrung nerves." [17] The transfer was effected. Meade then made a friendly explanation to Reynolds and was handsomely assured of the latter's support. Hooker took his leave; after a period of inactivity he was to have heavy duties, and perform them well, in the Chattanooga area.[18] To the scholarly Meade, unobtrusive officer that he was, the startlingly sudden promotion gave less of ambitious thrill than of "just diffidence" [19] as he rose to the soldier's challenge and obeyed the imperative order from Washington. Accepting extraordinary prerogatives conferred by the President, he prepared to fulfill a responsibility unexcelled, unless by Washington, in previous American history.[20]

For some days the talk, or hope, of a change of Union commanders had been floating about. The demand rose high for the recall of McClellan; it came with force and determination from many quarters —from the *National Intelligencer*,[21] from the New York board of councilmen, from the common council of Philadelphia, from A. K.

[17] *Ibid.*, 243.

[18] Neither defeat at Chancellorsville nor the humiliation of being displaced by Meade before Gettysburg served to spoil the spirit or blunt the fighting qualities of Joseph Hooker. For a careful study of his personality and career see Walter H. Hebert, *Fighting Joe Hooker* (1944).

[19] "By direction of the President of the United States, I hereby assume command of the Army of the Potomac. As a soldier, in obeying this order—an order totally unexpected and unsolicited—I have no promises or pledges to make. . . . It is with just diffidence that I relieve in the command of this army an eminent and accomplished soldier, whose name must ever appear conspicuous in the history of its achievements . . . ." Meade's General Order No. 67, June 28, 1863, *Offic. Rec.*, 1 ser., XXVII. pt. 3, 374.

[20] "Meade has . . . proved an excellent general, the only one . . . who has ever fought the army of the Potomac well. He seems the right man in the right place. Hooker was worse than a failure. Had he remained in command he would have lost the army & the capital." H. W. Halleck to Grant, July 11, 1863, MS., Ill. State Hist. Lib.

[21] Washington *National Intelligencer* (tri-weekly edition), June 18, 1863, editorial, p. 3, c. 1.

McClure (friend of Curtin and of Lincoln), from an audience addressed by Curtin, and from Governor Joel Parker of New Jersey.[22] Men of both parties joined in this earnest move, which expressed "a serious and powerful sentiment at the North." [23] Edward Everett had vigorously urged Lincoln to put McClellan back in command and had pleaded with the general, despite the interference of Halleck and Stanton, to accept.[24] It was indeed rumored that McClellan had been appointed general in chief of the army. The effect of the rumor, so the *Herald* reported, was "astonishing," as shown by a decline in gold and a "general revival of public confidence." Happening to be in New York City at the time, having come over from his home in New Jersey, McClellan was greeted by a "spontaneous ovation" which the *Herald* considered "unmistakable evidences of the extreme popularity of the General." [25] There was also a counter rumor, or fabricated whisper, that certain Democratic leaders in New York were planning to raise a force which, with McClellan at the head, would march upon Washington, and effect a *coup d'état* by which the Lincoln administration would be expelled.[26] From time to time similar reports had circulated concerning McClellan. A sensational account could be made up by putting these stories together, but they have no place except in the category of partisan falsification. It is a relief to note that men who were active against McClellan did not always traffic in this sort of slander. Referring, for instance, to an infamous tale concerning an alleged treasonable interview between McClellan and Lee before Antietam, Carl Schurz characterized such talk as "mere headquarters bluster." [27] Concerning the same canard a friend of McClellan wrote to him: "These are sad times when men can be brought to perjure themselves." [28] As for putting McClellan again at the head of the Army of the Potomac in the crisis of Lee's Pennsylvania invasion, it is clear that patriotic appeals to this end were made to Lincoln but that the old political prejudice against McClellan made such action impossible. Lincoln said virtually as much when he

---

[22] Rhodes, *Hist. of the U. S.*, IV, 277–278.   [23] *Ibid.*, IV, 277.

[24] ". . . I . . . urge[d] upon him [Lincoln] the expediency of replacing you in command of the army . . Notwithstanding the disgusts you have received . . . I hope . . you will not hold back." Edward Everett to McClellan, Boston, June 18, 1863, McClellan MSS.

[25] New York *Herald*, July 1, 1863, p. 6, c. 5.

[26] Edward Everett to McClellan, Boston, July 25, 1863, McClellan MSS.

[27] Myers, *McClellan*, 374–375.   [28] *Ibid.*, 375.

telegraphed as follows in reply to an appeal by Governor Parker:
". . . no one out of my position can know so well as if he were in
it, the difficulties and involvments of replacing General McClellan
in command, and this aside from any imputations upon him." [29]

III

One seldom reads of the Civil War in terms of blood and filth,
writhing men, spilled brains, and mutilated flesh. Even the terms
"sick," "wounded," and "dead" are so generalized as to be almost
abstract. Realities are so revolting that writers prefer to tell of flanking movements, of position and assault, of retreat or advance, of batteries opening up handsomely, of divisions doing this or brigades
doing that. The very word "war" is a euphemism for "human slaugh-
terhouse." Murder in drama usually occurs offstage. In historical accounts, especially military narratives, the war is offstage in the sense
that its hideousness and stench do not appear.

So it is with the shambles at Gettysburg. Richard Brooke Garnett
of Virginia, brigadier general under Pickett, went into battle ill but
upstanding. He came out of it dead. His "cool and handsome bearing
. . . devoid of excitement" won the admiration of his men. He was
shot from his horse at the mouth of Union cannon. Armistead, another of Pickett's brigadiers, fell with Garnett. Kemper, commanding
yet another of Pickett's brigades, received a serious wound. Where
fighting was closest there seemed almost a suicidal rivalry "to plant
the Southern banner on the walls of the enemy." [1]

When figured by regiments the losses under Pickett were appalling.
Of the Eighth Virginia, under Col. E. Hunton, fifty-four were re-
ported killed or wounded. It was an understatement; nearly all of
Hunton's men were slain, wounded, or captured. Other losses among
Virginia regiments included 87 of the Eighteenth Virginia, 77 of the
Twenty-Eighth, 62 of the Fifty-Sixth, 67 of the Third, 81 of the
Ninth, 108 of the Fourteenth.[2] The toll of field officers was enormous.
"Regiments that went in with colonels came out commanded by

---

[29] Telegram to Governor Joel Parker of New Jersey, *Works*, IX, 13–14 (June 30, 1863).
[1] Report of Maj. Charles S. Peyton, commanding Garnett's brigade, Pickett's division,
July 9, 1863, *Offic. Rec.*, 1 ser., XXVII, pt. 2, 386–387.
[2] Jesse Bowman Young, *The Battle of Gettysburg*, 426–427.

lieutenants." [3] The Twenty-Sixth North Carolina went in with over eight hundred; only 216 came out unhurt.[4] Heth's division of A. P. Hill's corps totaled about fifteen hundred effective men after the slaughter; it had numbered eight thousand.[5] Other Southern regimental losses, picked at random, were as follows: Of the Second South Carolina, 154 were lost at Gettysburg; of the Thirteenth Mississippi, 165; of the Seventeenth Mississippi, 200; of the Thirty-Eighth Virginia, 170; of the Fifth Texas, 109; of the Eleventh Georgia, 194; of the Forty-Eighth Alabama, 102.[6] In Garnett's brigade under Pickett it was officially reported that "the identity of every regiment . . . [was] entirely lost, and every regimental commander killed or wounded." [7] This brigade lost 941, Armistead's 1191, Kemper's 731, Pickett's division as a whole, 2888.[8] Captain Michael P. Spessard of the Twenty-Eighth Virginia was in Pickett's charge. "His son fell," so the report read, "mortally wounded, at his side; he stopped but for a moment to look on his dying son, gave him his canteen of water, . . . pressed on . . . to the wall . . . and fought the enemy with his sword in their own trenches . . . ." [9] Of the First Texas it was reported: " . . . many were killed and wounded, some losing their heads, and others so horribly mutilated and mangled that their identity could scarcely be established; but . . . all the men continued . . . unflinchingly to maintain their position." [10] Private W. J. Barbee of this regiment, "mounted a rock . . . , and there, exposed to a raking . . . fire from artillery and musketry, stood until he had fired twenty-five shots, when he received a Minie ball . . . in the right thigh, and fell." [11] The report of General Henry L. Benning, commanding a Georgia brigade, mentioned two of his colonels, William T. Harris and John A. Jones, killed on the second day—Jones by a fragment of shell which "passed through his brain," Harris by a ball that "passed through his heart, killing him instantly." [12]

On the Union side the roll of deeds and men was no less heroic. One Pennsylvania regiment, the One Hundred Fiftieth, known as

---

[3] *Offic. Rec.*, 1 ser., XXVII, pt. 2, 644.
[4] *Ibid.*, 645.　　　[5] *Ibid.*　　　　　[6] *Ibid.*, 338–339, 396.　　　[7] *Ibid.*, 387.
[8] *Ibid.*, 339.　　　[9] *Ibid.*, 387.　　　[10] *Ibid.*, 409.　　　[11] *Ibid.*, 410.
[12] *Ibid.*, 415. These losses are more impressive when compared with pre-battle strength. For example, for the brigade of General Alfred Iverson, C. S. A., it was reported that "out of the 1,470 officers and men present, June 30th, . . . there were but 400 left after the battle . . . ." Young, *Battle of Gettysburg*, 437.

"Second Bucktails," lost 264 men. The report read: "They all fought as if each man felt that upon his own arm hung the fate of . . . the nation." [13] Of the One Hundred Forty-Third Pennsylvania the losses were 253 out of 465; [14] the Twenty-Eighth Massachusetts lost one hundred.[15] General John Gibbon reported that his division "went into action about 3,800 strong; lost in killed and wounded over 1,600, and captured more prisoners than it had men on the ground at the end of the conflict." His "fearful" loss in killed and wounded was reported as especially high among field officers.[16]

IV

With no attempt to "cover" the battle of Gettysburg in these pages, it may be convenient to jot down some of the features of the three-day horror.

First Day, July 1, 1863. Lee's scattered forces, some of which had gone deep into Pennsylvania, were being cautiously concentrated at Cashtown, about nine miles west of Gettysburg, when Pettigrew's brigade of Heth's division (under A. P. Hill), moving toward Gettysburg in quest of shoes and other necessaries, "found a large force of cavalry near the town, supported by an infantry force." Getting no farther than the "suburbs of Gettysburg" (a rather amusing expression for a town that had 2390 inhabitants in 1860), Pettigrew returned to Cashtown and reported his observation (June 30); [1] the "enemy had now been felt, and found to be in heavy force in and around Gettysburg." [2] The Union cavalry was that of Buford; it was part of Meade's advance wing under Reynolds. Neither Lee nor Meade had planned that this should be the scene of combat, but their converging forces had met, and each commander now decided that Gettysburg was the place to fight it out. In making this decision while the choice to withdraw was still open, Lee was vigorously opposed by Longstreet, who advised him to swing around Meade's left and select a place to fight between him and Washington, with Meade making the attack. The battle of July 1 was a sharp preliminary fight which raged outside Gettysburg and through its streets as forces under Hill and Ewell met

13 *Ibid.,* 389.   14 *Ibid.*   15 *Ibid.,* 391.
16 *Offic. Rec.,* 1 ser., XXVII, pt. 1, 418.   1 *Offic. Rec.,* 1 ser., XXVII, pt. 2, 637.
2 *Ibid.,* 638.

those under Reynolds. Fierce attacks by numerically superior Confederates drove the Federals into retreat, but before the day closed a Union line of defense formed on Cemetery Hill, south of the town. There, with artillery support and reënforcements, they stood firm. The Confederates did not push their initial advantage to the point of dislodging the foe from that important position. Meade having not yet arrived, the Unionists at Gettysburg had been led by Reynolds, who was killed that day, then by Howard and later by Hancock; they had fought an excellent delaying action; there are those who say that the seemingly minor incidents of the first day determined the whole result.

A general battle had been precipitated not in terms of Confederate initiative, but of casual encounter. With tens of thousands streaming in on both sides a major engagement was on. Lee knew that he could not always control conditions and incidents; he also knew that a battle was inescapable. At the time it seemed reasonably promising of Confederate success. In the backward view it is evident that the attacking side was at a disadvantage. Conditions favored the defense if key positions could be quickly taken and held. Meade was growing constantly stronger; a few hours' delay meant everything to the Union cause.

Second Day, July 2. The morning was quiet. Action was delayed till past mid-afternoon. Then the Union left was badly threatened in a long and desperately fierce encounter, in the Peach Orchard and Devil's Den, between Longstreet and Sickles, the latter having detached himself in a rash forward movement instead of holding Little Round Top, key point in that part of the line. Sickles's move tended to expose and endanger the whole Union left; perhaps his ambitious thrust was in the hope of winning special prominence and glory; it became later the subject of a rankling dispute between himself and Meade. The wounding or killing of generals was one of the features of this battle; Sickles received a leg injury which necessitated amputation; in the controversy that followed there was a tendency for censure to be silenced in consideration of this costly sacrifice.

Longstreet's men in the powerful drive of their forward movement had all but taken Little Round Top, whose capture would have unhinged Meade's line. Fortunately for the Federals, however, General Warren hurried artillery and infantry into position just in time to repulse the on-rushing Confederates and keep both Round Tops in Union hands. On the Union right Edward Johnson's men of Ewell's corps made an attack upon Culp's Hill, east of Cemetery Hill, which was briefly successful. The hill was captured only to be released next day. Cemetery Hill was sufficiently well defended to withstand Early's strokes and with this vain assault the day ended. In a council of corps commanders that night Meade decided to strengthen and hold the Union line against Lee's attack next day.

Lee was disappointed. Confederate timing had gone wrong. Longstreet had been counted on to deal a crushing blow upon the Union left while Ewell struck the right and Hill took care of the center. These blows were expected to be delivered in advance of Meade's concentration. For success of the scheme, speed and coördination were essential and both were lacking. Longstreet was not only non-coöperative and "disgruntled"; he was so sincerely distrustful of Lee's strategy that he seemed determined to force his own plan "to be adopted in spite of Lee," while Lee's temperament was such that he did not sternly assert himself. It has been said by Lee's biographer that "on July 2 the Army of Northern Virginia was without a commander." [3]

Third Day, July 3. Though Pickett's charge in the afternoon was the chief event of the final day at Gettysburg, the morning's business on Meade's right was an essential factor. The basis for this phase of Union victory had been laid in the night hours by Geary's action in slipping Federal troops and artillery into inside positions along the Baltimore turnpike and on the rocky ground of Culp's Hill, then held by Johnson; all this was done "with the utmost silence and secrecy . . . within a few rods of the enemy's lines." [4] This part of the battle began at dawn (3:30) with a Union assault and raged with a series of shifting charges and countercharges for seven hours. It ended after terrible slaughter, with Federal recapture of Culp's Hill; and Meade's army occupied a hooklike position (a fishhook or reversed question mark), holding firmly on the Round Tops at the south, stretching for about two miles along Cemetery Ridge, and curving at the north on the now formidable positions of Cemetery Hill and Culp's Hill. Opposite stood Lee on Seminary Ridge; not

---

[3] Freeman, *Lee*, III, 149–150.   [4] *Offic. Rec.*, 1 ser., XXVII, pt. 1, 828.

quite a mile of open country separated the armies. From Confederate batteries there came at one o'clock a terrific and prolonged cannonade concentrated against the Union center; "the experience of the terrible grandeur of that rain of missiles and that chaos of strange and terror-spreading sounds, unexampled, perhaps, in history, . . . can never be forgotten by those who survived it." For almost two hours the artillery raged without shaking the Union position. The withstanding of that terrible test, with horses, men and carriages "piled together" and with limbers or caisson wheels shot off and replaced under fire,[5] was one of the chapters of bravery that contributed to Federal success.

Lee's supreme effort followed.[6] Against powerfully placed infantry and massed batteries there came in perfect order the "fearfully ir-resistible"[7] advance of the Confederates' best regiments. With colors carried high and a "precision and steadiness that extorted . . . ad-miration"[8] from their opponents they came on unhindered while tense moments passed as Union fire was withheld. The ensuing ordeal is beyond description. As the Confederates came within close range a deadly and destructive fire was opened upon them, mowing down thousands and throwing regiments into disorder. This, however, did not stop all of them; about a hundred penetrated to the low stone wall that marked the crest of the Union position, some even crossing the Union breastworks in an intensity of close and deadly combat which forced, momentarily, a partial Union retirement. For brief moments the battle seemed almost to waver, some of the Union batteries being nearly exhausted of ammunition, but soon it was over. Meade's line (Hancock's corps) had held; the magnificent Southern charge was utterly shattered and broken. Bloody Angle, apex of the assault, was too strongly covered for the utmost that an Armistead or a Garnett could do.[9]

---

[5] *Ibid.,* 437.

[6] This supreme Southern effort goes by the name of Pickett's charge, but of the forty-seven regiments in the attack, totaling about fifteen thousand men, less than a third (fifteen regiments) were those of Pickett. The brigades were those of Mayo, Davis, Marshall, Fry, Lane, Lowrance, Garnett, Kemper, Armistead, and Wilcox; the divisions were Pickett's, Heth's, Pender's (commanded by Trimble), and Anderson's. Hill's corps furnished more troops than did Longstreet's, which included Pickett's command.

[7] *Offic. Rec.,* 1 ser., XXVII, pt. 1, 439.   [8] *Ibid.,* 373.

[9] Longstreet's distrust of this assault is shown in his report: "The order for this attack, which I could not favor . . . , would have been revoked had I felt that I had that privilege." *Offic. Rec.,* 1 ser., XXVII, pt. 2, 360. See also Freeman, *Lee,* III, 121.

Only a desperate few had pierced the Union wall. Discharges from Meade's artillery [10] and infantry had broken up the main waves of Confederate advance on the plain between the armies. As for Pickett's men, who had been under terrific fire, the account of General Alexander, Confederate artillery commander, was that they "never halted, but opened fire at close range, swarmed over the fences and among the enemy's guns—were swallowed up in smoke, and that was the last of them." [11]

One of the reasons for Lee's failure was the uselessness of Stuart's cavalry. Having lost contact with the main army when Lee needed him most for intelligence, Stuart failed completely when counted on to strike Meade's rear simultaneously with blows on his front. On July 3, in a portion of the battle that has received small attention, Stuart's men, especially those commanded by Fitz Lee and Wade Hampton, made a dashing cavalry charge in approved style with sabers drawn, but Union cavalry under Gregg and Custer drove them back and defeated them at every point. In judging the nature of Stuart's failure, it is to be noted that his success in Meade's rear "would have been productive of the most serious consequences"; [12] also that most of the other mistakes on the Southern side resulted from the "injudicious use of the Confederate horse during the . . . campaign." [13]

Where there was all this superb sacrifice there was also bravery tempered with prudence, courage that stopped short of self-immolation. Some of the attackers in the confused hand-to-hand fighting, according to a Union report, "threw down their arms and were

---

[10] It was claimed, however, that Federal artillery had not done enough. Among the controverted points at Gettysburg (which cannot be treated here) was the statement of General Henry J. Hunt, able chief of artillery for the Army of the Potomac, that if his instructions had been followed on the third day, he did "not believe that Pickett's division would have reached our line." *Battles and Leaders of the Civil War*, III, 375. Correctly judging that the Confederate cannonade was preparatory to an infantry assault on the Union center, Hunt instructed Meade's artillery commanders to withhold fire for fifteen or twenty minutes, then to concentrate it accurately on those enemy batteries that were doing the greatest damage. (Many of them were doing virtually no damage at all, merely sweeping open ground in the Union rear.) As it turned out, the weight of Confederate assault fell at a point where Union projectiles had been exhausted during the preliminary cannonade, and the possible effectiveness of Federal artillery was partly lost. See also *ibid.*, III, 385–387.

[11] *Ibid.*, III, 365–366.   [12] *Offic. Rec.*, 1 ser., XXVII, pt. 1, 956.
[13] Freeman, *Lee*, III, 148.

taken prisoners of war, while the remainder broke and fled in great disorder." [14] Incidentally, in the shifting battle, retirement by one side or the other was essential where fighting organization was preserved; at times on each side the choice was between withdrawal and utter loss of fighting power. "With but two exceptions" wrote a Confederate colonel, "each and every man of the regiment proved himself a hero." [15] Another wrote: "Both officers and men, with scarcely an exception, did their duty . . . unflinchingly." [16] Censurable conduct sometimes found its way into reports. A Union colonel, reporting the capture of twenty battle-flags in "a space of 100 yards square," added: "Several colors were stolen or taken with violence by officers of high rank from brave soldiers who had . . . honestly captured them . . . , and were probably turned in as taken by commands which were not within 100 yards of the point of attack." [17] There were men "making to the rear as fast as possible"; [18] as in other battles men were posted behind the line to shoot stragglers.

To speak only of men enduring the fire at Gettysburg is to understate the fierceness of the battle. Longstreet, reporting on what is usually called Pickett's charge, referred to "wavering columns." Then, having indicated how some of his troops "advanced to the charge, . . . entered the enemy's lines, . . . and gained his works," he added: "About the same moment, the troops that had before hesitated, broke their ranks and fell back in great disorder, many more falling under the enemy's fire in retiring than while they were attacking." [19] The number of prisoners taken is another indication of how sharply the battle raged. The division commanded by General Alexander Hays claimed the capture of more than fifteen battle flags, not less than 1500 prisoners, and "2,500 stand of arms, besides an estimate of 1,000 left upon the ground for want of time to collect them." [20] Where there were willing prisoners, they became so usually by reason of the unmistakable decision of battle against them. In the close and confused fighting at Culp's Hill on July 3 General Geary re-

---

[14] *Offic. Rec.*, 1 ser., XXVII, pt. 1, 440. "Many of the enemy . . . crawled . . . under the sheet of fire, and, coming up to our lines, surrendered themselves prisoners." *Ibid.*, 450.

[15] *Ibid.*, pt. 2, 410.

[16] *Ibid.*, 572. Another statement read: "The whole regiment behaved admirably, with one or two exceptions." *Ibid.*, pt. 1, 286.

[17] *Ibid.*, pt. 1, 440. [18] *Ibid.*, 439. [19] *Ibid.*, pt. 2, 360. [20] *Ibid.*, pt. 1, 454.

ported large numbers begging to be captured: they had advanced, he said, "until met by our terrible fire, and then, throwing down their arms, rushed in with white flags, handkerchiefs, and even pieces of paper, in preference to meeting again that fire which was certain destruction." [21] This is but another way of saying that at Gettysburg there were artillery and infantry volleys which men could not withstand. As to the main generalization, reports of soldier conduct agree in emphasizing the superb performance of the troops. Over and over the officers reported in substance: "Where all behaved so nobly, individual distinction cannot with propriety be made." [22] In Peach Orchard or Devil's Den, at the stone wall or "clump of trees," each side met the fiery test with unstinted valor. It is this valor of both sides, rather than the unedifying spectacle of Americans killing Americans with furious intensity of purpose, that constitutes the chief tradition of Gettysburg.

V

Pickett's remnants staggered back and Confederate lines quickly formed to repulse a counter stroke, but it did not come. Meade's men had taken terrific punishment. Lee's army was to escape from the campaign. Despite that escape the Confederacy had passed what has been traditionally called its "high tide." From that hour it was to be a receding flood, and writers are expected to expatiate upon Gettysburg as *the* turning point of the whole war.

Such expatiating may be left to others; it will not be reproduced in these pages. One could argue that in the larger view the turning of the tide in September 1862, with McClellan in command, had been even more significant, particularly as to emancipation and as to policy abroad. One does no injustice to the importance of Gettysburg to say that in the phase which preceded Antietam the Confederacy stood at a high point in solid prospects which not even the Gettysburg phase could quite equal. The struggle, of course, was a continually shifting affair. Decisiveness in the whole war is hard to focus in any one battle or campaign, but in the uncertainty of military control at Washington the possibility of Union recovery in the event of Lee's offensive victory at Antietam was so low, and the situation abroad so

---

[21] *Ibid.*, pt. 1, 830.   [22] *Ibid.*, pt. 2, 406.

critical, that September of 1862 was at least as decisive as July of 1863. The averting of disaster at Antietam permitted the momentum of 1863–4–5 in both the East and West to develop. This was true despite those setbacks at Fredericksburg and Chancellorsville which prevented the Federals from exploiting the advantages that were reasonably to have been expected under more effective leadership than that of Burnside and Hooker.

This is a point which many writers have missed. Turning points are favorite themes and traditional viewpoints have great power of survival. It is hardly correct to speak of only one turning point in the war and that at Gettysburg. If a national cause escapes disaster more than once, each escape is as important as the whole cause. In that sense Gettysburg was of supreme importance, while in intensity of fighting it marked the peak of the struggle in the East. To speak of it as *the* turning point is unnecessary. It is to be remembered that the Confederacy never followed up a military victory with anything important in the political sense. Such a following up was certainly as much of a possibility in the event of a Confederate triumph at Antietam (before Grant had done much in the West) as at Gettysburg. If in each episode such a chance existed—if the cause, having been saved before, had to be saved again—that is enough tribute to the men of Cemetery Hill and the Round Tops.

As Confederates viewed the peaks and valleys of their effort, Gettysburg offered a devastating contrast to Chancellorsville. "Yesterday," wrote a Confederate general after Lee's defeat, "we rode on the pinnacle of success; to-day absolute ruin seems to be our portion. The Confederacy totters to its destruction." [1]

The fourth of July 1863 was a day of rare Union triumph as Grant at Vicksburg received the surrender of Pemberton's army of thirty thousand. This shining achievement was the culmination of a boldly conceived campaign that showed Grant at his best, yet the achievement was as much a matter of grim struggle as of brilliant execution; it came only after repeated failures to approach Vicksburg directly from the North, or to divert the Mississippi River, causing that stream to by-pass the famous city. Fighting the mighty river was no good; the day would come when the "Father of Waters" would go "unvexed

---

[1] Diary of General Josiah Gorgas, Chief of Ordnance, C. S. A., July 28, 1863, Gorgas MSS.

to the sea," but for heartbreaking months it refused to be enlisted on the Union side. The Yazoo approach had been no better; its creeks and bayous, bluffs and forested hills seemed made for Confederate defense.

Bitter frustration stopped Grant's early efforts, then he tried a new tack. He cut loose from his base, crossed his army to the Louisiana side, pushed it through a tangle of swamps and bayous to a point far south of Vicksburg, joined the fleet under Foote, who had daringly run the Confederate batteries, recrossed the Mississippi, and launched upon an almost faultless series of operations that sealed the doom of Pemberton as early as May 19, from which time Vicksburg was under tightly held Federal siege. The ending of that siege with Confederate surrender, coming dramatically on July 4 and coinciding with Meade's victory over Lee, gave Lincoln's cause the uplift in morale and the advantage in international standing which only military victory could bring.

To speak of the destructive effect of Gettysburg upon the Confederate cause is to refer to a long and slow process. Though checked, the military power that challenged the Union was still formidable. Great as was that Fourth of July, Lincoln had expected more.[2] Vicksburg had surrendered. As he wrote Halleck, if Meade could have effected the destruction of Lee's army the war would have been over. Instead of this, Lee got away keeping his army intact; the chance was lost. There had been almost incessant rains. Days passed while the Confederate host, with prisoners and wounded, was "compelled to await at Williamsport the subsiding of the river and the construction of boats." In this vulnerable position Lee expected attack; his position was "becoming daily more embarrassing." [3] The attack did not come; on July 13–14 he crossed the Potomac by pontoon bridge and ford. It seemed that Meade had wasted the ten days following Gettysburg. He had failed to pursue, and the possible stakes had not been won. A seemingly entrapped enemy had eluded its fate.

In his report Meade said in effect that he was preparing to attack, but the enemy got away.[4] One of Meade's difficulties was indecision,

[2] In response to a serenade on July 7, 1863, Lincoln said: "These are trying occasions, not only in success, but for the want of success." *Works*, IX, 21.

[3] *Offic. Rec.*, 1 ser., XXVII, pt. 2, 309.

[4] "The 13th [of July] was occupied in reconnaissances of the enemy's position and preparations for attack, but, on advancing on the morning of the 14th, it was ascer-

to which was added that fatal weakness, a council of generals. He submitted the question of an attack to his corps commanders; five out of six voted no; later there was reconnaissance with preparations for possible attack; it was too late; on advancing his army, he found the enemy lines evacuated.[5]

To Lincoln it had seemed that Meade had held Lee in his grasp. He was "close upon him"; the river was "so swollen as to prevent his crossing," wrote Lincoln on July 11. At that point the President was "more than satisfied," [6] but that was on the expectation that Meade would strike. Yet Lincoln had not actually ordered Meade to attack,[7] and now the chance was gone. The President had naturally been elated by hopes of putting an end to the war; the dashing of these hopes plunged him into deep distress. His thoughts may be read in a "draft of a letter" to Meade under date of July 14. This being the day of Lee's southward crossing, Halleck had informed the general that "the escape of Lee's army without another battle has created great dissatisfaction in the mind of the President"; he referred to the army as "not . . . sufficiently active." [8] Meade, conscious only of duty done, considered the censure "so undeserved" that he respectfully asked "to be immediately relieved from the command of this army." [9] Lincoln began his letter with a reference to Meade's request, dealing with the "supposed censure" by giving assurance of his gratitude for the general's "magnificent success . . . at Gettysburg." Then he frankly explained his distress of mind at "the magnitude of the misfortune involved in Lee's escape." "He was within your easy grasp, and to have closed upon him would . . . have ended the war. As it is, the war will be prolonged indefinitely. . . . I do not expect . . . you can now effect much. Your golden opportunity is gone, and I am distressed immeasurably because of it."

Lincoln generously explained that he wrote only because Meade had heard of his dissatisfaction, and that he "thought it best to kindly tell . . . why." Had the words of the Chief Executive reached Meade, no amount of kindness could have disguised the rebuke; the President's truest kindness in the whole matter was his withholding

---

tained he had retired the night previous by a bridge at Falling Waters and the ford at Williamsport." Report of General Meade, *ibid.*, pt. 1, 118.

   [5] *Ibid.*, 91–92.   [6] *Works*, IX, 25.   [7] *Ibid.*, IX, 28 n.

   [8] Halleck to Meade, July 14, 1863, *Offic. Rec.*, 1 ser., XXVII, pt. 1, 92.

   [9] Meade's resignation came in a communication to Halleck, July 14, 1863. *Ibid.*, 93.

of the letter. It was a "draft"; that was all. The pain that Meade would undoubtedly have felt if he had received such a letter from the President was not inflicted. Lincoln's own endorsement on the envelope read: "To General Meade; never sent or signed." [10] Next year, when sharp criticism of Meade appeared over the cloaking signature "Historicus" in the *Herald*,[11] and when it was thought that Sickles inspired if he did not write the stinging articles directed against the man who was still in command of the Army of the Potomac, Meade wanted a court of inquiry, but Lincoln discouraged the idea. Again Lincoln spoke in kindly terms: "The country knows that . . . you have done grand service; . . . it is much better for you to be engaged in trying to do more than to be diverted . . . by a court of inquiry." [12]

No such generosity characterized the Republican radicals of the congressional war committee. Pouncing upon Meade with the prejudiced fury that marked their "investigations," they "screamed taunts," [13] disseminated whispers, and created a publicity pattern of their own to rob the commander at Gettysburg of all credit. The radical version was that the success at Gettysburg was the achievement of the corps commanders and that Meade should have only blame for his "criminal vacillation" [14] in failing to pursue. When in February-March 1864 Wade and Chandler, of the war committee, demanded of Lincoln that he remove Meade, whom radicals disliked for politicians' reasons, and put Hooker in his place, Lincoln showed yet another favor to the harassed general by refusing the demand,[15] well knowing that his refusal would intensify the radical assault upon his administration in election year.

VI

The midway point in the war was reached before measures to raise an army became commensurate with the magnitude of the struggle. Not till March 1863, with Hooker poised for a desperate struggle with Lee and Grant for a duel with Pemberton, did Congress pass the first

---

[10] "Draft of Letter to General G. G. Meade," July 14, 1863, "never sent or signed." *Works*, IX, 28–30.

[11] For the bitter controversy between Meade and Sickles apropos of the "Historicus" contribution to the *Herald*, see *Offic. Rec.*, 1 ser., XXVII, pt. 1, 127 ff. See also *Battles and Leaders of the Civil War*, III, 413–419.

[12] *Offic. Rec.*, 1 ser., XXVII, pt. 1, 139.   [13] Williams, *Lincoln and the Radicals*, 304.

[14] *Ibid.*, 303.   [15] *Ibid.*, 337–341, 361–363.

strictly national conscription law for the United States. This warborn statute introduced a radical modification into the American military system. In January 1861 the United States army had consisted of 16,402 officers and men.[1] When war broke at Sumter Lincoln had summoned 75,000 three-months "militia" of the states (April 15, 1861). On May 3 he had called for forty regiments of volunteers for three years as well as for eight regular regiments and 18,000 seamen. After the shock of the Bull Run defeat Congress passed a series of acts authorizing the President to accept volunteers in such numbers as he should deem necessary, not to exceed one million; the service was to be for not less than six months nor more than three years. In the spring of 1862 there were 637,126 men in the service, according to the report of the provost marshal general.[2] There was a general impression that enough men had been raised, and on April 3, 1862, there came an amazing order of Secretary Stanton that recruitment be stopped. The whole elaborate service for raising men was discontinued, "the property at the rendezvous sold, and the offices closed throughout the country." [3]

In a short time, however, the mood changed and with it government policy, so that the recruiting service was resumed (June 6, 1862) and a series of far-reaching efforts was made toward the raising of new forces. A realistic study of the situation showed that, while the number of men drawn into the service might seem an impressive total, the effective strength of the army for combat duty was a far different matter. As the months passed that strength was depleted by many factors: time required for training, absenteeism, desertion, battle casualties, disease, military service far from the front, and a system of hospitals by which governors saw to it that many a man was brought back "first to his State and then to his home." [4] Along with this diminishing of the army there came a new realization of the military task which confronted the Union government in the summer of 1862 in the crushing of a formidable and determined Confederacy. On July 1 an impressive group of Union governors—eighteen of them from Maine to Missouri and from Michigan to Tennessee—insisting that the "decisive moment" was at hand to "crush the rebellion," presented a

---

[1] *Offic. Rec.*, 3 ser., V, 605.   [2] *Ibid.*, 608.   [3] *Ibid.*

[4] Emory Upton, *Military Policy of the United States*, 439.

paper urging the President to issue a new call for men. By this they meant that the governors were taking the initiative and that state agencies were to be used in the raising of volunteers. They meant also to organize a needless and inefficient number of new military units, with many new commissions, allowing the depletion of veteran regiments to continue. Their system also included other ineffective procedures.

In response to this appeal of the governors Lincoln issued a call for 300,000 men (volunteers for three years) on July 2, 1862.[5] He hoped that they would be "enrolled without delay, so as to bring this unnecessary and injurious civil war to a speedy and satisfactory conclusion." [6] The nation's law makers now added their contribution, tinkering with the machinery at a time when the war had produced small results in Union victory. Falling back on the system of short-term militia, Congress passed a militia act (July 17, 1862) by which the President was given a qualified power of conscription for Federal militia service through state machinery. Having been under the urging of governors, the President was now given a mandate by Congress, and on August 4 he ordered a draft of 300,000 militia for nine months' service—this on the heels of his July 2 call for 300,000 volunteers.[7] With many technicalities and complications as to shares and credits, this draft of 1862, though demanded by the general government and launched by orders of the President, was conducted by state authorities. Even in the midst of gigantic conflict the unmilitary American democracy was slow to go on a genuine war basis. The latter part of 1862, in this respect, was chiefly significant for the half measures and failures which, according to the provost marshal general, demonstrated "the necessity for a radical change in the method of raising troops." "The old agencies," he reported, "for filling the ranks proved more and more ineffective." Adoption of a drastic system, however, was dreaded, and it was not until after "a protracted, searching, and animated discussion" that the conscription act of March 3, 1863, was passed. "It was the first law enacted by Congress by which the Gov-

---

[5] Offic. Rec., 3 ser., IV, 1264–1265. Under this call 421,465 men were reported furnished.

[6] Works, VII, 250.

[7] Offic. Rec., 3 ser., V, 609. Under this call of August 4, 1862, for nine-months militia 87,588 men were reported furnished (ibid., 3 ser., IV, 1265).

ernment of the United States appealed directly to the Nation to create large armies without the intervention of the authorities of the several States." [8]

Under this ill-devised statute a Federal provost marshal general's bureau was set up and a vast national network of enrolling officials was spread over the country. Though in the long run its results were small, this elaborate machinery reached into every locality and into every home that included able-bodied men of military age. The thankless and dangerous business of these officials was to list the men liable to service, examine state "credits," equalize the burden by a process that resembled higher mathematics, determine exemptions, conduct the draft, make arrangements in the matter of substitutes and commutation money, and bear up as best they could against secret societies, newspapers, and politicians in the use of local pressure, intimidation, questions of legality, evasion, open violence, and every "imaginable artifice . . . to deceive and defeat the enrolling officers." [9]

The moment of adoption of national conscription was one of depression. As the provost marshal general reported, there was "general apathy" as to volunteering, recruiting had "subsided," and desertion had so "greatly increased" as to become a "formidable and widespread evil." [10] Defeats and setbacks were fresh in the public mind. Operations against Vicksburg had been frustrated; Stone's River had left Rosecrans inactive for months; Charleston had withstood Federal assaults; the gloom of Fredericksburg still lingered; in the same blood-soaked vicinity Lee was soon to win another triumph. Conscription was a "novelty." It was contrary to American tradition. "The people had become more accustomed to the enjoyment of privileges than to the fulfillment of duties under the General Government, and . . . beheld the prospect of compulsory service in the Army with an unreasonable dread." [11]

The mere manning of the administrative machine was highly elaborate, with the appointment of officials for each district and subdistrict. It required special care to see that dishonest persons were not appointed and that competent and patriotic men were put in charge of districts containing hostile elements. Beginning in late May 1863, the provost marshal general's bureau proceeded with its work

---

[8] *Ibid.*, 3 ser., V. 611. ,   [9] *Ibid.*, 618–619.   [10] *Ibid.*, 612.   [11] *Ibid.*, 611.

throughout the rest of the war. They found opposition "in almost every house, if not to the act itself, at least to its application to . . . particular persons." [12]

VII

It is not intended to indicate here the frauds, abuses, and fundamental defects of the conscription system. Exemption from military service was permitted to any who provided a substitute or contributed $300 commutation money. The number who escaped by the money provision exceeded 86,000.[1] Many localities, according to the bureau's report, entirely cleared themselves "by raising money and advancing it to the persons drafted." The report adds: "This appeared to be the favorite method adopted by disloyal sections to prevent the reenforcement of the armies . . . ." [2]

Along with the abuses of conscription as then applied there existed in Lincoln's day a wretched system of bounties whose purpose seemed not primarily to get men to go all the way in performing soldier duty, but rather to stimulate "enlistments"—i. e., to fill quotas, build up credits, and avoid or diminish the drafting of men. Local communities would often pay bounties in full at the time of enlistment, and this method of cash payment, as well as the whole mercenary principle, produced a medley of vicious effects and inequalities that can hardly be realized.[3] Exploitation by bounty brokers and substitute brokers added an odious element·to the system, which opened the door to that degraded individual, the "bounty jumper." This was the man who enlisted, collected bounties, deserted, reënlisted under a change of name, collected more bounties, and repeated the process until a final desertion left him free and enriched, or until caught. How far bounties encouraged fraudulent enlistment is hard to say, but the provost marshal general made the statement that by reason of the bounty system "profligate and corrupt men amassed fortunes from the money raised for . . . bounties to soldiers," and that veterans "who had enlisted early . . . , without expectation of bounty, had good cause to murmur when late in the war unworthy recruits came

---

12 *Ibid.*, 618.   1 *Offic. Rec.*, 3 ser., V, 720.   2 *Ibid.*, 718.
    3 Ably treated in F. A. Shannon, *The Organization and Administration of the Union Army 1861–1865*, II, 57 ff.

among them rich with bounty for one year's enlistment." The official report demonstrated that the whole bounty system was an expensive way of obtaining inferior soldiers.[4]

The provost marshal general's bureau calculated the number of Union desertions as 201,397,[5] the ratio of desertions to enlistment credits being 62 per thousand in the loyal states generally, reaching as high as 117 in some areas.[6] Men deserted for a variety of reasons. Sometimes the desertions, arising from an inadequate concept of military discipline, were technical; they were committed with no thought of abandoning the cause. Certain military practices produced disgust, as when election of unsuitable officers by men under their command caused intolerable dissatisfaction among an "often highly intelligent minority."[7] Other factors were false stories as to harsh conditions in the service, dread of becoming prisoners, the effect of physical exactions upon the less vigorous, and the urgency of home obligations. When such obligations coincided with inactivity at the front, a man might feel that his family needed him more than did the army.

Some of the opposition to conscription was due to "politics," some of it was no better than vulgar mob psychology; yet much of it was due to a genuine hatred of compulsion, resentment against the rich (supposed to be favored by the prevailing system), and dissatisfaction at what was believed to be unfair or partisan discrimination in the administration of the law. There was violence in Lincoln's own state; there was an "insurrection" in Holmes County, Ohio; there were disturbances in Wisconsin, Indiana, Kentucky, and Pennsylvania; there was rioting at Troy, Albany, and Newark; there was a flare-up of border violence in Missouri.[8] These, however, paled into insignificance beside the furious riot which raged in New York City from July 13 to July 16, 1863. As a center of busy industry and a port of entry for numerous immigrants, New York had more than the normal per-

---

[4] *Offic. Rec.*, 3 ser., V, 675.   [5] *Ibid.*, 677.

[6] *Ibid.*, 668. The figuring of percentages is complicated by the fact that there were more enlistments than troops and more desertions than individual deserters. With something like two million in Union army service (W. F. Fox, *Regimental Losses in the American Civil War*, 527), those who deserted constituted about ten per cent. Conscription fell short of making up the loss by desertion. See Ella Lonn, *Desertion during the Civil War*.

[7] *Offic. Rec.*, 3 ser., V, 678. Election of officers was abandoned later in the war.

[8] Randall, *Civil War and Reconstruction*, 412–413.

centage of adult males. It thus came about that an entirely just draft, proportioned to the total of men properly subject to military duty, would take more men from Manhattan, in proportion to population, than from rural areas; it was easy for agitators to represent this as deliberate discrimination. The fear that freed Negroes might come North and compete for poor white men's jobs was also a factor. Rational explanation, however, breaks down. The demons of party feeling, race hatred, and class prejudice were whipped up in one vast orgy of murder and destruction, precipitated at the moment when officers had come to the drawing of names from the wheel. Half-crazed rioters stormed through the city, overpowering police with rifles seized from an armory, pillaging, burning buildings, slaying hundreds of Negroes, assailing the *Tribune* establishment, destroying property, burning a colored orphan asylum, and fighting bloody battles on sidewalks and barricaded streets. Estimates of the number killed vary from three hundred to twelve hundred; F. A. Shannon considers five hundred the minimum.[9] Property to the value of some millions was destroyed. Finally, with the help of police, naval forces, militia, a company from West Point, and a detachment of Federal troops rushed north from the Gettysburg campaign, the rioters were suppressed and order restored. Next month the draft was quietly resumed and no resistance offered.[10]

Apropos of conscription there had arisen a controversy between the President of the United States and Horatio Seymour, Democratic Governor of New York. In the pages of Nicolay and Hay, the governor is made to appear in a very bad light. By their account, he denounced enrollment, demanded that Federal authorities submit to state control, asked to have the draft suspended, showed sympathy for the rioters, accused draft officials of frauds, directed "insulting charges" against Lincoln, and showed himself a partisan in his hostility to the execution of the law.[11] He and his friends, say Nicolay and Hay, made the proceedings of the government "the object of special and vehement attack." [12]

On the other hand it is shown by Alexander J. Wall [13] that Seymour stood firmly for the Union and the Constitution, sustained Lincoln

---

[9] Shannon, *Union Army*, II, 213. For other estimates see Wall, *Horatio Seymour*, 39.
[10] Nicolay and Hay, *Lincoln*, VII, 37.   [11] *Ibid.*, VII, 32 ff.
[12] *Ibid.*, 39.   [13] Wall, *Horatio Seymour*, 20 ff.

in essential war measures, and was all in all a loyal Democrat. He believed, however, that the South had rights, distrusted an abolitionist war, was vexed at the Republican party's claim to a "patent right for all the patriotism," [14] favored adherence to constitutional methods, considered conscription unconstitutional as well as unnecessary, and felt confident that recruitment, which he actively promoted in New York, would accomplish the purpose. He was not the politician type. The people of New York had elected him knowing his views, thereby rejecting Wadsworth who upheld Lincoln, and he felt that acquiescence in certain of the doubtful measures of the administration would be a kind of desertion from his party's and his people's standard. His opposition to Lincoln was genuine; it was not that of the demagogue; yet in the controversy between them Lincoln came through with the better showing. Perhaps it should be added that the nature of the contest gave Lincoln the advantage. To oppose conscription in time of gigantic and desperate war, and to do it with an unavoidable suspicion of party motive, is no easy task. When Lincoln wrote a frank and conciliatory letter asking coöperation, the governor sent a cold and guarded reply,[15] but it cannot be said that he showed actual noncoöperation with the Washington government in the more vital matters. Lincoln's approach was to treat the situation as if no difference or controversy existed, or at least to relegate disputes to the background. He addressed the governor with respect, spoke generously in conference with the governor's brother,[16] showed readiness for reasonable adjustment, and in the outcome was successful in upholding the draft law.

One does not need to single out Seymour, except for the prominence of his position. There were many Union men of both parties who opposed conscription in general and the odious Civil War brand of it in particular. Even Horace Greeley wrote that drafting was "an anomaly in a free State"; it oppressed the masses, he thought, and it would have to be "reformed out of our systems of political economy." [17] There were grave doubts of the constitutionality of the law of 1863, and so long as the Supreme Court of the United States remained silent on the issue, the legal question, after the manner of Americans with

---

[14] *Ibid.*, 30.
[15] Due to pressure of work, according to Seymour's biographer. *Ibid.*, 29.
[16] *Ibid.*, 29–31.   [17] Greeley to Stanton, June 12, 1863, Stanton MSS.

a law they distrusted, was considered open. The Supreme Court never passed on the constitutionality of the 1863 act, though a half-century later it unanimously upheld that of 1917, and Lincoln felt that the advantage of the Court's silence should not all be on one side. "I do not object," he said, "to abide a decision of the . . . Supreme Court, . . . but I cannot consent to lose the time while it is being obtained." He thought it impossible to match an enemy that used every able-bodied man "if we first waste time to reëxperiment with the volunteer system already . . . inadequate, and then more time to obtain a court decision as to whether a law [for conscription] is constitutional . . . ." [18]

VIII

Though the Supreme Court was silent on the validity of the conscription law, it is noteworthy that two high officials of the Federal government, the President and the Chief Justice, prepared undelivered opinions on this subject—the President upholding, and the Chief Justice emphatically denying the constitutionality of the statute. Taney's paper on the subject survived as a manuscript in his handwriting.[1] Though an undelivered opinion, it reads exactly as if it were a pronouncement from the bench in a specific case involving the validity of the draft law. It appears to have been prepared at the Chief Justice's leisure for future use if such a specific case should arise. Elaborately marshaling judicial and historical citations, the high justice comes through with the conclusion "that this [conscription] Act . . . is unconstitutional and void—and confers no lawful authority on the persons appointed to execute it." The reasoning starts with a restrictive interpretation of the whole American federal system, with emphasis on reserved powers of the states and limited powers of the nation; the argument then proceeds to the assertion that the power of Congress to raise armies does not confer authority to cause the militia of the states to be "of no practical value"; even more, it

---

[18] Lincoln to Seymour, Aug. 7, 1863, *Works*, IX, 60–61.

[1] That the Chief Justice prepared an opinion on conscription seems but slightly known. A copy of Taney's manuscript, made from the unpublished original for the use of George Bancroft, is in the New York Public Library. See Phillip G. Auchampaugh, "A Great Justice on State and Federal Power. Being the Thoughts of Chief Justice Taney on the Federal Conscription Act," *Tyler's Quarterly Historical and Genealogical Magazine*, XVIII, 72–87 (Oct., 1936).

is asserted that the law in question is invalid because it "enables the general government to disorganize at its pleasure the government of the States,—by taking forcibly . . . the . . . officers necessary to the execution of its law." [2]

Lincoln's opinion on the subject was left among his papers, but never issued or published during his lifetime. It is an opinion which cuts through to fundamentals and deals with the ethical justice as well as the legality of universal service. Getting down to bedrock, the President canvassed the elements of democracy, the dominance of patriotism over party strife, the need for doing things we dislike, the survival of republican institutions, and the integrity of the country. The legal objection he considered utterly flimsy. Congress had power under the Constitution to raise armies; that was the whole of it. Congress "must prescribe the mode, or relinquish the power." The country had gone as far as it could, thought Lincoln, with volunteering, yet more men were needed or it would lose all that already had been poured out. The cause required armies. Armies required men. "We have ceased to obtain them voluntarily, and to obtain them involuntarily is the draft . . . ."

To those who denied the need for conscription Lincoln appealed with the request that they prove their case by increased volunteering. He referred to the law itself apologetically, admitting that "it may not be exactly such as any one man out of Congress, or even in Congress, would have made it." As to its application he compared it to a tax law, which becomes "a dead letter" if no one pays until it becomes certain that all will pay equally, also to congressional apportionment, in which entire equality of population among the districts, required by the Constitution, is impossible in practice. He allowed that "errors will occur" in the draft and argued that the best the government could hope for was "an approach to exactness."

In a somewhat labored passage the President justified the clauses pertaining to substitution and to commutation money. Without the three-hundred-dollar clause he thought that rich men only, being able to pay a thousand dollars or so for a substitute, could escape the draft. In other words, the favoring of the more wealthy was due to substitution, to which, he said, the people did not object. Once substitution

---

[2] For quoted passages, see *ibid.*, 80, 83, 87. In Taney's paper "general government" appears in lower case while the words "State" or "States" are capitalized.

was permitted, the money provision was an advantage to men of moderate means, because it prevented the price of substitutes from going above three hundred dollars. If a man could not pay that much he could not escape, but he could come "as near escaping as . . . if the money provision were not in the law." "The inequality . . . pertains in greater degree to . . . substitution . . . , and is really . . . lessened by the money provision."

Conscription, wrote the President, was not new. It had been "practised in all ages." It was known to the framers who worded the Constitution so as to make it possible. "Shall we shrink," he said, "from the necessary means to maintain our free government, . . . ? Are we degenerate? Has the manhood of our race run out?" Early in the paper he had said with some sarcasm: "We are prone . . . to find false arguments . . . for opposing . . . disagreeable things." In his concluding passage he put his foot down: ". . . I feel bound to tell you it is my purpose to see the draft law faithfully executed." [3]

In this paper one finds Lincoln's rationalization of the draft in essence and his excuses for it in particular. It was an able document, worded and constructed in Lincoln's characteristic style. Why, then, did he never issue it? One can only speculate on the answer. If the President had used his usual publicity technique, the communication would probably have been addressed to some person or group. What person or group? That was something of a poser. There were passages in the document which made it appear that the Executive was exhorting those who were not doing their part. The paper would have been a plea for an unpopular law. It would have been depressing in its admission of the failure of recruiting. Its justification of the money clause, which was repealed in 1864 (less than a year after it was passed), would hardly have made pleasant reading. Some of its phrases, though understandable in the sense intended, were of a sort which the President's opponents might have twisted and used against him.

In any case the chief objection to the existing system, applicable both to substitution and to the commutation feature, was the matching of a money payment against the sacrifice of human life. There was, in this unissued paper, too much attention to what the citizen would have to do to "escape" the draft. Even Lincoln's reasoning would

---

[3] "Opinion on the Draft, never issued or published by the President" (Aug., 1863), *Works*, IX, 74–83.

hardly have convinced those who felt that the system as set up in 1863 did work for the benefit of the rich by putting a price on exemption, and fixing that price well above the ability of the average American laborer to pay. Millions of Americans were getting, for a year's average, less than a dollar a day. To poor men, the sum of $300, supposing it to have been laboriously saved, was a huge amount.

Taking it all in all, it was fortunate that this presidential defense of the conscription law of 1863 was never issued by Lincoln. To justify the concept and constitutional right of compulsory national service was one thing; to plead for the unsatisfactory law of 1863 was quite another. The vulnerability of Lincoln's argument, and the chance of its being misread, were doubtless canvassed in his own mind. The preparing of the paper and the decision not to issue it illustrated two things: Lincoln had the intellectual grasp and ability in debate which enabled him to argue a case well; he also had the restraint to withhold a product of his own thought. His caution in not presenting the paper to the public, thus avoiding a presidential misstep, is an interesting factor in the leadership of a rough-hewn man who seldom erred in his reading of popular sentiment.

For a basis on which to judge the matter one may turn to selective service as framed and administered during the World War. Universal service under Wilson was planned by the war department in advance, not left to Congress after the emergency had arisen. It was promptly enacted at the outset of the war. No stigma attached to the conscript; the whole emphasis was on the honor of national selection. Self-registration was wisely used; volunteer unpaid service by local officials made for economy; there were no bounties nor substitutes, and no provision as to commutation money; industrial deferments were provided. The Supreme Court unanimously upheld the law; opposition was never a widespread menace. In all administrative respects the system under Wilson was far superior to that of Civil War times, and in the total result its effectiveness was shown in the raising of two thirds of the nation's forces. Indeed the selective system was regarded by the war department not only as adequate for raising of all the troops, but as preferable to volunteering.[4]

---

4 "It is not certain . . . that the country . . . understood the imperative necessity of eliminating indiscriminate volunteering. . . To carry selection to its logical . . . end, there could be no deviation from the rule that each registrant must await his

At every essential point the conscription system of Civil War days presents to the historical student an unfavorable contrast to that of the Wilson administration. The law providing compulsory service came not at the outset, but midway in the struggle. Its adoption was a confession of failure; its very premise was the breakdown or inadequacy of volunteering, whereas the law of Wilson's day was based on the considered judgment that governmental selection was the most fitting and effective method of raising a huge army. Under Lincoln there was insufficient planning. Men in Congress, not military experts, wrote the statute. The drafted man was under a stigma; it was a stigma that hurt the pride both of the drafted man and of the community or state from which he came. A costly and elaborate system blanketed the country; enrolling officers laboriously made the lists instead of the men offering themselves for registration. Details of administration were lamentably designed, as shown by the abuses of substitution, bounties, and commutation. The constitutionality of the statute was vigorously assailed under Lincoln without being upheld by the Supreme Court, the Chief Justice, in fact, being under the strong conviction that the law was invalid. Serious disturbances, with hundreds of casualties, were encountered. Finally, when the results were cast up it was seen that about 46,000 conscripts and 118,000 substitutes were dragged into service for an army of about two million.[5]

For these defects Lincoln was not responsible, but an unconscionable amount of his time was occupied with patient adjustments and answers to complaining governors who in some cases seemed more concerned with minor inequalities, some of them imagined, than with the broad needs of the service. When the governor of Vermont complained of an unjust quota, Lincoln mentioned "keeping . . . faith" with New Hampshire, which had furnished a larger surplus and explained that it was "impossible to concede what Vermont asks without coming out short." [6] When Seymour of New York asked a suspension (postponement) of the draft, Lincoln adjusted the matter in terms of reënrollment. On the main matter of his executive duty he wrote to Seymour: "My purpose is to be . . . just and constitutional,

---

time and perform his military obligation only when his call, in orderly process, came to him." *Second Report of the Provost Marshal General* (1918), 6–7.

[5] Randall, *Civil War and Reconstruction*, 411.   [6] *Works*, XI, 6–8 (Feb. 8, 1865).

and yet practical, in performing the important duty with which I am charged, of maintaining the unity and the free principles of our common country." [7]

---

[7] *Ibid.*, IX, 61 (Aug. 7, 1863).

CHAPTER XXVIII

THESE HONORED DEAD

O N an autumn day in '63 Lincoln reached a high moment in
his life as he stood at tragic Gettysburg to deliver a simple
tribute to the nation's dead. If this formerly peaceful Pennsylvania town brings to mind Reynolds, Pickett, Armistead and
Garnett, if it connotes Lee's frustration and Meade's triumph, even
more does it suggest Lincoln's timeless words. By these words Gettysburg becomes more than a scene of carnage, for above the waste and
slaughter rises the challenge of a society founded and maintained in
enduring terms of democracy, order, and sanity. Without Lincoln's
ideal, Bloody Angle and Cemetery Hill produce only a shudder of
horror. In the bewildering excess of monuments at Gettysburg the
one most appealing is the undying flame of aspiration—the perpetual
light that points, albeit from a battlefield, to peace.

I

So famous is this dedicatory vignette and so inexhaustible the popular interest in Lincoln's smallest act that writers have probed every
corner of the episode.[1] In the voluminous literature covering Lincoln's address one finds less appreciation of its larger world significance
than minute inspection of its most trivial detail. What did the President wear? How did his white gauntlets look with otherwise black
attire? Did he ride his horse awkwardly or well? What kind of chair
was provided for the nation's Chief on the platform? Not a chair of

---

[1] For a fresh and competent study see F. Lauriston Bullard, *"A Few Appropriate
Remarks": Lincoln's Gettysburg Address* (1944). Where others have adorned the tale
with excessive verbiage Bullard gives the essential points in compact form; where less
careful writers have been misled he offers an important contribution in strict matters
of historical evidence.

state, according to a contemporary report, but "an old, dingy, uncushioned settee" which he shared with others.[2] What about his gestures? None, we are told, except a sweep of the hand at the words "these honored dead." [3] Did Lincoln smile? Only once, was one man's memory; that was when telling a story to a group that included Curtin and Seward.[4] How many times did he use the word "that" in the address? William E. Barton gives the answer: thirteen times! [5] How did he adjust his spectacles and hold his manuscript, how was his "Kentucky idiom" manifest, how did he pronounce his vowels? We have that too.[6] Were the words "under God" extemporaneously interjected? Competent investigators conclude that they were. When he spoke of government of, by, and for the people, did he stress the *of, by,* and *for,* or did he put the accent on the *people?* Barton would "like to think" [7] that he did the latter. How would the address read if rewritten in the manner of Theodore Roosevelt, or of Woodrow Wilson? Barton is "quite certain" that these men "would have said" so-and-so. Not only the big, solemn things, but the little things are presented to us. We are given the picture of Lincoln holding proofsheets of Everett's address as he sat to Gardner for what has come to be known as the Gettysburg portrait.[8] We are told who were in the President's party, how he was entertained, who were on the platform, who took notes, how the crowd felt (there are variant accounts here), what sources he drew from, what the papers said, what copies were made by Lincoln, and even, in the words of Barton, "what he wished he had said." [9]

There has been much speculation as to where and how Lincoln prepared the address. Did he jot it down while on the railway journey to Gettysburg? It is clear to scholars that this tradition has no foundation, but the story persists. It has gathered further details: a pencil

---

[2] Cincinnati *Daily Gazette,* Nov. 23, 1863.

[3] Interview (May 25, 1929) by the author with W. H. Tipton, lifelong resident of Gettysburg, who heard the address.

[4] *Ibid.*

[5] William E. Barton, *Lincoln at Gettysburg: What He Intended to Say; What He Said; What He Was Reported to Have Said; What He Wished He Had Said,* 147.

[6] As to the Kentucky idiom, see *ibid.,* 92.　　　　　[7] *Ibid.,* 83.

[8] In Barton's frontispiece the Gardner portrait is given with the erroneous statement that it was made in Gettysburg on November 11, 1863. It was made in Washington, as Barton correctly states on p. 54. The source for the Gardner portrait incident is Noah Brooks, *Washington in Lincoln's Time,* 285–286.

[9] Barton, *Lincoln at Gettysburg,* chap. xv.

was borrowed from Andrew Carnegie: the hasty jottings were put down on a yellow or brown envelope (some say a pasteboard), which reposed in the President's tall hat after the manner of his earlier technique as postmaster.[10] To unfounded tradition has been added obvious error; in an article giving "new facts" about the occasion it is stated that while Lincoln was in Gettysburg he received word "that his little son, Willie, who was very ill, had passed the crisis," a statement which overlooks the fact that Willie died in February 1862.[11] One could multiply such samples, but there is no need to go further into the unprofitable realm of Lincoln-at-Gettysburg apocrypha.

The first impulse toward the Gettysburg occasion was the imperative demand of decency and health. Where twenty thousand wounded had shocked Henry W. Bellows of the Sanitary Commission with their "unspeakable" suffering, the battleground presented a "fearful" spectacle.[12] The exposure of horse carcasses and soldiers' bodies,[13] hastily interred and soon uncovered by heavy rains, produced a press-

---

[10] This point has been covered by various writers, including J. G. Nicolay who rode with Lincoln (see *Century Magazine*, XLVII, 601 [1894]). In *Zions Herald*, CXVI, 1351 ff. (1938), F. Lauriston Bullard ably treats the sources of the legend, which he attributes to misstatements by J. G. Holland, Isaac N. Arnold, William O. Stoddard, Ben: Perley Poore, and others; he finds the "evidence . . . conclusive that the President did not prepare the speech on the train, that he did not borrow . . . paper from . . . Seward nor a pencil from Andrew Carnegie (p. 1351)." On other details of the preparation of the address Bullard finds Governor Curtin's recollections "curiously unreliable" (p. 1352). See also Charles Moore, *Lincoln's Gettysburg Address and Second Inaugural*. Moore states (p. 14) that the evidence is "conclusive" against the story that Lincoln wrote the address on the back of an envelope or sheet of brown paper borrowed from Seward.

[11] This is in a newspaper article giving the recollections of W. H. Tipton of Gettysburg, Pittsburgh *Sun-Telegraph*, Feb. 12, 1929, p. 3. It does not appear that Tipton himself made the mistake. The error was a matter of the identity of the "sick boy" mentioned by Lincoln (letter to Everett, Nov. 20, 1863, *Works*, IX, 211). It was Tad who was ill.

[12] H. W. Bellows to his wife, undated (evidently shortly after the battle), Bellows MSS. In referring to twenty thousand wounded, Bellows considerably understated the case. T. L. Livermore (*Numbers and Losses in the Civil War* . . . , 102–103), gives 14,529 as the number of wounded on the Union side, 18,735 on the Confederate side. Freeman (III, 154) gives the aggregate of all casualties in the Gettysburg campaign as 23,371 for the Confederates; 28,129 for the Federals.

[13] "In traversing the battlefield, the feelings were shocked . . . at the sights that presented themselves at every step. The remains of our brave soldiers . . . in many instances were but partially covered with earth, and . . . in some instances were left wholly unburied. Other sights, too shocking to be described, were . . . seen. These appearances presented themselves promiscuously over the fields of arable land . . . which would . . . be farmed over in a short time." *Address of Hon. Edward Everett* . . . [etc.] (Boston, 1864), 8.

ing problem of sanitation, while at the same time the need for a fitting
burial of fallen heroes, together with the motive of state pride, led to
the acquisition by the state of Pennsylvania of a seventeen-acre plot
on Cemetery Hill. Though from the outset the term "national cemetery" was used, the movement was at first a coöperative project of a
number of states with Pennsylvania in the lead. It was not until 1872
that the ground was ceded to the United States government, not till
many years later that the whole battle area became a great national
park.

Arrangements were in the hands of David Wills of Gettysburg, who
acted as Governor Curtin's special agent and later as head of a select
committee for the purpose. For the ceremony of dedication it was intended that the chief honors should be done by a distinguished orator
and a great poet. Edward Everett, orator extraordinary, ex-president
of Harvard, "master of elegance," [14] "Apollo in Politics," [15] full of
days and public honors at seventy, consented to be the speaker of the
day, but a poet was sought in vain. In the absence of a poet laureate,
who might have been expected to grow lyrical by official command,
unsuccessful approaches were made to Bryant, Longfellow, and other
bards of the time.[16] The failure was symbolic. Nobly conceived poetry
was and remained lacking during the Civil War; the verse that did
appear in enormous reams and bushels was unmitigated drivel.[17] A
noteworthy exception, which came just after the war, was Lowell's
ode recited at Harvard College on July 21, 1865, in commemoration
of the sons of Harvard who had given their lives in the war. The
most famous part of the ode, the sixth stanza devoted to Lincoln,

---

[14] Everett was thus characterized by Emerson, who spoke also of his "radiant
beauty of person . . . ; sculptured lips; . . . perfect utterance," and "florid, quaint,
affluent fancy." Paul Revere Frothingham, *Edward Everett: Orator and Statesman,*
63–64. Emerson was a fervent admirer, almost worshiper, of Everett.

[15] *Ibid.,* chap. v.

[16] Benjamin Brown French, commissioner of public buildings at Washington, assisting
in arrangements for the dedication, had sought to obtain an original ode for the occasion by a distinguished poet, and had appealed to Longfellow, Bryant, Whittier, and
George H. Boker. Unsuccessful in these efforts, French himself wrote a dirge or hymn
which was sung "in good style" after Everett's oration by "a delegation from the
Union Musical Association of Baltimore." Charles Moore, *Lincoln's Gettysburg Address and Second Inaugural,* 12; Cincinnati *Daily Gazette,* Nov. 23, 1863.

[17] In the twelve volumes of *The Rebellion Record: A Diary of American Events, with
Documents, Narratives, Illustrative Incidents, Poetry, Etc.,* ed. by Frank Moore, one
may find these forgotten lyrical atrocities embalmed. Their only significance is to
illustrate the low state of the muse when devoted to contemporary war themes.

"was not recited, but was written immediately afterward." [18] Lowell and Whitman were among the very few of Lincoln's time who could do justice to him in verse. As for a grandly conceived major poem on the theme of the war, that did not come until the appearance of Stephen Vincent Benét's *John Brown's Body* in 1928. It was in the same period that Sandburg's great interpretation of Lincoln, lacking none of the magic of poetry, took the form and substance of biography.

A poet and an orator had been the committee's first thought; the invitation to Lincoln came as a secondary matter. Plans were well advanced in August; Everett was invited on September 23; yet Wills's letter of invitation to the President came on November 2. By that time the date of the dedication, November 19, had been fixed to suit Everett, who asked more time for preparation than was at first allowed. It is not recorded that the President's convenience was consulted in setting the date. Lincoln gave ready acceptance; it was an occasion in which he plainly wanted a part.

II

In ancient Athens appropriate public attention was given to obsequies for those who died in battle. Famed Ceramicus held the remains of men who had fallen.[1] With their appreciation of the fine arts, one of which was oratory, Athenians would not be satisfied unless a master of speech was selected to deliver a panegyric; the elaborate care he would take in its preparation was considered comparable in the Greek mind with that of a sculptor. To have a great thing to say required that it be said well; to achieve great expression was to add to the world's indestructible treasure. The arrangements for the dedication at Gettysburg, especially the choice of Everett, a Webster of his day, gave advance notice of the dignity of the event.

The President and his party arrived by slow train from Washington on the evening of Wednesday, November 18, 1863, and the President was the overnight guest in the home of Mr. Wills on the central square or "diamond" of the town. That night Lincoln appeared in response to a serenade and made a few undistinguished remarks, mentioning

---

[18] Horace E. Scudder, *James Russell Lowell: A Biography*, II, 70.

[1] Soldier funerals among the Athenians are described, with details obviously taken from Thucydides, in the early paragraphs of Everett's oration.

that in his position it was important not to "say any foolish things." "If you can help it," said an impertinent voice in the audience!

This was not the only indication that some among the Gettysburg crowds failed to appreciate their President. Addressing a "large and clamorous" group John W. Forney, newspaper publisher and secretary of the Senate, upbraided his serenaders for inadequate cheers to Lincoln. To that "great man," he said, "you owe your name as American citizens." "He went on," according to the diary of John Hay, "blackguarding the crowd for their apathy" and "went back to the eulogy of the President, that great, wonderful mysterious inexplicable man who holds in his single hands the reins of the republic; who keeps his own counsels; who does his own purpose in his own way, no matter what temporizing minister in his Cabinet sets himself up in opposition . . . ." [2]

Throngs filled the town that night; next morning thousands more poured in, many of them traveling in covered wagons of the Conestoga variety. The unfinished work of re-interring the dead by wholesale at $1.59 per body had been temporarily suspended and coffins were much in evidence, while souvenir hunters roamed the battlefield to view the scene of death and pick up a dismal relic—a bullet, button, or fragment of uniform.

Smart young John Hay wrote of the night and the day of the ceremony with sophisticated sarcasm, recording various pranks and drinking parties, and indicating withal a restlessness as to what to do with himself. "[Wayne] MacVeagh," he wrote, "young Stanton, & I foraged around for awhile—walked out to the college, got a chafing dish of oysters then some supper and finally loafing around to the Court House where Lamon was holding a meeting of marshals, we found Forney and went around to his place, Mr. Fahnestock's, and drank a little whiskey with him. He had been drinking a good deal during the day & was getting . . . ugly and dangerous." [3]

Though many of the arrangements had been stupidly handled, the ceremony itself was elaborate and imposing. A procession, marshaled by Ward H. Lamon, moved in what Hay called "an orphanly sort of way" [4] to the cemetery, the homely President riding horseback.

[2] Diary of John Hay, Nov. 20, 1863 (Dennett, *Lincoln* . . . *in the* . . . *Diaries of John Hay*, 121).

[3] *Ibid.*, 119.   [4] *Ibid.*, 121.

The prepared order of procession included high military officers, the President and Cabinet secretaries, judges of the Supreme Court, the "orator of the day" (Everett), governors, commissioners, the Vice President, the Speaker, "bearers with flags of the States," members of Congress, a Gettysburg local committee, officials of the Sanitary Commission, religious committees, the telegraph corps, representatives of the Adams Express Company—and so on through the hospital corps, Knights Templars, and masons, to the press, loyal leagues, fire companies, and citizens of Pennsylvania, "citizens of other States" and of the territories.[5] During the march minute guns were fired which suggested to a reporter the "roar of battle, reverberating from the hills and mountains."[6]

There was a dirge followed by a prayer, the audience standing uncovered. Old Hundred was played by the band, then the "venerable orator" Everett rose and stood a moment in silence, regarding the battlefield and the distant beauty of the South Mountain range.[7] By the standards of that day Everett delivered a great speech, though for an audience unprovided with seats after a restless night and long travel, it was much too long. "Standing beneath this serene sky," the "Alleghenies dimly towering" before him, the orator raised his "poor voice to break the eloquent silence of God and Nature." He reviewed the funeral customs of ancient Athens, referred to Marathon, paid tribute to the dead, discussed the purpose of the war, and gave a closely documented summary of the three-day battle. Avoiding any flings at the common people of the South, he minced no words in denouncing the "foul revolt" as a crime. The heart of the people, North and South, he said, was for the Union. Some of his best phrases were devoted to "bonds that unite us as one people— . . . community of origin, language, belief, and law, . . . common . . . interests; . . . common pride . . . ." Elements of union, he said, were "of perennial . . . energy, . . . causes of alienation . . . imaginary, fictitious, and transient."[8]

Everett had not spared himself. He had avoided "sentimental or patriotic commonplaces."[9] He had delivered a learned and volumi-

5 Cincinnati *Daily Gazette*, Nov. 23, 1863.   6 *Ibid.*   7 *Ibid.*
8 Everett's address is reprinted in Barton, *Lincoln at Gettysburg*, 211 ff.
9 "The occasion is . . . not to be dismissed with a few sentimental or patriotic commonplaces." Everett to David Wills, Boston, Sep. 26, 1863. *Address of Hon. Edward Everett at . . . Gettysburg .,. .* [etc.] (Boston, 1864), 17. Commenting on the signifi-

nous address, had piled it high with historical and classical allusions, had omitted no effort to dignify the occasion. In contrast to all this stateliness and elaboration the impression of Lincoln's simple speech was that of almost shocking brevity. For the immediate occasion—posterity was a different matter—it was as if the highest official of the republic was playing second fiddle. The President's thought and manner were less conditioned by the immediate occasion than by the timeless aspect of his dedicatory duty, that quality being the greater because achieved in spite of tragic realities and official vexations. Mindful that the war was still raging and that armies were massed for doubtful combat in Tennessee, facing the unsightly work of reburial, immersed in hateful details of politics, surrounded in office by those who distrusted him, pressed, buffeted, roundly assailed, yet remembering that he stood in the presence of the dead, Lincoln looked beyond battles, politicians, and hatred to enduring verities. As revised by himself in the form that has become standard,[10] these were his words:

Four score and seven years ago our fathers brought forth on this continent, a new nation, conceived in Liberty, and dedicated to the proposition that all men are created equal.

Now we are engaged in a great civil war, testing whether that nation, or any nation so conceived and so dedicated, can long endure. We are met on a great battle-field of that war. We have come to dedicate a portion of that field, as a final resting place for those who here gave their lives that that nation might live. It is altogether fitting and proper that we should do this.

But, in a larger sense, we can not dedicate—we can not consecrate—we can not hallow—this ground. The brave men, living and dead, who struggled here, have consecrated it, far above our poor power to add or detract. The world will little note, nor long remember what we say here, but it can never forget what they did here. It is for us the living, rather, to be dedicated here to the unfinished work which they who fought here have thus far so nobly advanced. It is rather for us to be here dedicated to the great task remaining before us—that from these honored dead we take

cance of Everett's oration, Paul Revere Frothingham wrote: "Posterity has forgotten . . . that Everett . . . was the first to sound the note of reconciliation and eventual harmony between North and South" (Frothingham, *Everett*, 454). Whether he was "the first" need not be argued; the essential point is the importance which Everett placed on this factor.

[10] The text as here given is that of Lincoln's final and most careful autograph revision, known as the "Bliss copy" made for the Sanitary Fair at Baltimore in 1864, and used in a volume known as "Autograph Leaves of Our Country's Authors."

increased devotion to that cause for which they gave the last full measure of devotion—that we here highly resolve that these dead shall not have died in vain—that this nation, under God, shall have a new birth of freedom—and that government of the people, by the people, for the people, shall not perish from the earth.

III

It is not easy to recover the manner of Lincoln's speaking, nor the reaction of the immediate audience. According to John Russell Young, reporter for the Philadelphia *Press,* the perfection of Everett was "like a bit of Greek sculpture—beautiful, but cold as ice." It was "resonant, clear, splendid rhetoric." In contrast, he said, Lincoln spoke "in his high tenor voice, without the least attempt for effect." "Very few," wrote Young, "heard what Mr. Lincoln said, and it is a curious thing that his remarkable words should have made no particular impression at the time." He added that spectators were more interested in the efforts of a photographer to get a picture of the President while speaking (in which he unfortunately failed) than in the address.[1] Others, however, reported greater appreciation by Lincoln's auditors. The "right thing in the right place, and a perfect thing in every respect," was the description by the Cincinnati *Gazette's* correspondent, who reported long continued applause as the President concluded.[2] Mr. French, who was of the President's party, noted that the address was received with "a tumultuous outpouring of exultation."[3]

Some of the slighting remarks concerning the President's address were similar to the insulting voice at the President's serenade; some of the unawareness was traceable to the fact that humans cannot always be expected to hail a classic at birth. It is not true, however, as often stated, that the speech was unappreciated by contemporaries. On the day after the dedication Everett wrote thanking Lincoln for his kindness to him at Gettysburg, including thoughtfulness for his daughter's accommodation on the platform "and much kindness otherwise." "I should be glad," said Everett, "if I could flatter myself that I came as near to the central idea of the occasion in two hours as you

---

[1] John Russell Young, in *Frank Leslie's Illustrated Newspaper,* April 10, 1886, 119.
[2] Cincinnati *Daily Gazette,* Nov. 23, 1863.
[3] Diary of Benjamin B. French, MS., Lib. of Cong., quoted in Charles Moore, *Lincoln's Gettysburg Address and Second Inaugural,* 22.

did in two minutes." [4] Lincoln replied: "In our respective parts yesterday, you could not have been excused to make a short address, nor I a long one. . . . The point made against the theory of the general government being only an agency, whose principals are the States. . . . is one of the best arguments for the national supremacy." [5]

With equal promptness Longfellow pronounced the speech "admirable." This also was on the day after its delivery, while on the second morning "the *Springfield Republican* declared it 'a perfect gem' and that evening the *Providence Journal* described it as 'beautiful . . . touching . . . inspiring . . . thrilling.' " [6]

Column writers were few in those days, but a near approach to later columnists was George William Curtis, whose little essays on the world in general appeared in *Harper's Weekly* as the comments of "The Lounger." It is of interest to note what Curtis said of Lincoln at Gettysburg. "The few words of the President," he wrote, "were from the heart to the heart. They can not be read . . . without kindling emotion. . . . It was as simple and felicitous and earnest a word as was ever spoken." [7]

In Lincoln's own day the address became famous; this is shown by the demand for its text in Lincoln's hand. It is to this demand that we owe the President's careful attention to the final form of the address, which he rewrote several times and which has therefore come down to posterity as Lincoln wished it. This is not to imply that Lincoln changed his speech substantially, nor that he had failed to give careful thought to the text before delivery. For such an address to have been hastily prepared, or for the President to have trusted to the moment, would have been altogether contrary to Lincoln's habit. There were

---

[4] Nicolay and Hay, *Lincoln*, VIII, 203. In a letter to Mrs. Hamilton Fish, Mar. 18, 1864, Everett referred to "President Lincoln's singularly appropriate & much admired dedicatory remarks." Everett MSS.

[5] *Ibid.* Everett had argued that the authority established under the Constitution was the "Government of the United States" established by "the People of the United States." Noting that state officers were required to take oath to support the national government, he added: ". . . I never heard . . . of sovereigns being bound by oath to be faithful to their agency." Barton, *Lincoln at Gettysburg*, 241.

[6] F. Lauriston Bullard, in *Zions Herald*, Nov. 16, 1938, 1353.

[7] "The Lounger," *Harper's Weekly*, Dec. 5, 1863. George William Curtis was the "Lounger" (Frank L. Mott, *A History of American Magazines: 1850–1865*, II, 474). In 1859 he wrote: "I make my Lounger a sort of lay pulpit . . . ." (Edward Cary, *George William Curtis*, 120.) Curtis was also the "Easy Chair" of *Harper's Magazine;* as such he has been called the "American Addison" (William M. Payne, *Leading American Essayists*, 351).

times when the President appeared in response to crowds and frankly did not try to make a speech. His remarks on such occasions were conversational and intentionally casual, but no public man was more cautious of the public word, written or spoken, than Lincoln. He had more than two weeks in which to prepare for Gettysburg, and the well known correspondent Noah Brooks states that some days before the dedication Lincoln told him in Washington that the speech was short, and that it was "written, 'but not finished.'" [8]

That the President prepared the address carefully may be regarded as certain, and from a study of the evidence, including five autograph copies in Lincoln's hand which have survived to our own day, it is possible to reconstruct the development of the address as it evolved in successive versions. What is known as the "first draft," on official stationery of the Executive Mansion, is accepted as having been written (at least the first page of it) in Washington. The second page, consisting of ten lines, together with a substitution for words deleted on the first page, were written in pencil. In the two drafts that preceded the occasion one can see the turning of the literary lathe, the search for the effective phrase. Instead of the words "It is rather for us, the living, to stand here," the words " . . . to be dedicated here" were substituted. While in the Wills house on the morning of the day of dedication, Nicolay being with him,[9] the President probably worked over his first draft, then made the "second draft" which has survived in his handwriting, and which "is almost certainly that which Lincoln held in his hand when he delivered the Address." [10] It is a slight revision of the first draft.

The third stage in the evolution of the text of the address came a few days after the President's return from Gettysburg when he responded to a request from Mr. Wills, who desired the original manuscript for an official report of the proceedings which he was preparing. The President, as reported by Nicolay, directed his secre-

---

[8] Noah Brooks, *Washington in Lincoln's Time*, 286.

[9] Though he was with Lincoln in the Wills house on the morning of November 19, Nicolay seems to have been unaware that the President wrote the second draft on this occasion: the private secretary assumed that the President was merely doing over the latter part of the first draft. Nicolay's account appears in *Century Magazine*, XLVII, 596–608 (1894), esp. pp. 596, 601, but see Charles Moore, 16.

[10] Typed label accompanying the second draft of the Gettysburg address, MS., Lib. of Cong. (The Library of Congress has the originals of both the first and second drafts, being the gifts of the children of John Hay, 1916.)

taries to make copies of the Associated Press report; using this together with his original draft and his recollection "of the form in which he delivered it," Lincoln made "a careful and deliberate revision." [11] Just what form this revision took is a bit uncertain. Nicolay refers to it as "a new autograph copy," [12] but no such copy has survived and it is more likely that what Wills received was a version made under the President's supervision, [13] with secretarial help, while the President was sick. Though the original of this Wills copy has not survived, it is worth noting that as printed [14] it includes the words "under God" in the passage: "this nation, under God, shall have a new birth of freedom." The speech as prepared had not included these words, but the newspaper reports as well as all of Lincoln's later revisions, contain them; they were added by Lincoln as he spoke.

At the time of the address it was, of course, reprinted in the newspapers. Those papers that used the Associated Press report had an imperfect version; the report that is accepted as perhaps the nearest to an actual recording of the words which Lincoln uttered is that published on Friday morning, November 20, 1863, in the Boston *Daily Advertiser*. This version is reproduced herewith as an illustration, and the reader may be interested in its minor differences from the standard text as printed above.

Leaving aside the newspaper reports and returning to the evolution of the oration in successive versions, we may note that a third autograph copy by Lincoln was made at the request of Edward Everett, who "presented it, together with the manuscript of his own address, . . . to Mrs. Hamilton Fisn, . . . president of the . . . committee of . . . ladies having charge at the fair in aid of the sanitary commission . . . in New York in March, 1864, to be disposed of for the benefit of our soldiers . . . ." [15] It was bought by an uncle of Senator Henry W. Keyes of New Hampshire and remained for many years a possession of the Keyes family. In 1944 this Everett-Keyes copy, having been purchased from a private owner by hundreds of thousands of

---

11 Nicolay, as above cited in *Century Magazine*, 604–605.   12 *Ibid.*

13 Barton, *Lincoln at Gettysburg*, 103–104. Barton is of the opinion that Wills never owned an autograph of the address. See also William H. Lambert, in *Pa. Mag. of Hist. and Biog.*, XXXIII, 401 (1909).

14 It appeared in the official Gettysburg volume published by the state of Pennsylvania in 1863. Barton, *Lincoln at Gettysburg*, 104–105.

15 *Sen. Doc. No. 236*, 66 Cong., 2 sess. (1920).

small contributions from Illinois school children, was presented to the State of Illinois. Its place of deposit is the Illinois State Historical Library at Springfield.

A fourth autograph version was made by Lincoln at the request of George Bancroft. It was intended for sale at the Sanitary Fair at Baltimore in 1864, and for reproduction in a volume known as *Autograph Leaves of the Country's Authors.* Since it proved unavailable for this purpose by reason of being written on both sides of the paper, Bancroft was allowed to keep it, and Lincoln made yet another autograph, known as the "Bliss copy." This final version was done by Lincoln "with great care"; it was used both at the Baltimore Fair and in *Autograph Leaves,* edited by Colonel Alexander Bliss. Because it is in all probability the last copy written by Lincoln, and because of the obvious care devoted to it, it has become the standard form of the address.

In recapitulation, it may be noted that Lincoln made five autograph copies of his famous address which have come down to us: (1) the first draft, written probably in Washington, and perhaps partly revised at Gettysburg; (2) the second draft, written probably in the Wills house at Gettysburg and held by the President as he spoke; (3) the Everett-Keyes-Illinois copy, made at Everett's request and sold at the Sanitary Fair in New York in 1864; (4) the Bancroft copy, meant for the Baltimore Fair, but not used for that purpose; (5) the standard and definitive "Bliss copy," written carefully by Lincoln in 1864, sold at the Baltimore Fair, and reproduced in *Autograph Leaves of Our Country's Authors.* In addition, Lincoln directed and supervised the making of the version sent to Wills soon after the occasion, which was prepared with secretarial help and was probably not in the President's handwriting.

IV

In the Declaration of Independence Jefferson's authorship was no less important because he used concepts and phrases which were part of the currency of political thought. Similarly, it takes nothing from Lincoln's fame to find previous utterances which invite comparison with the famous reference to "government of the people, by the people, for the people." In a work published in London in 1794,

Thomas Cooper, formerly of Manchester, in advising Englishmen to come to America, wrote: "The [American] government is the government *of* the people, and *for* the people." [1] In 1798 Virginians of Westmoreland County sent an address to President Adams concerning the trouble with France, in which the following sentence occurred: "The Declaration that our People are hostile to a Government made by themselves, for themselves and conducted by themselves is an Insult . . . ." [2] Similar statements were made by Webster [3] and Marshall, [4] while Lamartine, paraphrasing Robespierre, wrote of a representative sovereignty "concentrated in an election as extensive as the people themselves, and acting by the people, and for the people . . . ." [5] Bibliographical search has also unearthed expressions of a like character by James Douglas in Edinburgh in 1830 [6] and by Matthew Fontaine Maury in a government report in 1851. [7] The most famous instance, however, and the one most often linked with Lincoln's phrase, is that of Theodore Parker, abolitionist preacher, who in 1850 used these words: "This [American] idea, demands . . . a democracy, that is, a government of all the people, by all the people, for all the people . . . ." [8]

---

[1] *Some Information respecting America, collected by Thomas Cooper, late of Manchester* (London, 1794), 53.

[2] In reply President Adams wrote: "The declaration that our People are hostile to a Government, made by themselves, for themselves, and conducted by themselves, if it were true, would be a demonstration that the people despise and hate themselves . . . ." *Proceedings of the American Antiquarian Society*, IX, 323, 326 (1894).

[3] "It is, Sir, the people's Constitution, the people's government, made for the people, made by the people, and answerable to the people." Webster's second reply to Hayne, Jan. 26, 1830, *Works of Daniel Webster* (Boston, 1851), III, 321.

[4] "The government of the Union . . . is . . . a government of the people. . . . Its powers are granted by them, and are to be exercised directly on them, and for their benefit." Chief Justice Marshall, in McCulloch *vs.* Maryland, 4 Wheaton 404–405.

[5] Lamartine, Alphonse de, *History of the Girondists* (Bohn ed., London, 1850), III, 104.

[6] Douglas referred to "a government where all power is from the people, and in the people, and for the people." James Douglas, *The Advancement of Society in Knowledge and Religion* (Edinburgh, 1830), 3rd. ed., 70. Quoted in *Century*, XLVII, 607 (1894).

[7] "Unlike Europe, . . . there are no disaffected people in this country for a foe to tamper with. The Government is by the people, for the people, and with the people. It is the people." M. F. Maury, in report on fortifications, *House Exec. Doc. No. 5*, 32 Cong., 1 sess., p. 190 (1851).

[8] Theodore Parker, *Speeches, Addresses, and Occasional Sermons* (Boston, 1852), II, 176. For the general subject of utterances parallel to Lincoln's, see J. G. Nicolay, in *Century Magazine*, XLVII, 606–608 (1894); Samuel A. Green, in *Proceedings*, Mass. Hist. Soc., 2 ser., XV, 92–94 (1901). The matter is treated also in Henry Steele Commager, *Theodore Parker*.

To point out that Lincoln had read Webster and Marshall is superfluous, nor is there much doubt that he was familiar with the saying of Parker, who had been a correspondent of William H. Herndon. That he consciously copied from any of these is less evident. As to the more obscure passages, they belong in the voluminous category of literary coincidence, dealing as they do with a concept whose universality among democratic minds constituted its main significance. Like Jefferson, Lincoln had the knack of taking an idea that was part of the heritage of the race and immortalizing it by pithy and unforgettable utterance. In the array of quotations here presented, it will be noted that the similarity of Lincoln's words to those of predecessors, while close, is not complete.[9] Whatever his sources, it was Lincoln who gave the phrase its setting, its precise form, and its dominant place in American tradition.

V

More noteworthy than literary parallels is the significance of the Gettysburg address as a tying together of Lincoln's fundamental concepts touching the basic theme of the American experiment. If one seeks passages for comparison, they are best to be found in Lincoln's own writings.

In the emotional release that had come with victory after so much delay, the President, on July 7, 1863, responded to a serenade at the Executive Mansion. Already Gettysburg to him meant dominant values: human liberty, democracy, aims of the Fathers, the Declaration, the cause of free government in the world. Frankly the President did not attempt a speech—he was always wary of impromptu utterance—yet in his casual remarks one can find the germ of the Gettysburg address that was to follow in November. The nation's birth "eighty-odd years since" was the point of departure. At one end of Lincoln's thought was Philadelphia in 1776; at the other, Gettysburg in 1863. From this it was a natural development to note the elemental importance of a nation founded on the "self-evident truth" of human equality, "the first time in the history of the world" that a nation had so founded itself by its own representatives. Coming to the present year and month, the President noted in victories just achieved "a

---

[9] Samuel A. Green, (see preceding note), 92.

glorious theme, and the occasion for a speech" which he was "not prepared" to make in a manner "worthy of the occasion." He briefly paid tribute to all who had "fought in the cause of the Union and liberties of their country"; then, mentioning no names lest he might wrong those unmentioned, he made his bow and called for music.[1] It was but a brief appearance before a celebrating crowd, yet the theme, and the clear call for a speech worthy of the theme, were not forgotten.

In his first inaugural Lincoln had expressed his central idea as to what the country was about in maintaining the republic against internal disruption. "A majority held in restraint by constitutional checks . . . and . . . changing easily with deliberate changes of popular opinions," he had said, "is the only true sovereign of a free people. Whoever rejects it does, of necessity, fly to anarchy or to despotism."[2] In the same address he had asked: "Why should there not be a patient confidence in the ultimate justice of the people? Is there any better or equal hope in the world?"[3] In his annual message to Congress of December 1, 1862, he spoke again of America's larger responsibility. Hoping his nation would choose the course which "the world will forever applaud," he warned: "We shall nobly save or meanly lose the last, best hope of earth."[4]

Shortly after the opening of the war Lincoln had said to Hay: "For my part, I consider [that] the central idea pervading this struggle is the necessity that is upon us, of proving that popular government is not an absurdity. We must settle this question now, whether in a free government the minority have the right to break up the government whenever they choose. If we fail it will go far to prove the incapability of the people to govern themselves."[5] When thus thinking aloud to his young secretary the President had been much occupied with composing his message to the special session of Congress of July 4, 1861, in which the following significant words, so like the theme of Gettysburg were used:

And this issue embraces more than the fate of these United States. It presents to the whole family of man the question whether a constitutional

---

[1] Response to a serenade, July 7, 1863, *Works*, IX, 20–21.

[2] *Works*, VI, 179.   [3] *Ibid.*, VI, 183.   [4] *Ibid.*, VIII, 131.

[5] Diary of John Hay, May 7, 1861, Dennett. *Lincoln . . . in the Diaries . . . of John Hay*, 19–20.

republic or democracy—a government of the people by the same people—can or cannot maintain its . . . integrity against its domestic foes. It presents the question whether discontented individuals . . . can . . . break up their government, and thus practically put an end to free government upon the earth. It forces us to ask: "Is there, in all republics, this inherent and fatal weakness?" "Must a government, of necessity, be too strong for the liberties of its . . . people, or too weak to maintain its own existence?"

. . . .

This is essentially a people's contest. On the side of the Union it is a struggle for maintaining in the world that form and substance of government whose leading object is to elevate the condition of men—to lift artificial weights from all shoulders; to clear the paths of laudable pursuit for all; to afford all an unfettered start, and a fair chance in the race of life.

. . . .

Our popular government has often been called an experiment. Two points in it our people have already settled—the successful establishing and the successful administering of it. One still remains—its successful maintenance against a formidable internal attempt to overthrow it. It is now for them to demonstrate to the world that . . . ballots are the rightful and peaceful successors of bullets . . . . Such will be a great lesson of peace: teaching men that what they cannot take by an election, neither can they take it by a war; teaching all the folly of being the beginners of a war.[6]

Where words were so simple it took something of genius to make them so meaningful. As Everett himself generously recognized, Lincoln said more in two minutes than the orator of the day in as many hours. Rarely indeed is Everett quoted for his own sake. Had Lincoln not participated, Everett's stately periods would have gone into oblivion, while Lincoln's phrases are the stuff of literature. Innocent of the cant of the patrioteer, they nevertheless touched the chord of elemental loyalty. It is for such utterance, and for the man he was, that Lincoln has become synonymous with fundamental Americanism.

Both in form and substance the address at Gettysburg was completely Lincolnian. Oratorically it had those elements that made Lincoln at his best a master of words. Fitness to the situation was the first element; the occasion made the speech. This was true, however,

---

[6] For quoted portions, see *Works*, VI, 304, 321, 322.

not in terms of exigent pressures or superficial demands of the moment, but rather with regard to the occasion as viewed in perspective. The second element, also typically Lincolnian, was a matter of the choice of words: thoughts that touched heights of exalted feeling were conveyed in language at once unpretentious and stirringly effective. Utter simplicity and restraint were somehow suffused with inspired dignity. It is as significant to note what was omitted as what was included in a speech whose brevity made every syllable valuable. There was not a breath of hatred, not a hint of vindictiveness, not a trace of vengeful judgment. Sensing the greater opportunity of the hour, Lincoln used the Gettysburg occasion for two purposes: in unforgettable phrases he paid tribute to those who had fallen; not failing in that, he coupled the deepest and most dominant sentiments of his people with the political idea that was central in his own mind: the wider world significance of democracy's testing, the enduring importance of success in the American democratic experiment as proving that government by the people is no failure. Standing at a cemetery, which men of classical turn were lugubriously calling a "necropolis," he did not confine his thoughts to the dead. Rather he showed that it is only by constructive deeds of living men that the sacrifice of the dead can have value.

SIFTING THE ANN RUTLEDGE
EVIDENCE

This appendix includes an account of how the Lincoln-
Rutledge story arose, an evaluation of the evidence, citations to
guide the questioning student, and, especially, emphasis upon
the need for historical criticism in dealing with a theme which has
been almost usurped by fiction writers.

FROM the Lincolns in Springfield and Washington to Ann
Rutledge is something of a digression. If one is treating only
the things whose reality and significance for Lincoln are matters of solid proof, the too familiar story of Lincoln and Ann may
be omitted altogether. To present the subject as one of the earlier
chapters in a book on *Lincoln the President* would seem inappropri-
ate. It would be out of key with the main emphasis. Yet popular
writing has created a stock picture, and the true state of the evidence
requires attention. For this reason the subject is included (in the
subordinate status of an appendix), not for any intrinsic importance
at all, but because historical criticism finds here a challenge and a
needful task.

From uncertain and conflicting memories of a courtship in picturesque New Salem the story has amazingly grown until the romantic linking of Abraham and Ann has become universal. In drama
it has usurped the spotlight. Perhaps the majority of those who think
of Lincoln not only believe that Ann Rutledge was the only woman
he ever loved; they go on from there to the fictional assumption that
an unambitious and lazy lad became a student of law and a man of
note only because of Ann, that her death left him crushed in spirit,
that her memory remained his inspiration through life, that his
tenderest emotions were always thereafter in retrospect, and that real
love for the woman he married was non-existent.

I

For the historian the problem is that of tracing the account to its sources, finding the evidence, noting how far the testimony holds together, and rejecting those elements that are but the froth and chaff of unchecked imagination. One may trace the popularizing—indeed the exaggerated exploitation—of the tradition to Herndon; it was he who gave it wide publicity, filled in the gaps, added his irrepressible contribution of psychoanalysis, and set the pattern which has become familiar to millions. Back of Herndon, to be sure, there were vague memories reaching to far-off New Salem days which in some manner tended to connect the name of Lincoln with that of Ann Rutledge.

An early mention of the story in print—a very obscure mention—was in an article written by John Hill and published in the *Menard Axis* of Petersburg, Illinois, February 15, 1862. Under the title "A Romance of Reality" the author, son of Sam Hill of New Salem, strung out an unflattering account of an awkward youth, a store clerk, a soldier who reached the field of action after the war was over, keeper of a stallion, day laborer, infidel writer, surveyor, hog drover, and love-sick swain. The reader was then informed that this was. none other than Abraham Lincoln, President of the United States. On the theme of the love-sick swain there was a passage telling how this youth had met an angelic lady, could think of naught but her, found his feeling reciprocated, and awaited the day when the twain would be one flesh. The lovely beauty died; melancholy fell upon the lad; friends noted his strange conduct; they kept him under guard to prevent suicide. That, in summary, was the story. Ann's name was not mentioned, but the identity was plain enough. This obscure mention of the matter was long buried, though contained in the Herndon collection; only recently has it been brought to light.[1]

Hill was not the best witness of New Salem days, he was addressing an anti-Lincoln audience, he was riding a theme, his memories were indirect (through his father), his account was pubished long after the supposed event, and there were flaws in his narrative.[2] His passage

---

[1] Jay Monaghan, "New Light on the Lincoln-Rutledge Romance," *Abr. Lincoln Quart.*, III, 138–145 (Sep. 1944).

[2] Hill was opposed to Lincoln in 1862 and his account is strangely belittling. He disparages Lincoln's service in the Black Hawk War, emphasizes his uncouthness and

has been summarized above because in the literature of the subject it has a certain priority in that it is pre-Herndonian.

From November 16, 1866, however, the subject was peculiarly Herndon's. On that date he delivered in Springfield a lengthy, lush, and sentimental lecture under the title "Abraham Lincoln. Miss Ann Rutledge. New Salem. Pioneering and *the* Poem." With fruity periods and lavishly bestowed adjectives he told the world that "Abraham Lincoln loved Miss Ann Rutledge with all his soul, mind and strength," that she "loved him as dearly," that they "seemed made in heaven for each other," that Ann was "honestly engaged" to two men at the same time, that she sickened under the conflict of emotion and duty and died, that Lincoln's heart was buried with her, that reason left him, that he was racked in heart and body, that he lost his logical faculty, speaking incoherently and wildly (Herndon supplied Lincoln's imagined words at great length), that he rose up a man once more after visiting "Bolin" Green, that from then he was radically changed (for the better), but that he committed the poem "Immortality" to memory and was ever thereafter influenced by the solemn contemplation of these deep thoughts.[3]

Paul M. Angle published an excellent study of this subject in 1927, but did not use the Herndon manuscripts, which were not then available to the historical profession. Concerning the familiar romance Angle concluded that "it is entirely traditional." He added: "No reliable contemporary record has ever been discovered. Instead, there are numerous reminiscences, put in writing at the request of Hern-

---

failure, makes him appear utterly unimportant, and gives an unfavorable twist to the lad's service in the little store by mentioning that an "opposition liquor shop" attracted the custom. In writing to Herndon several years after the article appeared, Hill admitted his error as to the stallion, and confessed that at the time of Lincoln's youth he "knew no more as to who he was than . . . of the inhabitants of the Fegee Islands." He mentioned James Short as one who could give more information than "any or all the men in the county"; it was Short who reported that he knew of no engagement or tender passages between Lincoln and Ann during the latter's life. For Short's statement see below, p. 330; John Hill's letters are in the Herndon-Weik MSS., June 6 and June 27, 1865.

[3] Brief summary of the last two columns of Herndon's lecture. It was given at Springfield on Friday, November 16, 1866, and was privately printed as a broadside on a large sheet, newspaper style. The original broadside is rare; the author has used a copy in the Illinois State Historical Library. The lecture was published in book form by H. E. Barker (Springfield, 1910). As for the poem, Herndon associated Lincoln's fondness for the lines "Oh, Why Should the Spirit of Mortal Be Proud?" with the tragedy of Ann Rutledge.

don, who, once given the lead, followed it tirelessly." [4]

This fits the case. Herndon did have something of a "lead" in none too reliable recollections. A careful study of the Herndon manuscripts reveals what those recollections were and confirms Angle's conclusion that all the material was non-contemporary—i. e., none of it belonged in or near the eighteen-thirties. In his lecture, Herndon invites all who doubt his story to come to his office and look over his records; now after nearly eight decades the author is happy to accept the invitation for this inspection.

As Herndon's papers reveal, old settlers, or in some cases their children, told of a friend of Lincoln's, a beautiful girl named Ann Rutledge, who had been engaged to one John McNamar and had died. Her lover was using the name McNeil; while building his fortunes in the West he did not want to be traced by his family. He had left New Salem, spending some years with his people in New York (sometimes misstated as Ohio); he had returned shortly after Ann's death. There was the tradition that Lincoln was greatly saddened by the girl's death; this, and the engagement to McNamar, are the factors that stand out most clearly in the mosaic of New Salem reminiscence.

The subject appealed to all the sentimentalizing and psychoanalyzing impulses of Herndon's nature.[5] He talked to survivors of those days or if he could not reach them he had them interviewed by proxy or got their statements by correspondence. He labored with an assiduity that gave importance to his very questions. The resulting mass of confused and contradictory evidence, found in his voluminous manuscripts, serves as the chief basis for the famous tradition so far as it had basis; the lecture and Herndon biography added the glowing details.

The vagueness of reminiscence given after many years is familiar to all careful historical students: if, in the haste of general reading, this matter is disregarded, the essence of the subject is overlooked.

---

[4] Paul M. Angle, "Lincoln's First Love?" *Bulletin No. 9*, Lincoln Centennial Assoc., Dec. 1, 1927, p. 5.

[5] "I being somewhat of a psychologist . . . ." Herndon to Ward H. Lamon, Springfield, Mar. 6, 1870, MS., Huntington Lib. It is impossible to evaluate Herndon without keeping in mind the vagaries of his amateur psychoanalysis. It amounted to an obsession. He even thought of himself as a kind of mind reader. He wrote: "You know my love of reading men—mind—moods—characteristics &c. . . . I love the science of the mind quite over all studies . . . ." Herndon to Weik, Feb. 21, 1891, Herndon-Weik MSS.

Huge tomes could be written to show the doubtfulness of long-delayed memories. Out of thousands of examples that could be cited, one may take the admitted case of Salmon P. Chase; it is exactly pertinent to the kind of problem we are handling. Chase had supplied from memory certain biographical details to J. T. Trowbridge, who in 1864 published a life of the Ohio statesman entitled *The Ferry Boy and the Financier.* After the book appeared Chase wrote to Trowbridge: "You have . . . thrown a great deal of attraction about . . . dry facts. Indeed, from information or fancy, you have collected some facts which are quite out of my recollection." Again he wrote: "It is strange to me how dim every thing is in that distant time. I see just one little part of things—glimpses of transactions—the (reality-totality?) hid behind clouds with little fissures revealing a part of an affair or person, and that little with mist clinging round and obscuring it. I dare not vouch for the entire authenticity even of what I seem to remember best." [6]

The historian must use reminiscence, but he must do so critically. Even close-up evidence is fallible. When it comes through the mists of many years some of it may be true, but a careful writer will check it with known facts. Contradictory reminiscences leave doubt as to what is to be believed; unsupported memories are in themselves insufficient as proof; statements induced under suggestion, or psychological stimulus, as were some of the stories about Lincoln and Ann, call especially for careful appraisal. If reminiscences are gathered, but only part of them used, that again is a problem. It is not so much a matter of taking Chase, a cultured man who confessed fallibility as to past events, and arguing that simple country people ought to be trusted even less; it is rather that proneness to uncertain recollection is a common human trait. The matter is brought to notice here because readers often overlook it, not being always aware of the basis for statements as to past incidents, while it is the very essence of historical study to find, sift, question, and evaluate sources of information. When faulty memories are admitted the resulting product becomes something other than history; it is no longer to be presented as a genuine record.

---

[6] Robert B. Warden, *Private Life and Public Services of Salmon Portland Chase,* 589, 56.

II

Looking into what Herndon collected, we find varying responses to his inquiries; the whole constituted a product he could not well digest. A Miss Berry and a Miss Short were mentioned mistakenly and a Miss Owens quite definitely as objects of Lincoln's attentions during Ann's lifetime.[1] Samuel Hill and William Berry were added to the list of Ann's suitors.[2] As above noted, it was generally agreed that the girl was betrothed to McNamar, and that Lincoln was plunged into gloom after her death. Mentor Graham, New Salem schoolmaster, briefly supported the tradition of the Lincoln-Rutledge engagement. In an interview with Herndon he is reported to have said: "Lincoln and she was engaged—Lincoln told me so—she intimated to me the same: He Lincoln told me that he felt like committing suicide often, but I told him God higher purpose . . . [etc.]." [3] These words were scribbled by Herndon; over his own signature Graham referred even more briefly to a "momentary derangement" in Lincoln caused in part by "the death of one whom he dearly and sincerely love[d]." [4]

Mrs. Lizzie Bell, daughter of Mentor Graham, furnished none too reliable glimpses of a quilting party where Ann kept her eye on Mr. Hill, while Lincoln flirted with another girl, with the result that "Lincoln & Ann had a fly up, but on her death bed she sent for Lincoln & all things were reconciled." Incidentally, Herndon's note on the page containing this reminiscence described both Mentor Graham and his daughter as "cranky—flighty—at times nearly non copus mentis—but good & honest." [5] In evaluating their contributions one should remember this comment. One should also remember that, by Mrs. Bell's own statement, she was a child at the time and did not know these things of her own knowledge.[6]

Though one does not wish to bear down too severely upon the schoolmaster, whose educational influence on Lincoln has probably

---

[1] G. U. Miles to Herndon, Mar. 23, 1866, Herndon-Weik MSS. (Concerning Miss Owens, see below, pp. 336–337.)

[2] R. B. Rutledge to Herndon, Nov. 21, 1866, *ibid.*

[3] Herndon's memo. of statement by Mentor Graham, Apr. 2, 1866, *ibid.*

[4] Mentor Graham to Herndon, May 29, 1865, *ibid.*

[5] Herndon's memo. of statement by Lizzie Bell, undated, *ibid.*   [6] *Ibid.*

been exaggerated,[7] one should note the following statement written by Graham to Herndon in 1865: ". . . I saw him [Lincoln] frequently when a lad about 12 years of age though was not personally acquainted with him this was at his residence at his place of birth in the winter of 1819 & 20 I went to school in the County of Hardin Ky . . . , during my attendance . . . I often past by old Mr. Lincoln's house & often saw his son Abraham out about the premises . . . ."[8] In this, of course, Graham was badly mistaken as to what he claimed to have remembered. The Lincolns moved from the birthplace location when Abraham was two years old (1811); they left Kentucky for Indiana when he was seven (1816). That the schoolmaster was at fault or confused (at least as to dates) in this case does not necessarily overthrow his New Salem recollections; but, taken in connection with Herndon's comment made in the period when he was interviewing Graham and his daughter, they do suggest the need for wholesome doubt. At any rate Graham's contributions on the Lincoln-Rutledge romance were meager, especially so in what he himself wrote. His account was more concerned with Lincoln's life in the New Salem period and with his own function in teaching the future President.

One of Herndon's principal witnesses—a lengthier one than Graham—was R. B. Rutledge, Ann's younger brother who was seventeen the year she died. After recounting Ann's engagement to John McNamar and the latter's long absence, Rutledge (in a statement attested by John Jones) declared:

In the mean time Mr Lincoln paid his addresses to Ann, . . . and those resulted in an engagement to marry, conditional to an honorable release from the contract with McNamar. There is no kind of doubt as to the existence of this engagement. David Rutledge [a brother long since dead] urged Ann to consummate it, but she refused until such time as she could see McNamar—inform him of the change in her feelings, and seek an honorable release. Mr Lincoln lived in the village, McNamar did not return and in August 1835 Ann sickened and died. The effect upon Mr Lincoln's mind was terrible; he became plunged in despair, and many of

---

[7] Kunigunde Duncan and D. F. Nickols, *Mentor Graham, The Man Who Taught Lincoln*. This book, rich in flavor and atmosphere, has been characterized as "neither sound biography nor reliable history" (*Abr. Lincoln Quart.*, III, 211). Graham's own considerable claims as to having taught Lincoln grammar and surveying are seen in his letter to Herndon, May 29, 1865, Herndon-Weik MSS.

[8] Mentor Graham to Herndon, July 15, 1865, Herndon-Weik MSS.

his friends feared that reason would desert her throne. His extraordinary emotions were regarded as strong evidence of the existence of the tenderest relations between himself and the deceased.[9]

At another time Rutledge wrote:

. . . the facts are Wm Berry first courted Ann and was rejected, after-wards Saml Hill, then John McNamar, which resulted in an engagement to marry at some future time, he McNamar left the Country on business, was gaun some years, in the meantime and during McNamars absence, Mr Lincoln Courted Ann and engaged to marry her, on the completion of the sudy of law. In this I am caroborated by James Mc [McGrady] Rutledge a cousin about her age & who was in her confidence, he say in a letter to me just received, "Ann told me once in coming from a Camp Meeting on Rock creek, that engagements made too far a hed sometimes failed, that one had failed, (meaning her engagement with McNamar) and gave me to understand, that as soon as certain studies were completed she and Lincoln would be married. . . . "[10]

Here is one person reporting what another person had written him concerning what that person recollected he had inferred from some-thing that Ann had casually said to him more than thirty-one years before! Anxious though he was to please, Rutledge could not accept Herndon's emphasis upon Ann's pining away because of conflicting emotions in her maiden heart. He courteously but firmly disagreed and reminded Herndon that Ann died of brain fever.[11]

There are inconsistencies and contradictions in Rutledge's asser-tions, and in reading his labored statements one can sympathetically understand his difficulty in reconstructing a picture of what happened. A writer of today ought not to put a higher value on his recollections than he himself did. He confessed uncertainty on points of Herndon's questioning and spoke of comparing notes with others.[12] In part this

[9] R. B. Rutledge to Herndon (in neat clerklike handwriting, not Rutledge's), attested by John Jones, Wintersett, Iowa, Oct. 22, 1866, *ibid.* This same Jones refers to him-self as an "eye-witness to the events" and adds: "As to the relation . . . between Mr Lincoln and Ann Rutledge, I have every reason to believe that it was of the tenderest character, as I know of my own knowledge that he made regular visits to her. . . . It was generally understood that Mr Lincoln and Ann Rutledge were en-gaged to be married." (Though an "eye-witness," Jones was qualifying his statements by such phrases as "I have every reason to believe," and "It was generally understood." Other testimony shows that it was by no means generally understood.)

[10] R. B. Rutledge (own handwriting) to Herndon, Nov. 21, 1866, Herndon-Weik MSS.

[11] R. B. Rutledge to Herndon, Nov. 18, 1866, *ibid.* What the pioneers called brain fever has been identified as typhoid.

[12] R. B. Rutledge to "Herendon," Burlington, Ia., Oct. 30, 1866, *ibid.*

consultation may have been intended to supplement his own knowledge, which he did not claim to be complete in itself. In the law of evidence, however, it is insisted that testimony ought to come straight. If witnesses arrange their recollections so as to make them agree, or if they seek to build them up where they admit uncertainty, the result lacks the validity of statements obtained from witnesses separately and unretouched. One must give full credit to the sincerity of R. B.'s effort to deliver the truth and some investigators might not consider that his product was rendered less valuable by this consultation. It is not an easy problem. Rutledge was not always able to make his words convey his idea as to the engagement between Lincoln and Ann. At one point he said it was "conditional"—i. e., dependent upon release from McNamar; elsewhere he stated that it was "not conditional . . . but absolute." [13] On Lincoln's mental suffering Rutledge wrote: "I cannot answer this question from personal knowledge, but from what I have learned from others at the time, you [Herndon] are substantially correct." [14] In contrast to this the attested statement had said: "The effect upon Mr Lincoln's mind was terrible; . . . [etc.]" [15] In R. B. Rutledge's letters there were cases in which he told his questioner that he (Herndon) was in error; yet he confessed liking Herndon's lecture, which, incidentally, had not been confined to Ann Rutledge, but had included a glowing description of the timber, bottoms, bluffs, meadows, hills, flowers, lichen, moss, rolling brook, wild fruit, birds, animals, fish, and more especially the early settlers of New Salem and the surrounding region.

The nature of Rutledge's recollections, however, is best indicated by a qualifying statement at the outset of his attested account:

I trust largely to your courtesy as a gentleman, to your honesty and integrity as a historian, and to your skill in writing for the public, to enlarge

---

[13] Rutledge's mention of the conditional engagement (in his statement attested Oct. 22, 1866) has already been noted. In his letter to Herndon in his own hand, Nov. 18, 1866, Rutledge said: ". . . during his [McNamar's] prolonged absence Mr Lincoln courted Ann, resulting in a second engagement, not conditional as my language would seem to indicate but absolute, She however in the conversation . . . between her & David urged the propriety of seeing McNamar, inform him of the change in her feelings & seek an honorable releas, before consumating the engagement with Mr L. by Marriage." (He doubts the word "conditional"; yet after all his explanation leaves the impression that Ann's marrying of Lincoln was not to be thought of except in terms of a release from her acknowledged and betrothed lover.) Herndon-Weik MSS.

[14] R. B. Rutledge to Herndon, Nov. 21, 1866, *ibid.*   [15] Quoted above, pp. 327–328.

wherever my statements seem obscure, and to condense and remove whatever seems superfluous. . . . Many of my statements are made from memory with the aid of association of events; and should you discover that the date, location and circumstances, of the events here named should be contradictory to those named from other sources, I beg of you to consider well the testimony in each case, and make up your history from those statements, which may appear to you best fitted to remove all doubt as to their correctness.[16]

Rutledge did his sincere best, but what we have in his testimony is dim and misty with the years; he became doubly indirect where he quoted James McGrady Rutledge and others; [17] and his record is qualified by his prefatory caution to Herndon as to how to use it. Yet if one adopts the familiar Ann Rutledge tale, this is a sample of the type of material he must accept.

III

The testimony of James Short, a close and true friend of Lincoln and of the Rutledges, deserves consideration if one has to deal with far-off rememberings. He lived in the Sand Ridge area near the farm where Ann spent the last few years of her life. (This farm was about seven miles north of New Salem.) There is a matter-of-fact quality untinged by sentiment in his statement. He said:

Mr L. boarded with the parents of Miss Ann Rutledge, from the time he went to New Salem up to 1833. In 1833 her mother moved to the Sandridge & kept house for me, until I got married. Miss R. staid at N. S. for a few months after her mother left, keeping house for her father & brothers, & boarding Mr L. She then came over to her mother. After my marriage, the Rutledges lived about half a mile from me. Mr L. came over to see me & them every day or two.[1] I did not know of any engagement or tender passages between Mr L and Miss R at the time. But after her death, which happened in 34 or 35, he seemed to be so much affected and grieved so hardly that I then supposed there must have been . . . something of the kind.[2]

---

16 R. B. Rutledge to Herndon, attested Oct. 22, 1866, Herndon-Weik MSS.

17 It will be noted above that he quoted a letter from James McGrady Rutledge "just received" (in 1866), which is different from reaching back into his own untouched memories.

1 Lincoln's surveying and various odd jobs took him all over the country around New Salem and he often stayed all night at the Short home.

2 James Short to Herndon, July 7, 1865, Herndon-Weik MSS. Lincoln had a very high opinion of Jim Short. On March 26, 1843, he wrote: ". . . I know him to be as honorable a man as there is in the world." *Works*, I, 265.

That Lincoln was deeply saddened by Ann's death was generally reported by these witnesses, several of whom retrospectively inferred, as did James Short, that if he grieved so much, he "must have been" in love with her.

John McNamar, Ann's fiancé who was in the East at the time of the alleged Lincoln-Rutledge courtship, wrote in 1866: "I never heard and [i. e., any] person say that Mr Lincon addressed Miss Ann Rutledge in terms of courtship neither her own family nor my acquaintances otherwise." [3] McNamar knew the Rutledges well not only because of his engagement to Ann but because he had bought half of the Rutledge farm, this being referred to as a "family arrangement." [4] If Lincoln did court Ann to the point of betrothal, and McNamar who was known to be engaged to her was not told of this fact when he returned to New Salem, human nature in country towns has radically changed! McNamar was respected by his neighbors and his word was trusted.[5] He said that two prominent men, personal friends of his, told him Lincoln "was Grieved very much" at Ann's death.[6] Bowling Green was said to have feared that the young man's grief might impair his mind; he took him to the Green home for a week or two and "succeeded in cheering him Lincoln up . . . ." [7] But Mrs. Green thought Ann loved McNamar as much as Lincoln, though the former had been absent so long, and one of Ann's aunts said she thought Ann would have married McNamar if she had lived.[8] Again Mrs. Green, sometimes called Mrs. "Bolen" Green, was quoted as saying that Miss Owens visited the New Salem region "for about a year next preceding the death of Miss Rutledge" and that "Lincoln went to see her frequently during that time She living handy to

---

[3] McNamar to G. U. Miles, May 5, 1866, Herndon-Weik MSS.

[4] Beveridge, I, 148; Thomas, *Lincoln's New Salem*, 81.

[5] "His [John McNamar's] conduct was strictly hightoned, honest and moral, and his object, whatever any may think of the deception . . . in changing his name, entirely praiseworthy." R. B. Rutledge to Herndon, attested Oct. 22, 1866, Herndon-Weik MSS. For unfriendly comment on McNamar, see Barton, I, 221–222.

[6] John McNamar to G. U. Miles, May 5, 1866, Herndon-Weik MSS. Miles sent this letter to Herndon, for whom it had been obtained.

[7] G. U. Miles to Herndon, March 23, 1866, *ibid.*

[8] *Ibid.* This aunt was Mrs. William Rutledge. Miles wrote: "Mrs Wm Rutledge who resides in Petersburg [1866] and did reside in the neighbourhood at the time of the Said courtship and who is . . . acquainted with the parties & all the circumstances . . . thinks that Ann if she had lived would have married McNamer or rather . . . liked him a little the best though McNamer had been absent in Ohio for Near two years at the time of her death though they corrosponded by letter."

Salem." [9] James Short denied that Lincoln refused to eat after Ann's death [10] and John Hill said that he bore up very well until, some days afterwards, a heavy rain fell which unnerved him. [11]

Various other witnesses contributed fragments of reminiscence. W. G. Greene, an intimate friend of Lincoln in New Salem days, agreed that Lincoln and Ann were engaged, and that his friends feared he would commit suicide after her death. Caleb Carman stated that Lincoln loved Ann but said he did not know "mutch" about it, as he was not in New Salem at the time. A cousin of W. H. Herndon, J. R. Herndon, referred to Miss Rutledge and said he had "know dout he [Lincoln] would have married iff she had of lived." L. M. Greene asserted they were engaged; William McNeeley presented hearsay evidence that Lincoln was "insane" after Ann's death; Henry McHenry described Lincoln's depression and desire for solitude, but added that some thought it was due to an increased application to his law studies. George Spears approved of Herndon's lecture, but remarked with refreshing candor that while he had lived through the time and events mentioned, he could not remember about them. Jasper Rutledge, relative of Ann born after her death and brother of James McGrady Rutledge, gave the traditional family version. He added the detail that McNamar's real name was revealed by his signing of some deeds (he had been using the name McNeil) and that Ann was suspicious of a man with two names. According to his account, correspondence between Ann and McNamar gradually ceased and Ann and Lincoln became engaged. Mrs. Sam Hill endorsed the main points of the Rutledge tradition, but gave it as her "honest opinion" that Ann would have married McNamar if he had returned before her death. Henry Hohhiner (?) expressed his "opinion" that Lincoln and Ann were engaged, while Jason Duncan thought Lincoln refrained from courting Ann because of her engagement to McNamar. [12]

---

[9] *Ibid.* In a postscript Miles wrote: ". . . in 1835 when Miss Rutledge died & when Lincoln was going to see Miss Owens this was Sangamo County—Menard being formed at the Session of 1838 & 9."

[10] Caleb Carman to Herndon, Nov. 30, 1866, *ibid.*

[11] John Hill to Herndon, June 6, 1865, *ibid.*

[12] For this paragraph the references, given in the order mentioned, are: W. G. Greene to Herndon, May 30, 1865; Caleb Carman to Herndon, Nov. 30, 1866; J. R. Herndon to Herndon, July 3, 1865; L. M. Greene to Herndon, July 30, 1865; William McNeely to

So the testimony runs—some *pro,* some *con,* some inconclusive, all of it long delayed reminiscence, much of it second- or third-hand, part of it consisting of inference or supposition as to what "must have been" true. The old settlers were contradictory among themselves. One of them wrote concerning an alleged bit of early Lincoln reminiscence: "If that old Lady . . . who says, Lincoln made a crop for her husband some time in 1831–32 or 33, was not a *woman,* I would say she *lied* like *hell* . . . ." [13]

One must now consider the statement of Isaac Cogdal regarding an interview he said he had with President Elect Lincoln in Springfield some time between November 1860 and February 1861. Cogdal was a farmer and former brick mason who studied law late in life, being admitted to the bar in 1860.[14] He lived in the Rock Creek precinct and had known Lincoln when they were both young men, being some three years younger than Lincoln. According to Cogdal's story as it comes to us, Lincoln asked him to come to his office in the State House and talk over old times and acquaintances of New Salem days. The manuscript record runs as follows:

Abe is it true that you fell in love with & courted Ann Rutledge said Cogdall. Lincoln said, "it is true—true indeed I did. I have loved the name of Rutlege to this day. I have kept my mind on their movements ever since & love them dearly"—said L [Just before this is the statement that Lincoln had asked Cogdal where the Rutledges were, an inconsistency not explained.] Ab—Is it true—said Cogdall, that you ran a little wild about the matter: I did really—I ran off the track: it was my first. I loved the woman dearly & sacredly: she was a handsome girl—would have made a good loving wife—was natural & quite intellectual, though not highly Educated—I did honestly—& truly love the girl & think often—often of her now.[15]

Herndon, Nov. 12, 1866; Henry McHenry to Herndon, Jan. 8, 1866; George Spears to Herndon, Nov. 21, 1866; Herndon's memorandum of statement by Jasper Rutledge, Mar. 9, 1887; Herndon's undated memorandum of statement by Mrs. Sam Hill; Herndon's undated memorandum of statement by Henry Hohhiner [?]; Jason Duncan to Herndon, undated. Herndon-Weik MSS.

13 W. G. Greene to Herndon, June 11, 1865, *ibid.*

14 *History of Menard and Mason Counties, Illinois* (pub. by O. L. Baskin & Co., 1879), 749.

15 Statement of "Isaac Cogdall," undated, Herndon-Weik MSS. In the manuscripts Herndon's spelling of the name seems to be "Cogdall" though it could be read "Cogdale." In the Herndon biography (Angle ed., 389) it appears as "Cogsdale." As shown by legal papers, newspapers, and letters by the man himself, the name was Isaac Cogdal.

The most obvious thing about this effusive statement is its unLin-
colnian quality. The record is Herndon's memorandum of an interview with Cogdal, who was presumably reconstructing from memory
what Lincoln had said to him some years before. Words ascribed to
Lincoln have been refracted by passing through two minds, and have
been exposed to the possible embellishment of both Cogdal and Herndon. It has been suggested that Lincoln's friends did not usually address
him as "Abe" [16] but in this record of jottings "Abe" and especially
"Ab" may have been abbreviations, for Herndon troubled himself
very little about periods. "Jas" without a period is used for James in
the same manuscript. On the other hand, Lincoln is quoted as having
addressed Cogdal as "Ike," and Cogdal may have called him "Abe"
when they were young men. Lincoln was a man of deep reserve about
personal matters. As President Elect he guarded his speech with the
utmost care. His lack of reticence here seems as unnatural as the
language attributed to him.

B. F. Irwin mentioned hearing the story of the Cogdal interview.
Irwin, who stated in an August letter that Ann died and Lincoln
took it very hard, wrote in September that his informants differed as
to Miss Rutledge's death. He followed this with a statement which
illustrates how twisted some of these recollections could become:
"Cogdal says she [Ann] was living in Iowa in 1860 as Lincoln told him
and Lincoln did say in 1860 that he . . . loved her still . . . ."
The same letter mentioned that Ann was unfavorably impressed with
Lincoln, who was poor and awkward, while McNamar and other
suitors had much more to offer.[17]

Cogdal's story comes to us with such indirectness in the telling as
to becloud with doubt what was actually said. Lincoln was not a man
to express himself so effusively to friends. "Lincoln never told Speed
nor Gallespie nor Judge Matheny—nor myself of this courtship—
death and unsanity" wrote Herndon. He added: ". . . he was the
most reticent & mostly secretive man that ever existed: he never

---

[16] Sometimes they used the contraction affectionately in the third person, but they
usually referred to him simply as Lincoln. Henry C. Whitney stated that Lincoln gave
no license for being called "Abe"; Horace White confirms this and refers to "pre
tended conversations . . . where his interlocutors addressed him as Abe this or Abe
that" as "imaginary." Roy E. Appleman, ed., *Abraham Lincoln From His Own Words
and Contemporary Accounts* (National Park Service Source Book Series, no. 2), 9.

[17] B. F. Irwin to Herndon, Aug. 27, 1866. B. F. Irwin to Herndon, Sep. 22, 1866.
Herndon-Weik MSS.

opened his whole soul to any man: he never touched the history or quality of his own nature in the presence of his friends." [18] That Herndon's lecture with its tale of Lincoln and Ann was news to Speed is known by his own statement.[19] In the face of such reticence the Cogdal record seems artificial and made to order. It was given out after Lincoln's death; it presents him in an unlikely role; it puts in his mouth uncharacteristic sayings.

There is, to the writer's knowledge, no thoroughly verified utterance by Lincoln, written or oral, in which Ann Rutledge is even mentioned, though one does find Lincoln's own statements concerning women whom he knew in this period—namely, Sarah Rickard [20] and Mary Owens.

IV

The effect of Ann's death on Lincoln seems to have been exaggerated by local gossip. Mrs. E. Abell, at whose cabin Lincoln was staying at the time of Ann's death, wrote in detail about his deep grief over the event, but added "the community said he was crazy he was not crazy but he was very disponding a long time." It is worthy of note that while she had first-hand knowledge of Lincoln's grief, she said she could tell little about the courtship.[1] Less than a month after Ann's death a close friend of Lincoln, Mathew S. Marsh, wrote his brother a letter containing a newsy paragraph devoted to Lincoln, which fails to mention any sorrow or abnormal condition of his at this time.[2] The letter establishes the fact that Lincoln was attending to his postmaster duties as usual,[3] and there is a record of a survey which Lincoln

---

[18] Herndon's MS. entitled "Miss Rutledge & Lincoln," 188—, *ibid.*

[19] J. F. Speed to Herndon, Nov. 30, 1866, *ibid.*

[20] For Lincoln's reference to Sarah Rickard, see Kincaid, *Joshua Fry Speed*, 47. Beveridge (I, 317) definitely states that Lincoln asked Sarah to marry him, but that she declined. Weik (*Real Lincoln*, 66–68) emphasizes Lincoln's attentions to Sarah; he also affirms that Lincoln proposed to her. (His material was the same as that used by Beveridge.) Sandburg and Angle, however, though pointing out that "Lincoln and Sarah went places together" (*Mary Lincoln*, 54) leave the impression that Sarah's interest was in Speed, whose departure left her disconsolate.

[1] Mrs. E. [Elizabeth] Abell to Herndon, Feb. 15, 1867, Herndon-Weik MSS. This lady, at whose cabin Lincoln was staying when Ann died, was Mrs. Bennett Abell, sister of Mary Owens.

[2] The original of the Marsh letter is in the collection of Oliver R. Barrett.

[3] Paul M. Angle, "Lincoln's First Love?" *Bulletin No. 9*, Lincoln Centennial Assoc., p. 7 (Dec. 1, 1927).

made, dated September 24, 1835, in his usual handwriting which shows that he was carrying on his surveying work.[4] This was at a time when, according to Herndon's embroidered account, Lincoln was a mental wreck. "He slept not," said Herndon, "he ate not, joyed not . . . until his body became emaciated and weak, and gave way. His mind wandered from its throne. In his imagination he muttered words to her he loved. His mind, his reason . . . walked out of itself along the uncolumned air, and kissed and embraced the shadows and illusions of the heated brain."[5] (A choice example, this, of Herndon's combination of soaring psychoanalysis with glowing language.)

By the statement of her brother, Ann Rutledge died on August 25, 1835.[6] The fall of 1836 found Lincoln absorbed in a prolonged courtship of Mary Owens. She had visited New Salem three years before —when Ann was living—and even then (i. e., in 1833), by his own statement, Lincoln considered her a desirable matrimonial partner.[7]

How did Herndon regard the known fact of Lincoln's courting of Mary Owens? He did not believe that Lincoln's profession of love for the lady could be taken otherwise than seriously. He thought "the letters expressed his honest feelings and his deepest convictions and that they were written sincerely—truthfully and honestly." Lincoln, he said, "was in love [with Miss Owens]—deeply in love."[8] Herndon had written effusively of the Ann Rutledge romance; now he spoke of Lincoln being thoroughly in love with Miss Owens; again he had it that Lincoln, in the period of his courtship of Miss Todd, "saw & loved an other woman—Miss Edwards and . . . desired to break away from Miss Todd & to join Miss Edwards."[9] In telling of Lin-

[4] *Bulletin No. 12*, Lincoln Centennial Assoc. (Sep. 1, 1928), 8.
[5] Broadside of Herndon lecture, Nov. 16, 1866, column 7, near bottom.
[6] R. B. Rutledge to Herndon, attested Oct. 22, 1866, Herndon-Weik MSS.
[7] "I had seen the said sister [Mary Owens] some three years before [i. e., before 1836], . . . and saw no good objection to plodding life through hand in hand with her." Lincoln to Mrs. O. H. Browning, April 1, 1838, *Works*, I, 88. In these words Lincoln admitted having a tender feeling for Miss Owens at a period two years before Ann's death. It has been noted how Mary Owens's sister, Mrs. Abell, knew little of Lincoln's attentions to Ann, though he was staying at the Abell cabin at the time of Ann's death. As to his courting of Miss Owens she had more to say. Lincoln, she wrote, told her sister he would rather have her "than any woman living." Mrs. Abell to Herndon, Jan. 13, 1867, Herndon-Weik MSS.
[8] Herndon's ms. fragment, "Lincoln's Courtship with Miss Owens," undated, Herndon-Weik MSS.
[9] Herndon to Lamon, Feb. 25, 1870, MS., Huntington Lib. One is dealing here with Herndon's comments—perhaps somewhat tentative—at a time long before he and Weik put their biography into shape.

coln's affections being given to Miss Edwards (this without adequate foundation), he mentioned the incident as "Miss Edwards flitting a cross the path"—this flitting made Lincoln "crazy *the second time.*" [10] Taking all that Herndon said, one gets the impression that he almost considered his hero weak-minded in the matter of women. As for Herndon's collaborator, he states specifically that Lincoln proposed marriage to at least four women: Ann Rutledge, Mary Owens, Sarah Rickard, and (of course) Mary Todd. [11]

In striking contrast to the Rutledge romance, there is ample documentation for the Owens courtship. We have several letters which Lincoln wrote her in which he discussed the question of her marrying him, and a complete account of the whole affair, including Miss Owens's refusal of his marriage proposal, which Lincoln wrote to his friend Mrs. O. H. Browning. [12] In 1866 Mary Owens herself (Mrs. Vineyard) wrote: "From his own showing . . . his heart and hand were at my disposal, ..." [13] This statement, indeed the full record on this point, fails to harmonize with the popular concept that Lincoln's whole life was influenced by his love for Ann.

Herndon treasured the Ann Rutledge story. Referring to Nicolay and Hay's articles in the *Century* he wondered if they were going to "suppress" the tale. He called it "the finest story in Lincoln's life." [14] It is the stuff of which poetry and song are bodied forth—young love, the picturesque life of a vanished pioneer town, the tragic death of a

---

[10] *Ibid.*   [11] Weik, *Real Lincoln,* 56, 66–67.

[12] Lincoln gave a long and chatty account of his courtship of Miss Owens in a letter to Mrs. Orville H. Browning, April 1, 1838. (*Works,* I, 87–92.) Some have stressed the April fool date and have discounted this letter as having been written in a joking spirit. Lincoln, however, is quoted as having said that it had "too much truth for print" (*ibid.,* 87 n.), and his own letters to Miss Owens (*ibid.,* 52–54, 55–57) indicate an intention to marry her if that should be her wish, combined with a rather excessive amount of plain speaking to make sure it was her wish. If Herndon took the courtship with Miss Owens seriously there was good reason for it; the fact of Lincoln's offer of marriage was confirmed by the lady herself in later life. In a letter to Isaac N. Arnold, November 25, 1872 (MS., Chicago Hist. Soc.), O. H. Browning tells of how he and Lincoln were at Vandalia in 1836–38, how the Brownings boarded at the same house with Lincoln, how Lincoln was very fond of Mrs. Browning's society, and how the above-mentioned April letter was received after they left Vandalia in 1838. For a long time they thought it was one of Lincoln's funny stories; later, wrote Browning, it was learned that Lincoln was writing "a true account of an incident in actual life."

[13] In the same letter she wrote: ". . . I thought Mr. Lincoln was deficient in those little links which make up the great chain of womans happiness . . . ." Mrs. Vineyard to Herndon, May 23, 1866, Herndon-Weik MSS.

[14] Herndon to Weik, Dec. 5, 1886, *ibid.*

beautiful young woman, the beating of rain and storm upon a new made grave, the age-long questioning concerning human mortality.

But there is repeated mention in the manuscripts of Herndon's worried doubts on the subject. The fact of Ann's engagement to McNamar seems greatly to have bothered him. Writing to Weik when the biography was in proof, he said: "Again the more I think of the Ann Rutledge story the more do I think that the girl had two engagements— i e that she was engaged to two men at one and the same. . . . I shall change my opinion of events & things on the coming of new facts and on more mature reflection in all cases—and so excuse me for 'sorter' wabbling around." [15] Herndon's account, which was to establish the story indelibly in the public mind, was already in printer's proof; yet here he is confessing that he is " 'sorter' wabbling around" in regard to the engagement of Lincoln and Ann.[16]

In the collection of Oliver R. Barrett in Chicago there is a stone (turtle shaped, about ten inches long) whose inscription records that A. Lincoln and Ann Rutledge "were betrothed here July 4 1833." (The carving is clear enough. The "J" in July is ignorantly reversed.) The pedigree of the stone, as often in such cases, is incomplete. One can get statements as to its having been found in New Salem, also as to its carving resembling that of an ax handle bearing Lincoln's name; back of that, information is lacking.[17] There are various counts against this stone if considered as a genuine record cut by Lincoln. Herndon, prominent advocate of the romance, said definitely that Ann stood firm in her feeling toward McNamar "up to 1834" and that Lincoln proposed to her in 1835. He said that "Soon after this . . . engagement Ann was taken sick . . . ," [18] this being her final illness. It has already been noted that she died in 1835. Without presuming to give a date to a matter that is alleged but not verified, it may be noted that those who would build up a case for the Lincoln-Rutledge

---

[15] Herndon to Weik, Jan. 11, 1889, *ibid.*

[16] He added, however, that he did not want the text of the book changed in its treatment of this theme. *Ibid.* At this point it is appropriate to note Weik's view that the story of Ann Rutledge was peculiarly due to Herndon's preservation. Her "melancholy history," wrote Weik, "but for the indefatigable and exhaustive researches of Mr. Herndon, would probably never have been preserved." *Real Lincoln*, 66.

[17] The writer has examined the stone through the courtesy of Mr. Barrett. The subject is discussed in *Bulletin No. 12*, Lincoln Centennial Assoc., 6–8 (Sep. 1, 1828). In this article it is stated that the stone was found at New Salem in 1900 and that the ax handle was dug up on the site of the Lincoln-Berry store in 1878.

[18] Herndon's MS. entitled "Miss Rutledge & Lincoln," 188—, Herndon-Weik MSS.

engagement will rely upon various recollections and upon the analysis of Herndon who believed such an engagement to have existed; they will therefore have great difficulty in arguing for the betrothal on so early a date as July 4, 1833. They will be confronted with Lincoln's own written statement that in 1833 he did not object to "plodding life through hand in hand" with Mary Owens. They will also have to remember that, where the Lincoln-Rutledge engagement was spoken of, it was related to a considerably prolonged absence of McNamar; in July 1833 Ann's lover had not been absent that long. (In a letter to George U. Miles, May 5, 1866, McNamar wrote that he left New Salem "in 32 or 33." The words "or 33" were then crossed out.) Another point to remember is that in 1833 (well on in his twenty-fifth year) Lincoln certainly knew how to form his letters; he would not have carved a reversed "J". To put the criticism of the stone in the very mildest form, too little is known of it to establish its authenticity. It is not known by whom or when it was made.

Space is lacking in which to show how other biographers have dealt with the Ann Rutledge theme. Many of them do little more than repeat Herndon. Beveridge bases his full account on Herndon's material and presents Lincoln's engagement to Ann largely along the line suggested by R. B. Rutledge, as above quoted. Yet he admits that Lincoln's courting of Ann was "misty" and states that "No positive [i. e., unconditional] and definite engagement resulted." [19] W. E. Barton accepts the tradition. "Abraham Lincoln and Ann truly loved each other," he writes.[20] Yet Barton adds on a later page: "We know very little about the Ann Rutledge incident. If Lincoln wrote any letters to Ann they were not preserved. If there is any other documentary proof of their love-affair, it is unknown. We know that much that has been told about it is unreliable." [21]

V

To recapitulate: In its origin the Ann Rutledge story rests on wavering memories recorded many years after the event. No proved contemporary evidence is known to exist. Herndon did not invent the romance. He loved the truth and sought it eagerly. Whether he always found it is another matter, but if he did we know that it had to

---

[19] Beveridge, I, 149.   [20] Barton, *Life of Abraham Lincoln*, I, 214.   [21] *Ibid.*, I, 225.

undergo his inevitable psychoanalysis before it emerged. He did elaborate the story, publicize it, and cast it into the mold which it has retained in popular thought. From the doubtful beginning of distant memory there has evolved a full-grown tradition; in the now classic form which the tradition has taken the main handiwork is that of Herndon. Few indeed were familiar with the episode prior to Herndon's sensational lecture of 1866, which came a considerable time after Lincoln's death. Other biographers, in presenting the story, have followed the Herndon line; but the reader will recognize that the quoting of many repetitions of Herndon and Weik adds nothing in terms of historical contribution.[1] Reminiscences gathered long after the event were not all in favor of the romance; they were contradictory and vague.[2] The two elements on which there is agreement are Ann's engagement to McNamar and Lincoln's grief at her death. Concerning the first of these elements it may be noted that in the popular conception of the Rutledge story, John McNamar is the forgotten man; yet it is worth while to note a passage that brings poignantly to light the feeling of the one who, after all, was Ann's acknowledged and accepted lover. ". . . I cut the Initials of Miss Ann Rutledge on a b[o]ard at the head of her grave 30 years ago,"[3] wrote McNamar to Herndon in 1866. It was McNamar, not Lincoln, who marked Ann's grave. As to Lincoln's grief it has been seen that his alleged derangement of mind is without adequate substantiation; in the "uncolumned air" of Herndon's lecture it is nothing more than fiction.

Whether Lincoln was in love with Ann, or grieved over the untimely death of one who was both a lovable young woman and a dear friend; whether his grief was due to a romantic attachment or to a

---

[1] Such repetitious "evidence" is found in Percival Graham Rennick, *Abraham Lincoln and Ann Rutledge: An Old Salem Romance* (1932).

[2] It is only by a study of Herndon's manuscripts that one can realize the uncertainty of his material. G. U. Miles, Herndon's father-in-law in Petersburg, Illinois, deputed to interview various persons concerning Lincoln and Ann, replied: ". . . the references you gave me knew little or nothing of what you wanted to know." Miles to Herndon, Mar. 23, 1866, Herndon-Weik MSS.

[3] McNamar to Herndon, Dec. 1, 1866, *ibid.* By way of further reference to the strangely neglected subject of McNamar's love for Ann, it is of interest to quote the following description in his handwriting: "Miss Ann was a gentle Amiable Maiden without any of the airs of your city Belles but winsome and comly withal a blond in complection with golden hair, 'cherry red lips & a bonny Blue Eye.'" McNamar to G. U. Miles, May 5, 1866, *ibid.*

temperament subject to gloom and deeply sensitive to the tragedy
of death; whether Ann loved him or was friendly to but unimpressed
by one who called himself a "friendless, uneducated, penniless boy"; [4]
whether there was an engagement between them or it was Ann's intention to marry McNamar when he returned, are matters open to
question. Ann's feeling and intent are left in considerable doubt by
contradictions in regard to an engagement between them, by the
opinion of some that she was unimpressed with him and would have
married McNamar if she had lived, and by the unanimous testimony
that she was engaged to McNamar.

Whatever may have been the true situation as to Lincoln and Ann,
that situation seems now well nigh unrecoverable. As to a romantic
attachment, it has not been *dis*proved. It is more correct to characterize it as *un*proved; as such it has been a famous subject of conjecture. It is a memory which lacks support in any statement recorded
in Ann's lifetime. Since it is thus traditional and not reliably established as to its nature and significance, it does not belong in a recital
of those Lincoln episodes which one presents as unquestioned reality.

As a historical puzzle or an exercise in the evaluation of reminiscence the Lincoln-Rutledge story is a choice subject; but its substance is far from clear while its fringe is to be discarded from the
record of established history. By that fringe we mean the elaboration,
the trimmings and embroidery, the fictional sentimentalizing, the
invented poeticisms, and the amazing aura of apocryphal material
that have surrounded the whole overgrown tale.

The present treatment has been concerned only with essential results in the telling, though masses of documents have gone into the
investigation.[5] To spin out the analysis into an extended account

---

[4] Lincoln thus described himself in terms of the recollections of "the older citizens";
he had just referred to "old friends of Menard." Letter to Morris, Mar. 26, 1843, *Works*,
I, 262.

[5] Not all of these documents are in the Herndon-Weik Collection. Some of the delayed reminiscence by those who had lived in the 1830's was as late as 1922. In that
year Mr. George P. Hambrecht of Madison, Wisconsin, received a letter from Sarah
Rutledge Saunders, written (March 18) by James Rutledge Saunders, her son, from
Lompoc, California; this Mrs. Saunders was Ann's sister. Concerning Ann's last illness
she said: "Finally my Brother David who was attending school at Jacksonville, Ill. and
Lincoln were sent for. I can see them as they each came, and when Lincoln went into
the sick room where Sister Ann lay, the others retired. A few minutes later Lincoln
came from the room with bowed head and seemed to me, at the time, to be crying. Soon
After this Ann died and was followed by my Father." She wrote also of seeing Lincoln

would, in the writer's view, not change the conclusion, though a full exhibiting of the subject would require a reproduction of numerous letters and jottings, an amassing of details about each witness with a studious examination of each bit of testimony, and withal a portrayal of the vanished background of New Salem.

Assuredly the effect of the episode upon Lincoln's later life has been greatly exaggerated—or rather, fabricated. Nor should one lightly overlook the shabby manner in which the image of Ann has tended to obscure the years of Lincoln's love and devotion for Mary, his wife, and to belittle her love and devotion for him. There is no need to comment on the expansive popular embellishment of the story— in novels, dramas, radio scripts and the like—nor to remind the reader of the voluminous flow of literary invention which has out-Herndoned Herndon in our own day.[6] Evaluation of the evidence, which one seldom finds anywhere but which has been attempted in the preceding pages, is the only answer to the inquiry as to where the pedestrian course of history ends and the limitless soaring of fiction begins.

"at our table and fire side." Well over ninety and very feeble, Mrs. Saunders confessed: "I am sorry to have so little recollection of the time . . . , being a mere child of six or seven." As to Lincoln and Ann in the final illness she added: "These are so dimly seen that I cannot speak of them with that degree of assurance that I would like." In this letter Ann's sister made no assertion that Lincoln and Ann were engaged. For a loan of the letter the author is indebted to the Abraham Lincoln Book Shop of Chicago.

6 Popular interest has stimulated the hand of forgery. For the "Minor Collection" hoax, whose day of deception was fortunately brief, one may consult the files of the *Atlantic Monthly* from December through April, 1928–29. See especially Paul M. Angle, "The Minor Collection: A Criticism," *ibid.*, vol. 143, 516–525 (Apr., 1929).

INDEX

Abell, Elizabeth (Mrs. Bennett Abell), quoted, **II**, 335.

Abolition, summary and characterization of the movement in the North, **I**, 86 ff.; and the churches, 88-89; degrees and shades, position of Lincoln, 89-91; Lincoln's 1861 attitude, 296.

Abolitionists, slight influence in North, **I**, 91; encounter opposition in Boston, 133; praise John Brown, 134; would consent to withdrawal from Sumter, 328; and Negro colonization, **II**, 139; and Lincoln's emancipation plan, 144; impatient for action by Lincoln, 151-153, 158-159; reaction to emancipation proclamation, 169 ff. *See also* radicals, Garrison, Weld, Higginson, Gerrit Smith.

Abraham Lincoln Association, **I**, acknowledgments (xv), 176.

Adams, Charles Francis (1807–1886), **I**, 276; **II**, 244; free soil policies, **I**, 91; on committee of thirty-three, 224; possible cabinet member, 261; appointed minister to Britain, 272, 372; and Civil War diplomacy, **II**, 31 ff.; and *Trent* affair, 37 ff.; on British reaction to emancipation proclamation, 179-180 and n.

Adams, Charles Francis (1835–1915), quoted, **I**, 292.

Adams, H. A., Union naval officer, prevents reënforcement of Fort Pickens, **I**, 332.

Adams, Henry, **II**, 346; on Sumner's speech concerning *Trent* affair, **II**, 50 and n.

Adams, John Quincy, on Jackson's nullification policy, **I**, 221; and slavery, **II**, 126; on martial law and emancipation, 182.

Adrian resolution, recommending repeal of personal liberty laws, supported by Republicans, **I**, 228.

Aiken, William, opposes secession, **I**, 219.

Alabama, Democratic delegation at Charleston, **I**, 140; vote in 1860, 192; secedes, 211, 212; Buell in, 261.

Alabama, The, case of, **II**, 52 f.; preys on Union commerce, 265.

Albany, N. Y., visited by Lincoln, **I**, 283; response to Lincoln's call to arms, 355.

Albany (N. Y.) *Atlas and Argus*, on Lincoln as President Elect, **I**, 292; on Lincoln's inaugural, 305.

Albany (N. Y.) *Evening Journal*, **I**, 146.

Albert, Prince, and *Trent* affair, **II**, 43-44.

Alexander, E. P., Confederate artillery commander, on Pickett's charge at Gettysburg, **II**, 283.

Alexandra, The, case of, **II**, 52 f.

Aliens. *See* Canisius, Knownothing party, nativism, *Deutsches Haus*.

Allen, W. J., **II**, 214, 234.

Alton, Ill., scene of final Lincoln-Douglas debate, **I**, 110; Lincoln's speech at, 117.

Altoona, Pa., conference of governors at, **II**, 229.

Amboy, Ill., Lincoln speaks at, **I**, 118.

America. *See* United States.

American Anti-Slavery Society, **I**, 87.

American party. *See* Knownothing party.

Anderson, Robert, Union army officer, commands forts in Charleston harbor, **I**, 316; and Sumter crisis of April 1861, 328-342.

Andrew, John A., governor of Massachusetts, possible cabinet member, **I**, 261; offers Scott help, 276-277; on colonization, **II**, 140-141; and Negro troops, 184, 185-186; differs from Banks, 222.

Angle, Paul M., **I**, 99; on Lincoln as lawyer, **I**, 34; on wedding default, 54-55; on Ann Rutledge, **II**, 323; bibl., 343.

Antelope, The, case of, **II**, 133 and n.

Antietam, battle of, **II**, 114 ff.; 229, 230, 258; importance, 285.

Antislavery. *See* abolition.

Anti-Slavery Society, **I**, 90.

Archives, **II**, 352.

Arkansas, in 1860, **I**, 192; votes against secession, 251; secedes, 357; response to

INDEX

375

inet, 291-292; advice on Lincoln's inaugural, 301-302; influence on Lincoln, 309, 368; approved by moderate Republicans, 313; and Sumter question, 319 ff.; dealings with Southern commissioners, 322 ff.; assumption of power, 324, 337 ff.; *Powhatan* incident, 337 ff.; attitude toward Sumter evacuation, 328, 333; "Some Thoughts" etc., **II,** 29-31; wartime diplomacy, 35 ff.; "bold remonstrance," 35 ff.; on wartime emancipation problem, 131-132; and emancipation proclamation, 155 f., 161, 168, 189; assailed by radicals, 241; denounced by Republican caucus, 242, 246; presents resignation, 243 ff.; criticizes opponents of slavery, 244; resumes post, 248.

Seymour Horatio, governor of New York, **I,** 270; **II,** 221; his supporters denounce emancipation proclamation, 173 f.; controversy with Lincoln on conscription, 295-296, 301-302.

Shannon, Fred A., quoted, **II,** 295.

Sharkey, William L., **I,** 143; opposes secession, 219.

Shaw, Lemuel, **I,** 240 n.

Shaw, Robert Gould, **II,** 183.

Shenandoah Valley, military operations (May–June 1862), **II,** 90 ff.

Sherman, John, **II,** 211; endorses Helper, **I,** 132 and n.; resolution on non-interference with slavery in any state, 224-225; and Cameron's confirmation as minister to Russia, **II,** 60-61.

Sherman, William T., Union general, under Frémont, **II,** 22; and advance in West, 66; serves under Halleck, 260; in Vicksburg campaign, 263.

Shields, James, Union general, duel incident and Lincoln-Todd courtship, **I,** 61-62; in Valley operations, **II,** 92.

Shiloh (Pittsburg Landing, Tenn.), battle of, **II,** 259.

Short, James, **II,** 323 n.; quoted, 330, 332.

Shurtleff College, **I,** 10.

Sickles, Daniel E., Union general, **I,** 229; at Gettysburg, **II,** 280; and newspaper criticism of Meade, 289.

Simpson, Bishop M., commends Cameron, **II,** 57.

Slade, William, colored, and the Lincolns, **II,** 203.

Slave insurrections, absence of, in Civil War, **II,** 195 ff.

Slave trade, domestic, and Compromise of

1850, **I,** 79; abolition of, Lincoln's attitude (1860–61), **I,** 235.

Slave trade, international, **I,** 84; treaty for suppression of, **II,** 136-137.

Slavery, Lincoln's abolition plan for District of Columbia, **I,** 17; territorial issue, 79 ff., 228-231, 237-241; Compromise of 1850, 79; Kansas-Nebraska act, 80 ff.; and sectional dissension, 85 ff.; and American churches, 88-89; Potawatomie massacre, 91-92; in Lincoln-Douglas debates, 122 ff.; Lincoln believes its extension should be checked, 131; denounced with polygamy, 157 n.; and German-Americans, 161, 163; and Republican platform of 1860, 171-172, 172 n.; territorial issue, 236-237; and Civil War, **II,** 126 ff.; and Democrats, 213.

Slidell, John, anti-Douglas leader in Louisiana, **I,** 141; and *Trent* affair, **II,** 37 ff.; mentioned, 212.

Smith, Caleb B., **I,** 169; **II,** 222; promise of cabinet appointment, **I,** 257; appointed secretary of the interior, 268-269, 271; advises concerning Sumter, 320, 333; quoted, 384; and McClellan's removal, **II,** 121; tires of cabinet, 242.

Smith, Charles F., Union general, and advance in West, **II,** 66.

Smith, Donnal V., quoted, **I,** 205.

Smith, E. Kirby, Confederate general, invades Kentucky, **II,** 261.

Smith, Gerrit, **I,** 90; **II,** 151; supports John Brown, **I,** 132.

Smith, John Gregory, governor of Vermont, and story of McClellan's alleged disloyalty, **II,** 122.

Smith, William Farrar, Union general, and McClellan's alleged disloyalty, **II,** 122-123; attempted dismissal by Burnside, 253.

Soldier vote, **II,** 235-236.

Solger, Reinhard, **I,** 163.

Soulé, Pierre, leader of Louisiana moderates, **I,** 141.

South, The, culture, **I,** 78-79; campaign of 1860, 190-192; popular vote for Lincoln, 201; not a unit in secession, 216-217; grievances, 237 ff.; pro-Union opinion, 245; military preparations, 251-253; representation in Lincoln's cabinet considered, 258, 267-268, 270; and Lincoln's inaugural, 306-309; opinion on Sumter negotiations, 324, 359; upper, attitude